Online Job Seeker's Bill of Rights

Online job searching, though still relatively new, is rapidly maturing into a whole new job-search frontier. I want to make sure that this new frontier is job seeker friendly, and I want to make sure that there are realistic standards, too. Here's my version of the new standards I'm looking for in online job searching — I encourage you to look for and demand these standards, too.

1. You have the right to expect resume privacy and confidentiality.

2. You have the right to expect that all jobs posted online are legitimate.

3. When someone requests your resume, you have the right to expect that the person is filling a specific job that is currently available.

4. You have the right to determine who has access to your resume online, if you choose to exercise that right.

5. You have the right to expect that, when you post your resume to an online employment site, your resume will not be copied or transferred to another online employment site without your permission.

6. You have the right to verify online job advertisements.

7. You have the right to expect employers to abide by all Equal Employment Opportunity Commission regulations in online interviews and e-mail communications as well as "traditional" forms of interviewing and job-search communications.

8. You have the right to expect integrity and honesty from all online employment sites.

9. You have the right to withdraw your resume from online postings at any time.

10. You have the right to post your resume online and view online job advertisements free of charge.

COMPUTER
BOOK SERIES
FROM IDG

Job Searching Online For Dummies®

Cheat Sheet

The Big Seven Online Employment Sites

These "Big Seven" sites are the largest and most prominent employment sites on the Web. I recommend that you check them out first:

- **America's Job Bank:** www.ajb.dni.us/
- **Career Mosaic:** www.careermosaic.com
- **CareerPath.com:** www.careerpath.com/
- **E.span:** www.espan.com
- **Monster Board:** www.monster.com/
- **Online Career Center:** www.occ.com
- **Yahoo! Classifieds:** classifieds.yahoo.com/ employment.html

Great Search Engines for Online Searching

Finding information on the Web can be an overwhelming task, to say the least. These search engines make that task a little easier:

- **For general Web searches:** AltaVista (www.altavista.digital.com/)
- **For finding electronic mailing lists:** Liszt Select (www.liszt.com)
- **For finding discussion groups and Web forums:** Reference.COM (www.reference.com)

Super-Quick General Reference Tools

If you need general Web reference information, try one of these tools:

- **Big Book** (www.bigbook.com): An online Yellow Pages–type of directory
- **HotSheet** (www.hotsheet.com): Your one-stop shop for finding quick reference sites
- **Ready Reference** (www.ipl.org/ref/ RR/): A great tool for finding in-depth reference material very quickly

Company Information on the Web

Don't even think about walking into an interview without having done research on the company first. For all the company info you desire, head to one of these sites.

- **BizWeb Business Guide to the Web** (www.bizweb.com): An online guide to more than 30,500 companies
- **Companies Online** (www.companiesonline.com/): Search for companies online by name, city, state, ticker symbol, or industry
- **EDGAR Database of Corporate Information** (www.sec.gov/ edgarhp.htm): Check recent SEC filings here
- **Hoover's Online** (www.hoovers.com/): A definitive online source for company profiles

JOB SEARCHING ONLINE FOR DUMMIES®

by Pam Dixon

Foreword by Ray Marcy

IDG Books Worldwide, Inc.
An International Data Group Company

Foster City, CA ♦ Chicago, IL ♦ Indianapolis, IN ♦ New York, NY

Job Searching Online For Dummies®

Published by
IDG Books Worldwide, Inc.
An International Data Group Company
919 E. Hillsdale Blvd.
Suite 400
Foster City, CA 94404
www.idgbooks.com (IDG Books Worldwide Web site)
www.dummies.com (Dummies Press Web site)

Library of Congress Catalog Card No.: 98-85427

ISBN: 0-7645-0376-6

Printed in the United States of America

10 9 8 7 6 5 4 3 2 1

1O/RS/QV/ZY/IN

Distributed in the United States by IDG Books Worldwide, Inc.

Distributed by Macmillan Canada for Canada; by Transworld Publishers Limited in the United Kingdom; by IDG Norge Books for Norway; by IDG Sweden Books for Sweden; by Woodslane Pty. Ltd. for Australia; by Woodslane Enterprises Ltd. for New Zealand; by Longman Singapore Publishers Ltd. for Singapore, Malaysia, Thailand, and Indonesia; by Simron Pty. Ltd. for South Africa; by Toppan Company Ltd. for Japan; by Distribuidora Cuspide for Argentina; by Livraria Cultura for Brazil; by Ediciencia S.A. for Ecuador; by Addison-Wesley Publishing Company for Korea; by Ediciones ZETA S.C.R. Ltda. for Peru; by WS Computer Publishing Corporation, Inc., for the Philippines; by Unalis Corporation for Taiwan; by Contemporanea de Ediciones for Venezuela; by Computer Book & Magazine Store for Puerto Rico; by Express Computer Distributors for the Caribbean and West Indies. Authorized Sales Agent: Anthony Rudkin Associates for the Middle East and North Africa.

For general information on IDG Books Worldwide's books in the U.S., please call our Consumer Customer Service department at 800-762-2974. For reseller information, including discounts and premium sales, please call our Reseller Customer Service department at 800-434-3422.

For information on where to purchase IDG Books Worldwide's books outside the U.S., please contact our International Sales department at 650-655-3200 or fax 650-655-3295.

For information on foreign language translations, please contact our Foreign & Subsidiary Rights department at 650-655-3021 or fax 650-655-3281.

For sales inquiries and special prices for bulk quantities, please contact our Sales department at 650-655-3200 or write to the address above.

For information on using IDG Books Worldwide's books in the classroom or for ordering examination copies, please contact our Educational Sales department at 800-434-2086 or fax 817-251-8174.

For press review copies, author interviews, or other publicity information, please contact our Public Relations department at 650-655-3000 or fax 650-655-3299.

For authorization to photocopy items for corporate, personal, or educational use, please contact Copyright Clearance Center, 222 Rosewood Drive, Danvers, MA 01923, or fax 978-750-4470.

is a trademark under exclusive license to IDG Books Worldwide, Inc., from International Data Group, Inc.

About the Author

Pam Dixon is an award-winning author, journalist, and speaker who is recognized for her contributions in the area of technology as it impacts education, business, and culture.

Dixon's first book, *Be Your Own Headhunter Online* (Random House, 1995), was recognized by the Computer Press Association as one of the best nonfiction computer books of 1995. One of her recent books, *TakeCharge Computing for Teens and Parents* (IDG Books Worldwide, 1996), was named one of three finalists in the prestigious 1997 Ben Franklin Awards.

Dixon is also the author of other ground-breaking books: *Virtual College* (Peterson's, 1996) is recognized by business and higher education leaders as the definitive book on distance education today. Dixon's latest, *Symantec Visual Café,* a book she coauthored on leading-edge Java technology, was published by John Wiley in May 1997. Dixon has written other books, including a book she coauthored on navigating the World Wide Web.

Dixon is a frequent contributor to national magazines and is a regular contributor to *The Orange County Register* and *The San Diego Union Tribune.* Her celebrity profiles and feature stories have earned her journalism awards, including a writing award from the Society of Professional Journalists. Dixon was the first writer to talk about the World Wide Web as it related to the entertainment business; two *Emmy* magazine articles she wrote before the Web went mainstream garnered high praise from top entertainment executives.

Dixon is the recipient of a Johns Hopkins University Fellowship for Outstanding Teaching. She speaks and lectures frequently on the topics of technology and education. *Fortune, U.S. News & World Report, Newsweek, BusinessWeek, Cosmopolitan, InfoWorld, The Los Angeles Times, New York Newsday, The San Francisco Chronicle, USA Today,* and many others have featured and quoted Dixon. The Associated Press has also featured Dixon in wire stories released for worldwide distribution. Dixon's television appearances have included segments on CBS News' *48 Hours,* NBC, ABC, CNN, Fox, PBS, MSNBC, and NPR.

Dixon, also a classically trained musician, writes about music and performs on the clarinet and recorder professionally whenever she can fit it in. She lives in Southern California.

ABOUT IDG BOOKS WORLDWIDE

Welcome to the world of IDG Books Worldwide.

IDG Books Worldwide, Inc., is a subsidiary of International Data Group, the world's largest publisher of computer-related information and the leading global provider of information services on information technology. IDG was founded more than 25 years ago and now employs more than 8,500 people worldwide. IDG publishes more than 275 computer publications in over 75 countries (see listing below). More than 60 million people read one or more IDG publications each month.

Launched in 1990, IDG Books Worldwide is today the #1 publisher of best-selling computer books in the United States. We are proud to have received eight awards from the Computer Press Association in recognition of editorial excellence and three from *Computer Currents'* First Annual Readers' Choice Awards. Our best-selling ...*For Dummies*® series has more than 30 million copies in print with translations in 30 languages. IDG Books Worldwide, through a joint venture with IDG's Hi-Tech Beijing, became the first U.S. publisher to publish a computer book in the People's Republic of China. In record time, IDG Books Worldwide has become the first choice for millions of readers around the world who want to learn how to better manage their businesses.

Our mission is simple: Every one of our books is designed to bring extra value and skill-building instructions to the reader. Our books are written by experts who understand and care about our readers. The knowledge base of our editorial staff comes from years of experience in publishing, education, and journalism — experience we use to produce books for the '90s. In short, we care about books, so we attract the best people. We devote special attention to details such as audience, interior design, use of icons, and illustrations. And because we use an efficient process of authoring, editing, and desktop publishing our books electronically, we can spend more time ensuring superior content and spend less time on the technicalities of making books.

You can count on our commitment to deliver high-quality books at competitive prices on topics you want to read about. At IDG Books Worldwide, we continue in the IDG tradition of delivering quality for more than 25 years. You'll find no better book on a subject than one from IDG Books Worldwide.

John Kilcullen
CEO
IDG Books Worldwide, Inc.

Steven Berkowitz
President and Publisher
IDG Books Worldwide, Inc.

Eighth Annual Computer Press Awards ➤ 1992

Ninth Annual Computer Press Awards ➤ 1993

Tenth Annual Computer Press Awards ➤ 1994

Eleventh Annual Computer Press Awards ➤ 1995

Author's Acknowledgments

I am *deeply* grateful to the many people who assisted me in the preparation of this manuscript. In the course of researching this book, I worked with over 50 career experts and top-flight recruiters. Without them, the information in this book would not be nearly as accurate, timely, or helpful.

Special thanks to Jim Lemke, resume, career, technology, and staffing and systems guru who gave me incredible insider info and great leads. Also to Michael R. Forrest, founder of CareerPath.com and general genius, who helped me think through key online job search issues. Ray Marcy, CEO of Interim, was key in helping me capture a picture of today's changing workforce and workplace, and Bill Warren graciously listened to my ideas and opinions and gave me crucial "road tested" feedback. Rick Miller also spent numerous hours letting me bounce ideas off of him — thank you for your technical help and recruiting knowledge!

Thanks also to Mike Silvester of Personics Software, Nayan Patel of Yahoo!, Suely Lohr, ace professional recruiter for GTE, Diane Hilton, Graham Spencer of Excite, Ed Stankiewicz, who was of enormous help, Angie Pantazopoulos, recruiting coordinator for Kilpatrick Stockton, Ron Cimino, VP of Paul-Tittle Associates, Rex Ballard, Evan Silver, director of recruiting for California Pizza Kitchen, Tricia Miller of Surgical Dynamics, Jane Paradiso, president of Talisman Technologies, Patrick Arnold of Attorneys @ Work, Jennifer Nelson, an amazing manager at Rollo Associates, Mark Neyhaber, senior professional staffing rep of the Disneyland Resort, Maria Perkins, Carol Lashman, president of ConsultLink, Don Machis, president and CEO of Alexus, Mark Sugalski, sourcing manager extraordinaire, Dara Quackenbush of Olicom, Jose Colmenares, recruiting team leader for Southwest Airlines, Linda Rose of Collaborative Communications, Pamela Hamilton, Jennifer Peters of Sterling Hager, and Bob Levinstein, VP of NationJob Bank, and Jennie Luke of CareerCast. Many of my other cohorts have requested anonymity, but you know who you are, and thank you!

Very special thanks to Joyce Lain Kennedy for her support, wisdom, and guidance. I am also grateful, as always, for Amanda Taylor's eagle eye. Also thanks to my faithful test readers, who patiently read several versions of each chapter!

Thanks especially to the entire IDG team: to Diane Steele, who is a true author's publisher, to Jill Pisoni for approaching me with this book project in the first place, and to the gracious and skillful Pam Mourouzis, project editor on this book, and her team of expert wordsmiths. Everyone worked hard to bring this book in on time and in great shape. Thank you very much.

And thanks to my agent and my good friend, Margot Maley of Waterside Productions, for encouraging me to take on this project and for all her support along the way. As always, heartfelt thanks to my family for their support: Dave, Abigail, Poppy, and Minnesota.

Publisher's Acknowledgments

We're proud of this book; please register your comments through our IDG Books Worldwide Online Registration Form located at http://my2cents.dummies.com.

Some of the people who helped bring this book to market include the following:

Acquisitions, Editorial, and Media Development

Senior Project Editor: Pamela Mourouzis

Senior Acquisitions Editor: Jill Pisoni

Copy Editors: Ted Cains, Kathleen Dobie

Associate Permissions Editor: Carmen Krikorian

Technical Editor: Amanda C. Taylor

Media Development Technical Editor: Joell Smith

Editorial Manager: Leah P. Cameron

Editorial Assistant: Paul E. Kuzmic

Production

Project Coordinator: Regina Snyder

Layout and Graphics: Cameron Booker, J. Tyler Connor, Lou Boudreau, Angela F. Hunckler, Jane E. Martin, Anna Rohrer, Brent Savage, Janet Seib, M. Anne Sipahimalani, Deirdre Smith

Proofreaders: Christine Berman, Kelli Botta, Michelle Croninger, Sarah Fraser, Rachel Garvey, Nancy Price, Janet M. Withers

Indexer: Sherry Massey

Special Help

Tere Drenth, Project Editor; Joe Jansen, Senior Copy Editor; Stephanie Koutek, Copy Editor

General and Administrative

IDG Books Worldwide, Inc.: John Kilcullen, CEO; Steven Berkowitz, President and Publisher

IDG Books Technology Publishing: Brenda McLaughlin, Senior Vice President and Group Publisher

Dummies Technology Press and Dummies Editorial: Diane Graves Steele, Vice President and Associate Publisher; Mary Bednarek, Director of Acquisitions and Product Development; Kristin A. Cocks, Editorial Director

Dummies Trade Press: Kathleen A. Welton, Vice President and Publisher; Kevin Thornton, Acquisitions Manager

IDG Books Production for Dummies Press: Beth Jenkins Roberts, Production Director; Cindy L. Phipps, Manager of Project Coordination, Production Proofreading, and Indexing; Kathie S. Schutte, Supervisor of Page Layout; Shelley Lea, Supervisor of Graphics and Design; Debbie J. Gates, Production Systems Specialist; Robert Springer, Supervisor of Proofreading; Debbie Stailey, Special Projects Coordinator; Tony Augsburger, Supervisor of Reprints and Bluelines; Leslie Popplewell, Media Archive Coordinator

Dummies Packaging and Book Design: Robin Seaman, Creative Director; Jocelyn Kelaita, Product Packaging Coordinator; Patti Crane, Packaging Specialist; Kavish + Kavish, Cover Design

♦

The publisher would like to give special thanks to Patrick J. McGovern, without whom this book would not have been possible.

♦

Contents at a Glance

Cartoons at a Glance

By Rich Tennant

page 67

page 229

page 185

page 137

page 7

Fax: 978-546-7747 • E-mail: the5wave@tiac.net

Table of Contents

Foreword

*T*he most effective route to advancing your career ten years ago was focusing on your job. Today, the best route is becoming an expert on the job search.

I'll explain.

In the past, people were consumed with job security — stick with a company, wait your turn in line, and eventually your employer will recognize and reward your efforts. Therefore, most people expected to go through the "upheaval" of changing jobs only two or three times throughout their work lives. When confronted with the task of finding a job only once a decade, they resorted to traditional methods: scouring through the Sunday classified section, networking with friends, blindly mass-mailing resumes, and registering with several employment agencies.

Luckily, the world has changed. The advent of reengineering and even downsizing has created a new mindset among workers. Instead of placing yourself at the mercy of "paternalistic organizations," you're taking greater control over your career, relying less on your employer. This means staying in touch with the job market, knowing which skills increase your marketability, and advancing your career through comparatively frequent job changes — whether with the same employer or with different ones. In short, job security is out and career security is in!

Unlike "the job hunt," the search for career security has no start and no finish. It is a process whereby you nourish your career on an ongoing basis. You should no longer wait until you are in a compromised position — miserably unhappy in a job or unemployed — to contemplate your career. Instead, spend one hour each month, when you can assess your career goals in a more proactive and accurate frame of mind. The Internet (and other entities, like Interim) is becoming an important career agent in this new paradigm. They are answering questions like

- What is the current demand for my skills in my region?
- What kinds of wages are people in my profession earning right now?
- What industries are presenting more career opportunities than others?
- What is the difference in cost of living if I were to relocate?

While a tremendous amount of information and energy has gone into the Internet to date, on a whole, it is still what I consider to be an undisciplined forum, with vast deviations in the quality of information found. In *Job Searching Online For Dummies,* Pam Dixon has created a road map for sifting through the Internet to find its true gems in career information. The Internet will continue to evolve, improve its ease of use, and become an integral resource to our workforce in the future.

The good news is that you already have your fingertips on some of tomorrow's best tools for managing your career today.

—Ray Marcy, CEO of Interim Services Inc.,
    Worldwide leader in comprehensive staffing,
    employment, and consulting solutions

Introduction

If you're looking for a job, then you're in luck! You picked up the right book to help you jump-start your job search in a big way. In this book, you get the inside scoop on everything you need to know about using the Internet to get a job in today's workplace.

I know how maddening it can be to feel like you're wasting away in a frustrating or dead-end job — you know, the kind where the headaches outweigh the money. And even if you have a great job, sometimes it's just time to move on.

I also know how scary it is to switch careers, and how jittery a big jump like that can make you feel. Getting a great job is always important, but it's especially so when that job is the first job of your new career.

In this book, I show you everything you need to know to capture the best job possible by using the Web and other online tools, such as e-mail. You may be quite surprised to learn that online job searching is so widespread now that between 40 and 80 percent of employers search for job candidates online.

Job searching online is fast and effective, and it can get your foot in the door when no other job-search method can. Interested? I hope so, because I'm all set to get started helping you find the very best job for you.

What's in This Book

This book contains the information you need to launch, maintain, and complete a successful online job search. It's divided into parts to make all that information easier to find. Here are the details about each part.

Part I: Getting Ready for Your Job Search

Part I is a power-pack of chapters that get you organized and give you an online job-search strategy. If you've ever felt like you were spinning your wheels in cyberspace, the chapters in this part will ground you and get you going on the path that you want to take. You discover online job-search tricks and techniques and find out about online job searching trends and numbers. You also get the lowdown on online privacy and your job search.

Part II: Building Your Electronic Toolkit

Putting together your electronic resume doesn't have to be the hardest part of finding a job. In fact, electronic resumes are a relatively simple matter. And after you have one going, you'll find using an electronic resume to be fast, efficient, and really effective. Part II shows you all you need to know about how to put together and use your electronic resumes and cover letters — with ease! You also get important information about online interviewing, plus telephone tips specifically geared to online job searching.

Part III: Communicating and Networking in the Digital World

Even the most silver-tongued folks sometimes find themselves with the taste of shoe leather in their mouths when it comes to the intricacies of e-mailing and online networking. In Part III, you get a complete cure to that foot-in-the-mouth feeling, with expert online networking advice that *really* works. You also catch up on the latest details about a hot new trend for job seekers: Web portfolios.

Part IV: Finding and Choosing a Job Online

Finding a job by using cyberspace as your search vehicle is easier than you may think. In Part IV, you get the complete scoop on where to look for jobs, plus tips on navigating online job databases like a real pro. Rounding out this part is important information about managing the tremendous results that you can expect from your online job search.

Part V: The Part of Tens

The Part of Tens contains five information-packed chapters that give you tips from employers, ways to improve your job-search odds, answers to common questions, and online no-no's to avoid. You also find general online job searching tips that can benefit everyone.

The Job Searching Online For Dummies Internet Directory

This is a long title for a simple idea — that is, the most definitive online job searching directory currently available! The directory lists for you the very best online job-search hot spots. You find reviews of the best online job and resume databases, including job sites for people working in professions from high-tech to legal to sales to communications and more. You also find information about tracking down company information online, and resume and cover letter help.

How to Use This Book

I know that everyone has completely different job-search questions and needs. That's why I designed this book so that you can jump around and read just those chapters you need to read. Feel free to hop and skip from topic to topic!

To assist you in your book browsing, I have a couple of suggestions that may help you as you pick and choose:

- ✔ **If you're a passive job seeker (that is, if you're just casually keeping an eye out for new job opportunities):** Make sure to cruise by Chapter 2 and look at the job-search strategies that apply specifically to passive job seekers. Also check out Chapter 11 so that you can start building your online network right away. You may also want to know about job search agents; check Chapter 14 for those details. And finally, because you're probably currently employed, be sure to look at Chapter 4 to read up on privacy and your job search.

- ✔ **If you need a new job yesterday:** You may want to jump right in and get your resume together; check out Chapters 5, 6, and 7 for resume information. Also, you want to start browsing job ads *immediately*. First check Chapter 2 to find a job strategy (the Blowout strategy may be a good one for you to try), and then go right to Chapter 14 to get going on job databases. When you take a moment to slow down, you may want to take a peek at Chapter 10 to make sure that your e-mail techniques are polished to a high gloss.

- ✔ **If you're a new college grad:** Follow the advice for people who need a new job yesterday. You may also want to check out the "Associations" section of the directory for extra help.

- ✔ **If you're a seasoned pro:** You'll probably take your time with a job search, because you want to find a job that fits your skills perfectly. I recommend that you follow the advice for passive job seekers, but with a twist: You may also want to get up-to-date with Web portfolios, which have become a very hot way for seasoned pros to both demonstrate computer knowledge and show samples of terrific work. See Chapter 12 for Web portfolio information.

- ✔ **If you're new to the Web:** You may want to begin with Chapter 1 and then go on to Chapters 2, 3, and 4, in that order. After you read those chapters, you'll be up to speed (and then some!). Next, you may want to graze through Chapters 13 and 14 to get a feel for where and how to look through online job databases.

Foolish Assumptions

I haven't made too many assumptions in this book, other than the following:

- ✔ I assume that you're looking for a job! I wrote this book specifically with job seekers in mind. I put front-and-center all the questions that job seekers have asked me and continue to ask me, and I answer those questions very directly in this book.

- ✔ I assume that you know what the World Wide Web is. I don't go into detail about definitions of the Web, give specifics about how to use Web browsers, or provide information about signing up for Web access. Instead, I focused the information in this book on job searching online. For details about the Web, take a look at *The Internet For Dummies* (also published by IDG Books Worldwide, Inc.), by Carole Baroudi, John R. Levine, and Margy Levine Young.

- ✔ Finally, I assume that you understand that Web addresses change frequently and that Web sites can "crash" from time to time. If you can't connect to one of the sites listed in this book, always try back at a later time, or check my Web site (www.pamdixon.com) to see if the address has changed. And if a site continues to give you problems, perhaps it has disappeared in a puff of digital dust. Never fear — you can still find plenty of job sites that work for you.

Conventions Used in This Book

I discuss the Web throughout this book. Most Web site names are pretty straightforward — for example, Career Mosaic is a pretty easy-to-understand name. But occasionally, you may find that names of Web sites look like URLs

(Web addresses) and even e-mail addresses. Though hip names like Reference.COM and Attorneys @ Work are catchy, they may be confusing to you as a reader.

So when I discuss resources available on the Web, I highlight the URL as follows:

`www.pamdixon.com`

If the URL appears within a paragraph, it appears like this: `www.pamdixon.com`. Real e-mail addresses look like this: `jobsearch@pamdixon.com`.

These conventions should help you distinguish between clever names and "real" links and addresses.

Icons Used in This Book

As you look through this book, you'll notice small pictures, or *icons,* to the left of the text. These icons are in the book as a convenience to you so that you can locate particularly helpful tips and advice in a jiffy. Each *...For Dummies* book contains slightly different icons. Here's a list of the icons you'll find in this book:

When you see this icon, you can count on finding insider tips and job-search information.

This icon "tips" you off to special online job-search tricks, techniques, and advice.

You see this icon highlighting road-tested suggestions and tricks.

This icon alerts you to definitions of technical terms.

Online job searching can save you time. This icon alerts you to specific time-saving methods.

This icon helps you remember important ideas so that you can always present yourself at your best.

If something may trip you up in your job search, this icon warns you about potential problems.

Launching Your Most Successful Job Search Ever

Getting a great job doesn't have to be drudgery! As you plan your job-search strategy, write your resume, and begin to contact employers, know that I'm here to help you in your journey. The majority of my help comes in the form of this book — it's chock-full of the latest online job searching advice.

If you read this book carefully, you'll find most of your online job-search questions answered. But occasionally, something new comes up. If you find yourself in a sticky online spot that I haven't covered, feel free to e-mail me (jobsearch@pamdixon.com) or visit my Web site (www.pamdixon.com).

Contacting me can help you out with your problem, and it will help future job seekers as I learn what's on job seekers' minds. I won't be able to send you an entire chapter on the matter, but I can usually point you in the right direction, or at least try!

Part I
Getting Ready for Your Job Search

The 5th Wave   By Rich Tennant

"NIFTY CHART, FRANK, BUT NOT ENTIRELY NECESSARY."

In this part . . .

Many job seekers want to use the Web in their job searches but are overwhelmed by the glut of information online. Other job seekers are hesitant to put any information online because they fear who might find out about their job-search efforts.

In this part, I show you how to tame the chaotic contents of the Web into usable, helpful job-search tools. You find super-effective help on developing a winning online job-search strategy, along with easy-to-follow online search techniques. And finally, if you're worried about your boss's prying eyes, you get the online privacy answers you need.

Chapter 1

Figuring Out What Makes an Online Job Search Work

. . . .

In This Chapter

▶ How effective online job searching really is

▶ What jobs are available online

▶ Who is likeliest to get a job by looking online

▶ What tools you need to succeed

. . . .

*F*inding a new job is a whole lot like going shopping for a new pair of shoes. If you take a friend, know where to shop, and know what you're looking for, you can actually make a pretty good time of the entire affair. (At least, I know that I can!) And at the end of the day, you go home with something new that fits you perfectly, that you really like, and that you'll use for some time to come.

In your job search, this book is that friend who goes along with you. It helps you figure out where to shop, gives you honest advice about what looks good, and helps you find not just any old job, but a job that really suits you. At the end of the day, my hope is that you find the job that brings out your best as a person and as a professional.

In this book, the particular store that I help you to shop in is that vast digital realm known as cyberspace. In this chapter, you find out what that kind of a shopping spree is all about. You'll be happy to know that when you go shopping for a job in cyberspace, your chances of coming back with what you really want are very good, indeed.

New Trends in Job Searching

Recently, I was inspecting a milk carton, checking to see whether the milk I was about to use was still fresh. The date stamp was just fine. What surprised me was the Web address I found, encouraging milk drinkers with questions to visit the dairy's Web site.

Huh? Since when does *milk* tie into the Web? And just when did a homey dairy get a Web site? Since the Web has pervaded just about every aspect of life, that's when.

The Web is a lot more than just a clever, creative place where nerds and geeks gather to catch up on computer trends. That whole notion of the Web as Geekville faded permanently at least five years ago.

Now, business interests have swept onto the Web, changing the landscape tremendously. Businesses from small to very large have made the Web a place that's extremely conducive to work issues, like productivity and — most important to you — job searching.

The Web holds a remarkably integrated position in today's business world. That is, businesses typically have one foot planted firmly on the Web and the other planted in "real" life.

Here are just a few of the big job-search trends that have sprung up from the way the Web has become so integrated with business and daily affairs:

- Company Web pages are playing host to company jobs — to the tune of millions of jobs posted via company Web pages.
- Businesses post tens of thousands of jobs per day to online employment databases.
- Employers regularly dedicate personnel and budget to facilitate online job seekers.
- Employers and recruiters have incorporated online candidate-seeking in their candidate-finding repertoire.
- Business e-mail — including job-search e-mail — accounts for over a trillion messages per year.
- Online resume databases are beginning to institute privacy policies due to the steady increase in high-level executives using the Web for job searching.
- Traditionally nontechnical professions have come online; for example, attorneys are a rapidly growing segment of the online job searching market.
- Online job databases have grown into full-fledged businesses as opposed to small one- or two-person proprietorships.

Today's job seeker, like my favorite dairy, needs to have one foot in the cyberworld and one foot in "real" life. Online job searching has officially become an integral part of a job search.

Looking at the Numbers

If you're wondering, like most people, exactly how many employers and job seekers use the Web to find each other, then this is the section for you. Here are some numbers to think about:

- ✔ According to a 1998 Ernst & Young/American Management Association HR Focus Survey, 70 percent of respondents use the Internet for recruiting, and half of human resources executives surveyed have employed "virtual" candidates in the past year.

- ✔ According to the Fordyce Letter, perhaps the most influential and widely read newsletter in the employment industry, employers and recruiters use the Internet and the Web to make 48 percent of all their hires.

- ✔ Coopers and Lybrand, an international professional services firm, issued a report about how employers found executives and middle managers. Web sites constituted 17.5 percent of hires for executives and 27.5 percent of hires for middle managers.

- ✔ According to William Warren, president of the Online Career Center, the OCC Web site receives over 1 million unique visitors per month. The OCC is independently audited, so these numbers are *real*. (An *independent audit* means that an unbiased third party reviews the OCC numbers.) The visits are about equally split between job seekers looking at job ads and employers looking at resumes.

- ✔ According to Nayan Patel, manager of the Yahoo! Classifieds section, Yahoo! Classifieds receives "millions" of visits every couple of weeks. Again, the Yahoo! numbers are independently audited.

- ✔ About 17,000 new jobs are posted online each week.

- ✔ Established online career sites are experiencing an average growth rate of about 22 to 27 percent per year, with some sites experiencing much higher rates.

- ✔ MRI (Management Recruiters International) surveyed 4,247 hiring executives responsible for hiring middle and upper managers and professionals. They found that about 37 percent of participants surveyed use the Internet to recruit. Here are some of the breakdowns by industry:

> Some 71.2 percent of technology firms use the Internet to recruit candidates, as do 42.6 percent of financial services firms, 39 percent of healthcare corporations, 45 percent of insurance companies, and 59 percent of telecommunication companies. Virtually all companies surveyed used the Internet to recruit at least a portion of candidates.
>
> ✔ According to a new survey by Lee Hecht Harrison, a major multinational career services firm, 41 percent of employers who responded used the Internet regularly to identify job candidates.
>
> ✔ Also according to Lee Hecht Harrison, the most common resource that employers use to post job opportunities are corporate Web sites, with 43 percent of employers posting jobs on their own sites, followed by 36 percent using job-posting Web sites.

These are just a portion of surveys containing numbers galore about online job searching. The essence of all the information is that, statistically speaking, you can miss a considerable number of opportunities if you don't shop for a job online.

Getting Hired by Getting Wired

Can you find a job online? Absolutely. Between looking at online job databases and looking at company Web sites, you can find jobs in pretty much every industry and profession posted online these days. Getting a job, in essence, has become almost as simple as e-mailing a resume.

Of course, you need to know what kind of resume to e-mail, you need to know what to say in that resume, and you especially need to know where to send the e-mail and whom to address it to! Anymore, the question isn't so much "Does this online thing work?" It's more a question of "How can I get this online thing to work for *me*?"

The bottom line? Yes, you can get hired by getting wired. As far as the "how" of a wired job search — well, that's what this book is all about!

Who Is Likeliest to Succeed in an Online Job Search?

You are likliest to succeed in an online job search! Though it's true that, five years ago, mainly techies could find jobs online; now, people from all professions can find jobs online. Some of the most *commonly* advertised types of jobs online include

- Technical jobs, including programming, computers, systems administration, and so on
- Engineering
- Financial services
- Sales and marketing
- Administrative
- Telecommunications
- Communications, including public relations
- Teaching, including academic and research
- Business and professional services
- Medical
- Legal, in increasing numbers

Even if you don't find a job posted on a job database, that by no means spells the end of your online job search. Online job searches are much broader and richer than that. A big part of online job searching involves visiting company Web sites. If you can think of a company, and if the company has a Web site, then you'll more than likely find jobs at that company posted there.

The Tools You Need to Succeed

Fortunately, the only items that you really need to conduct your online job search are

- The desire to find a job that's right for you.
- Access to a computer with Web access. It doesn't have to be your computer — you can rent a computer, borrow a friend's, or go to a public library.

The only other thing that you really need is the willingness to stick with it.

As far as skills, don't sweat it. Let me help you through your online job-search process. You find me in every one of these pages, walking with you every step of the way. I'm there when the going gets tough and when the going is smooth. I help you figure out where to look for a job, how to put your resume together, and how to cold-call an employer with your electronic resume. (And with style, too!)

The techie question

If you work in a technical profession, looking online for your job is more important than ever. It's not that you'll necessarily see a job advertisement that suits you; maybe you won't. But if you want to work for a particular company, you want to have a sharp, convincing electronic resume to e-mail to that employer.

Employers tell me that they don't even want to interview a technical candidate who isn't Internet-savvy; therefore, online job-search skills have become part of the filtering process. You probably knew that this trend was coming down the pike, so you're probably not surprised by it. I'm just confirming what you most likely already suspected.

The Web is not a complicated universe to understand, and getting a job via the Web is just a matter of understanding the new rules of the game. In this book, I take you job-shopping in this new cyber-universe and help you find a job that you'll enjoy for years to come.

Chapter 2
Winning Online Job-Search Strategies

*F*or most people, job searching has three initial steps:

1. **As soon as you know that you need a new job, you panic.**

2. **When you sit down to write or update your resume, you really panic.**

3. **When you try to find job leads, you really, really panic.**

Needless to say, all these steps come with a complete repertoire of uncomfortable feelings and thoughts. But before you start thinking that you're all alone in this endeavor, take a look at what most employers do when they need to *fill* a job:

1. **As soon as they need to fill a position, they panic.**

2. **When they can't find any good resumes, they really panic.**

3. **When they can't get anyone to agree to interview for the job, they really, really panic, and then they call a recruiter.**

Believe it or not, employers are just as panicked about getting jobs filled as you are about finding one. The trick in a successful job search (particularly an online job search) is to understand exactly how an employer panics and to insert yourself in the right place during the process.

That's what this chapter is all about. You get valuable information about what the job-search process is like from the inside. I interviewed hundreds of employers and dozens of recruiters and asked for the insider's view of the job-search process, and I'm here to share my knowledge with you.

Also in this chapter, you find out how to conduct your online job search step by step for great success. You find great job-search strategies, techniques, and tips. And you put a stop to your job-search panic in no time!

How an Online Job Search Works Today

An online job search is not a black-and-white matter; you find all sorts of gray tones blurring hard lines of distinction. That's because employers conduct a portion of their searches for candidates online, recruiters conduct a portion of their candidate searches online, and now, most job candidates conduct a portion of *their* job searches online. And everyone conducts the search slightly differently.

Certain major steps, however, are pretty much the same, and that's what I want to help you see.

An inside view of the job-search process

If you want to find a job and find one quickly, you need to understand the *entire* process of how jobs get filled. Otherwise, you're looking at a job search from just your vantage point and missing big pieces of the picture that can really help you fast-forward your job search.

A job search involves three essential components: the employer, the candidate, and the position to be filled. Recruiters may be a fourth component, depending on the job. How employers and candidates go about finding each other is what constitutes the job-search process. You need to remember that *employers have just as much of a process as you do.*

Realize that, as much as you're fretting over getting a job, the employer is equally fretting over filling that same job. From your point of view, somewhere "out there" the right opportunity is waiting to be found. And from the employer's point of view, somewhere "out there" the perfect candidate is waiting to be found. If you really know and understand how employers go about hiring for jobs, the inside info really puts some oomph into your job search.

Understanding the employer's candidate-search process

When employers set out to find candidates, they don't just look around one day and say to themselves, "Oh, I think I need to hire someone!" In very rare cases or in very small companies, you may find a casual scenario like that, but more often than not, the process is more formal.

Rick Miller, president of CareerCast (`www.careercast.com`), has years of experience as a corporate and third-party recruiter. Miller uses his experience to run a successful employment site and teach corporate recruiters in Fortune 100 and 500 companies how to do their jobs. According to Miller and others, when companies panic and think that a job will be hard to fill, they immediately jump for the phone to call a third-party recruiter to help fill the position.

But companies generally go through a longer, more thorough process before they reach for the phone. Here's the process that most mid-sized and large companies go through to make a hire when a position opens up, more or less:

1. **Someone within the company posts a requisition for a job. At the same time, the person posting the requisition goes through the resumes of existing employees to look for a fit.**

   The requisition, or "job req" as it's often called, is posted internally for a certain period of time. This ensures that talent within the company is exhausted before the company turns to hiring someone new.

2. **The job req goes public and becomes available to those not working for the company.**

   In larger companies, the job req goes to the human resources department. In smaller companies, the job req stays with the hiring manager.

3. **The human resources department or hiring manager performs a search for candidates in the company's resume database.**

   Candidates in a company's resume database include those whose resumes have come in "over the transom" from the Web and other sources.

4. **After searching the internal database, the employer puts out job announcements in a variety of low-cost places, including online job postings on a selection of job sites.**

5. **If online job announcements don't bring in candidates, the employer tries more expensive options, like newspaper and print ads.**

What is a recruiter, anyhow?

In case you have never worked with a recruiter, here are some quick definitions to help you get a general understanding of recruiters.

Recruiters come in two varieties:

- **Corporate recruiters** work for one company, typically as full-time employees within the human resources department.

- **Third-party recruiters** work for themselves or for recruiting firms, sometimes called *staffing firms*. Third-party recruiters typically handle many jobs for many different companies and are not full-time employees of any one company. Rather, third-party recruiters are contracted by companies for help filling hard-to-fill or special positions.

Recruiters also come in many flavors. Here are a few of the major ones:

- **High-tech recruiters** find candidates in high-tech fields, such as computer programming and engineering.

- **Executive recruiters** specialize in very high-end candidates, typically with six-figure salaries on up. They look for CEOs and board members.

- **Medical recruiters** find candidates within the medical industry, which includes everyone from doctors to researchers to biotechnologists.

Please note that I did not mention *online recruiter* as a specialty. Why? Because most recruiters work online now. To separate a regular recruiter from an online recruiter is to misunderstand how recruiters work today. Perhaps there are a few recruiters who don't use the Internet to find candidates, but those not using the Net constitute a minority. What works for recruiters is typically to do a little bit of everything — they use the phone, job ads, the Web, and all the other traditional candidate-search tools, such as networking.

6. **If none of the above works, the employer hires a third-party recruiter to find a candidate.**

    Meanwhile, the employer still continues with passive job advertisements online and on the corporate Web site to try to bring in candidates. (*Passive* means that the ad is a drawing-in device for candidates.)

7. **After the employer and/or the third-party recruiter finds a pool of candidates, the candidates are called on the phone and screened.**

    Those candidates who "win" the phone screening are invited in for interviews. Often, the pool of candidates includes those who have been brought in by recruiters and those who have come in through online or other job ads. (For more information on dealing with phone screening, see Chapters 9 and 15.)

8. **The interviews take place, and, ostensibly, the best candidate gets the job.**

Something to think about: If you're competing for a job and your skills are very similar to another person's, the person who came in through a recruiter often loses the bid. That's because the company has to pay a lot of extra money for candidates that a recruiter brings in. If you're the hands-down best candidate for the job, however, you don't need to worry about recruiters' fees.

Understanding how recruiters fit into the online job-search process

Nowadays, most recruiters do at least a portion of their business online, with some doing enormous amounts of business online. How likely it is that you will interface with a recruiter depends heavily on what area you work in and how high up the employment food chain you are.

Here's the reality that determines your relationship to a recruiter: The average recruiter gets paid 20 to 30 percent of your first year's salary. That 20 to 30 percent can mean a pretty hefty sum for an employer to pay out.

In some cases, employers are more than happy to shell out the cash because they're so grateful to have found the right candidate. In other cases, if you and another candidate are equally qualified, the person who came in via a recruiter typically loses the position.

The bottom line is that the higher up the employment ladder you are, the more likely it is that you'll interface with recruiters in your online job search. And the harder it is to locate professionals in your area of expertise, the more likely it is that you'll deal with a specialist third-party recruiter, like a medical or legal recruiter.

If you work in a high-demand niche specialty (like telecommunications engineers who specialize in cell-phone technology), your overall likelihood of working with recruiters increases dramatically. For example, the current high-tech market is so "dry" that a very high percentage of jobs in the high-tech area are going to recruiters.

In fact, more than 20 CEOs and executives told me that the only way to find high-tech workers in today's market is to hire them away from other companies. So if you work in a high-tech or high-demand industry (you know who you are!), prepare to work with recruiters in your online job search. If you don't find them, they'll find you!

Tips for working with recruiters

Recruiters have come online in *droves* to find candidates. As you search for jobs online, you may come across quite a few job ads that are offered by third-party recruiters. And if you post your resume online, you may also get calls from third-party recruiters.

The following sections give you some tips to help you work effectively with the recruiters you run across in cyberspace.

Keep good records so that you can go with the "First Contact" rule

An employer and a third-party recruiter can post an advertisement for the same position at the exact same time. Multiple candidates have told me that they got calls from both a third-party recruiter and an employer for the same job after e-mailing a resume to a company and posting that resume online. Which contact do you go with? Ethically, you need to go with the person who contacts you first.

Going with whoever contacts you first may sound simple to you, but the recruiter may have a real problem hearing you say that the employer contacted you first. How is the recruiter to know that you're not just handing out a line?

To keep everything on the up and up, keep very good records of where you post your resume and on what date. If you send your resume to a company Web site, note the date on which you send the resume. Otherwise, if you haven't kept good records, you really do have to go with the recruiter.

When you talk with a recruiter about a job, verify the job ad

If you're talking to a corporate recruiter, you don't need to worry about verifying a job ad. An in-house corporate recruiter is working for just one company and typically deals with real jobs (see the sidebar "What's a recruiter, anyhow?"). Corporate recruiters get paid whether or not they fill a position, so they don't need to place candidates at the same rate that many third-party recruiters do. On the other hand, some third-party recruiters — only a few — have been known to post phony ads in cyberspace in the hopes of raking in candidates left and right for future jobs that may come up.

To find out whether a recruiter is a corporate or third-party recruiter, simply ask what company the recruiter works for. If the recruiter says, "I work for Jane Doe and Associates," and the job he or she is offering is with GTE, then you're probably dealing with a third-party recruiter, and you need to verify the job ad. If the recruiter gives you a company name that matches the job, however — for example, "I work for Mobile, and Mobile is offering the position of . . ." — then you're probably dealing with an in-house or corporate recruiter.

The general rule when dealing with third-party recruiters (which I got from good third-party recruiters, by the way) is to immediately ask which company is offering the job. If you hear something like "I have relationships with many major corporations . . . ," skip it. The ad is probably phony.

But if you hear "Motorola is offering this job. The job entails . . . ," then you're dealing with a real job and probably with a decent recruiter. Remember, good third-party recruiters know the job descriptions of the positions they're trying to fill, typically by heart.

Just in case you think that I'm picking on third-party recruiters, I'm really not; my husband has found all his jobs via a third-party recruiter who is also a good friend of his. I just want you to be aware that, because the online environment makes it harder to check up on things, a few unethical recruiters do take advantage where they can.

Recruiters sound off

While researching this book, I had plenty of opportunities to get the inside scoop from recruiters. The only problem is that the more inside the scoop, the less the person wanted to be identified. This section lists some real insiders' tips that shall, by request, remain unattributed. Some of the tips fall in the category of how recruiters do business, and other tips fall in the category of general gripes.

Here are some general statements that recruiters made about the job-search process:

✓ "I kid you not, I live by the resumes and e-mail addresses I find on the Internet. Once I have a resume, I will keep it for a year or more and call the person with opportunities that come up."

✓ "I look mainly on free Internet sites for resumes, like Usenet and open databases. After I get the resumes, I keep them indefinitely for future reference. It doesn't matter if I have a current opportunity or not; I figure I eventually will, so I keep whatever I find."

✓ "I know a recruiter who posts phony ads online in order to collect resumes. He'll gather in all the resumes like a big fishing trawler with a net two miles long. Then he'll keep those resumes and work through them forever. Job seekers need to be aware of this so they know to verify job advertisements before they send a resume to a recruiter."

✓ "My advice to candidates is this: Put relocation information right in your resume somewhere, or I will call you assuming relocation is an option. I don't care about salary range, because I can usually figure that out from the resume."

- ✔ "I'm just an intermediary. After I match a candidate up with the hiring manager, I'm on to the next thing."

- ✔ "When I go to find a top executive, I head right for the Web. I search for a person who is active in professional associations and I look for repeat mentions in publications related to the field."

Recruiters' biggest complaints tend to fall into a couple of oft-repeated categories. Here is a sample of each:

- ✔ "I don't have time to go digging around a candidate's resume for a career objective. I want it to be obvious. If it isn't, I think that maybe the candidate doesn't really know what they want."

- ✔ "If I see a typo, I toss the resume. It's a liability for me to give that resume to an employer."

- ✔ "If you send a recruiter a resume, it had better be a good one, and you should be serious about finding a job — not just 'thinking about it.'"

- ✔ "When I see a new resume posted online, I call the person immediately. If I don't, 15 other recruiters will have gotten there before me and I'll lose the candidate. It doesn't matter if it's Sunday night — I have to get to that person first. I just can't believe it when people aren't expecting calls after they post a resume."

Your Part of the Job-Search Process

If you read the first part of this chapter, you know how employers and recruiters go through the process of finding candidates. Now it's time to look at how to go about finding a job online and fit yourself successfully into employers' and recruiters' candidate-search processes.

Essentially, your total online job-search process breaks into two sections:

- ✔ **Your step-by-step job-search process:** A job-search *process* involves everything you do to get a job, like creating a resume and researching companies. I like to break the online job-search process into ten general steps, which you can find described in the following section.

- ✔ **Your job-search strategy:** A job-search *strategy* is essentially how you choose to target specific online areas in your job search. I've discovered four main job-search strategies that you can use in your job search. I discuss these four strategies in "Ultra-effective online job-search strategies" later in this chapter.

Think of an online job search like a highway with off-ramps. Recruiters and employers drive full-speed ahead, looking for people like you. And you drive full-speed ahead, looking for the right employers and recruiters to match up with. The process of driving is your job-search process. The roads you choose to take are your job-search strategy.

Just remember that employers and candidates are on the road and in the same general areas, so all you have to do is see that the right employer takes the right off-ramp — the one that leads to you!

Job searching online step by step

The Web has invaded just about every aspect of life. I see busses with Web URLs plastered on the sides, newspaper ads with URLs lurking in the small print, and movie trailers with animated URLs. Even the nightly news anchors advise people to "check our Web site for more information on these and other stories."

Why, then, should it come as a surprise that the Web has become part and parcel of the job-search process? At this point, you're really hurting yourself if you leave out the online medium as you search for a job. The Net just isn't a good thing to leave out of any employment-related venture anymore.

The question remains, though, how to use the Net in the most *effective* way. I've helped lots of people find jobs by using the Net. Here, let me share my step-by-step advice with you. It really works!

Step 1: Put together a job-search notebook

Before you do anything else, start your job-search notebook. I've seen over and over again how many responses an electronic job search can generate. When the calls start flowing in, you need to be organized so that you can stay on top of things. Otherwise, you can miss opportunities because you lost that one scrap of paper on which you wrote phone numbers.

Your job-search notebook can be as simple or as complex as you like. The whole point of your job-search notebook is to help you keep good records, stay organized, and keep all your information within easy striking distance.

Here's a list of good basics to include in your notebook:

- A three-ring binder that's at least an inch thick.
- Paper that you never remove from the binder. Use the paper to note when you send out resumes, to which sites, and the pertinent contact information. (Figure 2-1 shows a sample job-search form.)

✔ Printouts of job advertisements to which you responded.

✔ Printouts of resumes that you send out. If you're sending out different versions of your resume as you respond to job advertisements, print out the resumes and attach each resume to each job ad that you send it to. That way, when you get phone calls, you won't be wondering which version of your resume the person is looking at. Trust me — you won't remember!

✔ A form to take each caller's phone number, title, company, and pertinent job information. (See Chapter 15 for a sample form.)

✔ Company research. If you're researching companies (and you should be!), keep all your research in your job-search notebook, too.

✔ Printouts of your follow-up notes, or at least a detailed record of whom you send notes to.

Some people like to use an electronic spreadsheet (like Microsoft Excel) to track their job-search efforts and print out the spreadsheet on a regular basis. If this method works for you, great! Just keep a printout of your spreadsheet in your binder, and make sure that you have a backup copy of your spreadsheet on a floppy disk.

In Figure 2-1, you see an example of an Excel worksheet that I use with people who are looking for jobs. If a person doesn't have a computer at home, I just print out the form — it still works organizational wonders.

Figure 2-1:
An Excel worksheet especially made for tracking your job-search efforts.

Date:	Site Name:	Posted/Sent Resume: Yes	No	Responded to Job Ad:	Company or Recruiter:
Jan. 18	Career Mosaic		X	Yes	MCI–via in-house recruiter
Jan. 18	Attorneys @ Work	X		No	
Jan. 19	Alt.Jobs.misc		X	Downloaded jobs ads	Various (see in notebook)
Jan. 19	MCI Web site	X e-mailed to T.J. Jones			tjjones@xyz.com

Step 2: Select a strategy

Getting a job is a lot like waging a military campaign. A definite strategic planning element goes into any military effort, and a job search is just the same.

An online job search lends itself to four distinct types of search strategies. Which strategy you choose depends on the kinds of results you want. I cover each strategy in detail later in this chapter. But for now, here's a quick list of basic strategies:

- ✔ **The Blowout strategy:** An all-out effort where you leave no digital stone unturned.

- ✔ **The Little Bit of Everything strategy:** The lesser cousin of the Blowout strategy. You try all sorts of things, but in moderation.

- ✔ **The Passive strategy:** The strategy where you let jobs come to you. This is a strategy for people who aren't looking hard for a job, but want to make sure that they're not missing anything.

- ✔ **The Precision Strike strategy:** The strategy for people who know exactly where they want to work. It involves going after a company and getting in the door.

Step 3: Put together your resume

If you're a former president of the United States, you may get away with not having a resume. But for pretty much everyone else, a resume is a job-search staple that you need at your immediate disposal.

If you haven't written an electronic resume before, I admit to you that they're a bit different from paper resumes. You need to use different words and a different style to make digital resumes as effective as possible. But a digital resume is not a difficult thing to create. Chapters 5 and 6 walk you through the entire process.

One quick recommendation: Make sure that your resume is scannable when it's printed out. Many companies take paper resumes and scan them into computer databases. If you aren't aware of this, you could end up out of the resume loop. Also, don't underestimate the new love that employers have for digital resumes. Get yours together as soon as possible. If you have any questions about scannable resumes, again, refer to Chapters 5 and 6.

Step 4: Choose the type of resume to send

The only standard for resumes in a job search is that a standard doesn't seem to exist. That's why, during the course of your job search, you may be asked for an electronic resume, a paper resume, a faxed resume, and maybe even a Web resume.

Each time you send out a resume, you need to determine which resume type is best to send out. In general, employers expressed to me a strong preference for e-mailed resumes in plain-text, otherwise known as ASCII, format. Employers also expressed a strong dislike of faxed resumes, stating that even though they list fax numbers, they list them only as a "just in case" precaution.

Typically, if an employer lists an e-mail address, the company prefers an e-mailed resume. If the employer specifically asks that you send resumes in a particular manner, then by all means follow the employer's lead. Just be prepared to switch off what type of resume you send at a moment's notice! (See Chapters 5, 6, and 7 for details about resumes.)

Step 5: Write sample cover letters, follow-up notes, and thank-you notes

This may sound corny, but I have always advised job seekers to write sample cover letters and follow-up notes. That way, when you really need a note or cover letter, it's already written and perfected. You can substitute the names and a little bit of pertinent information and get the note out without worrying about it or, worse, procrastinating.

When you need to respond to an employer, procrastination can really work against you. So set aside a few quiet moments to get your sample letters going. When I receive thank-you notes from job searchers, this is one piece of advice that people typically mention as very helpful.

Step 6: Have a friend read and reread your send-out material

If you've been following these steps, then you've written your resume and a few sample cover letters and thank-you notes. Before you send those resumes and notes to anyone, take them to a trusted friend or two and ask them to read your material for errors.

I recently wrote a letter of recommendation for a good friend. It was a very important recommendation that would help her get into a graduate program. Even though I read that letter at least five times, the person I asked to proof my letter spotted a typo in one of the sentences.

I don't know why, but all I can tell you is that if you wrote it, you won't necessarily see your own errors. But your friends sure will! Let them help you with this critical step in your job-search process.

Step 7: Send out practice cover letters and resumes

Unless you're an absolute pro at sending out electronic cover letters and resumes, I strongly recommend that you send out at least one or two practice rounds. That beautiful resume may not look nearly as wonderful after it goes through the e-mail process!

I keep three e-mail addresses active at all times so that I can test the things I write about. I send myself v-Cards (see Chapter 10), resumes, cover letters, and all sorts of things, just to make sure that they come over the wires the way I want them to. (A *v-Card,* by the way, is a virtual business card you can send along with your e-mail messages.)

Because I test my own systems so much, I have learned over and over again that e-mailed documents can look really different at the receiving end. I know that not everyone has three e-mail accounts going, so I recommend that you send your materials to either a family member or a friend, or that you sign up for a couple of free e-mail accounts. (See Chapter 10 for more information about free e-mail accounts.)

You may encounter some nervousness in sending out your resume and other documents digitally. If you're new to e-mailing your resume, don't feel at all bad if you get a little jittery. It's a common feeling! Practice takes that nervous edge away. Also, as you start to see for yourself what your resume looks like after you send it, your nervousness subsides.

Step 8: Research companies and online posting sites

You have your resume, you have sample cover letters, and you have a strategy. You're ready to get rolling. Now, all you need to do is to find the company Web sites that interest you and find the online employment databases that suit your skills and interests.

In the "Ultra-effective online job-search strategies" section later in this chapter, I help you decide which types of online areas to visit, depending on your strategy. But you need to go through and look at the specific sites to decide exactly which you like the best. Use the Internet Directory at the back of this book to read about the sites and help narrow your choices. Then take a look for yourself. You may find that the Monster Board and the Online Career Center are perfect choices for you, or you may find that Career Mosaic is more your style.

For more help with choosing online databases, see Chapter 13.

Step 9: Begin an online networking program

Online networking is definitely a fine art. Few people can network effectively online, but those who can have *major* advantages.

I discuss how to network online in Chapter 11. Please read that chapter very carefully! Then begin your online networking program in earnest. Fully reaping the rewards of your online networking program takes a bit of time, but no matter. Keep at it, and you'll soon understand why I list online networking as an important part of your job-search process.

Step 10: Based on the strategy you choose, go online and begin searching for positions and posting your resume

With your electronic resume at your command, it's time to get online and go public with your online job search. This is the part where you look for online job advertisements and post your resume. In essence, you have arrived at the meat and potatoes of your job search.

Of course, because you have practiced sending your resume, you have no worries. And because you've selected an online search strategy in advance (see "Ultra-effective online job-search strategies" for details), you know exactly which sites you're going to visit online and whether you plan to post your resume at the places you visit.

Now all you have to do is to be prepared for the responses to your online job search. I recommend that you scan Chapter 15 for preparation tips. And if you have any questions about which online job-search strategy you should use, read the next section for details. Remember that you can switch strategies if you need to.

Ultra-effective online job-search strategies

Strategy is *everything* in a job search. That's why I'm cutting loose with my strategy secrets in this part of the chapter. Here, I unveil road-tested online job-search strategies that really work. To use these strategies, all you have to do is choose the one that best fits your needs and then follow the steps in the strategy.

To understand and use the powerful search strategies that I outline in this section, check out the Internet Directory at the back of this book. In the directory, you can find a listing of online job databases to use in your online job search.

I refer to a number of online terms in this section, such as the "Big Seven" and niche databases, which I use in the directory and throughout the book. For clarity, here are some quick definitions:

- ✔ **Big Seven employment sites:** The Big Seven employment sites are the largest employment sites on the Web. These sites get the most traffic and have the highest visibility. Typically, the Big Seven sites receive millions of unique visitors per month, sometimes even millions of visitors per week.

- ✔ **Corporate Web sites:** A corporate Web site is simply a company's or an organization's Web site. Anymore, corporate Web sites house volumes of information that's relevant to a job search.

✔ **General job databases:** General job databases cover a broad range of employment interests, but they aren't large enough to number among the Big Seven. In essence, general job databases that aren't Big Seven sites are second-tier employment sites. Note that second-tier doesn't always mean second-best.

✔ **Geographic sites:** Geographic sites specialize in collecting jobs in one specific geographical area, such as Texas or the Twin Cities.

✔ **Niche sites:** Niche sites cover a specific career focus. For example, a niche site may specialize in high-tech, medical, or legal jobs.

✔ **Usenet:** Usenet is an area of the Internet where you can post information related to specific areas of interest. Each area of interest has its own discussion site, usually called a *newsgroup*. More than 17,000 newsgroups exist, and the numbers are continually growing.

The Blowout strategy

The Blowout strategy is for those job seekers who want a job *immediately*, and for those who don't care if the world sees their resumes. You want maximum impact, and you don't care if 5,000 people start calling you. You want a job *now*.

Please be aware that the Blowout strategy puts your resume in front of anyone with a connection to the Web. Your resume gets maximum visibility. I don't recommend this strategy for people who are currently employed or who work in senior positions. This strategy produces fast results, but at the expense of personal privacy.

If you're in a big hurry and you don't care about others seeing your resume, then here's a strategy that can get you fast results:

1. **After you create your resume, post your resume on every one of the Big Seven databases that accept resumes, including open resume databases like the Yahoo! Classifieds.**

2. **Go to each general job database that I list in the Internet Directory at the back of this book and post your resume there.**

3. **Select as many niche databases as apply to you and post your resume on those niche sites.**

4. **Go to Usenet — yes, Usenet — and post your resume on the relevant Usenet groups.**

   A good place to post your resume to Usenet is at the Career Mosaic site, www.careermosaic.com.

5. **Send your resume to recruiters.**

To do so, head to InterBizNet's top 100 electronic recruiters list at www.interbiznet.com/eeri/index.html. Select as many recruiting agencies as apply to you and send your resume to them. Also, be sure to check the Recruiters Online Network at www.recruitersonline.com.

6. **At each employment site that you visit, send your resume to at least three contacts listed in job advertisements.**

7. **Get ready for the phone to ring.**

The Little Bit of Everything strategy

This strategy is just what it sounds like — you try a little bit of everything! This strategy is probably the best one for most job seekers. It gets you solid results but keeps your privacy intact. This strategy takes longer than the Blowout strategy, but it's much faster-acting than the Passive strategy.

This strategy is a great choice if you're currently employed.

1. **Choose two or three of the Big Seven databases to monitor.**

   You can sign up for jobs to be sent to your e-mail address, but you also need to actively visit the sites, too. If the site offers complete resume confidentiality, then post your resume. Call first to assure confidentiality.

2. **Choose four to seven of the general job databases to monitor.**

   Again, search the databases regularly. You can also have jobs sent to you, but understand that you still get the best results by visiting the site. Again, post your resume, but only if you're guaranteed complete confidentiality. Always call and confirm resume-posting confidentiality.

3. **Select one or two niche and geographical sites to monitor on a regular basis.**

   The same rules about resume confidentiality apply here, too.

4. **Research companies for which you want to work. Find their corporate Web sites and e-mail your resume to those companies.**

   You can e-mail your resume to as many companies as you can stand, because the companies won't pass around your resume. Choose at least 20 companies for maximum impact.

5. **Add two value-added search strategies to your repertoire — that is, network online and work with online associations.**

   See Part III for more information about networking online.

6. **Keep at it! Check job sites and company Web sites at least once each week.**

The Passive strategy

Perhaps you aren't exactly thrilled with your current working environment, or maybe the project you're currently working on is boring you to tears. Or maybe you see that a year down the road, your project or group may be downsized. If any of these scenarios applies to you, then the Passive strategy is a good choice.

In the Passive strategy, you keep your eyes peeled for new opportunities, but you don't spend a lot of time going online and searching for them. You also need to be super-cautious about who gets and sees your resume, because you don't want to blow the whistle on your job-search efforts.

Here's your strategy:

1. **Look through the Big Seven job databases. Select one or two that will send job listings to your e-mail address. Sign up for the e-mail service.**

2. **Look through the list of general job databases. Select three or four that will send you opportunities. Sign up for the e-mail service.**

3. **Choose one or two niche databases, selecting those that will e-mail lists of job opportunities to you. Sign up to receive the e-mail listings.**

4. **Post your resume online only if you have 100 percent control of it.**

   That is, post it only if the only people who ever see your resume are those to whom you send your resume.

5. **Wait and see which job opportunities come your way via e-mail.**

   When you see an opportunity that appeals to you, print out the advertisement and then send your resume to the contact person, stating in your cover letter that you are currently employed and that you need to keep your resume private.

   If you send your resume to a third-party recruiter, it's particularly important that you insist that the recruiter not pass your resume around to others. If you can't get a verbal agreement of confidentiality, don't send your resume to that person.

6. **As time goes on, you begin to see which databases have jobs that suit you. Narrow your database choices to just those that send you the best jobs.**

   Also, keep an eye out for new databases to try.

You can continue job searching passively until you find something you like, or until you decide to switch to a more active strategy. The real advantage of beginning with a passive job search is that you get a feel for what's available and for salary ranges.

The Precision Strike strategy

In the Precision Strike strategy, you go after just one or two companies for which you really want to work. This strategy is particularly effective for high-level executives and for people with hard-to-find skills:

1. **Research companies in your field.**

   Choose no more than five target companies or organizations to pursue. (See Chapter 3 for research tips.)

2. **Find the company Web sites.**

3. **Scour the Web sites for detailed contact information.**

   Collect e-mail addresses, company information, and philosophy, and check for job openings.

4. **Research the company thoroughly, using all possible online research methods.**

   Think depth of information, not breadth. (See Chapter 3 for extensive research tips.)

5. **Go on Usenet and Web forums to glean personal information about your target companies. For example, find other employees who work at the target company and strike up a conversation with them.**

   See Chapter 11 for details on how to do so smoothly.

6. **Loaded with background information and, hopefully, target names, take the plunge and send a very targeted cover letter and resume to one or two contacts at each company.**

7. **Follow up with one telephone call or with e-mail.**

8. **Check for job openings on the target Web sites continually, and keep up your networking efforts and follow-up notes. (See Chapter 11 for more information about networking and using follow-up notes.)**

Value-added job-search strategies

If you're interested in adding extra power to any of the standard online job-search strategies, then you can add one or more of the following bonus strategies to your search arsenal. These bonus strategies won't get you a job by themselves — they're definitely add-ons to your main strategies.

But these value-added job-search strategies can indeed help you uncover more jobs. These strategies may even help you realize better long-term career success if you stick with them.

Tapping into online associations

Finding an association relevant to your career interest used to be a whole lot of work. I distinctly remember going to the library and looking up associations in a huge — and I mean *huge* — monster of a book. Typically, the book had out-of-date information and was a chore to read.

But now, several people have created lists of associations that are on the Web. (See the "Associations" section of the Internet Directory at the back of this book for information about the lists.) The lists are extraordinary and can take you to literally thousands of associations.

After you find an association related to your area of expertise, put on your networking hat and get to work! For blow-by-blow details on using associations to network, see Chapter 11.

Here are just a few of the associations that I found online by visiting just one Web site, www.ntu.edu.sg/home/ctng/assoc.htm:

- ✔ American Accounting Association
- ✔ American Bar Association
- ✔ American Communication Association
- ✔ Direct Marketing Association
- ✔ International Television and Video Association
- ✔ National Association of Home Builders
- ✔ National Education Association
- ✔ Society of Women Engineers

Online networking — really

I've discovered that very few people network effectively, online or otherwise. Therefore, online networking is actually a value-added strategy. I bet you're like me in that you know all sorts of people who never network and still get good jobs.

But I must tell you, I have witnessed networking's power to help you get into a job you really want. That's where networking really comes into play — in a highly targeted job search. Another time when networking becomes important is when you have serious, long-term career goals in mind. Networking can help you reach your career goals much more easily and perhaps even more quickly. For online networking secrets, see Chapter 11.

Online corporate scouting

A highly underestimated value-added strategy is *corporate scouting,* or digging up all the possible companies you could work for. In any field, there are the high-profile front-runners — you know, the companies and organizations that stand tall. But then there are the unsung heroes — those high-quality organizations that you may not have heard about.

For example, just about every journalism school grad would leap at the opportunity to work for *The Wall Street Journal* or *The New York Times.* But what about all the other papers? The *Orange County Register,* for example, is a Pulitzer Prize-winning major metro daily that journalism graduates may never have heard of. That doesn't mean that the *Orange County Register* isn't a major paper or a good paper!

In your field, look for all the companies you *could* work for, not just the big players. That way, you can dramatically increase your chances of finding a job in your field. For detailed help in locating this kind of information, see Chapter 13.

Chapter 3

Getting the Information You Need Online

· ·

In This Chapter

▶ Super-effective search methods and tools

▶ Finding hard-to-find Web sites and quality information

▶ Scouring a Web site for information

▶ Super sample information searches

▶ Search tactics to avoid

▶ Bonus: Unusual search methods and tools

· ·

*A*t some point during your job search, you may come up short on information. And if you do, you'll probably want to go online to take care of your info-crisis.

No problem! The Web is a great place to find all sorts of job search–related information. The only problem is that most job searchers aren't Web specialists or professional researchers, so finding the right information in a timely manner can pose a challenge.

I could no doubt wax cyber-poetic for hundreds of pages about how to search the Web for information. But I know that you don't have time to read a tome about online searching. I also know that you may need at least a little bit of help, though; otherwise, you may risk being stuck paging through a list of 5,000 or more useless results from a search that didn't work out quite the way you wanted it to.

In this chapter, I save you from taking frustrating hikes through mounds of irrelevant information. Here, I give you a batch of specific, focused methods to use when you need to go online to hunt for employment-related information. You'll have the Web at your command in no time.

General Search Tools That Work in a Hurry

Just like in "real" life, to get anything done using a computer, you need the right tools. And along with those tools, you need a good plan. After all, the best tools available won't do you any good if you don't know how to use them properly or don't have a clear plan for using them. I can think of more than one truly horrible haircut I've gotten, and the fault didn't lie in the make or grade of the scissors that the stylist used!

Perhaps preparing to search the Web by collecting tools and getting a plan together sounds like way too much fuss. But as complicated as the Web has become, when you set out to find information on the Web, lining up your tools and tactics in advance is a good idea. This section talks about the tools; for information about the methods, see "The Tried and True Search Methods" section later in this chapter.

If you think of the Web as a mountain of data to be conquered, then your climbing tools of choice are search engines, meta lists, indexes, and word-of-mouth information. And along the way, you definitely want to put keywords to work for you.

TIP

Keyword tips

A *keyword* is simply a word or group of words that you use to search online databases and search engines. Because an online search is only as good as your keywords, making sure that your keywords are right on target is a good idea.

The secret to success with keywords is to have more than one or two that you can use. I advise you to choose a minimum of four keywords to describe the job you want or the topic you're researching — the ideal is to have around 12 keywords to choose from.

Try to choose keywords that range from very broad to very specific; that way, you can haul in the maximum results. If you're a psychologist, for example, good general keywords include *psychology, psychologist,* and *therapist.*

More-specific words defining your specialty are also good additions. For example, a forensic psychologist could add keywords like *forensic, clinical,* and, if interested in teaching, *professor.* Additional words can come from even more detailed research areas, such as specific behavior disorders.

Search engines

Search engines are programs that act a lot like a card catalog for the Web. Literally hundreds of search engines exist. Some engines search the Web at large; others are dedicated to searching one specific database.

AltaVista is an example of a well-known search engine that's designed to search the entire Web. The search engine at the Online Career Center is an example of a search engine that's designed to search just the Online Career Center's job and resume database.

Here are some facts about search engines:

- ✔ Search engines sport a *search box,* which is the blank or space into which you type keywords or questions.
- ✔ Different types of search engines exist — some are definitely smarter than others!
- ✔ The best way to find out how to use an individual search engine is to read the directions at the search engine site.
- ✔ A search engine is only as good as the database it's searching. Good data is the foundation of a good search. Even the best search engine can't manufacture good data out of bad or incomplete information. Conversely, a great database with a bad search engine doesn't produce good results, either.
- ✔ Many search engines enable you to perform a more advanced or detailed search, which involves filling out more keywords or maybe more forms.

In Figure 3-1, you see a search engine. This particular search engine is HotBot (`www.hotbot.com`), a solid, stable search engine. To conduct a simple search, all you do is type your keyword of choice into the search box and click on the Search button.

But notice the SuperSearch link just above the search box — that's where all the truly great searching begins. In Figure 3-2, you see a portion of HotBot's SuperSearch page. You have many more options to fill out, and if you scroll down the page, you find even more options.

Though you may find the increased options of SuperSearch to be too much of a good thing, try to get used to the idea of searching the Web with more, rather than fewer, options. The Web has become such a crowded place that every bit of detail you add to your searches makes the results more precise and thus more helpful.

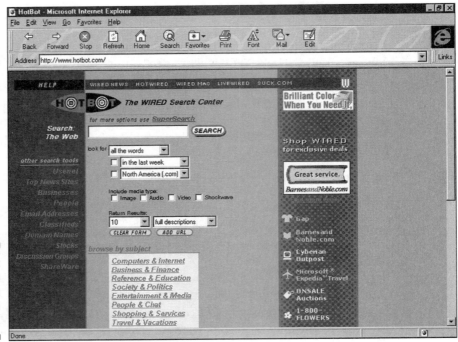

Figure 3-1:
HotBot's main search page.

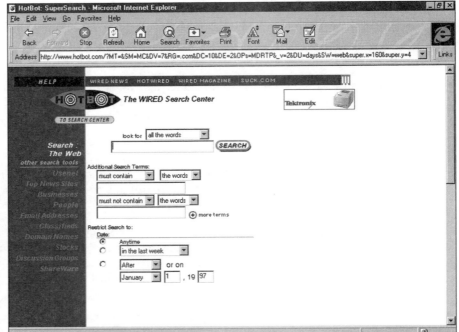

Figure 3-2:
HotBot's SuperSearch page, a more detailed way to get Web info.

Quick search engine tips

Even if you've been searching the Web for years, take a few minutes to read and practice these tips. I've found that they can make a big difference in the quality of information you find when using a search engine.

- ✔ Read the directions! Almost every search engine has a help section that describes in enormous detail exactly how to best use the search engine.

- ✔ Make sure that you have at least four keywords on any given topic so that you can use the search engine most effectively.

- ✔ Always try your keyword searches in more than one search engine. You can get vastly different results from different search engines!

- ✔ If you're having trouble using a search engine, use it to search for a hobby or interest that you're very, very familiar with. For example, if you're a runner, search for *running*. When you search for familiar items, you magically see exactly how good the search engine is.

- ✔ Even if you're new to the Web, I bet that you already have a couple of search engines that you've been using over and over again. Well, allow me to change all that by introducing you to some of my favorite search engine meta lists. These lists give you immediate access to hundreds of search engines all gathered together in one place. I use the search engine meta lists constantly!

    Here are a few of my favorites:

    - **Beaucoup:** www.beaucoup.com/engines.html
    - **The Internet Sleuth:** www.isleuth.com/
    - **The All-in-One search site:** www.albany.net/allinone/
    - **Dr. Webster's Big Page of Search Engines:** www.drwebster.com/search/search.htm

Professional indexes or directories

Professional indexes or directories are maintained as a business, not as a hobby. Typically, professional directories are very thorough and contain a wealth of links. Yahoo! (www.yahoo.com), for example, is a professional directory, as are the Excite (www.excite.com) and Galaxy (www.einet.net/galaxy.html) directories. In Figure 3-3, you can see the opening page of the Galaxy directory.

Settling on a directory that you like is a matter of chemistry. I've heard people argue over which Internet directory is better than another. Life is too short for that. Take a look at the various directories and decide for yourself which one suits you. (For a list of directories, refer to the Internet Directory at the back of this book.)

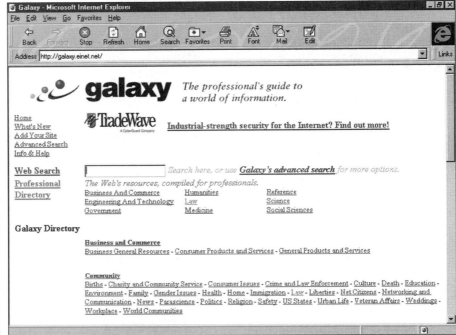

Figure 3-3:
Galaxy's
opening
page is
a great
example
of a
professional
index page.

Quick tips for using directories

Directories are so popular because they're truly easy to use. Nevertheless, here are a few tips to help you with them:

- ✔ Think of directories as a giant bookmark list. Click at will!

- ✔ Even if a directory has a search box, try to click on the subject links to search for information. Sometimes directory search engines aren't nearly as good as their subject links.

- ✔ Don't be afraid to explore "out of category." For example, if you're researching foreign statistics and trends, don't just click on a Foreign Statistics subject link. Also take a look at general statistical trends, and maybe even explore general reading sources. In a directory, you never know what treasure may have been put in an odd category.

Meta lists

A *meta list* (sometimes called a *meta index*) is just like a professional directory, but a meta list is typically maintained by a very idealistic individual, a college, or a business. Some of my favorite meta lists are those like JobSafari (a meta list of company Web sites at `www.jobsafari.com`), the Beaucoup page (a meta list of search engines at `www.beaucoup.com/engines.html`), and Webpages of Scholarly Societies, a giant meta list of associations maintained by the University of Waterloo (at `www.lib.uwaterloo.ca/society/overview.html`).

You use a meta list just like you use a professional directory — simply click on the links and follow your interests. The main thing you need to remember to do is to bookmark everything that interests you as you go along. In Figure 3-4, you see another of my favorite meta lists, the Nonprofit Resources Catalogue (`www.clark.net/pub/pwalker/`) — one of the most extensive collections of nonprofit information on the Web.

A meta list that focuses on one topic or subject area is sometimes called a *topical index* or *topical meta list.* The Nonprofit Resources Catalogue is a good example of a topical meta list.

Word of mouth

As I discussed the Web with my agent one day, she mentioned a regional Web site that one of her clients had created and remarked that the client had done a great job with it. She recommended that I take a look at it. I wrote down the URL and, when I got back to my office, logged on to the Web and indeed did take a look. Thus began my love affair with one of my favorite sites on the Web! (If you're curious and want to take a look for yourself, the address is `www.zoomsd.com/`. The site is a virtual guide to San Diego.)

Web pages have become like books in the sense that a personal recommendation for a site can carry a lot of weight, depending on who's doing the recommending. Fully one-third of my bookmarks have come from word-of-mouth recommendations. I know that when I come across a great Web site through word of mouth, I feel lucky to have found it, and I bookmark the site immediately.

In a way, the Internet Directory at the back of this book is like a word-of-mouth recommendation. In the directory, you find plenty of my favorite professional and career-related sites, like HotSheet, All in One, Research-It!, Business Wire, the Online Career Center, CareerCast, and hundreds more. Also check my Web site, `www.pamdixon.com`.

Word of mouth is certainly not an exact way to search the Web, but it sure turns up a lot of great starting points!

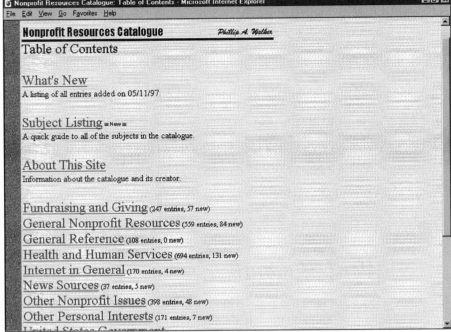

Nonprofit Resources Catalogue   *Phillip A. Walker*

Table of Contents

What's New
A listing of all entries added on 05/11/97.

Subject Listing ═ New ═
A quick guide to all of the subjects in the catalogue.

About This Site
Information about the catalogue and its creator.

Fundraising and Giving (247 entries, 57 new)
General Nonprofit Resources (559 entries, 84 new)
General Reference (108 entries, 0 new)
Health and Human Services (694 entries, 131 new)
Internet in General (170 entries, 4 new)
News Sources (37 entries, 5 new)
Other Nonprofit Issues (398 entries, 48 new)
Other Personal Interests (171 entries, 7 new)

Figure 3-4:
A great
meta list,
the
Nonprofit
Resources
Catalogue.

The Tried and True Search Methods

In this section, I talk about personal search methods that I have used and refined over the years. I've taught many people how to research the Web by using these methods — I haven't found anyone yet who hasn't had success with at least one of them!

The key to success with all Web search methods is to know what you want to find. Even if you have only a broad idea, like "I'm looking for law firms on the Web," that's okay. Having an idea of what you want is the major requirement.

Something else to consider is that, when you combine two or more search methods, you get outstanding results. When I research books and papers, I use all the methods I share with you here. Often, I go through each method several times just to make sure that I've really scoured all the information available.

I'd like to share a secret with you: One of these methods will naturally suit you much more than any of the others. So I encourage you to try all the methods. I used to teach, and through observation I learned that people's minds tend to be comfortable with certain search patterns. The trick is to find which search pattern fits you best and then go with it.

Bookmarking

I mention bookmarking quite a bit in all my search methods. Bookmarking lets you save the URL of a Web site that you like in a list called a *bookmark list* or a *hotlist*. After you bookmark a site, all you have to do is click on that site's bookmark in your bookmark list to open the site. You don't have to type in a long URL.

Every browser is set up to bookmark differently. If you don't know how to bookmark, take the time now to read your browser's help file and figure out how to bookmark — it really helps you get around the Web more quickly.

Also, I recommend that you set up a bookmark folder called "Search" just for your Web searching results. Again, check your browser's help file for specific details on setting up bookmark folders.

I prefer the Comparison and the Narrow It Down search methods. You may, however, find that the Popularity Contest method suits you best. But no matter — the key is to find a good fit and then utilize what you know.

The Quick and Dirty search method

The quickest search method involves going to an index and rooting through the contents. If you need to find a quick reference or maybe locate some directories in a subject area, the Quick and Dirty method is a good one to try. But for locating in-depth information on the Web, I don't recommend it as a number-one option.

Estimated time per search: 2 to 5 minutes

Key: Relying on one index to get you to information fast

Benefit: Quick search for information tidbits

Here are the search steps:

1. **Decide what you're searching for.**

2. **Head to a large index or directory.**

   For a Quick and Dirty search, I like to use HotSheet (www.hotsheet.com) or Yahoo! (www.yahoo.com).

3. **Either do a keyword search for information or click on categories.**

4. **Keep your eyes peeled for any topical directories listed for your area of interest.**

   For example, Job Hunt (www.jobhunt.com) is a topical meta list of job-search links.

5. **Explore the meta lists and links that you find in your subject area of interest.**

   You should be able to find relevant links right away.

Variation One

You can perform a Quick and Dirty search with Internet directory books, too. I'm very fond of Brad Hill's directory book, *Internet Directory For Dummies,* published by IDG Books Worldwide, Inc. Brad is a great writer, and he chose excellent sites for the book.

An especially good place to begin all your job-related searches is in the Internet Directory at the back of this book. I did all sorts of searching for you, so why not take advantage of the work I've already done?

Variation Two

I also like to do a quick keyword search of one or two Web search engines as a Quick and Dirty search. If you're looking for a personal home page or a company, this variation can work wonders for you. Just head to a Web search engine like AltaVista (www.altavista.digital.com), type in your keywords, and go! Note that this works only for very basic information.

The Narrow It Down method

The essence of the Narrow It Down method is to start big and get small. I'm not talking about diets here! Rather, I'm referring to the scope of the information you're looking at. You start by scanning huge amounts of info and keep narrowing down your choices to get more in-depth.

For researching books, Narrow It Down is one of my favorite Web research methods. The key to this method is to use different types of search databases.

Estimated time per search: At least 30 minutes

Key: Using different *types* of search vehicles

Benefit: Most thorough information

Here are the Narrow It Down steps:

1. **Decide what specific information you want to find.**

2. **Head to a *minimum* of three or four different kinds of search vehicles.**

   I suggest a directory, a meta list, and a search engine as a minimum search.

3. **Start with a directory or two. Search through the directories for the information you seek, either by keyword or by clicking on the correct topics in the directory. (This method works better if you click on topics.)**

   Some good directories to try are Yahoo! (`www.yahoo.com`), Galaxy (`galaxy.einet.net`), HotSheet (`www.hotsheet.com`), Planet Oasis (`www.planetoasis.com/`), and Excite (`www.excite.com`).

4. **If you see a description of a page that looks even remotely good, bookmark the page and quickly move on to the next item. (Most browsers allow you to bookmark pages by simply placing your mouse pointer over a URL and then right-clicking. With Internet Explorer, I right-click and then select the Add to Favorites option. With Netscape Communicator, I right-click and then select the Add Bookmark option.)**

   Make a habit of bookmarking pages that mention the word *directory* somewhere in the description.

5. **Also look at two or more very good search engines. Perform a keyword search on your topic and then look through at least four pages of the search results, again bookmarking quickly and moving on.**

   Good engines to try are AltaVista (`www.altavista.digital.com`) and HotBot (`www.hotbot.com`).

6. **Scan Usenet and listservs for information.**

   To do so, perform a keyword search on Reference.COM (`www.reference.com`). Again, bookmark anything that looks relevant.

7. **Select one of the "Best of the Web" sites and do a quick search on that site, again bookmarking any relevant results.**

   See the "Popularity Contest method" section later in this chapter for a list of "Best of the Web" sites.

If you're aware of one, also search a meta list relating to your topic. If you don't know of any meta lists yet, don't worry. You'll find one as a result of your Narrow It Down search!

After you whip through all the search tools and bookmark interesting links, settle in with a glass of water or a cup of hot tea and carefully scour the sites on your list. Take the time to explore all the relevant links you find. When I find particularly great information, I print it out and store the pages in a binder for easy reference.

The Popularity Contest method

The idea of the Popularity Contest method is to quickly get to a broad range of information by using site review indexes. Though the Popularity Contest search method doesn't necessarily net you in-depth information, it does get you reliable information very, very quickly.

Estimated time per search: About 5 to 10 minutes

Key: Relying on others to narrow the search for you

Benefit: Very fast results

Here are the steps:

1. **Decide on your search topic.**

2. **Choose two to three "Best of the Web" sites. Good ones to try include:**

   • **Luckman's Best of the Web:** www.bofw.com/

   • **Best of the Web:** www.botw.org/

   • **Lycos Top 5% Sites:** point.lycos.com/categories/

   • **10 Best on the Web:** www.10-best.com/

   • **Starting Point:** www.stpt.com/

3. **Scour the "Best of" sites for Web pages relevant to your search. Bookmark each page that is of value to you, quickly moving on to the next page.**

   After you have worked your way through at least two of the "Best of" sites, you should have at least five to ten Web sites to view.

4. **View the pages that you bookmarked. If the pages are good, link-mine them.**

   See the section "Scouring a Web Site for Job-Related Information" for more information about link-mining.

Please note that the results of a Popularity Contest search are typically not in the least bit comprehensive. But this method gives you a fast start on your search.

People often ask me why I suggest that you use *two* popular site guides. The reason is that the "most popular" lists tend to be arbitrary, which is great, as long as you get two opinions for balance.

The Comparison method

The Comparison method involves looking across a broad range of directories, indexes, and meta lists in order to find the most frequently mentioned Web sites. This method is good for figuring out what's popular on the Web.

For the Comparison method to work well, you need to know which directories and meta lists to look through. If you don't have access to good meta lists, start by locating meta lists with a Quick and Dirty search. Then return to the Comparison search.

Estimated time per search: About 15 to 30 minutes

Key: Comparing at least four information sources

Benefit: Great for finding well-known sites in a particular subject area

To perform a Comparison search, here's what you do:

1. **Decide what you're searching for.**

2. **Gather a collection of meta lists and directories to compare.**

   Four is the number that seems to produce the best results, but comparing two or three sources works, too. If you don't have meta lists to compare, you can always use large directories as your comparison tools. (Galaxy and Yahoo! are probably the two best directories to use in this case.)

3. **Go to your first meta list or directory and read through it without bookmarking anything.**

4. **Go to your second meta list and read it all the way through, looking for mention of the same sites that you saw in the first list. If you see a site name on the second list that you also saw on the first list, bookmark that site.**

   Bookmark only repeat sites!

If you have the patience, you can repeat this process with up to ten lists. After you have finished your comparison, look at your bookmarked sites and explore them. The point here is to find repeat sites.

The results of a Comparison search give you a very good idea of which sites people in a particular industry think are the definitive or highest-quality sites. Please note, though, that bookmarking only repeat sites takes discipline; you may be tempted to bookmark every good site. But the point is to find only sites that repeat, so stick with the process if you want the best results.

The Bunny Rabbit method

The Bunny Rabbit method is a much-derided method of searching the Web. You won't find me laughing at it, however, because I know that it can help you find information in a way that no other search method can.

The number-one rule of using this method is to make a quick decision at every link you click on. When you click on a particular link, follow it to the end, the end being a Web page. Period.

If you do anything else, you're hedging into the Narrow It Down method. Trust me on this one — to really break open the treasures of a Bunny Rabbit search, choose links until you reach a home page.

Estimated time per search: About 3 to 7 minutes per "trail"

Key: Relying on good intuition and synchronicity

Benefit: Can find unusual or hard-to-find sites of great value

The method:

1. **Decide what you're searching for.**

2. **Go to a major index like Galaxy (`galaxy.einet.net`).**

3. **Perform a keyword search for your information or click on a relevant heading.**

   I like to click on a relevant heading.

4. **Follow one link trail all the way down to the Web page level.**

   For example, from the Galaxy home page, I clicked on the Law category. Then I clicked on the Legal Profession category. Then I clicked on a publication I saw listed, the Rodent (an official underground publication for associates). I didn't know what it was before I clicked on it, but when the Rodent page opened, I couldn't believe what good luck I had — the Rodent is a part of EmplawyerNet, the nation's largest legal employment database on the Web. (That's what they say, at least.) Not bad for following one link trail, eh?

5. **After you reach the "destination" Web page, explore every link on the site, no matter how banal the links look. (I call this process *link-mining*.) Bookmark everything that's relevant.**

   I can't tell you how many fabulous link collections I've found by doing this.

6. **After you fully link-mine the page, you have a choice: Either follow one of the great links you found to a new destination page, or go back to Step 1 and start over again.**

   I tend to follow the new links I find on Web pages.

7. **Keep following link trails and keep link-mining every site you see.**

   After you've link-mined eight to ten Web sites, you probably have a great start on the information you need.

By the way, I call this method Bunny Rabbit searching after one of my favorite professors in college, who simply couldn't give a lecture without digressing all over the place. Whenever he digressed, he would eventually recover and say, "Now that we've explored that bunny trail . . ." and get back to the subject. Of course, his bunny rabbit lectures are the ones I remember!

Search Samples to Get You Started

In your quest to master cyberspace in a hurry, you're sure to make some glaring errors and have some resounding successes. To get you started in your forays, I've put together a few positive and negative example searches.

Time-saving searches

These three searches get you the information you need quickly. Remember, though, that I could have arrived at the information by using any number of search methods. As always, the idea is to choose the searches that are best suited to you and that uncover the information the quickest.

Time-saving search #1: Finding an obscure company Web site

My advice here is to head right for a Web browser and type in **www.companyname.com**. If you aren't sure of the company name, or if the company name trick doesn't bring up the right Web site, then head to AltaVista (www.altavista.digital.com/) and do a simple keyword search.

If you're looking for the Thunderstone Web site, for example, type in the keyword **Thunderstone** at the AltaVista site and wait for the results; then scroll down the list until you notice a likely candidate. When I performed this keyword search, I found the Thunderstone Web site mentioned right on the first page of results.

If you try this method and the company you're looking for still doesn't come up, try looking in some of the company meta lists. The one at JobSafari (www.jobsafari.com) is a good one to try. If that still doesn't work, try looking the company up in an online Yellow Pages, such as the Big Book (www.bigbook.com). (JobSafari and the Big Book are listed in the Internet Directory at the back of this book.)

If none of this works, start over with a new spelling of the company name and try different search engines and meta lists.

Key: You're essentially performing a Quick and Dirty search and then a Narrow It Down search in this example.

Time-saving search #2: Looking for the latest information in your profession as you prep for an interview

Say you're teaching in sub-zero temperatures and have had it with the winter weather. Florida sounds really good to you. Much to your surprise, after you send out a resume to a school district in Florida, you get a phone call. Later, you get another call requesting an interview. Now you're nervous and you want to make sure that you nail this interview.

To find information about Florida's geography, head to the Excite index and click on City.net, which gives you details about every major city in the United States. At least you can figure out what it's like where you're interviewing, where you can stay, and what to wear!

As far as what to say in your interview, you want to make sure that your educational lingo is completely up-to-date. You settle on two indexes, the Excite index and the Yahoo! index. You decide to look through both indexes and compare offerings.

After about an hour of plowing through all the education-related links at both sites, you realize that this ERIC site you keep seeing must be pretty hot. (It's available at `ericae.net`.) You visit the ERIC site and about 14 other sites that you saw mentioned in both places. Now you have enough information for an in-depth interview and then some!

Key: For finding the latest information in a field, the Comparison method often works best.

Time-saving search #3: Looking for a specific job

If you're looking for a specific type of job, such as a public relations specialist, immediately head to the back of this book and look at the listings of employment databases. After perusing the list, choose a few and then go to the sites and perform keyword searches for your specialty. For a public relations job, you might try keywords such as *communications, PR, marketing, public relations, writing,* and *corporate communications.*

Also go to the Yahoo! index and the Galaxy index and explore the public relations links (or whatever links pertain to your specialty) to see if you can find any extra information about companies that are hiring in your area.

If you get really serious, take a look at the associations and employment meta lists, too, and begin exploring further. Also, start looking for public relations companies on the Web. (See Example #1 for help in getting information from a Web site.)

Key: This search relies on word of mouth for narrowing down information quickly and then moves to a Bunny Rabbit type of search.

Lost in cyberspace: Time-wasting searches and ways to fix them

It happens to everyone. You've just spent a half-hour clicking around aimlessly on the Web and you have absolutely nothing to show for it — at least, nothing substantive. Often, the problem is simple to fix.

Here are the most common Web time-wasters and the fixes for them.

Time-wasting search #1: The search engine that couldn't

You go searching for information to help you prepare for an interview. Say you're looking for salary information. You hop on the Web, go right to AltaVista (or any Web search engine), and type in the keywords *salaries* and *Minneapolis*. Though you receive over 40,000 documents that match your query, none of them relates to what you really want. You have a time-waster on your hands.

Key mistake: Your search pattern isn't broad enough.

The fix: Use more than one type of search tool.

To fix the problem, all you have to do is to switch to one of the search methods I outlined earlier in the chapter. For this particular problem, I would start with a Quick and Dirty search. You only need one little tidbit of information, so why not start with a directory or index? Because you have this book, your answer is super-easy; I list salary calculators in the Internet Directory at the back of this book. If I don't list the info you need, though, head to Yahoo! or Galaxy to try to track it down quickly.

Time-wasting search #2: Keywords? What keywords?

A keyword is a term that you use to get information from a database.

Say you're looking for a job as an accounts manager. You log on to CareerPath.com (CareerPath.com is a top employment site found at www.careerpath.com/) and type **accounts manager** in the search box. One minute goes by. Then two minutes. Finally, your results come back — a giant list of more than 1,000 jobs! You scan the first page, and none of the jobs is even remotely what you're looking for. You've just landed yourself a time-waster.

Key mistake: If you don't know what you want, a computer surely won't. And if you're too general, the computer will be, too.

The fix: Gather and use a healthy assortment of keywords. (*Healthy* typically means four keywords or more.)

Keywords are critical to any online information search. Typing the wrong keyword in a search box is a lot like ordering the wrong food at a restaurant. The person taking your order can't read your mind — you have to indicate exactly which item you want from the menu, preferably using the same words that are on the menu.

So what's the "wrong" keyword? Any keyword that doesn't give you the results you want. In the sample CareerPath.com search, you can fix the search by coming up with tighter, better keywords. For example, instead of the extremely broad term *accounts manager,* how about *customer service manager* plus an industry term, like *medical, technical,* or *biotechnology*? The point is to develop and use as many specific words as possible. (See the "Keyword tips" sidebar earlier in this chapter.)

Time-wasting search #3: The "always" trap

You want to find out about a company. Because you always start your searches at Yahoo! (or any major directory), you start this search there, too. You dig around the index and you can't find the company listed. Frantically, you begin keyword searching the index for any mention of the company. You've tried everything and you're finding nothing. You have a frustrating time-waster on tap.

Key mistake: You're stuck in a rut as far as searching goes.

The fix: Try a new search method and new search tools.

Realize that even the very best index has its limitations. For your company search, try a Quick and Dirty search using a different directory than the one you normally use. Or use Variations One and Two of Quick and Dirty searching: Use a book-based directory and try a simple keyword search of a Web search engine. And if those methods don't turn anything up, try a Popularity Contest search.

Because the Web changes so much every day, you need to always try something new to keep up with it.

Scouring a Web Site for Job-Related Information

Web sites are mines of information — you just need to know how to tap into their veins. To do that, you need to learn how to scour a Web site for information, an information art that I call *link-mining*.

Unfortunately, even though the technique I show you here works wonders, it's only as good as the Web page you use it on. Though company Web pages and info sites have gotten pretty good, not every corporate Web site is "mineable." You know that you've hit an unmineable site when you type in a URL and think to yourself, "There isn't anything on this Web site!"

But for this example, I want to show you how to scour and link-mine one of the best-organized company Web pages I've ever seen: the Thunderstone Web page. If you haven't heard of Thunderstone, don't worry. I quiz you at the end of this section — you will figure out a lot about this company when you see the site!

Here are the steps for scouring a Web site for info:

1. **Open the URL and immediately scan the front page.**

   The hallmark of a great company or information site is that you can find certain information right away. That information includes

   - A search feature
   - A contact link
   - An employment link
   - A company information link
   - A product link, if the company produces something
   - A list of recent customers

   If you find all these elements, as you do in the Thunderstone opening page, you're in luck. Bonus information includes corporate bios and photos. Check for all the elements in Figure 3-5.

2. **Scan the customer list first.**

   It should give you a very good indication of how high on the food chain the company is. Take a look at Thunderstone's last 100 customers: AT&T, Anheuser Busch, Boeing, and so on. These are big-time customers.

3. **Take a look at the company information area.**

   In the Thunderstone site, the company info area gives an entire company profile and then a chronological history of company milestones. The company profile discusses corporate mission, which includes the key goals of being high-quality and low-profile. That nugget of information is a giveaway to the corporate culture.

4. **Systematically work through every major link.**

   The Literature link lets you request printed materials from Thunderstone, such as product brochures. If you wanted to work at Thunderstone, you would want to see this material. Thunderstone also has a nifty demonstration page that shows how its products work.

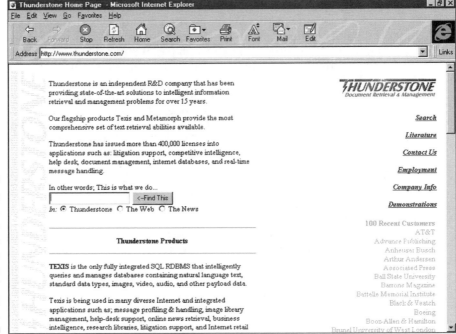

Figure 3-5:
Looking at the Thunderstone home page with an eye for gathering information.

5. Head to the employment page.

The Thunderstone Employment page lists more information about corporate culture and expectations. The page lists some jobs and then requests that you do not call, but rather e-mail an ASCII resume, if you're interested in one of the jobs. Thunderstone also lists a postal address.

If a company you're interested in lists an e-mail address, e-mail your resume and any follow-ups, when appropriate.

6. As two last info-efforts, check the contact page to see whether you can locate any executives.

At the Thunderstone site, you can't. Still, you can head to the Search area to try to uncover any information you still want. The Thunderstone search area (shown in Figure 3-6) happens to be one of the best you'll probably ever find.

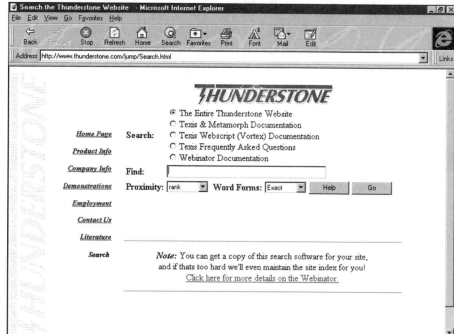

Figure 3-6:
The
Thunderstone
search area
for digging
information
from its
Web site.

A quick Thunderstone quiz

Now it's time for your quiz. To take it, log on to the Thunderstone Web site (www.thunder-stone.com) and use it to answer the following questions. If you can't answer these questions, you need to take more time to scan the Web site.

✔ What kind of corporate culture does Thunderstone have?

✔ Will it be difficult to find a job at Thunderstone?

✔ What products does Thunderstone produce?

✔ What is Thunderstone's position in its industry?

✔ What is the process for applying for a job at Thunderstone?

✔ What colleges does Thunderstone recruit from?

All the answers are on the Thunderstone Web site.

If you ask yourself these questions at every company Web site you visit, you'll find yourself much more knowledgeable about what kind of environment you're sending your resume off to!

Esoteric Search Tricks and Tools

Sometimes even the best search methods come up empty. When this happens, it's time to get esoteric — that is, to go for the oddball search. On the Net, sometimes the unusual methods can help you find that stray bit of information, like how many high-tech companies are in Beijing, China, or when and where the next conference on office automation will be held.

Unearthing local info: Geographical search tricks

I estimate that fewer than one-tenth of one percent of all Web surfers have tried a geographical search. The reason for this low number is not that this search method doesn't work, but that it's time-consuming. However, if you really want to uncover information about a particular region, this method is one of the very best for doing so.

A geographical search involves digging into what is commonly called the Master Web Server Directory. This directory is maintained by the World Wide Web Consortium and contains a list of all the computers that host Web pages. (You can view a user-friendly version of the Master Web Server Directory at Virtual Tourist, www.vtourist.com/.)

Essentially, you're visiting one computer at a time and rifling through all the Web pages on just that one computer. Again, the point of the exercise is to find local information. If you look at all the Web pages hosted on computers in Ireland, for example, you find all sorts of information about Ireland.

I use a geographical search when all my other search methods fail to turn up the amount of information I want. For example, say I wanted to find a job in Ireland. The first thing I would do would be to perform a Comparison search. I would consult three or four job meta lists to see if anything related to Ireland showed up. Then I would try a Narrow It Down search to see what that turned up. Because I did in fact do those searches, I can tell you that I found only about five Irish job database sites.

My next step would be a geographical search. I would look for Irish companies and organizations for which I might want to work. Certainly, I would be on the lookout for all company home pages, too!

Estimated time per search: At least 20 minutes, often longer.

Key: Looking at one computer at a time in a specific place produces a depth of information about that area.

Benefit: A geographical search turns up the very best information about a place. It can't be beat for that.

Here are the steps for a geographical search:

1. **Open the Virtual Tourist site at** www.vtourist.com/.

   Virtual Tourist is a clickable map of all the Web servers in the world. You can see what Virtual Tourist looks like in Figure 3-7.

2. **Select a region you want to view — for example, Europe or Asia. Then select the country you want to explore.**

   I selected Ireland.

   What you see next is a list of all the Web servers in the country you selected. The servers are organized by category and by city.

3. **Click on the topic or city that interests you.**

   I clicked on the Business link to see what businesses I could find in Ireland. I found over 600 Irish company home pages, plus a directory of Irish businesses on the Internet. The list included accounting firms, architecture firms, organizations, manufacturers, retail stores, banks, you name it. My search took about 15 minutes and yielded excellent results. To find a job, I would then scour the company Web pages and e-mail my resume to the appropriate people.

Figure 3-7: The opening page of the Virtual Tourist Web site.

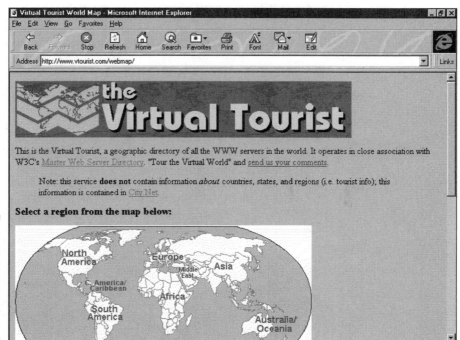

Geographical searches can help you uncover hard-to-find information in any region or city that's home to one or more Web servers.

Unusual search tools to try

In the Internet Directory at the back of this book, I list some excellent search engines. But I had to be painfully selective! *Hundreds* of search tools are available. I'd like to point out a few of the more interesting search engines, just in case you need to look for something a little bit off the beaten path.

You can find the search tools I mention in the following section by typing in their URLs, or you can find the tools on the four search meta sites that I list in the "Search engines" section earlier in this chapter.

- ✔ **Internet Legal Resource Guide** (www.ilrg.comw/): A searchable index of over 3,100 Web sites. The site intends to serve as the most comprehensive online resource concerning law and the legal profession.

- ✔ **Economic Indicators** (www.access.gpo.gov/congress/cong002.html): A search engine, updated monthly by the Council of Economic Advisors, that gives you access to the latest figures on economic indicators.

- ✔ **Ahoy!** (ahoy.cd.washington.edu): A search engine that helps you locate personal home pages. I've found that Ahoy! is by no means foolproof, but it's still worth a look.

- ✔ **Ecola's Tech Directory** (www.ecola.com/archive/computer/): An incredible search tool that collects most of the online computer publications in one giant meta list. It's very helpful if you're researching computer trends or information.

- ✔ **Worldwide Event Database** (www.ipworld.com/EVENT/SEARCH.HTM): You can find conferences, shows, and classes related to your profession at this search engine. On a recent swing-by, I found events sponsored by the National Sporting Goods Association, the BSR Archaeological Search Team, and the International Quality and Productivity Center. I even found a conference on organic geochemistry!

Chapter 4

Keeping Your Resume and Your Job Search Private

● ●

In This Chapter

▶ Controlling who sees your resume

▶ Guarding against resume theft

▶ Tips on pre-employment screenings

▶ Important info for the currently employed

▶ Preparing for the close of your job search

▶ Maintaining your privacy sanity

● ●

*P*utting yourself "out there" to get a job is exposure enough for many people. I've talked to a number of job candidates who absolutely detest the idea of sending a resume filled with a life's worth of experience to total strangers.

If all the cogs and gears work smoothly, at least one of those "total strangers" eventually becomes your boss or co-worker. But in between the time you send out your resume and the phone call you get saying "You're hired," a whole lot can go awry. And you know the old saying: When something can go wrong, it generally does.

The whole notion of privacy in the workplace and in your job search is increasingly troublesome. In this chapter, you find out how you can keep your resume, your personal information, and your job search private.

What Every Job Seeker Needs to Know about Privacy

Privacy seems to have taken on an entirely new meaning in the digital age. I hate to sound alarmist, but consider the following job search–related privacy issues:

- ✔ Anymore, pre-employment background checks are a matter of phoning an information brokerage and paying a mere $50 for an extraordinary amount of personal information, most of which the brokerage collects digitally.

- ✔ Resumes are being *reverse-spammed* with alarming regularity — that is, they are being collected from databases and cross-posted to places that *you* never would have dreamed of placing them.

- ✔ Studies show that 25 percent of employers admit to reading and monitoring employee e-mail. Imagine how many more employers read employees' e-mail and simply don't admit it!

- ✔ Identity thieves troll open resume databases on the Web for seasoned pros whose identities and credit ratings they can latch onto. Preventing this particular problem is easier than solving it after it happens.

- ✔ Employers actively look out for their employees' resumes on the Web. Just hoping that no one sees your resume is not enough anymore. The best cure is to keep your resume private in the first place!

Just about everyone who has ever had a privacy problem inevitably says, "I can't believe it happened to me." Well, more and more job seekers are saying that to themselves and those closest to them. The good news is that privacy problems don't have to happen. With just an ounce of prevention, you can solve the vast majority of your privacy problems before you land in hot water of any kind.

Keeping Your Boss Away from Your Online Resume

I'd like to relay a surprising revelation that I made while researching this book. I was conducting a standard phone interview with a highly placed executive at a Fortune 1000 company, getting all sorts of great info for job seekers. It started off like any interview that I conduct while researching a book. But when I asked about resume privacy, my source immediately clammed up, asked to go off the record, and asked me to stop rolling my tape. I agreed.

My source went on to explain that her company had just initiated a "find and tell" policy, whereby any employee who found another employee's resume on the Net was to inform a supervisor immediately. The person who was caught with a resume on the Net, according to company policy, would be let go at worst or, at best, interviewed extensively by the human resources department to try to be "salvaged."

Yep — you read it right. Salvaged! Unfortunately, this incident is not an isolated one. I spoke with six other major, well-known companies who recently placed similar policies on the books. If you're a new grad or are currently unemployed, you may have an advantage in the sense that you don't need to worry about a current employer finding your resume. You can put your resume just about anywhere (within reason) and not have a worry in the world.

If, however, you are currently employed, protecting your resume and controlling who sees it and when have become extremely important. Gone are the days when you could just think to yourself, "Oh, my boss isn't even computer literate! Why should I worry about him or her ever finding my resume online?" Let me be very clear: Times have changed!

Fortunately, you have real options. The following sections discuss the best ways to protect your resume and keep it in front of the people who can hire you — not fire you!

Be aware of reverse spamming

Bill Warren, president of the Online Career Center, alerted me to a trend that I subsequently found running rampant in cyberspace: *reverse spamming*. As mentioned earlier, reverse spamming is when your resume is taken from one database and copied to others without your permission.

Warren told me that he and his crew at OCC had to take extreme measures to guard the OCC resume database from reverse spamming. He said that *agents* — programs that search and index material on the Web — come to OCC trying to collect all the resume data, copy it, and deposit it somewhere else, like in a new database. To solve the resume-theft problem, OCC has installed a password-protected database that only qualified employers can access. And if by some chance someone hacks into the OCC system, the intruder gets bumped off the OCC site automatically.

But for resume databases that are *open* — that is, that have no password protection and leave your resume available for all to see — I have to warn you: You never know where your resume may show up again. Warren says that if you post your resume on an open site, like Usenet, you may find your resume floating around "for years."

Another real problem with reverse spamming is that you can post your resume to a reputable board where you don't think your boss may ever look, and then five days later, your resume may have been copied to over a dozen employment sites without your permission or knowledge. The lesson? Never post your resume to a place that's not password-protected.

Don't post your resume on Usenet if you're currently employed

If you're currently employed, the absolute worst place to put your resume is on Usenet. I talked with one candidate who put his resume on Usenet and was getting calls eight months after he had accepted a job. He liked getting his job, but the fallout was hard to take.

The big problem with putting your resume on Usenet is that it will get reverse-spammed — you'll find it *everywhere*. Also, anyone with a Web connection can see your resume, and that includes your boss as well as would-be identity thieves.

Before you post your resume on any employment database, call the people who maintain the database

A lot of employment databases will probably be unhappy with me for suggesting this. But I think your resume is so important that you need to be absolutely clear about where your resume goes and how it gets there. Some employment databases, like Attorneys @ Work, the Online Career Center, and others, make a very strong stand for privacy. Others have strong privacy language but don't really do anything to ensure your privacy. Still other employment databases share resumes with partners; meanwhile, you never knew that your resume was going to ten databases instead of one. And maybe one of those ten databases is not password-protected. . . . You get the idea.

Call before you post. Ask who can see your resume. Ask whether your resume is shared with other databases. Ask whether you can decide on a case-by-case basis who can view your resume. If you're employed, these are the questions that will keep your resume out of your boss's hands.

Password-protect your Web resume

If you have your resume on the Web, you may want to protect your resume with a password box. That way, the only people who can see your detailed, personal resume information are those to whom you give the password.

Each Web-hosting service (*Web hosts* are businesses that house your Web pages) is slightly different. Be sure to sign up for a Web-hosting service that lets you password-protect your Web pages easily. The service that I use lets me just drop a password box onto my page; setting up password protection takes about three minutes. If you're searching for a job and want to use a Web resume, seriously consider using a Web-hosting service that allows you to password-protect pages.

Take promises about "blocked" access with a grain of salt

Quite a few employment databases told me that they block certain employers from seeing a candidate's resume. That sounds like great privacy in theory, but when you see how it really works, you realize that the theory doesn't pan out too well.

The way a blocked-access system typically works is that if an employer has a certain domain name, like www.ford.com, and you work for Ford, you can specify that no one from www.ford.com can see your resume. This works great about 75 percent of the time. But what about when that Ford employee logs on to the database from a different account, such as a personal America Online account? The answer is that the resume blocking just stopped working.

Know what you want: A password-protected, confidential resume database where you decide who sees your resume

If you're worried about resume privacy, I have an answer for you. Or rather, leading employment databases have an answer for you. That answer is password-protected databases that enable you to send your resume only to those individual employers whom you want to see the resume. More and more employment sites are moving to this type of database, which I discuss in detail in Chapter 14. So far, going with a privacy-guaranteed database is the only way to be assured of resume privacy.

Staying Safe from Identity Bandits

Identity bandits are people who latch onto your personal information and make it theirs. The real problem that identity thieves pose for you, other than the obvious financial headaches, is that they destroy your pre-employment background checks by giving you a bad digital reputation.

You may have heard about how identity thieves rack up tens of thousands of dollars in bills by using their victims' names. But what you may not know is that many identity thieves also commit all manner of crimes by using other people's identities. Unfortunately, a background check with your social security number and work history could become dirtied by criminal activity that you don't even know about.

I've heard story after story of people who got interviews and then were abruptly dropped from the short list. After this happens dozens of times, you begin to wonder — is it something I did? Maybe not. Maybe an identity thief is working in your name.

 If you're a new grad, it's unlikely that an identity bandit will target you. But the more work experience you have and the farther up the career ladder you have climbed, the more important it is for you to follow these bandit-busting guidelines:

- ✔ **Never, ever put your social security number on your resume.** I don't care what the situation is; don't put your social security number on any resume at any time — ever! The only time that you need to hand over your SSN is after someone hires you. If an employment database asks for your SSN, then that employment database is not legitimate, and you should avoid it.

- ✔ **If you want to be as safe as possible, don't post your resume on Usenet or on any open, non-password-protected database.** The more experienced you are, the more important it is for you to keep your resume in a password-protected database. That way, only qualified employers have access to your resume. Even if you aren't currently employed, to be safe, keep your resume off Usenet and other open databases. Identity thieves won't come after you if you're an unemployed new grad because you probably don't have much money yet. But why take the risk?

- ✔ **If you insist on posting your resume on an open database, then don't put your address or your full name on your resume.** Also, try to mask your gender by using a first initial only. If you post your resume in a public area, then omitting sensitive personal information is about the only thing you can do to protect yourself.

Surviving Pre-Employment Screenings

Talk about tossing privacy out the window! *Pre-employment screenings,* where employers dig for information about your credit and your past, are on the rise. Being ready for what the screenings may bring your way is up to you, because, unfortunately, you don't get a chance to defend your pre-employment screening. You may not even know that it occurred. That's why you want to make sure that the information employers find about you is correct.

If you have never been through a pre-employment screening, then you may be in for quite a surprise. Before I worked for the federal government in a series of summer jobs, I was screened thoroughly, as I was before each teaching position I ever accepted. Those screenings were nothing compared to what candidates must endure now.

Due to the enormous amount of information that has been cataloged and put online, the amount of personal information that shows up in background checks has increased dramatically. For a mere $50 to $300, employers can get your complete credit history and reports, spending habits, voting records, magazines that you subscribe to, places you travel, and a whole lot more, depending on which state you live in. (Privacy laws vary by state.)

There are quite a few arguments about what information an employer can and can't get, and for now, I'll leave those arguments for the attorneys. The most important thing to know in your online job search is that, more often than anyone would like to admit, pre-employment screenings can go wrong.

Two scenarios account for negative pre-employment screenings:

- ✔ An identity bandit has grabbed your information and has run amok with it.
- ✔ A computer error has given your past an undeserved digital black eye.

If you want to preempt problems in the pre-screening area, your best bet is to get there first. In the Yellow Pages, you can find a heading called Investigative Services. These are the folks who do pre-employment screenings.

A basic screening can cost as little as $50; a thorough screening costs $200 to $300. My advice is, before you start your job search, hire an investigator to do a basic search on you. Your goal is to make sure that the facts are accurate and reflect your real history.

If you find erroneous credit, educational, criminal, or other records, act to get those records corrected immediately. Doing so takes a long time! If you find erroneous information, you need to contact all the relevant computerized databases to get the error corrected. To enlist help, check the "Privacy Resources" section of the Internet Directory in this book. There, you can find a list of privacy organizations that can help you.

For people who have common names

If you have a common name, like me, then you may want to check the Net for other occurrences of your name. For example, several people with the name Pam Dixon chat on Usenet. None of the posts are mine — I never post on Usenet. The posts are pretty harmless, but I like to keep an eye on them nonetheless.

If you do a search on your name and find that a person with your exact name likes to spend an inordinate amount of time posting weird or obscene messages on Usenet, then you may want to put your middle initial or entire middle name on your resume to differentiate yourself from that other person.

Managing Headhunters Who Call, Call, and Call Some More

If you're in a high-demand field, you may want prepare for the time you want to bring your job search to a close. I know that, when you're looking for a job, thinking ahead to the time when you will have one is difficult. But in this case, do try and think ahead.

Corporate recruiters and third-party recruiters work hard to find qualified candidates and will really go the extra mile to bring you in if you have a desirable skill set. The thing is, recruiters in some areas (like high-tech) will keep on trying long after you've said yes to another position. They don't know that you've found a job, and in some cases, they may wisely wait it out and see whether you maybe, just maybe, don't like your new job.

If you want quick closure on your job search, I suggest that you install a separate phone number dedicated to your job search. Use your new phone line on your resume and for your call-back contact phone number. Depending on which phone service you use, a second or third line can cost as little as $7 a month, depending on where you live. Believe me, those few extra dollars are worth it when you can shut off the flow of calls at your discretion. When you're ready to end your job search, you can simply let an answering machine answer the extra phone line, or you can disconnect the line. That way, your home number isn't floating around for years in recruiters' Rolodexes. See Chapter 15 for more advice about bringing closure to your job search.

Part II
Building Your Electronic Toolkit

By Rich Tennant

All through high school he wouldn't talk to anyone - hardly said a word. Now he's graduating from an Ivy League college with an advanced degree in communications.

In this part . . .

*1*t's true — in a job search, a good portion of your job searching fate rests on the information that employers find in your resume and cover letter. That much hasn't changed in an online job search. But the resumes and cover letters that you send sure have!

Part II gets you up to speed on creating and using an electronic resume. You get all the latest information and resume style trends so that you'll look super-savvy to employers. And if you've been worrying what to do about cover letters, this part takes care of those questions, too.

After reading through the chapters in this part, you won't be at all concerned that your resume matters so much — you'll be glad that it does!

Chapter 5

Choosing Your Electronic Resume

● ●

In This Chapter

▶ Exploring the types of electronic resumes

▶ Examining new resume basics for a new, wired workplace

▶ Choosing e-resumes for maximum effectiveness

▶ Avoiding the pitfalls of e-resumes

● ●

*A*nyone who's ever looked at an online clothing catalog knows that some things are better suited to paper and ink.

But other things, like resumes, adapt wonderfully to an electronic medium. Perhaps that's why employers have by and large embraced the concept of electronic resumes.

In the process of embracing new digital technology, however, employers have unwittingly created a whole new way of approaching resumes. The old rules definitely don't apply anymore! Unfortunately, the rules of the resume road have changed so rapidly (and continue to do so) that job seekers are having a tough time keeping up with all the changes.

Five or so years ago, you could have managed a job search without worrying about electronic resumes. But that was then. Now, electronic resumes have become the resume standard in business. Unfortunately, if you don't know the electronic ropes, you can find yourself on the outside track, instead of on the inside track, where you want to be.

In this chapter, I provide an overview of the types of electronic resumes that you need to know about. Plus, you find out which resume to choose for specific types of job-search situations. After you read this chapter, you can get back to the business of worrying about *what* you want to say in your resume rather than wondering what *kind* of resume you should be using!

Taking a Big-Picture Look at Electronic Resumes

Do you want to know just how you've come to be sending out electronic resumes as opposed to those pretty linen paper resumes of a decade ago?

In the mid to late 1980s, two companies, Restrac and Resumix, began selling very expensive resume tracking systems to high-end businesses. The resume tracking devices enabled employers to scan or manually input a resume and then store the resume in a database in which employers could search and track all the stored resumes by keywords and other criteria. Because of the high cost of the systems, only the very largest companies signed on.

Now, a total of about 400 to 600 Fortune 500 and other large companies use Restrac or Resumix. That isn't a lot, but the companies using the systems are high-impact, high-profile companies like GTE, Northrop Grumman, and Southwest Airlines. This high-end cluster of companies definitely got the electronic ball rolling.

Of course, Resumix and Restrac evolved with the times. Now, both systems allow e-mailed resumes to sail right into the databases, and Resumix also has a Web product that helps employers manage resumes and jobs via the Web.

But far more revolutionary than the evolution of Restrac and Resumix is that, about four years ago, offshoot companies started springing up, claiming to be low-cost competitors to the expensive Restrac and Resumix systems. And competitors they were! Corporations like Personics, Inc., now offer much lower-cost electronic resume tracking systems.

Though you probably don't care about the behind-the-scenes competitive wrangling, you should know that systems like Personics' are really taking off. That's news you can use because, now, electronic resume-tracking software is permeating mid-sized and small businesses.

Also, new features of resume tracking software enable a company's hiring managers to access resumes right from their desks, whereas before only human resources departments typically had access to the resumes.

These big changes in how companies handle resumes spell *big changes* in what kind of resumes you need to send. Now that resume tracking software has gone mainstream, you can count on computers handling your resume more often than people.

The bottom line in all this is that, if you aren't using an electronic resume, your resume may not be getting the play you want it to get. You can't assume that only the corporate giants use resume tracking systems anymore.

To bring your resume into the "new generation" of resumes, you need to know only a few basics. Those basics are not difficult to learn, so bear with me as I walk you through them.

New resume basics

I haven't talked to an employer recently who doesn't accept e-mailed resumes, and I haven't talked to an employer in the last year who told me that he or she dislikes e-mailed resumes.

The reason is simple: The growth in the use of electronic resume tracking systems has coincided with the surging popularity of e-mail as a business communication tool. The result is that employers can pop e-mailed resumes right into their electronic resume tracking systems. Direct e-mailing is quick and efficient, and it cuts down dramatically on paperwork, not to mention scanning errors.

What does all this mean to you as a job searcher? You need to know what kind of resume employers want you to send, and how they want you to send it. If you can get your mind around just four basic ideas and really hang on to them, you're right on top of today's resume realities. Here are the new resume basics:

- ✔ Have two resumes: a scannable paper resume and a plain-text electronic resume. Format your plain-text electronic resume as a keyword resume. (See Chapter 6 for more details about keyword resumes.)

- ✔ Use your beautifully formatted paper resume and/or your Web resume as your bonus resume.

- ✔ Know how to e-mail an electronic resume to an employment database, to an employer's Web site, and to an individual's e-mail address.

- ✔ If you have a choice of how you send a resume, know the preferred breakdown, according to employers:

    - E-mailed plain-text resumes are the number-one preference of most employers.

    - Scannable resumes that are printed out on white paper and mailed flat via postal mail are employers' second choice.

    - Faxed resumes that are scannable are employers' last choice. I received numerous complaints from employers about the poor scanning quality of faxed resumes.

Knowing the Types of Electronic Resumes

In high school biology class, I clearly remember memorizing the hierarchy of all living things: kingdom, phylum, class, order, family, genus, and species. Though resumes aren't nearly as complicated as biology, they do share a definite hierarchy. I place resumes in a hierarchy like that shown in Figure 5-1.

✔ You can break resumes into two broad categories, electronic and paper.

✔ Within the paper category, you have formatted paper resumes and scannable paper resumes.

✔ Within the electronic category, you have plain-text or ASCII resumes, formatted electronic resumes, and Web resumes.

✔ Finally, all resumes have a style, such as keyword, chronological, or functional.

This book focuses on electronic resumes plus scannable resumes, because those are the resumes that pertain to an online job search. If you want more information about paper resumes, see *Resumes For Dummies* by Joyce Lain Kennedy (also published by IDG Books Worldwide, Inc.).

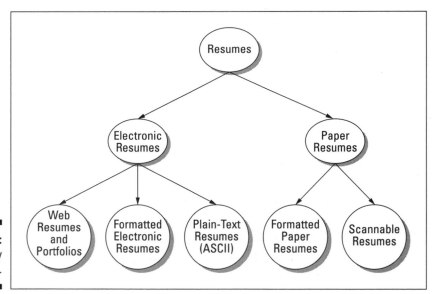

Figure 5-1:
A hierarchy of resumes.

Plain-text or ASCII resume

Plain-text resumes are so named because they're digitally unadorned. Plain-text resumes are text and that's it — they include no extra frills whatsoever.

Another name for a plain-text resume is an *ASCII resume* (pronounced *ask-ee*). This is because ASCII (American Standard Code for Information Exchange) is a very simple form of text that almost all computers can read and understand. ASCII text involves those characters that you find on your keyboard: letters, numbers, and a handful of symbols, such as the dollar sign and the asterisk.

ASCII is not limited to platform — that is, both PCs and Macs can read ASCII text. Neither is ASCII text limited by special formatting placed in a document by an application such as a word processor. Please note that in this book I use the terms *plain-text resume* and *ASCII resume* interchangeably.

You can find examples of ASCII resumes in Chapter 6.

Plain-text resume features

A plain-text resume has the following features:

- ✔ It contains no italics, underlining, bold, hollow bullets, or any type of "pretty" formatting.
- ✔ It looks just like a plain e-mail message.

If you see a plain-looking resume online, it's almost certainly a plain-text resume.

Choose a plain-text or ASCII resume when . . .

Your plain-text resume can do nearly 98 percent of your online resume work for you. It's your hardest-working resume! As such, there are few situations in which your plain-text resume won't work for you.

Here are some key times to use a plain-text resume:

- ✔ When you e-mail a resume to an employer
- ✔ When you post on online employment sites and databases
- ✔ When you send a resume to a corporate Web site
- ✔ When a contact asks you to e-mail a resume
- ✔ When a job advertisement lists an e-mail address

Note: The plain-text resume is your default resume. When in doubt, send a plain-text resume!

Formatted electronic resume

A *formatted electronic resume* is a resume that you create with all the pretty formatting — fancy fonts, headlines, underlining, special characters like bullets, and even color if you want. These are the resumes that make you as a job seeker feel more confident, because you present your words in a visually pleasing format.

Although ASCII resumes are your bread-and-butter resumes, employers may still ask you for a formatted electronic resume. A high-level recruiter at Rollo Associates told me that she asks candidates to send a formatted resume so that she can get a sense for the person's personality. And that's just what a formatted resume enables you to do — you get to express your creativity much more than with a plain-text resume, because many more design options are available to you.

You can see a formatted electronic resume in Chapter 6.

Formatted electronic resume features

A formatted electronic resume can contain bullets, special typefaces, extra symbols, clever spacing, tabs, vertical lines, shading, and other design elements.

Choose a formatted electronic resume when . . .

You may seldom use your formatted electronic resume. But if you do need to use a formatted electronic resume, here are the most common circumstances in which you will get such a request:

- ✔ Occasionally, a job advertisement indicates that you can send in a Word document online. This means that if you use Microsoft Word as your word processor, you can send your Microsoft Word resume to the employer via e-mail as an attachment (see Chapter 7 for an explanation of how to do so).

- ✔ A *very* recent trend is that a few online job sites allow candidates to post Microsoft Word resumes. (Net-Temps and E.span are two examples.) In this case, send your Word resume as is via e-mail to the employment site's contact address.

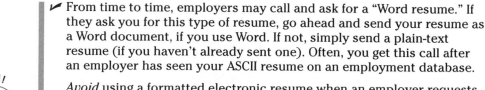

✔ From time to time, employers may call and ask for a "Word resume." If they ask you for this type of resume, go ahead and send your resume as a Word document, if you use Word. If not, simply send a plain-text resume (if you haven't already sent one). Often, you get this call after an employer has seen your ASCII resume on an employment database.

Avoid using a formatted electronic resume when an employer requests that you e-mail a resume. The preferred method of e-mailing a resume is to send a plain-text resume.

Scannable resume

A *scannable resume* is a paper resume that employers can scan electronically into a computer database. Most paper resumes that you send to companies are scanned into a database, whether you know about it or not.

And that's where the problems come in. If you don't know how to create your resume in such a way that it passes muster with a computer scanner, then your resume typically won't make it into the company database. Even though you're sending a paper resume, your paper resume needs to be able to enter the digital realm smoothly and with a minimum of transitional trauma.

Sure, some major employers — Southwest Airlines, for example — hire squadrons of people to take your paper resume and hand-key it into a database. But Southwest Airlines is a rarity in the business. Most employers will take a non-scannable resume and do one of three things with it:

✔ Call you and ask you to e-mail a resume

✔ Call you and ask you to send a scannable resume

✔ Toss the resume into the reject pile

Your best bet is to understand scannable resumes before you ever send out your first resume. You can see an example of a scannable resume in Chapter 6.

Scannable resume features

Scannable resumes are basic, simple resumes without any special formatting. A good scannable resume sports a complete absence of the following elements:

✔ Boldface

✔ Underlining

✔ Hollow bullets

- ✓ Italics
- ✓ Fancy fonts
- ✓ Tabbed columns (columns do not scan well)

Interactive Search, Inc., a company that processes thousands upon thousands of paper resumes by scanning them into electronic databases, has lots of experience with scannable resumes. The CEO of the company described to me the various types of scanners that are on the market today and how each scanner accepts various elements.

Some scanners accept bullets; others don't. Some scanners accept bold; others don't. The Interactive Search CEO's advice: Keep your paper resume as simple as possible, because you never know what technology an employer will use to scan in your resume.

Choose a scannable paper resume when . . .

Here are the times when you want to use a scannable paper resume:

- ✓ Whenever you send a *paper* resume to an employer — period, no exceptions, unless the employer specifically requests that you send a different type of resume
- ✓ When an employer requests that you fax a resume

Web resume or Web portfolio

A *Web resume* is one that you can place on the Web. Web resumes come in two flavors:

- ✓ A formatted electronic resume that you've placed on the Web is typically referred to as a *Web resume*. A Web resume looks like a paper resume, but it's on the Web. The only difference is that your Web resume can also contain a photograph.
- ✓ A multimedia Web site that contains a resume and significant samples of your work is typically called a *Web portfolio*. A Web portfolio can contain graphics, sounds, and video clips.

You can see an example of a Web portfolio in Chapter 12, and an example of a Web resume in Chapter 6.

Web resume features

Chapter 12 gives additional information about Web resumes and portfolios. But the important features that I want to point out are the following:

✔ Web resumes are typically used as follow-up devices. Typically, you don't send a Web resume to an employer. Rather, you list your URL or Web address on the electronic or paper resume that you send, and you wait for the employer to visit your site at his or her discretion.

✔ Web portfolios are used in today's job hunt as a portable portfolio of work samples. You can refer to your Web portfolio during interviews. If an employer doesn't have access to the Web, you can print out Web pages and carry them as a paper portfolio.

The way you put together a Web resume or portfolio depends completely on what you want. Currently, there are no strong Web resume guidelines suggesting fonts or other elements. The only major guiding factor in a Web resume relates to photos: Do you want to risk putting a photograph of yourself on your Web resume?

Employers told me "no photos" over and over, but again, ultimately, the decision is yours. A good work-around for photos is to add a snappy graphic to your resume, which can add spice but doesn't create a potential discrimination problem for employers. (See Chapter 12 for more details about working with graphics.)

Choose a Web portfolio or resume when . . .

Here are the times when you want to use a Web portfolio or resume:

✔ You work in a creative field that doesn't lend itself well to verbal description. For example, if you're an opera singer, you want a Web resume that includes a photo, because how you look is part of your job. You also want to include sound clips from recent performances and reviews of your work. An excellent example of this type of creative resume is mezzo soprano Adria Firestone's Web resume, which is located at www.adriafirestone.com.

✔ You want to stand out from the competition as being very up-to-date and computer-savvy. Even if you have only a text resume on the Web, that's still more than most people have; thus it makes you look good.

✔ Another situation in which a Web resume is helpful is when you place a short version of your resume online. When employers begin calling and asking you to send a more detailed resume, you can simply refer them to your Web site, which hopefully contains a longer, more detailed resume as well. Both job seekers and employers tell me that this is a time-saving, effective method of getting information quickly.

You *don't* want to use a Web resume at most online employment sites. You also don't want to e-mail a Web resume to an employer as a cold call. Again, use your Web resume as a referral, a way to give more detailed information.

Chapter 6

Constructing Your Electronic Resume

In This Chapter

▶ Elements of electronic resumes

▶ Benefits of keyword formatting

▶ Steps to create an electronic resume

*E*lectronic resumes are a lot like school uniforms: They level the style playing field. Now, instead of worrying about which paper to use, what size of envelopes to choose, and what font best expresses your personality, you essentially need to concern yourself with getting your electronic style in order, and that's it. Because everyone's online resume is plain as can be, you don't need to worry about looking plain yourself.

When it comes down to it, electronic resumes, just like uniforms, are actually simpler to work with in the long run. If your opinion differs, perhaps I can help you. In this chapter, I show you the elements of electronic resumes. I also walk you step by step through the process of creating an electronic resume, as well as creating all the electronic variations of the same.

Getting Your Resume in E-Style

Electronic resumes are definitely different from paper resumes in terms of looks and function. An electronic resume is a digital animal that lives by an entirely different set of rules — rules that a computer dictates.

To please the digital powers that be, dressing your resume for digital success is important. That involves a few key items: You need to include keywords, and you need to get your resume in the right style, or *format,* for employers.

A quick note about resume length

Online electronic resumes are generally one to three pages in length, with the average being one and a half pages. Mark Sugalski, a sourcing manager and ace recruiter, told me that he likes to see what he calls a "bikini" resume used online — that is, a short one- to one-and-a-half-page resume. If he's interested, he calls the candidate and asks for a more detailed resume. (You have one ready, I hope!)

Keywords are words that describe skills related to your profession. Because employers search resume databases for nouns and noun phrases such as *teacher, manager,* and *accountant* instead of *teaching, managing,* and *accounting,* stacking plenty of skill nouns into your resume is important.

As far as keywords are concerned, they're the lifeblood of electronic resumes. When you e-mail an electronic resume to an online database, employers use keywords and phrases to find your resume. When you e-mail your resume to a company Web site or HR department, your resume lands in a database where, again, employers use keywords to find you.

About the only time employers don't use keywords to find you is when you e-mail a resume directly to them.

Therefore, in the interest of simplicity, create an electronic resume that you can use in either situation! Hedge your bets and pack your resume with keywords from top to bottom. (For more help on keywords, see Chapter 3.)

As far as electronic style elements, well, you have a lot to think about. I cover each type of electronic resume in "Creating and Formatting Your Electronic Resume," later in this chapter.

One more thing: In dealing with electronic resumes, you likely will encounter the term *ASCII* with some regularity. ASCII (pronounced "ASK-ee") is the acronym for American Standard Code for Information Exchange. It is the very simplest form of text that almost all computers can read and understand. ASCII is sometimes called "plain text."

Looking at the Elements of an Electronic Resume

Here are the parts of an electronic resume, pulled apart and analyzed piece by piece.

Name and contact block

Position your name and contact information in a block at the very top of your resume. You want to present your name first, followed by your physical contact address, phone number, fax number, and e-mail address. If you have a superb Web site or a Web portfolio, list your URL as well.

For scannable resumes and plain-text resumes, place your name and contact block at the far left side of the page, with each element on its own line (see the samples later in this chapter). Each element gets its own line to help computers read your information clearly.

For plain-text resumes, place parentheses around your area code. For scannable resumes, remove the parentheses and just use hyphens. (No slashes, please!) The reason for the digital wrangling is so that each type of computer system can read your information accurately.

Job objective

A job objective can take several different forms. Most notably, your job objective states what you want. Take about five to eight words to state your job objective, or simply list a job title. Most often, the job objective comes right after your contact information. (See the sample layouts later in this chapter.)

I need to tell you right away, though, that career experts argue vociferously about job objectives. The problem? Some think that you should use a summary instead. The solution? Decide which works best for you. According to current practice, which is nebulous to say the least, you can include an objective alone, a summary paragraph alone, or use both. (See the next section for details on summaries.)

For electronic resumes that will be used online, I recommend that you use an objective plus a keyword summary or paragraph, for the simple reason that you need to please a computer above all else.

Here are some tips and samples to help you make a decision:

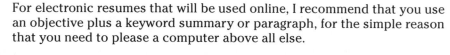

- ✓ If you're very sure of the exact type of job you want, using an objective is a good option.

- ✓ If you have a long or complicated resume, an objective makes it easy for your readers to grasp what you want very quickly. Sometimes, speed is the name of the game.

- ✓ If you see a specific job that you want to pursue, listing the job title in your objective is perfectly acceptable.

- Many recruiters and employers report that a clear, concise objective is very important to them.

- If you are a new graduate or are new to the workforce, including a career objective is usually a good idea.

Now for the downside of using an objective:

- If you look at resumes of CEOs and high-level executives, many don't list objectives. More often, you find them listing a snappy summary paragraph (see the "Summary or keyword paragraph" section).

- If your career objective is too specific, you could talk yourself out of a job right at the top of your resume.

Here are some well-written objectives. Remember, keep objectives short, short, short!

- Corporate finance, long-term risk analysis, and management

- UNIX systems administrator in an engineering environment

- Position as an academic advisor for adult education students

- Marketing position in the biotechnology industry

Avoid putting something like "seek to use my degree in a fulfilling job" in your objective. Focus your objective on the *job* that you want to do, emphasizing particular *skills*.

Summary or keyword paragraph

Your summary or keyword paragraph is a condensed paragraph that highlights your skills. If you're writing an electronic resume, including a summary paragraph that contains numerous keywords is very important.

This is because your electronic resume will go into a computer database, where keywords are the major way that employers find you. Though including a job objective is a matter of choice, you can hurt your chances with a keyword-hungry computer if you omit a summary or keyword paragraph in an electronic resume.

Currently, many different types of resume tracking systems exist. Some of the systems use different "logic" than others to search for resumes. One type of tracking system goes through your resume and records the first 100 keywords. Because of this type of system, most experts agree that for electronic resumes, getting your keywords way up at the top of your resume is pretty important. Thus, the keyword format was born. (A *keyword-formatted resume*

is simply a resume with a strong emphasis on keywords. Keyword-formatted resumes almost always have a keyword summary or a keyword-heavy summary near the top of the resume.)

As you may expect, experts and recruiters disagree about keyword paragraphs.

- ✔ Some like to see keyword paragraphs placed right after the contact information.
- ✔ Others prefer to see the keyword paragraph placed after the job objective.

My position is that the placement is up to you, and that both work just fine. Because your job or career objective is so short anyhow, you probably won't harm yourself by placing your keyword paragraph after your objective. In a keyword paragraph, the important thing is to make sure that it's *either* the second or the third major element of your resume.

As far as what goes into your summary or keyword paragraph, you have a lot of options. If you work in a technical field, you can simply list your relevant skills one right after the other, with each noun or noun phrase separated with a comma. This treatment is a *keyword summary,* or just a *summary.*

If you're a high-level executive and you're sending a resume to a company's human resources department, you may want to call your keyword paragraph an "executive profile" or "career profile." An executive profile type of summary, while still containing numerous keywords, is more effective if you do a little bit more verbal smoothing. Please note that though some CEOs and executives do list a career objective, more often than not they simply use a thorough summary paragraph and leave off the career objective.

Here's an executive profile loaded with enough keywords to please a computer and smooth enough to please human eyes, too:

> Award-winning corporate comptroller with more than ten years' experience in two $500 million corporations. Impressive record in implementing new financial database architecture that saved over $2 million annually. Proficient in Oracle, Prism, Red Brick, and SAP systems as well as MS Project, Excel, Word, PowerPoint, and FrontPage.

Technical skills, such as in the following example, are good bets to place right after the contact information and before the objective. Readers can glance over your skills immediately, and so can a computer.

Here's a keyword summary chock-full of nouns and noun phrases that will get noticed by a computer:

Skills:
Languages: C, SQL, C++, Assembler, Pascal
Software: Oracle Developer 2000, Informix NewEra, Foxpro
OS: UNIX, Windows NT/95/3.11, MS-DOS
RDBMS: Oracle 7, Informix 7

In this sample, note that I did not use the label *keyword summary.* You don't have to label your paragraph a keyword summary, even if it is one. You can label your skills paragraph *qualifications, skills, career profile,* or *professional history summary.* For most professionals, labeling your paragraph *skills, qualifications,* or *keyword paragraph* is a great option.

Work experience

You can arrange the content of your resume in essentially three basic ways:

- ✔ Chronologically (according to time)
- ✔ Functionally (according to skill)
- ✔ A blending of the two

In this chapter, I stick with a basic chronological format, which means that after your contact information, objective, and summary paragraph, you include information about the following items:

- ✔ Your employment history arranged in reverse chronological order (you begin your resume with your most recent experience). For online purposes, cover about the last ten years of your employment.
- ✔ Your education and training.
- ✔ Awards and special achievements, if applicable.

The important point to know about writing about your employment history is to include dates, job titles, and places of employment. Even if you're intentionally masking these items for online confidentiality purposes, you still want your basic resume to include these items.

Please understand that I'm presenting only one resume organization option! You have *many* others to choose from. I selected a reverse chronological organization for this chapter because it works very well in computer databases and is widely accepted.

An important note about e-resumes and keywords

As you create your resume, remember to load it with nouns and noun phrases that fit your industry, your skills, and your goals. Sure, you need verbs, but you also need to add as many different keywords to the body of your resume as you can. Try not to repeat your keyword paragraph or skills summary verbatim if possible.

When you put a resume online, your resume is usually searched by keywords. And if your resume goes to a company that uses resume tracking software, again, your resume is searched by keywords.

Keywords are crucial to your eventual job-search success! Add them liberally to your resume, and even to your cover letter.

Because my focus in this chapter is on electronic resumes, not on the infinite points of how to organize your resume, I'd like to refer you to *Resumes For Dummies* by Joyce Lain Kennedy (IDG Books Worldwide, Inc.) for detailed advice in the resume organization area.

Creating and Formatting Your Electronic Resume

If you've been dreading the process of creating an electronic resume, fearing that it will be about as pleasant as doing your income taxes, you needn't worry. Word-processing software makes going digital fast and simple.

Before you start, you need a few tools:

- ✔ You need access to a computer with word-processing software such as Microsoft Word or Corel WordPerfect.

- ✔ If you're creating a scannable resume, you also need white paper (the brighter the better) and access to a good printer. A laser printer is best, but a very good ink-jet printer also works. The old dot-matrix printers are completely unacceptable for printing scannable resumes.

- ✔ If you want to create a Web resume, you have more flexibility and options if you have a *Web editor,* which is a piece of software that helps you create and edit Web pages. Popular Web editors include Microsoft's FrontPage and Corel's Web.Designer. Please note that the newer versions of word processors enable you to save documents in HTML format.

Step by step to a basic electronic resume

In this section, I walk you through the steps for creating a basic electronic resume, which is essentially a plain-text or ASCII resume. This is your "base" resume that you use to create all your other electronic style variations.

1. **Open a word-processing document and immediately set the margins at 0 and 65, or set the margins to allow for about 65 characters. (Each letter and each space counts as one character.)**

   You set these margins so that your words don't run off electronic screens, which most often display only 60 to 65 characters.

2. **Give your document a name and save the document.**

   I know that you haven't written anything, but why risk losing data? Don't worry about format yet — just save your document so that you don't lose it. Remember to keep saving your document throughout the writing process.

3. **Select a simple font such as Times New Roman or Courier. Select a 12-point or 10-point type size.**

4. **Type in your resume elements, using all caps to highlight your name and major headings.**

   Be sure to use parentheses around your phone and fax area codes, and separate the rest of your phone number with hyphens. Place your contact information one item to a line. Justify to the left, avoiding centering or flush-right formatting. *Use your spacebar to indent items.* (If you use tabs to space your document, all your tab formatting will be lost when you save it as ASCII.) If you wish, you can use a single hyphen to highlight bullet points.

5. **Spell-check your resume, and then have a second person read it for accuracy to make sure that you didn't miss anything.**

6. **Double-check all your resume information for accuracy.**

7. **After you're very sure that the information in your resume is accurate, save your resume as a text file.**

   To do so, go to your File menu and choose Save As. From your word processor's Save As pull-down menu, select ASCII or Text Only. You see what my word processor's options look like in Figure 6-1. I selected Text Only with Line Breaks to save my plain-text resume.

8. **Now for the test: Close your file.**

   Often the program asks whether you know that you will lose formatting. Don't worry about this message. Click on Yes or OK and close the file.

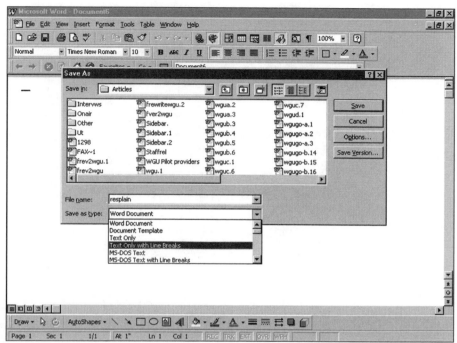

Figure 6-1:
Saving a file
as ASCII in
a Microsoft
Word 7
document.

9. Reopen your text resume.

It appears as genuine ASCII text at this point. Now you can go in and fix spacing problems *with your spacebar.* You can also add hard returns after lines for spacing. Please be aware that you must not skip this step, as your formatting often looks different when you reopen the document as Text Only. After you've finished fixing the spacing, save, close, and reopen your document again to double-check spacing.

10. Perform a trial e-mailing.

See Chapter 7 for details about how to do so.

If your resume checks out via e-mail, you're all set! If not, usually the only changes you need to make are spacing fixes.

Figure 6-2 shows an example of a basic electronic resume. (This is also an ASCII resume.)

```
YOUR NAME
Address
City
State, Zip Code
Telephone: (000)000-0000
Fax: (000)000-0000
Yourname@email.com
www.yourURL.com

Job Objective: State what you want to do or what you are
qualified to do. You can also list a job title. (You can
combine your objective with your keyword or summary
paragraph if you wish.)

Summary of Qualifications: This is a keyword summary
listing nouns that describe your skills. (Some experts
like to put the keyword paragraph first, before the job
objective.) Note: If you are a CEO or high-level
executive, you may want to skip the objective and call
your summary an  executive profile.

PROFESSIONAL EXPERIENCE

19xx - Present Employer, Location of Employer
          Job Title
          Name job accomplishments and skills, noting your
          actions and the results of your actions. Use nouns
          and noun phrases to describe equipment, procedures,
          tasks, awards, promotions, raises, increases in
          leadership, and special projects. Add new keywords
          wherever possible.
          - List accomplishment
          - List accomplishment

19xx - 19xx  Employer, Location of Employer
          Job Title
          Name job accomplishments as above. Try to broaden
          your keywords.

19xx - 19xx    Employer, Location of Employer
          Job Title
          List accomplishments as before, but take less room
          doing so.

19xx - 19xx  Employer, Location of Employer
          Job Title
          List accomplishments as before, taking even less
          room.

EDUCATION

List your educational achievements here. Be sure to
include professional certifications, seminars, and
training.
```

Figure 6-2:
An ASCII or
plain-text
resume.

Theme and variations: Getting your resume in e-style

After you've created your basic electronic resume, fashioning it into a new electronic style is just a matter of a few moments of extra tweaking. That's one of the great benefits of using electronic resumes: They're adaptable and flexible tools that you can use in many forms with a minimum of effort.

Here's how you can take your basic electronic resume (which really is an ASCII resume) and quickly transform it into new stylistic variations.

Plain-text or ASCII resume steps

You have very little to do to ensure that your basic electronic resume is in ASCII style, because the essence of your basic e-resume is that it's an ASCII resume! Nevertheless, it doesn't hurt to do the following:

1. **Open your basic electronic resume.**

2. **Check that you've included parentheses around the area code portions of your phone and fax numbers.**

   The parentheses help computers identify the phone numbers. Also check that you've added hyphens between the numbers (refer to Figure 6-2). Also make sure that each item of your contact information is on a separate line so as not to trip up computers.

3. **Scan the first 100 or so words of your resume.**

   Double-check that you've packed your resume with numerous non-repetitive nouns and noun phrases (keywords) that highlight your skills.

4. **Fine-tune spacing, if necessary.**

   Do so with your spacebar, not with tabs!

5. **Save your resume.**

   You may wish to save a copy of your finished ASCII or plain-text resume on a floppy disk to ensure that you don't have to rewrite it in case you have a hard disk crash.

Please refer to Figure 6-2 to see a good example of a plain-text resume.

Scannable resume steps

To create a scannable resume from your basic resume, you take just a few extra steps. Plus, you need to have access to a good printer and white or light-colored paper.

Here are the steps:

1. **Open your basic electronic resume in your word processor.**

2. **Immediately save your basic resume with a new name so that you don't overwrite your basic resume.**

3. **Take out all parentheses from your basic resume, including those around phone and fax numbers.**

   This step is crucial because parentheses hang up some types of scanners. Also, avoid using slashes in phone numbers.

4. **For aesthetic purposes, change font sizes from 10 to 16 points.**

   In my sample scannable resume, I use 16 points for the name, 14 points for the main resume headings, and 12 points for the rest of the resume. I also remove headings that are in all caps for visual reasons, but this step is not essential. To do so, I retype the heading using just initial caps. For example, instead of HEADING, I use Heading.

5. **If your resume runs longer than one page, place your name at the top of the second page on a separate line.**

6. **Save your scannable resume and print it out, preferably using a laser printer.**

   Use bright white paper — the higher the contrast between the paper and the text, the better. Remember, scannable resumes go right into a computer database!

7. **When you send your scannable resume, mail it flat and without staples.**

   Use a paper clip to hold two or more pages together.

8. **If you fax your scannable resume, turn on the fine print feature of the fax machine you use.**

You can see an example of a scannable resume in Figure 6-3.

Formatted resume steps

Creating a formatted electronic resume from your basic electronic resume is more fun than it is work! Follow these steps:

1. **Open your basic electronic resume and immediately save it with a new name.**

   You don't want to overwrite your basic electronic resume.

2. **Decide how you want your resume to look, and then add the design elements you desire.**

   You can add bullets, horizontal and vertical lines, shading, special fonts — in essence, whatever you want, within reason.

```
Your Name
Address
City
State, Zip Code
Telephone: 000-000-0000
Fax: 000-000-0000
Yourname@email.com
www.yourURL.com

Job Objective: State what you want to do or what you are
qualified to do. You can also list a job title. You can combine
your objective with your keyword or summary paragraph if you
wish.

Summary of Qualifications: This is a keyword summary listing
nouns that describe your skills. Some experts like to put the
keyword paragraph first, before the job objective. Note: If you
are a CEO or high-level executive, you may want to skip the
objective and call your summary an "executive profile."

Professional Experience

19xx - Present Employer, Location of Employer
     Job Title
     Name job accomplishments and skills, noting your
     actions and the results of your actions. Use nouns
     and noun phrases to describe equipment, procedures,
     tasks, awards, promotions, raises, increases in
     leadership, and special projects. Add new keywords
     wherever possible.
          - List accomplishment
          - List accomplishment

19xx - 19xx     Employer, Location of Employer
     Job Title
     Name job accomplishments as above. Try to broaden
     your keywords.

19xx - 19xx     Employer, Location of Employer
     Job Title
     List accomplishments as before, but take less room
     doing so.

19xx - 19xx     Employer, Location of Employer
     Job Title
     List accomplishments as before, taking even less
     room.

Education

List your educational achievements here. Be sure to include
professional certifications, seminars, and training.
```

Figure 6-3:
A
scannable
resume that
pleases
computers.

3. **After you've given your resume a design makeover, save your resume as a standard or default document.**

   For Microsoft Word, simply save the document as an MS Word document. If you use Corel WordPerfect, save the document as a WordPerfect file. Don't save your document as text, or you'll strip out all your new design!

4. **If you wish, print out your nicely formatted resume for your records.**

   A formatted resume is a good item to bring with you to interviews so that you can leave a good-looking copy of your resume with each employer.

Figure 6-4 shows a fully formatted electronic resume.

Web resume steps

Depending on the software you use, changing your basic electronic resume into a Web resume can involve a varied number of steps. Here's one option to try:

1. **Open your basic electronic resume in the word processor that created it.**

2. **Decide whether you want a formatted resume or a plain-text resume on the Web.**

3. **If you want a formatted resume on the Web, follow the steps for creating a formatted resume, but rename your resume file something like webres so that you know which resume to put on the Web.**

4. **After your resume looks the way you want it to, save the document again as HTML.**

   The most recent versions of some word-processing programs enable you to do so. Please note that HTML has its limitations; you may need to work with your resume for a while before you're happy with how it looks.

5. **Preview your HTML resume in a Web browser.**

   To do so, simply open your browser and then, instead of opening a URL, open a local file. (A *local file* is a file that's stored on your computer.) Most browsers have a menu selection like Open File that lets you open a local file.

6. **If you like the way your resume has translated to HTML, publish it to the Web.**

   If you don't like it, go back and fiddle with it in your word processor, or you can fiddle with the HTML version. If you have a lot of troubles, you can simply save your basic electronic resume as HTML and get that up on the Web right away.

Your Name
Address
City
State, Zip Code
Telephone: 000-000-0000   Fax: 000-000-0000

Yourname@email.com   www.yourURL.com

Job Objective: State what you want to do or what you are qualified to do. You can also list a job title. You can combine your objective with your keyword or summary paragraph if you wish.

Summary of Qualifications: This is a keyword summary listing nouns that describe your skills. Some experts like to put the keyword paragraph first, before the job objective. Note: If you are a CEO or high-level executive, you may want to skip the objective and call your summary an "executive profile."

Professional Experience

19xx - Present Employer, Location of Employer

   Job Title

   Name job accomplishments and skills, noting your actions and the results of your actions. Use nouns and noun phrases to describe equipment, procedures, tasks, awards, promotions, raises, increases in leadership, and special projects. Add new keywords wherever possible.

   • List accomplishment

   • List accomplishment

19xx - 19xx   Employer, Location of Employer

   Job Title

   Name job accomplishments as above. Try to broaden your keywords.

19xx - 19xx   Employer, Location of Employer

   Job Title

   List accomplishments as before, but take less room doing so.

19xx - 19xx   Employer, Location of Employer

   Job Title

   List accomplishments as before, taking even less room.

Education

List your educational achievements here. Be sure to include professional certifications, seminars, and training.

Figure 6-4:
A formatted electronic resume with extra design details.

Your second option for creating an HTML or Web resume depends on using Web creation software like Microsoft FrontPage. Please refer to Chapter 12 for more information about Web portfolios and resumes.

1. **Open a Web page creation tool (also called an HTML editor).**

2. **Use the import feature to import your basic electronic resume into the HTML editor.**

   Or simply cut and paste text from your word processor into the HTML editor. (Most allow you to do so.)

3. **After the basic resume is in the HTML editor, edit the resume to look as you want it to look.**

   Rearranging the resume to your liking may take you a while.

4. **Save your HTML resume as an HTML document, again using your HTML editing software.**

5. **Publish your HTML resume to the Web.**

   You can see what a Web resume looks like in Figure 6-5.

 I know that you *can* add a photo to your Web resume. But don't! Many employers shy away from photographs with resumes because of Equal Employment Opportunity Commission rules and regulations about discriminatory hiring practices. In fact, I know employers who won't consider a resume with a photo for this very reason.

Figure 6-5: A resume transformed into HTML and published to the Web.

Chapter 7

Putting Your Electronic Resume Out There

....

In This Chapter
- ▶ Choosing a resume send-out strategy
- ▶ Getting your resume online
- ▶ E-mailing your resume
- ▶ Mastering Web resume forms
- ▶ Protecting your resume privacy

....

I have several rather dramatic older sisters, so I grew up hearing the continual lament: "I'm all dressed up with no place to go!" They seemed to bleat out this particular cry most frequently on Friday nights. That's when they felt stuck at home and out of touch with what they considered to be critical teen social action.

My sisters have long since stopped complaining about their lack of social opportunities. In fact, I suspect that they wistfully long for those quiet nights! Now, though, I get a variation on the "stuck at home" theme from my friends and readers when I hear this frequently uttered phrase: "I have a great resume, but I have nowhere to send it!"

Well, consider yourself cured. In this chapter, I show you what to do with your perfectly dressed and raring-to-go resume. In just an hour or so, you can get your resume in front of the right people — those who can offer you the job you've been looking for!

Resume Send-Out Strategies

To get your resume in front of the right people, you need to make some decisions about where and to whom you want to send it. That's both difficult and easy at the same time. First, the easy stuff.

Despite the numerous resume databases and the seemingly dazzling array of online options you have, your resume opportunities really boil down to these three basics:

✔ Posting your resume to online employment sites with resume databases (not all employment sites accept resumes)

✔ Submitting your resume to company Web sites

✔ E-mailing your resume directly to individual employers as a result of a job advertisement or a lead you found via research

Now for the tougher stuff. This is where you need to dig in and do some poking around on the Web and, most important, make some important long-term decisions about how you want your job search to work.

These particular steps can help you get a resume strategy together fast:

1. **Make a decision about what you want in terms of a job.**

2. **Choose a job-search strategy.**

   This strategy forms the backbone of *how often* and *where* you post your resume. I discuss job-search strategies extensively in Chapter 2; please check that chapter for details about which strategy is right for you. Finding the right one is really important!

3. **Based on your job-search strategy, decide whether to post to open, confidential, password-protected, or candidate-controlled resume databases.**

4. **Go through the listings in the Internet Directory at the back of this book and find those databases and resume hot spots that match the level of visibility and privacy that you require (see the sidebar "A quick course on resume privacy" for more details).**

To figure out which resume database sports which privacy features, you need to take it on a database-by-database basis. Read the fine print, and when in doubt, call or send an e-mail to the database with your questions. Again, see Chapter 2 for more details about job-search strategies.

Paying to post your resume is almost never worth it. Currently, the strong trend is that you don't pay to post your resume.

A quick course on resume privacy

Resume databases come in a full range of privacy options. So far, no standards or laws exist that encourage employment sites to protect your privacy, so you must fend for yourself. I've found that your best protection is to be very aware of your options and to vote with your feet. (That is, if you don't like a site, leave it behind!)

Here's a rundown of the types of privacy that you can find online right now:

Open resume databases allow anyone with a Web connection to view the resumes that are posted at the site. As of this writing, Yahoo! Classifieds, Usenet, and many other sites fall in this category.

Password-protected resume databases require a password from anyone who wants to search the resumes. Sites using this feature allow only legitimate employers and recruiters to access the resumes. CareerCast, NationJobs, Net-Temps, and, in fact, most sites offer at least password-protection for you.

Confidential resume databases strip your personal information off your resume so that your employer can't zing you for looking for another job if he or she sees your resume online. Online Career Center, E.span, and other sites offer this feature. But you have to really look for it — not nearly enough employment sites offer a confidentiality feature.

Candidate-controlled resume databases are the ideal. Your resume is password-protected and confidential, and you decide who sees your resume on a case-by-case basis. I love candidate-controlled databases because you control your resume every step of the way. You don't need to worry about the wrong person stumbling across your resume. Attorneys @ Work and the Online Career Center are two excellent examples of this type of database. (As of this writing, E.span also plans to implement a candidate-controlled resume database.) I wish that all databases gave you this level of control over your resume!

E-Mailing and Posting Your Resume Online

Getting your resume online is quick and simple — that is, if you know the digital ropes. Here's the lowdown on e-mailing your resume and submitting it to online databases.

E-mailing resumes

You e-mail your resume more often than any other task you perform with your resume. That's because e-mailing is fast, fast, fast.

When an employer or anyone else requests that you e-mail a resume, the assumption is that you will send a plain-text resume pasted into the body of an e-mail message. The only exception to this is when an employer asks you to send a text attachment or another type of attachment. The following sections give you all the details.

If you have questions about how to use a cover letter with your e-mailed resume, refer to Chapter 8 for detailed information.

Copying and pasting

Copying and pasting is computer-speak for a wonderfully lazy method of copying text from one place to another. It's pretty much universal, no matter what kind of computer you use. And best of all, it saves you from having to retype text.

Here are the general steps for copying and pasting your resume into an e-mail message.

Note: These steps reflect that I use a PC running Windows 95. For Windows 3.1 and Mac users, the steps may differ slightly . Also, my e-mail program, Eudora Pro, may look slightly different than yours if you use a different program.

1. **Open your plain-text or ASCII resume.**

   See Chapters 5 and 6 for information about plain-text resumes.

2. **Highlight your entire resume from top to bottom.**

   You can see what this looks like in Figure 7-1. To highlight text, click over the text and drag down the page until all the text is highlighted, or *selected.* Most word-processing programs also have a Select All option on the Edit menu. This option automatically highlights all the text of the document that's currently open on your screen.

3. **Right-click on the highlighted text and choose Copy, or go to the Edit menu and choose Copy.**

4. **Switch to your e-mail program.**

5. **Create a new e-mail message.**

6. **Place your cursor inside the e-mail message area.**

7. **Right-click and choose Paste. Or choose Paste from the Edit menu.**

   Your plain-text resume appears in the e-mail message area, as shown in Figure 7-2. You may need to fix some of the spacing, which you can do with your spacebar.

8. **After you're happy with how your resume looks, send it off!**

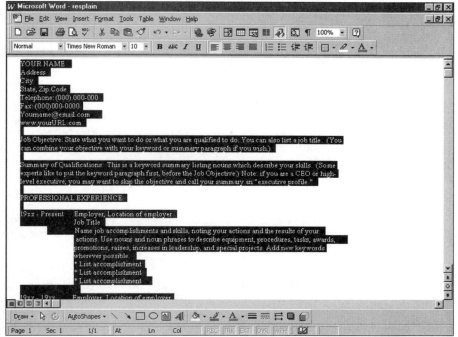

Figure 7-1:
Getting
ready to
copy text in
a copy-and-
paste job.

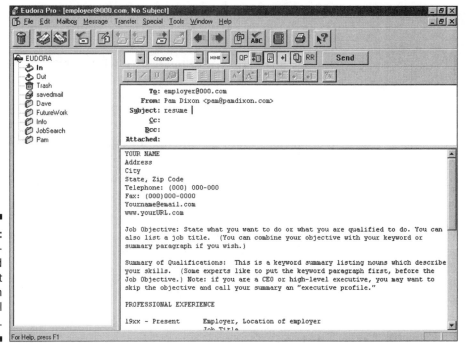

Figure 7-2:
A copied-
and-pasted
plain-text
resume in
an e-mail
message.

Send a practice copy-and-paste e-mail to a friend so that you can road-test your resume. You may find that it doesn't travel well over the wires. If not, you can reformat your resume so that it travels with less digital mussing. The most common problem is incorrect spacing. If you notice spacing that's off, simply correct it with your spacebar.

Sending attachments

An *attachment* is simply a document that you add to your e-mail message. Most employers vastly prefer that you not send attachments, so I advise against sending an attachment unless an employer specifically requests that you do so.

You'll usually use one of two types of attachments in your job search:

- ✔ **Text attachments:** Text attachments are simply plain-text or ASCII documents that you add to your e-mail message. Most computer users can open text attachments without difficulty.

- ✔ **Formatted or binary attachments:** Formatted attachments, also called binary attachments, are those like Corel WordPerfect or Microsoft Word documents that contain elements unique to the software. If you don't have the particular piece of software that was used to create the formatted document, you may not be able to open the document. That's why you should send a formatted attachment only upon request.

To add an attachment to your e-mail, take these general steps:

1. **Begin a new e-mail message.**

2. **Look at the menu of your e-mail program for a selection called Attach File or something similar to that.**

3. **Choose the Attach File option.**

   A dialog box displaying your files opens.

4. **Browse through your files and double-click on the file that you want to attach.**

   Your e-mail message now shows that you have attached a file to the message. All you need to do now is to send your e-mail message in the standard manner.

Note: If you send a formatted attachment, your message may take longer to send than normal. This is not at all out of the ordinary, so don't sweat it if this happens to you.

Posting your resume to employment databases

Posting your resume to an online employment database is relatively simple — you'll find that most employment databases require you to fill out some kind of form or copy and paste your resume into an e-mail message.

Because each employment site is set up slightly differently, you need to visit sites individually to see what each one requires. In general, though, you can expect to find the following types of posting methods on your visits:

- ✔ Most often, you post via some type of rather lengthy online form.
- ✔ Less frequently, you copy and paste an ASCII resume into a simple e-mail form.
- ✔ Very infrequently, you fax or mail (regular mail) a resume to a database.

Here, I walk you through the resume form submittal procedure at the Online Career Center, which is very similar to what you find at many employment sites.

1. **Open the OCC site at** `www.occ.com`.

2. **Scroll to the bottom of the page and click on the Submit Resume link.**

   You arrive at the OCC Resumes page.

3. **Click on the Job Seekers — Post Resume link.**

   You see the OCC login page.

4. **Enter your personal e-mail address to create an account.**

   This is a common feature. After you enter your e-mail address, OCC sends you a user name and password via e-mail. When I logged in at OCC, I received my user name and password at my e-mail address in less than two minutes.

5. **To retrieve your user name and password, open your e-mail software and check your mail. Copy the information you need and then return to the OCC login page.**

6. **Enter your user name and password, as I've done in Figure 7-3.**

   As is the case in many password boxes, the characters of the password appear as asterisks for privacy reasons.

   You go immediately to the OCC Submit Resume online form.

Figure 7-3:
Logging in
to the OCC
resume
submittal
area.

7. Fill in the following:

- Your contact information

- Where you want your resume placed

- Relocation information

- What kind of job you want

- What salary you want

- Your education

- A resume title (This is what you want your resume to be called — for example, writer, accountant, attorney, and so on.)

8. Type or paste the body of your resume into the large message area.

You see the bottom part of the form in Figure 7-4, along with the message area I refer to. Fill out the form completely and paste your plain-text resume in the "resume body" section. Double-check to clean up the spacing if you need to, making corrections with the spacebar. I have filled out a little bit of information so you can see what it looks like.

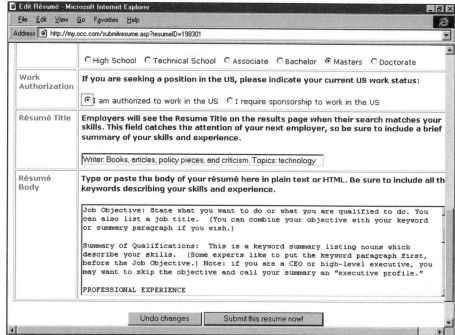

Figure 7-4:
The Online
Career
Center
resume
form.

I looked at the "inside" view of several online resume databases. The most common mistakes I found were misspellings in the online form, particularly in the resume titles. When you fill out an online form, spelling *really* counts. Be extra careful, because making a typo or spelling error in an online form is especially easy.

9. After you finish filling out the form, click on the Submit button.

You can then view your resume, edit it, or manage the results of your job search. In Figure 7-5, you see what my completed resume looks like to an employer. Please note that your resume is private and candidate-controlled on OCC, which is why your resume appears to the employer without contact information.

If you look closely at Figure 7-5, you can see that my spacing is slightly off. Even though my spacing was perfect when I created my resume, it got a little bit skewed when it got to the OCC site. I left my spacing skewed so you can get a feel for the kinds of problems that you typically encounter with submitting resumes. The fix? Either reformat your resume so that it's flush left, and therefore 100 percent unflappable, or fix the spacing in the edit section of OCC.

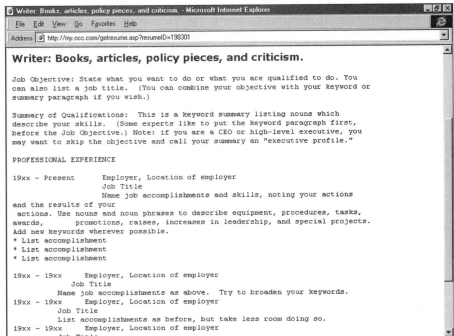

Writer: Books, articles, policy pieces, and criticism. - Microsoft Internet Explorer

File   Edit   View   Go   Favorites   Help

Address   http://my.occ.com/getresume.asp?resumeID=198301

Writer: Books, articles, policy pieces, and criticism.

Job Objective: State what you want to do or what you are qualified to do. You can also list a job title. (You can combine your objective with your keyword or summary paragraph if you wish.)

Summary of Qualifications: This is a keyword summary listing nouns which describe your skills. (Some experts like to put the keyword paragraph first, before the Job Objective.) Note: if you are a CEO or high-level executive, you may want to skip the objective and call your summary an "executive profile."

PROFESSIONAL EXPERIENCE

19xx - Present   Employer, Location of employer
                      Job Title
                      Name job accomplishments and skills, noting your actions
and the results of your
 actions. Use nouns and noun phrases to describe equipment, procedures, tasks,
awards,   promotions, raises, increases in leadership, and special projects.
Add new keywords wherever possible.
* List accomplishment
* List accomplishment
* List accomplishment

19xx - 19xx   Employer, Location of employer
                   Job Title
            Name job accomplishments as above. Try to broaden your keywords.
19xx - 19xx   Employer, Location of employer
                   Job Title
            List accomplishments as before, but take less room doing so.
19xx - 19xx   Employer, Location of employer
                   Job Title

Figure 7-5:
My finished
OCC
resume.

Getting your resume to a company via a company Web site

To get your resume to a company Web site, you generally encounter two submittal options:

- ✔ **E-mail:** Many company Web sites provide you with an e-mail contact address. In this case, all you need to do is to send a plain-text electronic resume to that address. You can send your resume along with a cover letter, as long as you keep the resume and cover letter in just one document.

- ✔ **Form:** Corporations are turning more and more toward online forms to manage resumes. Most often, the company is trying to be helpful. It may also be making sure that resumes come into the database correctly. If you have your resume together already, you can copy your resume into the message area of the form.

In Figure 7-6, you see a portion of the Kimberly-Clark Corporation Web site (www.kimberly-clark.com), a good example of a well-designed site. Plus, it's pretty typical in that it asks you to complete a form in order to submit a resume.

Figure 7-6:
Filling
out the
Kimberly-
Clark online
resume
submittal
form. (Used
with
permission,
©1996-97
Kimberly-
Clark
Corporation.)

To get to most corporate resume submittal areas, simply look for Join Our Team, Employment Opportunities, or Send a Resume types of links on the corporate Web sites. Most often, after you arrive at the resume submittal site, you find an e-mail link that says, "E-mail us if you're interested" or something similar. After clicking on the e-mail link, often a form pops up.

That's what happens at the Kimberly-Clark Web site. You can see a portion of the Kimberly-Clark resume submittal form in Figure 7-6. To fill out the form, just click on the boxes and type in the information. In the message area at the bottom of the screen, you can copy and paste your resume into the area. In Figure 7-6, you can see a little bit of information that I began to fill in.

Employers get turned off when you send your resume to too many departments within the company. Decide on one or two key departments and let it go at that.

Prescreening forms

Recently, some companies have been getting so deluged with electronic resumes that they're putting up prescreening devices to help people decide whether sending a resume is the best idea.

Typically, prescreening forms require that you answer a series of questions before you can send in your resume. If you come across a prescreening form, simply answer the questions to the best of your abilities.

If the form doesn't invite you to submit a resume, scour the Web site for appropriate e-mail addresses. Or call the company and ask the human resources department directly how you can send a resume, mentioning that you're qualified and that you had trouble with the Web site.

Chapter 8

Building and Using Your Electronic Cover Letter

*I*n discussing online job searching with employers, I discovered that although some things about a digital job search are similar to a traditional job search, other things — like cover letters — have been transformed completely.

Cover letters used to be those crisp, perfectly typed pieces of paper that you sent to an employer along with your paper resume. The best cover letters highlighted your achievements and expanded on your resume, compelling the employer to read your resume with interest.

But that cover letter scenario is by and large a rare thing anymore when you're making first contact with an employer. Now, if you're sending a paper cover letter and a paper resume to an employer, it probably means that you've landed the interview and the employer has asked you to send a detailed resume. And even then, you'll probably send an electronic cover letter with your detailed electronic resume.

Confused about what to do with your cover letter in your online job search? You needn't be. In this chapter, you discover exactly how job searchers and employers use cover letters today. You get the inside scoop on how to craft a modern cover letter that shows you at your best and doesn't irritate employers. You also get the information that you really need about exactly what happens to your cover letter when you send it to a large corporation.

And of course, you get some sample cover letters to look at. So before you fire off that cover letter, read this chapter.

Cover Letters: From Appetizers (Then) to Desserts (Now)

When I'm being good, I go to a gym that has a 1950s look to it. The signage is old-timey, and the notes and posters in the gym are all retro in some way. The gym's newsletter is likewise retro, filled with old '50s advertisements that have become amusing due to the way times and attitudes have changed. What's most interesting to me is what makes the advertisements look so dated: first off, the use of language. But the biggest giveaway is the clothing — it's a complete stylistic picture of the times.

Likewise, cover letters give a picture of the job searching times. Here's a little secret: A *vast* stylistic change is occurring in how people use cover letters in job searching. The cover letter used to be the first thing that an employer saw after opening a job seeker's carefully addressed envelope. The cover letter was a perfectly crafted hors d'oeuvre for the resume that followed. But not anymore.

Now, cover letters have completely different functions:

- ✔ Companies that use resume tracking software scan cover letters into their resume database systems. Companies almost always place your cover letter in a separate file from your resume and rarely read it.

- ✔ Some companies routinely discard cover letters and keep only the resumes.

- ✔ Electronic cover letters best serve as short introductions to resumes that you e-mail to individual employers. The emphasis is on *short*.

- ✔ When employers like your resume, they do one of two things: pick up the phone and call you, or read your cover letter, if they still have it. In any case, employers read cover letters second, not first — that is, unless you have written a *cover quip*. (See the section "An Overview of Great Electronic Cover Letter Styles" later in this chapter.) Employers will take the time to read a one-paragraph "cover letter."

- ✔ When an employer asks you to come in for an interview, the employer may ask you to send a more detailed resume. This is when you send a detailed resume and a complete cover letter. This complete cover letter is going to a person who is thinking about making an employment commitment to you. This person reads the cover letter carefully and definitely won't discard it.

Because of resume tracking software, resume tracking and management guru James Lemke says that many cover letters are seen *after* the resumes now. According to Lemke and others, some electronic tracking systems take a picture of the cover letter and store it in a file for employers. But that file doesn't come before the resume — it comes after the resume, if at all.

John Reese, President, CEO, and founder of Interactive Search, Inc., concurs with Lemke. (Interactive Search takes literally millions of resumes and cover letters from companies all over the world and places the documents in private electronic databases for employers.) Reese says that if you want to say something, you need to say it *in your resume* because a potential employer may never read your cover letter.

Essentially, if an employer is interested in you, the employer will take the time to find your cover letter file and read it. So your cover letter still needs to be good — but you need to know that your cover letter comes *after* your resume in most situations. So instead of pre-resume appetizers, cover letters have become dessert — they're the finishing course to your resume.

An Overview of Great Electronic Cover Letter Styles

In the electronic world, you have your choice of three major types of cover letters: the electronic cover letter quip, the longer electronic cover letter quip, and the complete electronic cover letter. This section describes each type of cover letter.

The electronic cover quip

The *electronic cover quip* consists of one power paragraph that opens with a bang and closes quickly. Cover quips are one paragraph plus a closing line, and that's it. Typically, you send an electronic cover quip in response to an online job advertisement or to a company Web site as a cold call.

For example, here's a great cover letter quip:

Dear Jim Anderson:

I saw the position of Senior Account Executive with Anderson Sales, Inc. advertised on the Monster Board. (Requisition #35466.) Although I am currently employed by one of your primary competitors, I am considering excellent opportunities such as yours. Attached please find my resume.

I will e-mail you this week to see if we can arrange a meeting to discuss this opportunity.

Best,

Andrea Jobeston
(000) 000-9999
andrea@jobsearch.com

The longer electronic cover quip

The *longer electronic cover quip* is made up of one to three power paragraphs plus a power closing line. The higher up the employment food chain you are, the more likely you need just a little more room to explain why you are the best person for the job.

Longer cover quips are best sent in response to higher-level job advertisements (CFO, CIO, and so on). Longer quips also work well when sent in response to a phone call from a recruiter or to a meeting (on the phone or in person) in which an employer invites you to send a resume.

The longer cover quip needs to be a maximum of one screen long, which is about three paragraphs. Each paragraph must really count.

The complete digital cover letter

The *complete digital cover letter* consists of three to seven paragraphs, with the average being about five. It's an electronic corollary to the standard paper cover letter that you're used to writing. The complete digital cover letter best serves when you know the person you're sending the letter to, when you and the recipient have a mutual acquaintance, when you have been invited to send a more detailed resume, or if you're a very high-level executive.

I'm well aware that most people are used to sending complete cover letters in response to all job advertisements. Believe me when I tell you that you need to be very careful when you unleash a full cover letter in the digital realm! Because the medium of e-mail is so different from paper, it has changed the rules a bit.

Take my hints with this one, even if they seem odd to you. If you can't get used to sending shorter cover letters, then at the very least opt for the longer cover quip of three paragraphs. But save yourself the time of writing long cover letters — unless you have targeted the cover letter correctly, it may never be read.

Knowing What to Say in Your Cover Letter and When to Say It

Writing cover letters in the electronic world is relatively simple. You have an opening, a message, and a closing. That's it. You don't need to worry about the color of your paper or the color of the ink that you use. Just the content. To help you, here's a quick course on building the contents of a cover letter:

1. **Choose your cover letter type: cover quip, longer cover quip, or complete cover letter.**

2. **Decide on your opening line.**

   Look at the sample cover letters in this chapter and read the power writing tips for ideas. In general, though, if you can drop a name, do. If you can't drop a name, then make a power statement of what you want and why.

3. **If you're writing a cover quip,** write a power opening line, round it out with basic information, and then close.

   If you're writing a longer cover quip, decide on two additional ideas that you want to get across after your opening. You essentially have one paragraph to express each idea.

   For a complete cover letter, choose three to five ideas or facts that you want to get across after the opening, and give each idea one to two paragraphs. Ideas that you may want to emphasize include your unique skills, your long experience, your contributions to your last or current job, things you appreciate about the employer's company, ways the company and you are a great fit, and how you can jump right in to become part of a team.

4. **Decide on a closing statement.**

   Don't wimp out at this point — make it strong. Choose proactive statements like "I look forward to talking with you about this opportunity," or "I will e-mail you on such and such a date to inquire about setting up a meeting."

Power Writing Suggestions for All Electronic Cover Letters

The ultimate point of any cover letter, electronic or otherwise, is to alert the employer to your qualifications and to show why you are the best person for the job. But in an electronic cover letter, you have less time than ever to make your point.

Remember that your cover letter is likely to be read on a computer monitor, so you're subject to the scroll-down rule. That is, you have one screen to interest someone, or he or she probably won't scroll down to read any farther.

Here are some opening lines and power paragraphs designed to keep readers a-scrolling:

- ✔ "Although I am currently employed by one of your competitors, I have long understood that [name the company] represents the industry leader, and I would welcome the opportunity to work with you." Go on to describe your skills.

- ✔ "I was pleased to discover your opening for [job title] on [name where you saw the ad and the date]. As my attached resume shows, my background and experience demonstrate precisely the qualities you require in a [name the title] candidate."

- ✔ "While I was browsing [name the electronic employment database and the date], I noticed your opening for [name the title]. Although I am currently employed, your advertisement caught my eye because I have been looking for the right opportunity to work with your company." Go on to explain why you like the company — what values and priorities do you share? What about the company's product or philosophy do you really like?

- ✔ "I enjoyed (talking with you) (meeting you) last [date and place]. In response to your request, attached is my resume. Since our discussion, I have looked into the company projects that you discussed and find them to be closely aligned with my skills and goals." Name the common ground, pointing out how your skills enhance current company projects.

- ✔ "Our mutual friend, [name the person], suggested that I send you a resume. [Name the contact] mentioned that you may be looking for someone who has my skills and qualifications. [Point out some salient skills.] As I have been interested in your company for [name a period of time that is honest], I welcome the potential opportunity to work with you."

Getting Digital: Creating Super Electronic Cover Letters

Now that you have what you want to say down pat, it's time to sit down and get your cover letter into e-mailable bits and bytes.

To create any of the electronic cover letters in this chapter, you must first have access to a word-processing program like Microsoft Word or Corel WordPerfect. (Any program that enables you to create documents on a computer will do.)

Here are the exact steps to follow:

1. **Open up your word-processing software.**

2. **Open a new document.**

3. **Before you start typing, create a name for your document and save it so that you don't lose your information.**

   I recommend saving the cover letter as cldraft so you know that the file is a draft and not a final copy of your cover letter.

4. **Open with a salutation of** Dear [Person's Name]:.

   Include the entire name, omitting Ms., Mr., or Mrs., and follow the name with a colon.

5. **Press Return or Enter twice to create two lines of space.**

6. **Begin writing.**

   For a cover quip, write no more than one paragraph of three to four sentences. For a longer cover quip, write two to three paragraphs at most, and for a complete cover letter, write about five paragraphs.

7. **After the body of the text, press Return or Enter twice and write the close.**

   "Sincerely" or "Best Regards" is an appropriate closing line.

8. **Press Return or Enter once or twice after the closing line and type your name, followed by your phone number and e-mail address.**

9. **Save your document normally.**

10. **Save a second version of your document in ASCII, or plain text.**

    To do so, go to your File menu as choose Save As. (Most word-processing programs have this option.) You see a dialog box that asks you for the filename and the file type. Change the name of your file to reflect the fact that this is the final copy of your cover letter. I suggest something like covlettr. From the File Type pull-down menu, choose Text Only or ASCII.

11. **Click on Save and then close your document.**

12. **Reopen your text-only document to see how it looks.**

Typically, I need to add some spacing and paragraph breaks to my documents. Go ahead and save your document again, making sure to save it as Text Only.

You're all set! All you have to do is remember the filename. When you want to send your electronic cover letter, just do the following:

1. **Open your word-processing program and open your cover letter.**

2. **Highlight the entire letter.**

3. **Choose Copy from the Edit menu.**

4. **Open your e-mail program, create a new message, and copy your letter into your e-mail message.**

To copy your cover letter into your e-mail message, position your cursor in the message portion of your e-mail and choose Paste from the Edit menu.

Every word-processing program is slightly different, but the steps for your program should be nearly identical to the ones I just outlined. If worse comes to worst and you can't copy and paste your cover letter into your e-mail message, you can always type it in.

Electronic Style Tips

Just in case your cover letter is placed in a resume tracking database, keeping your cover letter in a simple format is important. (That's why you should save your cover letter in ASCII, or plain text.) Here's a list of quick tips that can help you keep the computers happy:

- When you put your contact information in the cover letter, put your e-mail address, phone number, and physical address on separate lines. Computers can understand and sort this information much more easily.

- Put parentheses around the area code of your phone number. This tips off certain computer systems to the fact that the numbers you list are phone numbers.

- Avoid any extras in your cover letter. "Extras" means italics, underlining, boldface, fancy fonts, and bullets.

- Avoid using asterisks and emoticons in your cover letter. They do not translate well! (Emoticons are symbols that replace body language; for example, ;-) is an emoticon that symbolizes a person winking.)

Using Your Electronic Cover Letter

Again, nothing has changed more than cover letters in a digital job search. A brand-new set of rules has grown up surrounding the modern use of cover letters. Already, employers hold strong opinions about what they do and don't want to see.

General guidelines

I know that some of these guidelines may run contrary to long-held cover letter wisdom. All I can tell you is that times have changed, and cover letters have, too.

✔ **Any information that you want an employer to notice must appear within the body of your resume.** You absolutely can't count on your cover letter staying with your resume as a package, and you can't count on your cover letter being read before your resume. I can't emphasize this point enough: Put all the meat and potatoes in your resume.

✔ **The more "cold" your resume is coming in, the shorter your cover letter should be.** Specifically, if you send an electronic resume in response to a _job advertisement,_ send a cover letter quip only. If you send an electronic resume to a company via the _company Web site,_ again, send a cover letter quip.

✔ **If you are responding to a job advertisement, be sure to mention the job title as well as the job number in your cover letter.** The person reading your cover letter may not be familiar with the job number, but he or she likely knows the title.

✔ **Don't submit a cover letter with an electronic resume that you send to an employment database.** Cover letters are discarded from almost all the employment databases that accept resumes.

✔ **Send your cover letters in business-letter style, no matter how short the cover letter is.** (See the "Electronic Style Tips" and "Looking at Sample Cover Letters" sections in this chapter for more details.)

✔ **Your cover letter should immediately precede your electronic resume, with both in one e-mail message.** (See "Sample Cover Letters" to see how this looks.)

Which cover letter to use in which circumstances

If you're like me, you must have experienced at least some frustration in grammar classes. Just when you learned one "rule," the teacher would subsequently introduce all the "exceptions to the rule." Unlike grammar exercises, you won't find any hard and fast rules in job hunting. But you'll find all sorts of special circumstances. Here are a few that you may have questions about:

✔ If you know the person to whom you are sending an electronic resume — that is, if you met in person or talked on the phone — send a longer cover letter quip. Stick to three paragraphs max, and emphasize the conversations that you have had with that person.

✔ If you have been recruited or headhunted and have been invited to send a resume to a corporation, ask the recruiter outright if the corporation wants a cover letter. If yes, send a longer cover letter quip. If no, send a cover letter quip.

✔ If you're a high earner sending an electronic resume cold to a third-party recruiter who works in high-level executive recruiting, send a complete cover letter with a detailed electronic resume. But keep your electronic cover letter to one page maximum.

✔ If someone you haven't met invites you to send a first resume, send a longer cover letter quip with it. That covers the bases without going overboard.

✔ If you've already sent in an electronic resume to an employer and the employer has invited you for an interview, the employer may request a more detailed resume. This is a good time to write a compelling and complete cover letter. (But keep it to one page.)

✔ If you're sending a resume cold to an employer's Web site, keep the cover letter short. Choose a cover letter quip length.

✔ If you're responding to a job announcement, send a cover letter quip. If you have ten or more years of experience, send a longer cover letter quip.

Looking at Sample Cover Letters

Here are some sample cover letters to help you see what works well in the electronic cover letter arena.

Cover letter quip plus resume in
response to a job advertisement.

Dear Eber Andrews:

I am sending you my resume in response to the XYZ Company's position announcement for a sales trainee (Job #754893). I discovered the advertisement on Monday, July 3, on the Monster Board and found the position to be an excellent fit with my background and experience.

I look forward to talking with you soon regarding this opportunity.

Sincerely,

Anne Albright
(800) 555-1212
aalbright@jobsearch.com

(begin resume here)

Note that the key elements of the cover letter simply take care of business. The cover letter states where and when the candidate found the job advertisement, and it lists the job title as well as the number.

Cover letter quip plus resume sent cold to a person via a company Web site, not in response to an advertised job opening.

Dear Bobbi Jones:

My award-winning graphics experience in the field of computer animation is an excellent fit for your company's goals and projects. I have long been an admirer of your company and have taken the opportunity to send you my resume, which is attached. Although I am currently employed and I did not see a position advertised on your Web site, I am willing to wait for the right opportunity at your company.

I am looking forward to discussing possible positions with you.

Sincerely,

Christopher Dodd
Chris@candidate.com
(800) 555-1212
1212 Garden Way
Anycity, USA 99999

_____

(begin resume here)

This cover letter sells the person sending it from the very first line, plus it indicates that the sender has researched the company. (All pluses!) The energetic close is an upbeat way to finish a cold-call type of letter.

Cover letter quip plus resume sent in response to a position advertised on a company Web page.

Dear Bernard Johnstone:

I was pleased to read of your job opening for a senior forensic accountant on the Online Career Center on Monday, February 12. You will find that my resume, which is attached, outlines why I am an excellent fit for the position. Beyond my 10 years at XYZ accounting firm, I have specialized in forensic accounting for over 7 years.

I am looking forward to discussing this opportunity with you and setting up a meeting.

Sincerely,

Rod S. Ande
(800) 555-1212
RodAnde@candidate.com

(begin resume here)

Longer cover letter quip sent with a resume after talking on the phone with a potential employer and being invited to send a first resume.

Dear Ms. Andres:

As you requested in our telephone conversation on Wednesday, October 11, attached is my resume for your review.

After learning of the specific skills and qualifications that you are looking for in a senior UNIX systems administrator, I am confident that my broad background will prove to be an excellent and productive match with your company.

As you will see in my resume, I have over 15 years' experience on diverse platforms including HP, Sun, and Silicon Graphics. I also have experience with maintaining workstations in an NT environment. On the database support side, I have extensive experience in Oracle database construction and maintenance.

I will call you next Thursday to see when we can meet. I am looking forward to discussing how my skills can help you meet your company's challenges.

Sincerely,

Frank A. Pillar
(800) 555-1212
pillar@jobsearch.com

_____

(begin resume here)

This cover letter reflects the fact that a conversation has taken place. The writer uses Ms. Andres, which is perfectly appropriate following a phone conversation. The writer emphasizes the skills that Ms. Andres said she was looking for and points out highlights of the resume. The closing statement reflects the candidate's confidence and desire to move forward with the opportunity.

Complete cover letter sent in response to an employer's request for a more detailed resume.

Dear Mary Bene:

Thank you for your call inviting me to come and interview with you on Friday, April 20, for the position of medical technical writer. I am looking forward to discussing how my skills and experience can benefit your company's projects and goals.

As promised, attached is my complete curriculum vitae, which includes details of the projects I have worked on in the last ten years. You will find that I have the technical writing experience you are looking for in the specific cross-section of areas you need. As you know, there are many technical writers, but very few have the broad medical experience that I do.

I have written over 25 medical instrument manuals, working with teams of top-flight researchers and doctors. Additionally, I have written six pharmaceutical manuals describing medications and the related technical and medical information about each drug.

As I am adept at working with teams of diverse professionals, I particularly welcome the opportunity to interface with the teams of medical professionals that you described to me on the phone. I have worked with teams ranging from four to eighteen members, and I have even worked on a telemedicine team where members of the team were as far away as 3,000 miles.

I am looking forward to our meeting next Wednesday.

Sincerely yours,

Beth Graeme
Beth@jobsearch.com
(800) 555-1212

_____

(begin curriculum vitae here)

This letter points up the specific work experience and skills the job seeker has that the employer is looking for. Pointing out rare skills is always a plus, as is showing off the ability to work on a team and participation in new technology.

Deciphering Modern Cover Letter Etiquette

The essence of good cover letter etiquette is basically that a good cover letter is respectful, pleasant, and businesslike. These specific etiquette guidelines can work well for you in a modern job search:

- Do open the cover letter with a salutation, but leave off titles. Stick with the person's first and last name for first contact. After you learn the gender of the person, you can loosen up a little.

- If you're sending a cold-call resume and don't have the person's name, call the company to inquire who is the best person to send the information to. It's rare that absolutely no one will be able to give you the name of the right person.

- If you're sending your cover letter to a company Web site, you don't know whether the company uses resume tracking software. Assume that they do. Make sure that your cover letter can function as a dessert, so to speak.

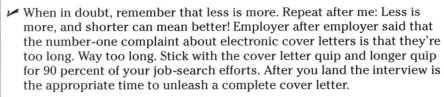

- When in doubt, remember that less is more. Repeat after me: Less is more, and shorter can mean better! Employer after employer said that the number-one complaint about electronic cover letters is that they're too long. Way too long. Stick with the cover letter quip and longer quip for 90 percent of your job-search efforts. After you land the interview is the appropriate time to unleash a complete cover letter.

- Avoid hyping yourself as the best person for the job. State why you're a good match, but then drop it. If you need detailed guidance as to what to write and not write in a cover letter, I recommend *Cover Letters For Dummies* by Joyce Lain Kennedy (also published by IDG Books Worldwide, Inc.). Her book is loaded with sample cover letters.

- If you currently have a three-page cover letter that would make Shakespeare proud, rethink your approach. You can keep your three-page cover letter, but definitely don't send it out until you're invited to do so. Even then, take out the trimmers and pare down your cover novelette to one page. You'll have better results.

- Don't get casual and chummy in your cover letter. Stick to business style and formatting. Just because you're e-mailing a cover letter doesn't mean that you can afford to let go of standard business etiquette.

Chapter 9

Acing Interviews, Online and Otherwise

- -

- -

*O*f all the aspects of job searching that have changed since the Web entered business life, interviewing has changed the least. When it comes down to it, interviewing is all about seeing whether you have the right chemistry with an employer, and technology doesn't appear to change chemistry. (At least not yet!)

Nevertheless, an online job search does subtly alter your experiences prior to an interview, and on the rare occasion that you actually interview online, well, that definitely constitutes a change of pace.

In this chapter, I help you with all the pre-interview preparation that you need to do to ace your interviews. I also give you some great techniques for showing off your work to its best advantage during your interview. And just in case you're one of the rare people who interview online, I give you lots of inside tips and hints to make your online interview as smooth and positive as possible.

Pre-Interview Preparation

The art of interviewing hasn't changed, but a few things leading up to the interview have. Namely, in an online job search, you find yourself taking more phone calls. You also find yourself getting a few more "fishing expedition" phone calls than you may be used to.

But if all goes well in your interview process, you can expect to go through a general routine of a screening call, a second call inviting you to an in-person interview, and then the actual interview. An interview can be over the phone or in person. Depending on the size of the company, you may go through more than one round of interviews.

As far as I'm concerned, some of the most important interview actions are those that you take before the interview process starts rolling. That's where pre-interview preparation comes in. By doing great interview preparation online, you can influence the eventual outcome of your interview.

In Chapter 3, I discuss detailed online search methods that you can use to find information online. And in the Internet Directory at the back of this book, you can find a whole section that lists online interview resources.

Industry research

Before you step into an interview, be sure to catch up on the general state of the industry that you work in. You can bet on numerous questions about general industry trends from savvy interviewers. The more you're trying to advance in your career, the more important this type of research is.

The following sections give you some suggestions for researching your industry.

Check the periodicals for your industry

Every industry has its own trade publications, and many of those trade publications are online now. If you can, read at least three online trade-related publications. Also try to read about four months' worth of back issues so that you can talk about industry news events if you need to.

You want to be sure to have read the same things your interviewer has read, or you may look behind the times.

Find the industry's Web hot spots

Every industry has definitive Web sites. Being the host for your industry's Web hot spot would be incredibly ideal. But just in case you aren't, you need to find out who is, or at least be familiar with the pages. Why bother? Because if you look Internet-savvy, you look that much better to today's employers.

In my profession, I can rattle off at least a dozen of the top job spots on the Web, complete with URLs that I've committed to memory. I've learned these hot spots because knowing the hot spots is a lot like having read the right books in high school and college — it's just something you need to have going for you if you want to be at the top of your game.

To find industry hot spots, check major indexes like Yahoo!
(www.yahoo.com) and Excite (www.excite.com). If you see a Web site listed
in two or more major indexes, it's a very good bet that you're looking at a
well-known site.

Locate hot discussion groups in your industry

If you've been missing out on a discussion list, now's the time to find it, read
the archives (or back issues), and keep up with it regularly. Again, it is a
matter of being up-to-date with trends and industry info. You want to know
more, if at all possible, than the person interviewing you! (Or at least stack
the odds in your favor.)

A great place to find information about mailing lists is at a search engine
called Liszt Select (www.liszt.com), which you can find described in the
Internet Directory at the back of this book.

Using Liszt, you can keyword-search for just about every discussion group
available. This is significant, because more than 80,000 mailing lists are
currently available. Again taking my profession as an example, a major
mailing list is called JobPlace. I don't contribute to the list, but I sure do
read it regularly so that I know the latest gossip.

Company research

Researching companies is a skill well worth developing. The learning curve
is minimal, and the results can be very profitable for you, particularly in
interviews. You find yourself with a depth of knowledge that sets you far
apart from other candidates. Imagine being able to refer to last year's profit
margin when you discuss your abilities. Statements like "I know that your
profit margin last year was at a record high of 32 percent, and I bring skills
that can help maintain that high productivity . . ." are interview gold.

Using AirTouch Cellular as an example company, the following sections talk
about ways to research a company prior to an interview.

Find the company Web page

To find the company home page, always try the domain name trick first.
That is, type in **www.** followed by the company's name and then end it with
.com. So for AirTouch, you might try www.airtouchcellular.com and
www.airtouch.com. Actually, the latter URL proves to be the correct one.

If the domain name trick doesn't take you to the company Web site, try a
keyword search in a search engine. AltaVista has an excellent business
search facility built right into its search engine. Just go to the AltaVista
home page (www.altavista.digital.com) and click on the Find a Business tab. You can find extensive help for locating a company's Web page.

Last but not least, if the search engine doesn't work, try looking up the company in Big Yellow (www1.bigyellow.com/), an online national Yellow Pages directory.

After you find the company Web page, read it thoroughly, and study it to get a handle on corporate culture and find other information.

Check the company's stock

Checking a company's stock is so simple that it's just about a no-brainer. You want this information as part of your basic financial information about a company. Simply log on to Yahoo! (www.yahoo.com), click on the Stock Quotes link, and type in the name of the company for which you want stock information. You won't want to walk into an interview and not know the general price range of a company's stock — you may well be asked a very direct question about your knowledge of the company's current stock.

Sometimes you may not have the exact name that the company uses for trading. The Yahoo! Stock Quote engine returns possibilities for you. For example, I typed in **AirTouch**. Yahoo! returned with AirTouch Communications, Inc., which is the complete trading name.

Locate the SEC filings of the company

The best source for locating SEC (Securities and Exchange Commission) filings is to access the EDGAR database at www.sec.gov/edgarhp.htm. The whole point of locating the SEC filings is to get very detailed financial information on companies.

If you've never looked up a company's information on EDGAR before, you may be pretty surprised at the incredible level of financial detail you find yourself privy to. The federal government requires that certain types of companies file vast amounts of financial information for the public's perusal. By all means, take advantage of it. You may find that the company with the beautiful marble building actually is in debt and is losing money left and right. Or you may discover that the interview you landed with a company in an unimpressive little corner office building is growing over 400 percent a year!

Look for company profiles

One of the best places to look for company profiles is in Hoover's Online (www.hoovers.com). In Figure 9-1, you see the AirTouch company profile that I found on the Hoover's site. The profile details AirTouch's products, joint ventures, sales, net income, key executives, number of employees, employee growth, and top competitors.

Other good sites on which to find company profiles include the job meta lists that I name in the Internet Directory at the back of the book. Chiefly, JobSafari, Companies Online, and Business Wire offer help in this important area.

Figure 9-1:
A look at
AirTouch
Communi-
cations'
corporate
profile on
the Hoover's
Online
Web site.

Look for company news

Often, a company's Web site contains a press release area. That's good — if
a press release area is available, download the press releases and read them!
But all too often, companies omit the press release page. No matter. If the
company is publicly traded, the press releases are likely to be sitting on
another site.

I like to look for company news in a few places:

- ✔ My first choice is almost always PRNewswire (www.prnewswire.com/),
  which is a huge collection of company press releases that's updated
  every hour.

- ✔ Another option I like to check is Business Wire at www.businesswire.com/.
  Business Wire also contains thousands of recent press releases. (Plus,
  Business Wire keeps selected corporate profiles on tap.)

- ✔ Both Hoover's Online and Yahoo! offer company news. To find company
  news in Hoover's, perform a keyword search for the company. To find
  company news at Yahoo!, go to the Stock Quote section of Yahoo! and
  perform a keyword search for the company. If the company is publicly
  traded, Yahoo! lists the most recent stock information, plus links to the
  latest news about the company.

When you want to get really serious about looking for company news, you can go to all the various newspapers on the Web and begin searching those.

A fast way of searching various online sources is to use the Electric Library. The Electric Library is a for-pay service, but it does offer a free 30-day trial period.

Competitor research

I think that researching the competitors of a potential employer is a much-overlooked factor in the interview preparation process. Because finding this kind of information isn't exactly easy, you really set yourself apart from other interview subjects when you do it. When you have competitor information at your fingertips, you let the employer know that you truly care about working for the company, and you also reveal that you're on the ball.

The following sections provide some tried-and-true suggestions and resources for looking at competitors.

Find the competitors

I hate to keep plugging Hoover's Online, but it really is a fast way to find competitors. When you perform a search in Hoover's, if the company is listed, you also find a list of the company's primary competitors. It's a four-star method of quickly finding competitors for publicly traded companies.

The competitors' links are nicely highlighted and are ready for you to click on and explore. Also on Hoover's, you find recent news stories mentioning the company you searched for. Sometimes, the stories mention competitors.

Another way to find competitors is to do an all-out keyword search of the industry that you work in using what I call the Narrow It Down search method. (See Chapter 3 for exact details about how to perform this type of search.)

For now, though, the search basics involve looking at all the references to a key industry — for example, cellular technology. I have performed many such searches for competitive information, and I can tell you that it doesn't take too long (about 15 minutes) for you to start seeing certain company names over and over again.

Make a list of the company names that you see repeated, and you have a list of competitors. If you don't see your target company's name in that list, it probably means that the company you're interviewing with is not a first-tier competitor. That's something to think about, too.

Last but not least, the Yahoo! index (biz.yahoo.com/research/indgrp/) has a search page that enables you to search by industry. I strongly suggest that you visit this page and take a look around your particular industry. Typically, you can find competitors lurking in the lists.

Investigate the competitors

After you've located the competitors, it's time to do company research on them. Go through all the steps you went through to research the company you're interviewing with.

What invariably happens is that you come away from your research with an extraordinarily sound and strong grip on industry trends, insight into the movers and shakers, and a wealth of knowledge about recent happenings.

You don't need to worry about letting your interviewer know about your research efforts — your advanced knowledge will shine!

Creating a Portfolio

It doesn't matter what profession you're working in or aiming for — almost anyone can put together a portfolio of work to show to an employer during an interview. But the more communications-oriented or graphics-oriented your profession is, the more important a portfolio becomes in your job search.

Why bother with a portfolio?

A portfolio gives your resume an extra dimension that words alone can't always convey. And an *online* portfolio conveys all sorts of good information about your computer skills, too. You have nothing to lose and everything to gain by creating a portfolio, so why not try it?

Here are some good qualities an online portfolio effortlessly conveys about you:

- ✔ General computer knowledge
- ✔ Web page building skills
- ✔ Internet savvy
- ✔ Design savvy
- ✔ An up-to-the-minute technical attitude

You can't very well lose an online portfolio. (It would certainly take some doing.) As such, your online portfolio can serve as a great backup copy of your physical or paper portfolio.

Portfolio basics

Your portfolio can be as simple or complex as you want it to be, but the minimum is usually about 4 pages and the maximum is about 20 pages (except for graphic designers — the maximum goes up to about 50 pages).

I suggest that you create your physical portfolio first and then put your portfolio online via your Web page. If you need help getting your Web portfolio going, see Chapter 12.

Always remember that if you just don't have time to get your portfolio online, you can hire someone to help you. Scanning in photos and the like shouldn't cost an arm and a leg anymore, as many office-supply stores offer low-cost scanning. If it does cost an arm and a leg, ask a college or high school student to help you.

I like the idea of putting something extra in your online portfolio so that you can mention your online portfolio during your interview. For example, if you're interviewing for a job as a Web page designer, you want to bring in printouts of your Web page designs. But you want to have even more samples up on the Web.

If you have very large diagrams, blueprints, or other unwieldy items, putting samples online can be a whole lot easier than lugging them around, particularly if you're flying to an interview.

In putting together your portfolio, here are some suggestions:

- ✔ **Engineers** can collect schematics of projects and scan them for use on your Web page.

- ✔ **Public relations workers** can put together press releases and campaigns. New graduates can write samples of these items.

- ✔ **Teachers** can put highlights of successful units that you've taught in a portfolio, along with students' art and writing samples, if you have them. If not, you can substitute other creative materials.

- ✔ **Salespeople** can collect visuals of big successes and make a visual record of big sales and accounts. For example, collect company logos and present them as a snazzy visual for your portfolio.

- ✔ **Administrators** can create a diagrammatic portfolio that graphically illustrates successful changes or campaigns that you launched. Look for creative visual ways to represent your success.

- ✔ **Graphic- and text-oriented professions** lend themselves very well to portfolios. Pictures and other samples of your work are all good choices to include in your portfolio. Figure 9-2 shows an example of a Web portfolio for a writer.

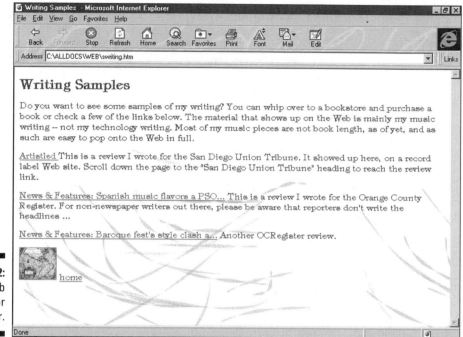

Figure 9-2:
A Web
portfolio for
a writer.

During your interview, be sure to mention your portfolio at an opportune time — for example, when you're asked about recent work projects. If your portfolio is on a Web page, you may want to call in advance to make sure that the person interviewing you will have access to the Web during your interview. Otherwise, bring your paper or physical portfolio.

If you want to be extra safe, you can always take a backup paper copy of your online portfolio with you to the interview.

Winning Telephone Interviews

Getting a job is an art, and like any art form, the beauty is in the eye of the beholder. I could name about a dozen well-known career experts who differ substantially on what you should and shouldn't say during telephone interviews.

But if you take everything that the experts say and distill it, the essence of the matter is actually pretty simple: Stay positive, do your research, and rehearse your answers. For very detailed and reliable information about interviews, please consult Joyce Lain Kennedy's book *Job Interviews For Dummies* (IDG Books Worldwide, Inc.).

Here are my tips for telephone interview success with an online edge:

✔ **Be positive.** There's no arguing about this point! Stay upbeat, even if tough questions come your way. For example, if you're asked why you left your last job, don't talk about how you and your boss didn't get along or how the company was such a dud. Instead, focus your answer on what was good about your last job. One engineer who abruptly changed jobs told me that he detested his boss. He won a new job by emphasizing how well he worked with his co-workers, never breathing even the slightest complaint about his old company. He landed a great new job within five weeks.

✔ **Conduct a virtual portfolio tour over the phone.** While you're on the phone for your interview, you can "show" your interviewer your portfolio if it's on the Web. In fact, you can arrange a virtual portfolio tour in advance with the person interviewing you. All you need to do is request that he or she interviews you at a desk where the Web is easily accessible. During your interview, you can talk the interviewer through your samples and successes.

✔ **Navigate salary questions carefully.** This is an area where experts disagree vehemently. Some say to ask about salary; others say to wait until the employer opens the door. My advice is that if you're a hot commodity, you can always negotiate your salary, so waiting is the safer bet. Simply wait for the employer to ask you what kind of salary you're expecting, and be prepared in advance with your answer. Remember that you can research salaries online at The Salary Calculator (www2.homefair.com/calc/salcalc.html).

If you're talking with a recruiter, you can clear away questions about salary at this stage of the game. If you think that you may be interested in an opportunity, you can say something like "I'm looking for a job in a range of $_____ per year. Is this job in that range?" That way, you don't waste time with opportunities that pay $20,000 or more below what you want!

✔ **Prepare for phone interview questions in advance.** Anticipate the questions that an interviewer may ask you and practice your answers out loud. If you aren't sure what kinds of questions you may be asked, check out the World's Biggest Job Interview Question Bank at www.sunfeatures.com/~jlk. For specific instructions on reaching the questions at this URL, be sure to see the entry for this site in the Internet Directory.

Bringing Your Online Research into Your In-Person Interviews

One of my favorite success stories falls into the area of preparing for interviews online. Jennifer Peters, an account coordinator for Sterling Hager, Inc. (a large, Boston-based, high-tech public relations firm) graduated from college with a great degree and lots of networking experience from her volunteer efforts. But she lived in Florida, and she wanted to move farther north.

Jennifer found the offer on CareerPath.com, sent in her resume, and waited. She had to wait about a month and a half, which she found nerve-wracking since all the friends she graduated with had already taken local jobs. But Jennifer waited it out and eventually got the call inviting her up for an interview. Jennifer paid for the plane ticket out of her own pocket and saw to it that she was extremely well prepared for the interview.

Jennifer says that she researched Sterling Hager's Web site and knew it by heart. She also researched trends in public relations and researched Web trends, all online. And then she delivered what ended up being her winning coup: She put together a portfolio of work and brought it with her to the interview.

I talked with the person who actually hired Jennifer and asked him what made Jennifer stand out. He told me that Jennifer was clearly up-to-date with current Web trends, which was very important to him. He also said that Jennifer's research on the firm really made her stand out from the competition. Finally, her portfolio clinched the deal.

Believe me, every bit of online research that you do on company background and competition enters the interview with you. Your answers to questions are more informed, and you're more confident. And if you have taken the time to create a portfolio and put it on the Web, that's just one more factor in your favor.

If you're heading off to an important in-person interview, here are some tips to help you bring your online research with you to the interview table:

- ✓ **Print out the company's Web page and bring it with you as a reference.**

- ✓ **Put letters of reference on your Web site, preferably in a password-protected area.** Chris Brady, an engineer I interviewed, put his reference letters and information on a password-protected portion of his Web page. When the interviewer asked him for references, Chris talked about his Web page and gave the password. According to Chris, employers were unanimously impressed and typically looked at the reference letters during the interview.

✔ **If you have put your portfolio on the Web, be sure to mention it to the person interviewing you.** Interview subjects told me over and over again that employers appreciated the portfolio and respected the skills that it took to get that portfolio on the Web.

Breezing through Online Interviews

Talk about a "trend" that never happened! About three years ago, when desktop videoconferencing technology finally started to come up in quality and down in cost, some career pundits began predicting that widespread online interviewing was just around the corner.

That corner sure has been a long time in coming. For whatever reason, online interviewing has never taken off. Maybe, just maybe, you'll end up interviewing online. But I doubt it.

The only exceptions are for people working in the high-tech industry. There, you may find an online interview or two coming your way — throughout your entire career. You're far more likely to use online videoconference technology to take classes and hold corporate business meetings.

But just in case you're one of the rare few who do find themselves in online interviewing situations, here are some tips:

✔ **Show up early for your online interview.** Invariably, the company will ask you to go to a corporate location where you have the interview. Usually, making sure that the equipment is all set up and everyone is online together takes about five extra minutes. Sometimes employers assume that you understand that you need to arrive a few minutes early. Fifteen minutes early is a good amount of buffer time for an online interview.

✔ **Don't worry about your personal computer equipment.** The interviewer is responsible for providing all the equipment and paying for any costs incurred. If the interviewer asks you to provide equipment or to pay for costs, consider it a red flag — making the interviewee pay is absolutely not industry standard.

✔ **Know that even the best online videoconference technology still has some delay time.** The important thing that you need to know about delay time is that you need to avoid sudden movements and long pauses. I'll never forget a tape I made of myself and some friends via online videoconferencing. I looked ridiculous! I looked like I was gesturing wildly with my arms, when I really wasn't. But the videoconference system had skipped some frames, thus my jumpy motions. To avoid this, keep your arms at your sides, look straight into the camera, and keep still.

✔ **Consider keeping a low-key smile on your face between questions.** If you get "frozen" in a frame with a frown, the interviewer sees your frown for about two to seven seconds, depending on a host of technical variables.

✔ **Wear solid, muted colors.** Stripes, plaids, and screaming reds wreak havoc with inexpensive camera systems. (Desktop systems are most definitely inexpensive camera systems!)

✔ **Speak carefully; don't rush through your sentences.** Your pronunciation can seem slightly fuzzy during an online videoconference, so make sure that you articulate your words clearly.

Special Pointers for Combination In-Person and Online Interviews

Sometimes, you find yourself in the awkward position of both sitting in an office with a person interviewing you and interviewing with someone from a remote location via online videoconferencing. If this happens, focus on the person with you in the office, even if the remote person is the bigwig.

I have been in this situation several times, and I should warn you that it's disconcerting. I always feel like I'm ignoring the person on the video-conference system if I don't spend every minute looking at the camera. But in a "double" situation, you have no choice but to turn away from the camera when the person sitting with you talks to you.

The trick here is to understand that everyone is as uncomfortable as you are, most particularly the remote person. Decide right away that the situation isn't perfect and that you can triumph over it. Here are some tips that help in a technologically imbalanced situation:

✔ **Focus on one main person.** Otherwise, your attention is split and you may find it difficult to concentrate.

✔ **Be prepared to have difficulty understanding the person who's in a remote location.** Don't be afraid to reiterate the question by saying something like "That last question came through a little fuzzy. Did you ask if . . ." and then repeat the question. If you haven't a clue as to what the person said, politely ask him or her to repeat the question. Be prepared for the remote person to ask the same of you.

✔ **Work hard to avoid interrupting the remote person.** Sometimes, due to the lag time, you need to wait a few seconds before proceeding with a response. Those few seconds can seem pretty long in an interview situation, but wait it out!

✔ **Follow up with both interview parties.** Be sure to ask for the remote person's e-mail address before you close the interview so that you can whip out a follow-up thank you e-mail right away.

Part III
Communicating and Networking in the Digital World

"Keep in mind, should you decide to hire me, I can't promise horsey rides every time I come by your office."

In this part . . .

Perfecting your online communication and networking skills is an art form that you can master with just a little bit of extra effort. And that extra effort is worth it — online networking and communication is one area where your efforts can yield big payoffs.

This part is all about how you can use e-mail effectively in your job search, sidestepping digital blunders that could hamper your job-search efforts. You also find out how to do something very rare: to use the online medium to build and grow a vast, global, helpful network of peers and other people who can help you in your job search.

Finally, this part gives you the latest on Web portfolios and how you can use these terrific tools in your job search.

Chapter 10

Using E-Mail in Your Job Search

• •

In This Chapter

▶ Putting e-mail to work in your job search

▶ Winning e-mail style

▶ Understanding employers' e-mail expectations

▶ E-mail bloopers

▶ Resume e-mailing tips

• •

*W*ouldn't it be great if you could just turn on your computer, fire off an e-mail, and get a job? Well, in a sense, you can — that is, if your e-mailing skills are fully up to snuff and in line with current business practices.

You know how the real business world works: Most companies have a quiet, unwritten set of rules. If you can understand and follow the unwritten company code, then you're on the inside track. And so it is in the digital realm of bits and bytes.

In this chapter, I help you see and understand the unwritten codes that employers hold about the e-mail you send them. From e-mailing resumes to cover letters to follow-up notes, I cover all the electronic bases. I help you get the skills that can help you get your foot in the door of where you want to be.

What You Need to Know about What Employers Expect

Ten years ago, employers barely had computers on their desks, let alone e-mail. But all that has changed. Now, about 2.6 *trillion* e-mail messages flit across the Net per year, and a good portion of those trillions of tidbits directly relate to work and work issues. In fact, a recent American Marketing Association survey revealed that e-mail is now used more often than any other business communication tool.

Because e-mail has become so interwoven into the business world, it has also become interwoven into the art and science of getting a job. In fact, during the past few years, a veritable set of unwritten expectations has grown up surrounding e-mail and getting a job. You may not be aware of the expectations, but that doesn't mean employers don't expect you to know the rules of the digital road.

That's why I want to let you in on the scoop! In your job search, you need to know going in that potential employers expect the following things from you.

Employers expect you to have an e-mail address

When you begin e-mailing your resume to employers, they want two things from you in addition to your resume: a phone number and an e-mail address. Nowadays, you look out-of-date if you don't have an e-mail address listed somewhere on your resume.

I know that it isn't necessarily fair, but employers really look out for candidates who display a certain amount of basic computer knowledge. Having e-mail is a bare minimum. If you don't have your own computer, you needn't worry. With a little bit of extra effort, you can get access to a computer and an e-mail address, too. Check out the "Don't have e-mail? No problem!" sidebar in this chapter.

Employers expect you to check your e-mail every day

Are you the kind of person who lets unopened or old mail pile up into giant, skyscraper-like stacks of paper? If so, then you may also go a few days without checking your e-mail. Uh-oh. Employers expect you to respond to e-mail more quickly than snail mail, otherwise known as postal mail. Employers expect that, within 24 hours of sending you an e-mail, a response is forthcoming.

Unfortunately, not everyone can check e-mail every hour on the hour. The best possible solution I can offer is to set a regular time to check your e-mail, particularly during your job search. If you don't have a computer at home, make arrangements to get Web-based e-mail and ask a neighbor or a friend if you can work out a deal for borrowing computer time during your job search. Or you can use the library every day. Whatever you do, set a time for yourself and be diligent about checking your incoming e-mail consistently every day.

Don't have e-mail? No problem!

Most employers I talk with today view a private e-mail address as a basic necessity of a job search. What's more, you also need an e-mail account to access some of the newer features of the majority of the employment databases on the Web.

Now, I know that not everyone has a personal computer sitting at home. But even if you don't have a computer, that shouldn't stop you from having your own e-mail address. To get online, stop by a local public library that has Internet access, or rent computer time at a copy shop that provides computers with Internet access.

As soon as you're online, sign up for a free e-mail address. It only takes a minute, and you have an active e-mail account within minutes. The following e-mail sites offer free Web-based e-mail, which means that using

your e-mail is as simple as surfing the Web. With Web-based e-mail, you can access your personal e-mail from any computer that has access to the World Wide Web. Just remember your password!

Here are some freebies to sign up for:

- ✔ **Hotmail (free, Web-based e-mail):** www.hotmail.com
- ✔ **RocketMail (free, Web-based e-mail):** www.rocketmail.com
- ✔ **MailExcite (free, Web-based e-mail):** www.mailexcite.com
- ✔ **Juno (free, but not Web-based, e-mail):** www.juno.com

The CD included with this book also contains e-mail software called Eudora Light.

Employers assume that you have copy-and-paste and attachment skills

Employers expect you to be able to paste your resume into the body of your e-mail. I discuss how to do this step by step in Chapter 7. Employers also expect you to be cozy with sending all manner of e-mail attachments, from documents to pictures to even video.

If you have never sent an attachment in your life, and if you're unfamiliar with cutting and pasting text into e-mail, please head to Chapter 7 and brush up on these areas right away. Don't let a big job opportunity be your first time out practicing these skills.

Employers expect spelling perfection in e-mail messages

There's no question about it — when you send e-mail to potential employers, spelling mistakes are outright unflattering to your image. Unfortunately, when you're writing an e-mail, spelling errors can be difficult to catch.

Save yourself by using an e-mail program with a spell checker. If you don't have access to an e-mail spell checker, write your e-mail text in a word-processing program where you can spell-check it, and then copy and paste the text into your e-mail message. Of course, you also want to read your work carefully for all those errors that your spell checker didn't catch.

If I'm sending out an important e-mail, I also print it out before I send it. I go over the e-mail word by word. I don't know why, but I know that for me, printing out e-mail makes it a lot easier to catch those small mistakes that otherwise can slip by.

Top Ways to Use E-Mail in Your Job Search

I like to refer to e-mail as a ground-floor communication tool. By "ground floor," I mean that you can use e-mail to get the basics done, but that's about it. E-mail in a job search is always a beginning, an entrée into something more.

Think about it: When you e-mail your resume, you send off a shot in the dark. If people look at your resume and decide to respond, they *call* you to get a read on you. They want to know how articulate you are, how you interact with them, and all those other things that are pretty difficult to determine via e-mail alone.

And when employers decide to interview you, they call you on the phone or, in most cases, bring you into their offices for a face-to-face meeting. They want to know how you as a person fit into the corporate culture, and again, that fit is best determined in person, not by e-mail.

So, in your job search, e-mail is typically a way to open the door, say thank you, and confirm schedules. If you're *very* skillful, you can network with e-mail (see Chapter 11 for online networking advice). But basically, the best uses of job search-related e-mail break down into the following categories:

- ✔ **E-mailing your resume to employers and employment databases:** E-mailed resumes are standard practice in today's job hunt.

- ✔ **E-mailing cover letters:** You need a brief digital introduction to your e-mailed resume. An e-mail cover letter is that intro (see Chapter 8).

- ✔ **Sending follow-up e-mail to telephone calls from potential employers:** E-mail is a very effective way to say thank you and to remind employers how right you are for the job.

✔ **Networking:** Making and developing contacts via e-mail takes great skill, but you can do it if you work at it.

✔ **E-mailing questions to experts and others related to your job search:** If you have a quick question, e-mail is an appropriate way to get an answer.

Now that you know how to use your e-mail in a job search, it's time to turn to getting your e-mail looking perfect.

Winning E-Mail Style

Every year, *People* magazine comes out with its infamous style issue. In the style issue, the magazine's editors choose the most and least stylish people of the past year. The winners appear in full-color pictures wearing gorgeous gowns and buff tuxedos, looking stunning. The losers appear in similar full-color pictures, looking probably the worst that they ever have in their lives.

When using e-mail, you can choose your own destiny. Unlike the poor celebrities who get picked arbitrarily for the style losers list, you have the power to make your e-mail win every time. All it takes is a little bit of know-how and attention.

Style tips that help you make the grade

These style tips can help you dress your e-mail for job-search success:

✔ **Keep your e-mail messages short.** A good general rule is to try to keep your e-mail shorter than one page, excluding your resume. If you have to take more than five or six paragraphs to explain yourself, you've taken too long! In e-mail, less is more.

✔ **Write short, snappy paragraphs.** Do your paragraphs look like the beginnings of the next great American novel? I hope not, because it's the short, snappy paragraphs that count in your job search. What is short and snappy? Short is about two to four sentences. Snappy means short sentences.

✔ **Watch your tone.** Could you speak the contents of your e-mail to a potential employer and sound natural but not chummy? If so, then your tone is probably right on. You want to sound respectful and slightly reserved, but not ridiculously so. Employers frequently relay to me that people have lost job offers because they were too casual during the interview process.

- **Open and close your e-mail like a standard letter.** Open your e-mail with a salutation and close it with a standard business close line. Just because you're sending e-mail doesn't mean that you get to forget everything you know about writing a letter! Good openings include "Dear [the person's name]:"; good closings include "Sincerely," "Regards," or if you're sending an e-mail to a very formal company, "Sincerely yours."

- **Format your message in business style.** Just because you're using e-mail doesn't mean that you should throw all formatting concerns to the wind. Take a little extra effort and make your e-mail look polished. After the opening of the e-mail, leave two blank lines and then begin your message. After your message, leave one blank line and write your closing. Then skip at least two lines and write your name and contact information (see "Putting E-Mail to Work: Samples of Great E-Mail Style" to look at formatting).

- **Contextualize your message.** When I send out important letters, I use my letterhead and type the letter. When I send out less critical, less formal letters, I use my smaller memo letterhead paper and write my letter by hand. In the paper world, letterheads and paper size signal how serious or formal the letter is. But in the digital world, you don't have to worry about such a thing, at least not yet. Until that time, you need to immediately set your e-mail in context. Do so by stating your purpose right in the first sentence or two of the message. Also, keep standard business letter spacing for e-mail that you send to potential employers. See "Putting E-Mail to Work: Samples of Great E-Mail Style," later in this chapter, for examples of what I mean.

- **Always include your name, e-mail address, and other pertinent contact information at the bottom of the e-mail.** Some Internet providers strip return information out of your e-mail. I know that one of my e-mail accounts regularly eats up return e-mail information, leaving me at the mercy of the return e-mail information that the sender placed in the e-mail message. Protect yourself from this woe and always include your phone number and e-mail address at the end of your messages.

- **Keep characters per line to 64 or less.** One of my friends who works at a local paper has the most annoying e-mail system — it sends her e-mail in one long, straight line. To read her e-mail, I just keep scrolling to the right, reading one single, very long line of text! Always be on the lookout for this kind of glitch. As you write your e-mail, make sure that your lines are about 64 characters or 10 to 15 words long. If your e-mail gets any longer than 10 to 15 words per line, employers may not see your entire e-mail message in one glance, and that's something you don't want. Just press the Return or Enter key if you see your message expanding indefinitely and running off the digital page.

- **Never use all caps, even for emphasis.** Please don't use all caps, even in single words. Doing so typically comes off as shouting. USING ALL CAPS is never pleasant for a recipient, and it gives the wrong impression of you to an employer.

E-mail terminology

If you're new to e-mailing, here are a few common terms that you want to be familiar with:

- **BTW:** One of the most common acronyms that I use within e-mail messages. It translates to "by the way."

- **Emoticons:** The symbols you occasionally see in e-mail, like :-), :-o, or ;-). (Tilt the book sideways to view the faces!) The point of emoticons is to add "body language" to e-mail. Emoticons are best used in personal e-mail communications — avoid using emoticons in your job-search e-mail.

- **Firing off an e-mail:** To send an e-mail message.

- **FYI:** Another common acronym, which stands for "for your information."

- **Signature:** A short, electronic ending that you can place on each piece of e-mail you send. A job-search signature should contain your name and return e-mail address at the very least.

- **Slam-o-gram:** A rude e-mail message.

- **Spamming:** Sending multiple e-mail messages to employers or others. Employers refer to multiple submissions of e-mailed resumes as *spammed resumes.*

- **v-Card:** A virtual card attached to an e-mail. Everyone can read the v-Card just by clicking on it. You find v-Cards attached to more and more e-mails these days.

- **Virtual persona:** Who you appear to be online, based on your e-mail communications. Your virtual persona may or may not reflect the real you.

- **If you're sending e-mail to someone you don't know, identify yourself in some way.** In your e-mail closing line, make sure to add a quick identifier that gives a clue as to your area of expertise. That way, when the employer prints out your e-mail, he or she has an instant reminder of who you are. You can add a one-word description such as writer, accountant, programmer, and so on. If you want to get fancier, you can create a v-Card in addition to your one- or two-word description (see "Bonus: v-Cards" later in this chapter for directions).

- **Be careful with your salutations.** Avoid using Mr., Mrs., and Ms. in salutations. You never know whether Les is a man or a woman's name! Opening first contact letters with just "Dear Les Smith" is better. After you have talked with the person, you can always go to "Dear Mr. Smith," or "Dear Ms. Smith." It's better to be safe than incorrect!

- **Avoid using e-mail acronyms.** E-mail acronyms like FYI are in the same category as emoticons. They're great for corresponding with people you already know or with whom you have a casual conversation going. But for job searching, leave the acronyms out.

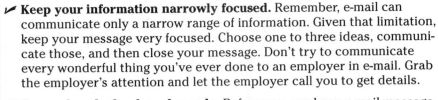

✔ **Keep your information narrowly focused.** Remember, e-mail can communicate only a narrow range of information. Given that limitation, keep your message very focused. Choose one to three ideas, communicate those, and then close your message. Don't try to communicate every wonderful thing you've ever done to an employer in e-mail. Grab the employer's attention and let the employer call you to get details.

✔ **Remember the loudspeaker rule.** Before you send any e-mail message, imagine your e-mail being read over loudspeakers. And not just any loudspeakers, but loudspeakers that your boss, family, coworkers, and friends hear. If you get squirmy about any part of your e-mail being read over loudspeakers, then change your message! E-mail is not necessarily private communication, particularly in a job search, so always apply the loudspeaker rule. It can save you a great deal of heartache in the long run.

Bonus: v-Cards

I first learned about v-Cards, or virtual cards, from Jennie Luke, a computer and resume expert who works with the CareerCast employment database. She sent me an e-mail with a v-Card attached. It was great! I double-clicked on Jennie's v-Card, and a teeny business-card-sized document popped up in my e-mail with business information about Jennie, such as her title, address, and other pertinent contact information. After I received Jennie's v-Card, I started seeing more and more v-Cards attached to e-mail messages. Figure 10-1 shows what a v-Card looks like in a message. In Figure 10-2, you see what an opened "generic" v-Card can look like.

Believe me, you don't need to have a v-Card in your e-mail. But it's a nice little bonus if you want to make the extra effort.

You can create a v-Card in two ways. If you use Netscape Communicator 4 and above, v-Cards are built in. The only problem with using the Netscape v-Cards is that, as of this writing, they don't work perfectly with all e-mail programs. Here's how you create a v-Card by using Netscape Communicator:

1. **From the Edit menu, choose Preferences.**

2. **Choose Mail and Groups.**

3. **Choose Identity.**

4. **From the Identity window, click on the Edit Card box. Fill in the v-Card tabs as you wish.**

    You find tabs for address, phone number, job title, and additional comments.

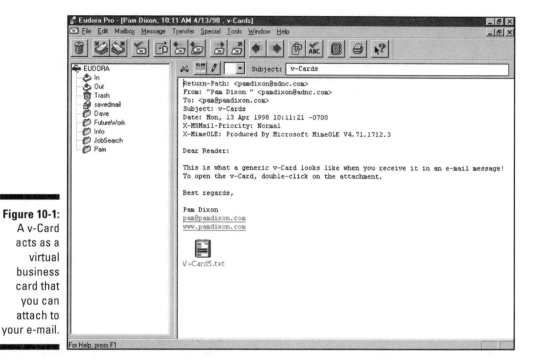

Figure 10-1:
A v-Card acts as a virtual business card that you can attach to your e-mail.

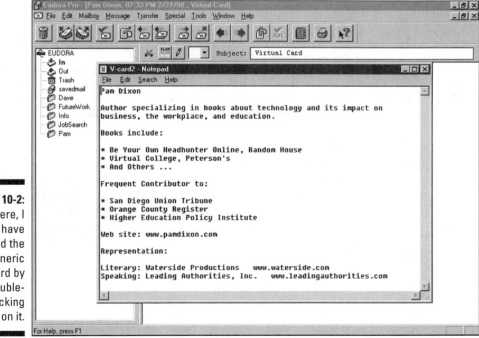

Figure 10-2:
Here, I have opened the generic v-Card by double-clicking on it.

If you want to create a more generic v-Card, which is what I like to do, here are the steps:

1. **Open a document in your word processor and create a short file that lists your name, address, phone number, job title, e-mail address, and place of employment.**

   You can add other information if you wish.

2. **When you have finished, save your document as a plain-text or ASCII file.**

   Keep your lines short — they may not "wrap" automatically for you.

3. **Name the file "v-Card" and save it in a place that will be easy to find again.**

   I keep my v-Card on my computer's desktop area for easy access.

4. **When you write an e-mail, attach the v-Card to the message.**

   See your e-mail program for directions for attaching files.

   Because you created your v-Card as a text file, anyone can read it just by double-clicking on it.

Just remember, though, that a v-Card is a *bonus!* Don't depend on people opening and reading it. Always place your critical contact information in the body of your e-mail.

E-mail bloopers to avoid

In your personal e-mail to friends and family, you can get as creative as you want with emoticons, jokes, and opinions. But in the e-mail that you send out for your job search, being more conservative in your communications is wise. Here are some key snafus to stay as far away from as you can.

Cold-call e-mailing top executives without some form of introduction or entree

If you e-mail a top exec because you know a friend of a friend of that exec or because you met him or her at a party, that's perfectly acceptable. But when you send a resume to a company or organization cold — that is, not in response to an introduction or to a specific job announcement — sending the resume to the employment contact person listed on the company home page is really important.

Please save yourself the embarrassment of sending your resume to just whomever. Executives very rarely handle the initial stages of the hiring process, so even if you do find the vice president's e-mail address on the home page, restrain yourself from firing off an e-mail. Typically, top execs are brought in toward the end of the hiring process, when a company is getting ready to make a final decision about you.

Another factor to consider is that a high percentage of companies use resume-tracking software these days. Typically, resumes go to one or two key people. The key first contacts are responsible for getting your resume in the database, but that's it.

E-mailing a resume to an employer more than once every three to four months without specifically being asked to do so

If an employer is interested in you, they may ask you to send them multiple copies of your resume so they can pass it around. But if you sent a resume to an employer less than three months ago and you haven't heard a thing, wait it out.

Don't keep sending resumes thinking that your resume didn't get noticed or didn't get into the system correctly. Typically, just a few people in a company collect resumes. One employer told me of a candidate who e-mailed him a resume every week, just to be sure. The person who kept e-mailing the resume got noticed, but not hired.

A good rule for e-mailing resumes is that if you haven't heard in three months, then go ahead and send in a new resume with a very brief cover letter stating that this is your second attempt and that you're still very interested in the company.

Sending a negative e-mail message to anyone at any time or place

E-mail leaves a long, long trail. Unlike its paper counterpart, e-mail can be distributed to dozens of people in a minute or two. Long after the moment that got you upset has passed, that hot e-mail you sent can still be circulating.

I once read an interview in which television journalist Barbara Walters gave 20 golden rules for succeeding in any career. One of them was never to put anything negative in writing, ever. Barbara Walters was absolutely correct.

If you find yourself writing an e-mail in which you make a statement such as "Warning: This may sound grumpy," or "I hate to sound rude, but . . . ," stop yourself. Your statement *will* sound grumpy, and a few years from now, you won't want to see that grumpy e-mail resurface.

Using emoticons in your job-search e-mail

Emoticons are cute, but they aren't appropriate for business e-mail, and especially not for job-search e-mail. Leave the emoticons for your friends and family.

Using your work e-mail address as a contact address

One of the biggest e-mail bloopers of all is using your work e-mail address as your personal e-mail for your job search. Just don't do it. Your employer can fire you for it, and you'd have no legal recourse. Other employees have been fired for job-search e-mail flowing through company resources. Court decisions thus far favor the employer. Think about it: The employer provides the computer, the e-mail software, and the Internet account.

Personal use (and your job search is considered personal use) of company equipment is not acceptable, unless an employer specifically states that in written policy. Please see the sidebar "Workplace privacy and legal issues related to e-mail" for more reasons not to use your employer's e-mail in your job search.

Sending your resume as an attachment

I discuss the nitty-gritty of attaching, copying, and pasting your resume into an e-mail message in Chapter 7. But here, let me just say that employers strongly prefer that you include your resume in the body of the message that you send — that is, unless the employer specifically asked you to send your material as an attachment.

In general, though, if you e-mail a resume to an employer, place your resume in the body of the e-mail so that the employer can read it as soon as he or she opens up the message.

Workplace privacy and legal issues related to e-mail

If you're currently employed, you want to be aware of the current laws that do and don't protect your e-mail at work. In 1986, Congress officially passed the Electronic Communications Privacy Act (ECPA), which became federal law. The ECPA bans a third party from intercepting your e-mail messages, but it doesn't currently ban your employer from monitoring your e-mail content. In court cases dating from 1990, employers consistently win when it comes to monitoring employee e-mail. The point? Don't use your work e-mail for job searching, period.

Putting E-Mail to Work: Samples of Great E-Mail Style

Figures 10-3 through 10-6 show some prime examples of e-mail that get the job done in your job hunt.

> Dear Bessie Cohen:
>
> I found your company's announcement for a UNIX systems administrator today on the Online Career Center. In the body of this e-mail, you will find my most recent resume and contact information.
>
> I look forward to hearing from you soon.
>
> Sincerely,
>
> David Andrew, UNIX systems administrator
> Phone: 800-555-1212
> e-mail: david@jobsearch.com

Figure 10-3:
E-mail
cover quip
with
resume.

> Dear Mark Saganawski:
>
> Thank you for your interest in my resume. I was pleased to talk with you today about the marketing position for XYZ Company, and I look forward to further communication with you about this opportunity.
>
> Sincerely,
>
> Dana Jones
> Marketing Specialist
> Phone: 800-555-1212
> e-mail: dana@jobsearch.com

Figure 10-4:
E-mail
thank-you
note for a
follow-up
call.

Dear Sally Jones:

In perusing your company Web site, I found your name listed as the correct contact person for job inquiries. I understand that you do not currently have any positions open in my specific area, but I am very interested in working for your company.

As such, I have included my resume in this e-mail. If a position that suits my skills becomes available, I would welcome the opportunity to discuss such an opportunity with you.

Sincerely,

Anna Jones
Phone: 800-555-1212
E-mail: anna@jobsearch.com

(place resume here)

Figure 10-5:
Resume
cold-call
e-mail.

Dear Mr. Tyler:

Thank you for your call today. Attached are three copies of my complete curriculum vitae, as we discussed.

I enjoyed talking with you about the opportunity at XYZ Company, and I look forward to meeting you in person to discuss the possibilities with you.

Sincerely,

Ron Andres
Phone: 800-555-1212
E-Mail: ron@jobsearch.com
Address: 1212 Cedros Avenue
Anywhere, USA 88997

Figure 10-6:
After a long
screening
conversation
with an
employer.

What if you lose an employer's e-mail address?

I hope that this doesn't happen to you. If it does, you basically have three options:

✔ Go low-tech and simply call and ask the employer or someone in the office for the correct address. Of course, if word gets out that you lost the address, you don't look very organized.

✔ Check the company Web page and hope, hope, hope that it lists the appropriate e-mail address.

✔ If all else fails, try Four11, a collection of millions of e-mail addresses (www.four11.com). The only problem with using Four11 is that it doesn't list everyone. Plus, if the person you want to reach has a common name, like mine, you find lots and lots of e-mail addresses to choose from. On my last visit to Four11, I found hundreds of e-mail addresses for Pam Dixon, and not one of them was mine!

E-Mail Checklist for Job Seekers

Here's a checklist that can keep you looking good in cyberspace:

✔ Have I spell-checked my e-mail message?

✔ Is this message worded as though I were talking face to face with the recipient?

✔ Are my paragraphs short?

✔ Are my lines less than 65 characters long?

✔ Have I written more than one page (resume excluded)?

✔ Have I included my name and contact information at the bottom of the e-mail address?

And here's a resume-specific e-mail checklist:

✔ Have I attached my resume as a text file or placed it in the body of the e-mail message? If I've attached another type of file, is it because the employer specifically requested such an attachment?

✔ Have I attached the *correct* file?

✔ If copying and pasting, have I pasted the entire message?

✔ Have I pasted ASCII text only?

Chapter 11

Finding the Right People and Making Contact

● ●

In This Chapter

▶ Online networking strategies

▶ The right approach

▶ The best online networking haunts

▶ Blunders that unhook you from the online grapevine

● ●

*A*nyone who has worked in a corporate environment knows all about the fabled grapevine — that nebulous, all-powerful string of shared information that reaches farther than Jack's mythical beanstalk ever could.

If you're currently employed, you're probably very willing to tap into the office grapevine as well as participate in general office networking. Entry into an office-level grapevine is relatively easy, and most people can manage at least some form of office networking with a minimum of social skills. An office grapevine is difficult to ignore, and if you choose to ignore your office grapevine, others may perceive you as an outsider or, worse, as downright unfriendly. Plus, your lack of key gossip makes you much more vulnerable to the whims of employment fate.

But as powerful as the office grapevine is, office networking plays only a minuscule piece of the overall networking picture. Genuine networking means a whole lot more than knowing how to plug yourself into a corporate environment, and those few people who have learned genuine networking skills can tell you mythical tales of its extraordinary power.

The only problem is that *very* few people actually understand how to network.

I was one of the lucky ones — I learned networking skills early on from watching my parents. I grew up in the Northern Virginia/Washington, D.C. area, surrounded by diplomats, think-tank experts, and four-star generals. I watched keenly as key golf games brought in multimillion dollar deals, meetings of the minds over the best chocolate cake on earth procured important introductions, and favors granted at the right time were never forgotten and were always repaid.

Then, as now, the business of work had an awful lot to do with how a person could form business relationships. One of the big changes, though, is that the Internet has entered the picture and has added a completely new — and exciting — dimension to networking.

In this chapter, I introduce you to true online networking, perhaps one of the most neglected people-arts of our time. I cut loose with all sorts of insider information about online networking that pertains specifically to your job search. If you've been wondering what you're missing in terms of online networking, and if you're wondering how anyone could possibly make use of the Net's fabulous, but hard to tap, networking potential, then this chapter is for you.

The Limits and Potential of Online Networking

Online networking involves two things: forging new relationships online and maintaining face-to-face contacts via the online medium.

Make no mistake — even if you're an expert face-to-face networker, online networking can still throw you for a loop. Online networking is more difficult and time-consuming than "regular," or in-person, networking because your typical online communication medium, e-mail, is primarily text-based. That leaves out a lot of body language! Online networking also requires that you learn a whole set of new social rules. By heart.

"Then why bother?" you may ask, and rightly so. You may want to bother because a mature online network has the potential to be global, instant, and infinitely more powerful than your local in-person network. You can go farther, faster.

But the caveat is that online networking takes a high degree of skill — so high, in fact, that I consider online networking to be an art form. Although online networking is extremely powerful in potential, the limitation comes in your ability to actualize the potential and really pull it off.

If you really want to go for it, you need to learn three basics: what the online networking "rules" are, where to network, and what kinds of things to say online.

Masterful Online Networking Strategies

Recently, a newspaper reporter I know ran a story about online job search-ing. She mentioned my name in her article, as well as my e-mail address. The story, which was originally for a smallish newspaper, got picked up by papers across the country, and lo and behold, the e-mail started pouring in. Big time.

I found myself reading through over 40 e-mail messages a day, with each message asking for my help in some fashion or another. I responded to some messages immediately and in detail, simply because I was compelled by the sender. I sent a more general response to other messages, offering general advice and broad pointers.

What made the difference in my response? Everyone asked for help, but some knew how to ask for help in such a way that they elicited a much better and more personal response from me. The people who got a good response from me were good networkers, either naturally or from reading books or talking to others.

The following sections give you tips that can help you become a good networker, too. Commit to these strategies, and you take the first step toward building a powerful cyber-network that no computer can crash.

Have a caring, giving attitude

I always surprise people when I tell them that the single most important element in networking is to have a caring, giving attitude. This simple secret can revolutionize your networking, online and otherwise.

What do I mean by a caring attitude? Simply that you have something to offer other people, and you actively go about finding ways to offer your help to others in appropriate ways and at appropriate times.

Even if you're e-mailing someone to ask for help outright, you can ask in a way that values the person's time and expertise and that hints that you're not just a "taker" but that you're a person who remembers a favor.

You don't need a formula of the right words to say in your networking communications; your attitude comes through loud and clear and does a lot of your talking for you. So my advice is to make sure that you approach every networking relationship with these questions:

What can I give to this person? What favor can I do now or someday in the future for this person?

Have a goal

This is one of those pieces of advice that's a lot easier to say than do. But the reality is that if you know what you want to accomplish, your networking gets a lot easier (see the sidebar "Lessons from Peter Wong"). You know what company sites to explore, who to strike up relationships with, and which associations to tap into. In fact, you may, like Peter, concentrate all your networking efforts on one target company.

Targeting and focusing your networking is a superb way to build a network that's truly functional — that is, your network relates completely to where you want to work, what you want to accomplish in your work, and where you want to be in five or ten years. The only problem is that, if your goals change, your network has to change, too.

I remember well-known television network figure Barry Diller commenting about his Rolodex after he left the Fox Network (a network that he helped build from the ground up). He commented — and I paraphrase — that his Rolodex was 80 percent useless after his departure. I remember thinking, "Aha! Now that was a good network!" Can you imagine having 80 percent of the people you know being able to actively help you in your current job? That's quite a good figure. Most people could cite only about 20 percent of the people they know as actively able to help them in their careers or jobs.

Understand networking timing

In an online networking situation, *timing is everything.* The key is that you want to begin your networking efforts *while you're employed.* Even if you know that you'll be laid off in a month, it doesn't matter. Begin your networking from a position of strength, not neediness.

Online networking works exponentially better if you're employed at least part-time. Where you're employed doesn't necessarily matter, either. I've received networking messages from people who worked as chefs, file clerks, scientists, psychologists, teachers, radio broadcasters, part-time temp workers, and janitors. As a networker, a person's job title doesn't matter to me; the fact that the individual is gainfully employed does matter.

Having a job says something good about you as a person, and loudly. Remember that, in the online world, communication is by and large text-driven. Your innate charm or winning smile won't bring you nearly as many points as face-to-face networking. So the facts about you, such as whether you're currently employed, take on added significance and weight.

Lessons from Peter Wong

Peter Wong, a software design engineer for Microsoft's Accessibility and Disabilities group, arrived at his job via an interesting route: As a blind engineer, he encountered numerous difficulties in getting his operating system (Windows) to work with the special screen-reading software that he used to operate his computer. Because Windows was becoming the pervasive operating system that businesses used, Wong knew that it was only a matter of time until he had to switch careers.

After all, if Wong couldn't get a computer to work for him with the new Windows operating system, how could he continue to work as a computer programmer? So, thought Wong, why not solve the problem from the *inside?* Why not go to work for Microsoft and help change the operating system itself?

That's exactly what Wong did. He approached Microsoft "cold" with his ideas about accessibility. Much to his surprise, he landed a plum job helping to refine Microsoft's MSAA (Microsoft Active Accessibility) technology, which will be built into the new operating systems of all Windows-based computers. The MSAA technology enables people with special needs to use Windows easily, and it's now available for Web browsers.

The reason Wong is so passionate about getting Windows and online technology to work easily for visually disabled people is that, nowadays, computer use is pretty much imperative for everyone. If a standard computer doesn't work for those with disabilities, that poses a huge obstacle for future employment. "I hope that Windows truly lives up to its name so that it becomes a window of opportunity for all people," says Wong. "To me, the opportunity should be available for everyone who's interested in learning computers."

Thanks in part to Peter Wong, now it is.

Being currently unemployed, however, can work against your online networking efforts. I suggest that you try temping or working as a consultant until you find a job that you want to settle into. Your employed status not only helps your networking, but it also makes you much more attractive to employers.

If you're a student, you want to begin your networking while you're a student. After you graduate, you fall under the same rules as everyone else: Employment, any employment, really helps you out.

Begin early

The best time to begin networking is while you're employed, and as soon as possible. The reason you want to start early is that an online network takes a long time to mature and begin working. You can always get a person or two to give you some quick advice, but you need something more long-term for your career than just a quick networking "hit."

To build a base for a long-term network, get in the fray as early as possible so that you can start contributing and building up a good reputation. If you've been neglecting your networking, start now to remedy the situation. You want to build a good, solid network *long before you ever need to use it.* Just as Rome wasn't built in a day, neither is a personal network. (See "Knowing What to Say Online" later in this chapter for more information.)

Focus on quality, not quantity

In the online world, finding a large quantity of networking contacts is ridiculously easy. But the real point is to forge quality relationships over a long period with people who can eventually help you, and people you can eventually help, too.

If you know "only" ten people online, but each of those online contacts is truly helpful, then consider yourself very lucky. And if you're keeping up contact with "only" a dozen people via e-mail, also consider yourself lucky. Those people you currently talk with online on a regular basis form the base of your online network.

One person I know e-mails me only once or twice a month. She just keeps in touch and keeps me up-to-date. I do the same with her. Because we have a good idea of what the other is doing, we've been able to trade writing assignments over the years. Sometimes I have an opportunity that I'm not quite right for, but my friend is perfect for the job. I'm happy to pass her the opportunity, because she's done exactly the same thing for me. She's a high-quality contact for me, and I work hard to be a high-quality contact for her.

Follow your hobbies (the "gym rule")

Some of the best online contacts come via what I call the "gym rule" — that is, if you follow your hobbies online, you have a natural basis for communication that works networking miracles.

Take, for example, the virtual training team that I'm a member of. This team has members across the United States and is composed of runners of varying abilities. We share success stories, tell race-day war stories, and trade advice about everything from losing weight to soothing our aching feet. And we share all our tales online via a *listserv,* or e-mail message list.

On the virtual racing team are professionals from all walks of life: record producers, retired government officials, librarians, professors, doctors, teachers, accountants, you name it. I've gotten to know these people pretty well now and would find it easy to ask for career help from them if I needed it.

The point is to follow your passion and look for others who share it with you. Get talking about things, and over time, you'll find that you have an incredible network of professionals whom you know pretty well!

Get and stay active in relevant associations

Everyone knows that you're supposed to be active in associations, but who has the time? Here's a tip: If you participate in associations online, you can take some of the sting out of the inevitable time drain that an association can represent.

Many associations have listservs, or online message lists. These lists are super ways of keeping your name in front of the right people and staying in touch with the movers and shakers in your industry.

Bring online networking traffic to you

In online networking, one of the great equalizers is to create the definitive Web site for your profession. Chris Brady, a plastics engineer, set up a plastics engineering Web site while he was getting an M.B.A. The idea of his site was to provide plastics engineers with a way to network and help each other find referrals for materials, which evidently is a big part of plastics engineering.

Chris's Web site took off — to the point where the movers and shakers of his industry now hobnob on Chris's Web site. Chris told me that he pays just under $20 a month for his Web site. For an investment like that, Chris has been repaid 100 times over. He receives plum job offers on a regular basis, and needless to say, he's become a well-known and well-respected name in his industry thanks to his Web site.

The whole idea is that Chris volunteered his time and effort in setting up and maintaining a Web site. Even though the Web site takes Chris extra time, it's time well spent. You can visit Chris's site at `www.NetPlastics.com/Millennium`.

Show deep respect to a major online principle: The Net remembers

When you network in person, it's possible to have bad chemistry with someone and then move on, forgetting all about it. But when you network online, your bad chemistry is a matter of record, perhaps even public record. That's because online networking leaves a textual trail.

Because of the trail of words that your online efforts leave, staying positive in your online networking efforts is super-important. A single grumpy e-mail may float around the Net for years, haunting you like a permanent social scar.

If you've fallen prey to *flaming,* or sending nasty e-mail notes to a person or online message board, confess immediately. Apologize, plead guilty, and, if you flamed a board, promise publicly to amend your quick-tempered ways. You do this so that the person you burned doesn't one day end up being the networking contact you wished you'd never made.

Knowing Where to Network Online

If you ask expert online networkers where they network, they launch into a long diatribe describing the dozens of online groups they chat with and the dozens of chat rooms they frequent. Listening to the fitful digital trail can leave even the most enthusiastic would-be networker feeling discouraged and time-crazed.

But don't be discouraged. Figuring out where to network is actually very simple. Even if your networking takes on gargantuan proportions, it still boils down to tracking the following three groups of networking contacts:

- ✔ The people you have met in person whom you e-mail
- ✔ The people you have never met whom you e-mail and chat with only online
- ✔ Online "cold-calling," which involves contact with an employer or an expert who doesn't know you

A big part of knowing where to network online involves knowing an individual's e-mail address. That's because online networking, like networking in the "real" world, depends on communicating with people, one-on-one and in groups. Keeping track of individual e-mail addresses is up to you, but I *can* help you figure out where to find people online.

The following sections show you the most popular and fruitful online areas for building a cyber-network that you can come to count on.

Discussion groups/Usenet

Discussion groups, otherwise known as *Usenet,* are online groups in which you discuss a topic through text messages posted in a public discussion area. Tens of thousands of online discussion groups exist. You can probably find a discussion group on any topic you can think of. And if a discussion group doesn't exist, you can start one!

The positive aspect of discussion groups is that you can find hundreds of experts in no time flat. If I wanted to, I could go online, go to Usenet, and collect at least 100 e-mails from experts in a matter of minutes. But the downside of Usenet is that your discussion is public, and you need to abide by definite rules if you want to be an accepted member of the online discussion group. Snobbery is alive and well in cyberspace!

To get to know people and truly build a network via Usenet, you need to look good in all your messages. You also need that giving attitude that I mentioned earlier in this chapter.

In terms of networking, I like Usenet for the following tasks:

- ✔ Finding experts to e-mail privately or publicly.
- ✔ Finding peers with whom you can discuss industry trends and hobby interests. You have real possibilities of building true friendships online via discussion groups.
- ✔ Finding people who work within your target companies.

When I discuss Usenet with job seekers, I frequently encounter a lot of panicked looks. A lot of people seem to have heard about discussion groups, but they don't know how to access them. But it's simple. Here's the procedure for easy Usenet surfing:

1. **Read up on *netiquette,* or Net etiquette.**

   Usenet adheres to a very particular set of social standards. Knowing the social rules well in advance of making any networking moves is best. A netiquette guide that I particularly like is Virginia Shea's, which is available at `www.albion.com/netiquette/index.html`.

2. **Open the Deja News search engine (`www.dejanews.com`).**

3. **Either do a quick search from the opening page or perform an Interest Finder search, which is available by clicking on the Search for Interests link.**

   - A **quick search** gives you a list of *messages* that have been posted about the topic.
   - An **Interest Finder search** gives you a list of relevant *groups* to explore.

   For example, I used the keyword *running* to search for hobby interests. In the quick search, I received a list of over 7,000 messages on Usenet related to running. In the Interest Finder search, I found about a page of Usenet groups that matched my interest. I recommend that you try both searches.

4. **After you get your results list, simply click on the messages or the group to explore.**

   In Figure 11-1, you see a list of Usenet groups related to running that I found. To find a group of like-minded individuals and begin to forge relationships with them, all I have to do is begin *posting* (or e-mailing) messages to the group. You can find complete posting directions on the Deja News Web site.

Reference.COM, a search engine that I discuss later in the "Mailing lists" section, is another excellent tool to use when looking for Usenet groups. In fact, my search of Reference.COM for running-related groups turned up over 200 relevant groups, which was a larger result list than Deja News gave me. Try both search engines and see which one you prefer — both are good. Also, the CD included with this book has two newsreader programs, InterNews and FreeAgent, that help you access online discussion groups.

Web forums

Web forums are like Usenet discussion groups, except Web forums exist only on the Web. Currently, Web forums are much less inhabited than Usenet. Therefore, your messages and online communications stand out on Web forums much more than on the crowded Usenet.

In my experience, finding a high-quality Web forum is more difficult than finding a high-quality Usenet group. Nevertheless, when you do find a high-quality Web forum, you'll have an easy time getting to know the handful of people who frequent the forum. If you find a good forum, you have a potentially great networking situation.

A great tool for finding Web forums is Reference. COM (`www.reference.com`). Reference.COM allows you to search for Web forums specifically, and, to my knowledge, it's the only search engine that has this feature.

To use Reference.COM to search for Web forums, open the URL and choose Web Forums from the pull-down menu situated right over the search box. Type in a keyword and then click on Search. Reference.COM displays a list of results for you. (You can see what Reference.COM looks like in the Internet Directory at the back of this book.)

Mailing lists

Mailing lists are public or private group discussions carried on via e-mail. Sometimes, mailing lists are also called *listservs.* Mailing lists get high marks from me for networking impact. One thing I need to make immediately clear, though, is that there are two types of mailing lists: public and private.

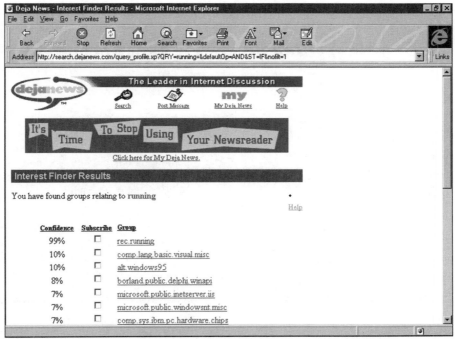

Figure 11-1:
The results
of a Deja
News
search on
the topic of
running.

✔ Public mailing lists are generally *archived,* or stored, on Usenet.

✔ Private mailing lists are just that — private. They're not archived on Usenet. The virtual racing team list that I enjoy so much is a private mailing list. If you aren't sure whether a mailing list is private, simply ask someone on the list or e-mail one person privately and ask.

Currently, about 85,000 mailing lists exist. Many of the mailing lists discuss scholarly and professional topics; others are devoted to avocations and hobbies.

Using mailing lists is simple. After you find a list that you like, you simply subscribe to the list. (Each list has its own directions for subscription.) When you want to make a statement, you post a message to the list. Posting to a list is a matter of sending an e-mail message to a designated e-mail address.

I subscribe to a number of professional and avocational mailing lists. I've "met" numerous people over the years this way, and I often meet up with my online buddies at professional conferences.

Investigative networking gossip tips

To find people who work within a company that you want to work for or plan on interviewing with, perform a keyword search for the company name in Deja News. You may find thousands of e-mail messages related to the company. You may also find e-mail messages from people who work for the company, if that company has a clear domain name.

For example, Ford Motor Company employees have a *name*@ford.com e-mail address. A search of Deja News for *Ford* brings up gossip about Ford, as well as Ford employees' posts. When I searched under the keyword *Ford*, right at the top of my results list I found a post from a Ford employee discussing charter boats.

After you find employees, bring every smooth networking ability that you have to bear in developing a relationship with that person. When the time is right, you can inquire about the company's working environment, or maybe even ask about job leads.

Again, this is why you want to start your networking early. If you know that you want to work for a company, don't wait until the day before the interview to begin building relationships with the company's employees!

To find lists that are right for you, I have two great tools to share with you: Liszt Select (www.liszt.com) and Reference.COM (www.reference.com). Both tools are search engines that look for mailing lists, both public and private. To use either of the tools, follow these steps:

1. **Open the URL.**

2. **In Liszt Select, type in a keyword relevant to your interests and click on Search.**

   In Reference.COM, choose the kind of search that you want to perform from the pull-down menu sitting above the search box on the opening page. Then type in your keyword and click on Search.

   The selections on the Reference.COM menu include

   - Mailing List Directory (use this to search for any mailing list, public or private)

   - Usenet & Mailing List Archive (select this to search for public mailing lists)

   - Mailing List Archive (this searches for archived messages of mailing lists)

3. **When you get the results list, click on the mailing lists that interest you.**

   The links in Reference.COM and Liszt Select take you to an information page that tells you how to subscribe to the list. Note that Liszt Select typically gives you fewer results than Reference.COM.

After you subscribe to a list, read the messages for a week or two without posting any messages. Try to get a feel for the cast of characters and for the tone of the list. When you do post your first message, introduce yourself and be sure to list the URL of your Web site and your e-mail address in the message. Be upbeat and let the group know that you're happy to participate. Then the hard work of developing online friendships begins. As always, have a sharing, giving attitude!

Web pages, especially company-, association-, and hobby-related

Web pages are great sources of contacts. You can typically find a person's e-mail address listed on a Web page, along with a bio or statement of the person's relationship to an industry, association, or company (or hobby, if that's what you're looking at).

All this free information gives you a real "in" with a person, as long as you make the right approach. An example of this is approaching an executive with your resume, e-mailing an expert with a question or comment, or e-mailing a person with an invitation to discuss a mutual avocational interest.

I receive a lot of visitors on my Web site, and quite a few e-mail me resumes and career questions. The people I respond best to are those who take the time to find something nice to say about the Web site or about my work, or who show me that they've read my Web site well enough to find a common interest to mention. You can glean important networking lessons from this example — I'm just like everyone else out there in how I like to be approached.

Here are some tips that can help you elicit positive responses from e-mail messages that you send to people you find on the Web:

- ✔ **Read the Web site.** Find any and all information about current projects, hobbies, samples — you name it. If material is on the Web site, find it, read it, and *take something from that material and put it in your e-mail message.* To an employer, you might write about the company's latest project. To an expert, you may want to say something about your mutual interests in a research area. If you're pursuing a contact in an association, you may want to mention your goals in the field and your admiration of the association's activities. One time, a smart e-mailer noticed a teeny sentence on my Web site in which I mentioned my love for greyhound dogs. This person — with whom I'm still in contact, by the way — mentioned her love of greyhounds. How smart she was! She got an immediate, positive reply from me.

✔ **Don't presume that the person you're e-mailing speaks English as a first language, has a gender that matches the name listed, or anything else.** I have sent e-mail to a lot of people over the years, and I have seen over and over again how important it is not to presume anything. When you send an e-mail based on Web site information, keep it neutral (see Chapter 10 for more hints in this area).

✔ **Understand that, if you e-mail an executive, a secretary or other intermediary may read the message first.** Executives who have their e-mail addresses listed on Web sites often have someone screen their e-mail. Keep this in mind in your communications. Keep your e-mail short, giving, and easy to read. Also, give the screeners time to get through the e-mail before you fire off a follow-up reply. Wait a minimum of a week before you send a follow-up message.

For extensive tips about finding the right Web sites, refer to Chapter 3.

Chat rooms

Online chats allow you to type messages to a group of people in real time — that is, you don't have to wait for the messages to arrive in your e-mail in-box. In a chat session, you type a short message and press Enter, and your message appears in a communal chat area. To see what a live chat looks like, head over to an online chat area, such as Talk City at `www.talkcity.com`, and try it out.

Chat rooms are by and large a *bonus* part of networking. The discussion in most chat rooms is quick-paced and difficult to follow, even if everyone is well-behaved. Furthermore, chat rooms tend toward quippy conversations as opposed to substantive conversations. You're not going to make a lot of great networking contacts in even the best chat rooms, unless you simply luck out.

Nevertheless, I like chat as a networking tool for accessing experts and getting a quick networking hit. To find experts chatting online, here are some tried-and-true steps to follow:

1. **Go to the Yahoo! Net Events area at** `events.yahoo.com`.

2. **In the search box, type** chat **and a keyword of your choice. Click on Search.**

   In a sample search, I typed **chat engineer**.

   You see a result list according to your keywords.

3. **To access any chat you find on the list, simply click on the high-lighted link and follow the directions.**

4. To see a list of all scheduled chats, type chat **in the search box.**

You get a list of thousands of chats to look at.

In Figure 11-2, you see a list of three chats I found as a result of my query, *chat engineer.* The chats are high-quality and are professionally related. I would imagine that, at the very least, you could catch up on industry trends. With effort and luck, you may meet a networking contact.

To see listings of good online chat sites and tips for navigating the sites, please see the "Chat" section of the Internet Directory at the back of this book.

I want to mention two cautions about networking on chat sites:

✔ Chat sessions are sometimes recorded and stored as archives. Anything you say can be researched later on. This has happened to me several times as a result of author talks on chat sites. Those author talks hang around for a year or so before they go away.

✔ Not all chat sites are equally useful. Check the Internet Directory at the back of this book for site suggestions. If you find yourself in a time-wasting or even unseemly conversation, you can always log off.

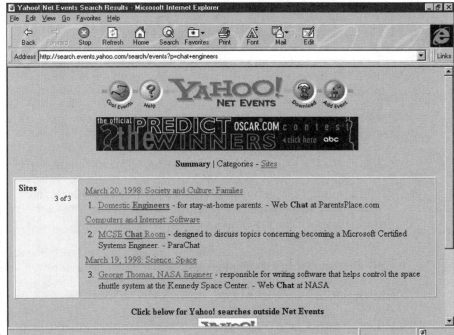

Figure 11-2:
A list of engineering-related chats from Yahoo! Net Events.

Online courses

Distance education, sometimes referred to as *virtual college,* is quickly becoming a standard feature in America's top schools and universities. New York University has an entire virtual college program, and the University of California, Los Angeles, just dramatically expanded its online course offerings. About 250 other colleges and universities offer distance education courses and degrees.

In distance education courses, you can take classes via the Internet from all manner of schools, no matter where you live. I have interviewed hundreds of distance education students and professors and want to share with you that taking an online class in your area of expertise is one of the best ways to build a high-quality online network.

Kevin Kimma, a former online student, built up a significant network of peers while earning an online M.B.A. He told me that now, years later, he still stays in contact with the people he met and learned with online. He shares work ideas, strategies, and leads with his former classmates. For more information about online education, you can take a look at *Virtual College* (Petersons), a book I wrote about the subject. You can also look at www.petersons.com, a large distance education Web site.

Knowing What to Say Online

Networking is all about being personal, being helpful to others, and staying in there for the long haul. Sure, you have occasional quick hits in networking — for example, sending your resume to an employer is a networking quick hit, as is e-mailing an expert for advice. But quick hits aren't what comprise the backbone of your networking Web. You want to develop long-term relationships and grow them over the course of your entire career.

Unfortunately, you won't find a single "style" or format to use in your networking communications. My advice is to use good, solid e-mail style and follow online netiquette rules before you post to public forums like Usenet. (For e-mail information, see Chapter 10. For Usenet tips, see "Discussion groups/Usenet" earlier in this chapter.)

The other advice that I offer is in the way of general help. Because so few people actually follow through on tips like these, you improve your skills dramatically — and with them, your effectiveness — if you do even a little bit of this in your networking.

What works

The things that help you build an online network are the same things that help you build an in-person network. However, when you go online, you need to be more obvious about everything because, most of the time, you have only words to help you convey your message.

Being polite

Being civil is so simple, particularly online, where you have time to formulate a response. In your online communication, whether on Usenet or just via e-mail to another individual, always be polite.

If you must say something negative to someone, call that person on the phone and have a discussion. If it's not important enough to call the person about, then it isn't important enough to put into writing.

What you write in online networking will stick around for a long, long time, so you need to make sure that what's sticking around is always positive. Save your grumpiness for the appropriate time and place. With the widespread use of data archiving, the hot reply that you sent to someone on Usenet may still be searchable and available ten years from now. And the person you burned may remember you, too.

Having a helpful attitude

When you go online with the idea that you want to build a network, you need to keep a helpful attitude at the top of your agenda. Don't jump online and post messages saying something like "I need a job, help me please" to every newsgroup you can think of. Not only will you not get help, but you'll get a few *flames,* or negative e-mail responses, too.

The reason you'll get a bad response is that what you've done is essentially walked up to a group of strangers and begged. Walking up to a group of strangers, introducing yourself, getting to know everyone, and *then* asking for help is much better. Hopefully, you will have helped other people long before you ask for help the first time.

Doing favors for others whenever you can

If you're in a position to help one of your online friends, then do so. If it involves setting up a meeting, sending some information, or just pointing a person in the right direction, great! Consider yourself lucky. Every time you help someone out, you strengthen your network.

The best kind of online favors are unobtrusive and natural. You don't want to do too much of a favor, because that puts a person too far in your debt. Do small, quick things for others. Then you can do more favors and help more people.

Maintaining good follow-up

Keep in touch with people at least once a month, and you'll go a long way toward building your online network. I know people who e-mail a newsletter once a month to all their networking pals. I receive several such newsletters and enjoy them immensely.

To grow your online network, begin with your in-person contacts. When you meet someone in person, be sure to get that person's e-mail address so that you can send a good follow-up note after your in-person meeting. You have a good chance of adding this person to your online network if you can keep up communication over a long period of time. You don't need to send e-mail every day — once a month or so is perfect.

Saying thank you

Having to say this seems silly, but the words *thank you* are all too uncommon today. When someone in your online network does something for you, e-mail that person a thank-you note immediately, before procrastination sets in. The thank-you note takes three to five minutes of your time at most, and it preserves and enhances your relationships. Saying thank you is an unwritten rule of networking — especially in online networking.

I once went way out of my way to help someone who was about to sign a book contract. I located the very best literary attorney in New York City to look over her book contract, plus I got her a special rate with the attorney. I indebted myself to the attorney in the process, and I found a way to help the attorney later on. But the person I helped didn't play her networking cards right.

She used the attorney, but never thanked me for the referral. I heard through the grapevine that the person I helped was thrilled with the attorney. Too bad she didn't tell me that, because I won't go out of my way for her again. All it would have taken is a one-liner: "Hey, thanks for the referral!"

When it comes to saying thank you, silence is not golden.

What doesn't work

I bet that you already have a very good idea of what doesn't work online. Just in case, the following sections give you some pointers.

Having a gimme, gimme, gimme attitude

One of the worst possible things you can do is to go online with a "gimme" attitude. It's an ugly way to approach people, and it's bound to turn off the very people who could help you. The hallmarks of gimme messages are those statements that make the recipients feel used, like some sort of meat in the networking market.

I get my share of gimme messages. Here's one I received just yesterday:

I saw your book about job searching online while I was in the bookstore the other night and got your e-mail address. I would like to know more about how I can look for a job online. Please help me.

I e-mailed a reply to this person asking if they had a more specific question related to the book. The person sent me a reply stating that he had simply copied my name out of the book! Now that's a gimme attitude.

Communicating sporadically

After you begin networking online, you need to maintain your efforts consistently. Unfortunately, you won't be able to disappear from the digital domain for months and have everyone wait patiently for you to get back. When you leave, the digital seas close behind you, and it's very difficult to get back in. That is, those people who were so warm to you just two months ago may not view you with the same enthusiasm when you decide to get back online. Because you're dealing with people, you need to remember that consistent contact is important.

Know in advance that this is the way it is, and develop a consistent pattern of communicating. If you only have time to feed your network once a week, then stick to once a week, and people will know to expect that timing from you. But if you work your online network once a day and then suddenly stop when you have a crunch at work, you need to let people know that you'll be gone and for how long. If you leave your network for longer than three weeks, though, you jeopardize your networking efforts. Once a month or every three weeks is the minimum amount of time you can go in the online networking world.

Disrespecting someone's time

In your e-mail cold-calling, respecting another person's time is very important. E-mail messages that are longer than one page send a negative message in the time department, for sure.

Keep your e-mail short and to the point. Somewhere in the message, acknowledge that the person is busy and that you value the time he or she spends responding to you and helping you. Even something as simple as "I know how busy you are. Thank you in advance for taking the time to look at this" works wonders.

Sending an unsolicited resume with anything but the best manners

As far as sending an unsolicited resume, you find two camps of thought. One camp states that e-mailing your resume to the right people within companies, completely unsolicited, is important. One of the primary ways executives find jobs (other than through networking) is by sending an unsolicited resume to the right person.

The other camp says that you shouldn't bother busy executives with your resume, unless an executive specifically invites you to send one.

My feeling is that you must find the *right* person to send your resume to, and then send it only after you've *first* sent a resume to the human resources department so that your resume gets into the company's resume database.

When you send an unsolicited resume, you need to find a way to be unselfish about it, or it will *never, ever* work. Employers told me that they don't like getting mediocre "gimme a job" resumes, but they do like getting good resumes sent with the right attitude.

Here are some tips for making a good impression with your cold-call resume:

- ✔ **Make your unique skills clear right up front and show how your skills can *help the company*.** Ask directly to meet with the person to discuss job possibilities.

- ✔ **Keep your cover letter to one page.**

- ✔ **Send your resume as ASCII text, not as an attachment.**

- ✔ **Show the person reading your resume that you've put thought and research into the company, and that you're willing to invest even more time in learning about the company.**

- ✔ **Show a giving attitude.** Congratulate the person on a recent promotion that you read about in the company press release section. Wish the person well in the new company initiative that you noticed on the corporate Web site. Talk about the person.

- ✔ **Don't say in your cover letter that you want to "find fulfillment in a job that lets you use your degrees."** You won't get many bites. Why? Because your letter talks only about what *you* want — it doesn't offer a single thing to the person reading it, and it makes you look selfish, even if you aren't. To be effective as a cold caller, you need to be giving and generous in your communications.

- ✔ **In the last line of your cold-call cover letter, mention that you've also sent your resume to the HR department for their convenience.**

Networking with a false virtual persona

This may come as a complete shock to you, but plenty of people decide to protect their online and networking privacy by altering their name or gender. My advice? If you're a man, network as a man, and if you're a woman, network as a woman. Don't go about pretending to be someone you aren't.

If you're any good at networking, you'll eventually meet or work with the people you're in contact with online. When you do meet, you want to present yourself without fear of being "discovered" as a phony. And if you present yourself as other than what you are, the news will spread like wildfire when you're discovered — online, of course.

Chapter 12

Marketing Yourself with Your Web Page

*Y*our Web page figures into your job search only as much as you want it to. Certainly, having a Web page is not a requirement for getting a job. But it's a really nice extra to have at your disposal.

In this chapter, I discuss the latest on Web pages as they relate to your job search, including current Web page trends and tips.

Tapping into the Power of a Job-Search Web Page

Essentially, a job-search Web page is any Web page that's appropriate for you to use in your job search. The best job-search Web pages contain enough information about you to make an employer want to invite you in to talk more about yourself. Of course, the corollary is that a poor job-search Web page sends employers running — in the opposite direction!

A job-search Web page that contains extensive samples of your work can also be referred to as a *Web portfolio*.

Currently, there are no hard-and-fast rules about job-search Web pages. You have tremendous latitude in deciding what may or may not work for you. That latitude can be both good and bad!

In any case, I've spent a good amount of time looking into how Web pages are used and viewed in the job market. Here's what I've discovered:

✔ Employers view it as a plus when a candidate has a Web page, provided that the Web page *doesn't contain a picture of the candidate*. A photograph exposes the employer to potential charges of discrimination.

✔ The employers I talked with unanimously dislike Web pages that are loaded with hobbies and other information unrelated to a job search. The bottom line is that, if you're going to tell an employer about your Web site, you need to make sure that your Web site is ready to "go to work."

✔ If you have a Web page loaded with hobby interests, save that page and create a new one for your job search. Or you can do what I do with my Web page: I simply take out links to my hobby interest pages when I need to. The pages are still there, but without the link to the page, no one knows that it's there or can access it.

✔ Employers really appreciate being able to access a detailed text resume from a candidate's Web site. It's a time-saver for everyone.

✔ When a candidate creates a Web portfolio of work samples, employers are generally impressed beyond words. Because Web portfolios are still rare, they make the bearers stand out in a positive way. Great info to add to your Web portfolio includes schematics, drawings, models of projects, writing samples — really, anything that demonstrates visually what you do in your work. (See Chapter 9 for more examples.)

✔ A Web page that's viewed as the definitive hub of an industry gives the creator of the page a real head start on the competition in a job search.

Something to think about is that you usually market yourself with your Web page after an employer has "bitten" at your resume and wants to learn more. I personally have talked to only three people who were offered jobs because employers stumbled across their Web sites and were so impressed that they contacted the Web site creators to invite them in for interviews.

The point is that a job-search Web site isn't an *initial drawing-in* device; rather, it's something that you use as an impressive *follow-up* device.

Web pages are great for

- Giving an employer more detailed information about you and your skills
- Showing off work that doesn't translate well to verbal descriptions — for example, musical compositions or graphic art samples
- Showing an employer that you're Web-savvy and up with Web trends

As such, it's fair to say that a Web page serves as a deal-closer as opposed to a lure.

What to Include in and Exclude from Your Web Resume

I'd like to repeat that no hard and fast guidelines for Web resumes and portfolios exist. However, I can point out a few items that may help you as you put your Web page together.

Do!

Here's a list of things to try:

- **Do list your URL on your text resume that you send to employers.** Doing so gives employers an opportunity to check you out prior to talking with you.

- **Do print out the contents of your Web pages and take them with you to interviews, just in case an employer doesn't have access to the Web.**

- **Do create a separate link for each relevant section of your Web page.** For example, create a link for your resume, a link to samples of your work, and a link to reviews of your work, if appropriate. Put all these links on the opening page of your Web site.

- **Do make sure that your opening Web page loads quickly.** Quick loading encourages busy employers to stick around to read your information. Remember that not everyone has a rapid modem connection and a fast computer!

- **Do stick to one theme for your Web site.** Some Web sites are wry, others are scientifically inclined, and others are artsy. Decide on a tone and a look and stick with them; your site will be more memorable and will create more of a pulled-together, job-oriented impression.

✔ **Do put nifty graphics and even sound on your site, but also provide a text-only page.** Not everyone enjoys heavy graphics, and some employers may be visually impaired and may prefer a text-based site. Ditto for frames. If you use frames, provide a non-frames version of your site.

✔ **If your Web portfolio depends on a graphical presentation, do make sure that all your graphics have good titles.** That way, if a graphic doesn't display correctly, at least readers have an idea of what they aren't seeing.

✔ **Do experiment!** Consider your Web page a work in progress. You can tweak it and improve it for as long as you have it.

Don't!

What's a Do list without a Don't list? Here are some real Web page no-no's that you want to steer clear of:

✔ **Don't put your photograph on your Web site if you're actively seeking employment with a company.** I don't care how wonderful you look; unless you're a model, an actor, a performer, or a newscaster, leave your online photo gallery off your Web site. Current EEOC (Equal Employment Opportunities Commission) regulations make it very clear that if an employer discriminates against you because of race, gender, or other factors, the employer is legally liable. Traditionally, employers view photographs with extreme distaste and caution because photos open the door for a candidate to say, "You discriminated against me." Some employers go to the extent of throwing away all resumes with photos in order to avoid even a hint of EEOC problems.

✔ **Don't clutter your Web site with endless information that's unrelated to your job search.** Of course, you don't have to make every morsel of your Web page business-related, but you may want to cut down the extras during your job search. You can always put the information back up later, after you land a job.

✔ **If you're currently employed, don't go around your current place of employment bragging about your Web portfolio.** Your current employer probably won't find your Web site unless you broadcast the URL, so why tempt fate?

Fabulous Web resumes and portfolios

This section is a very biased, very arbitrary, and very short list of Web sites that I think are knockouts. Each of these Web sites has something compelling about it that's well worth checking out. See for yourself!

Elizabeth Parker's Web page

`www.byteit.com`

Elizabeth Parker is a Web page designer and book author. Her Web page is a terrific example of a page that's warm and friendly yet still gets down to business. I consider Elizabeth's page to be a complex, artsy page that's well worth a job seeker's visit, particularly for those people working in graphic arts.

By the way, Elizabeth's book, *Home Page Improvement* (IDG Books Worldwide, Inc.), is an excellent book on creating a great Web site. It's one of my favorite Web page self-help books.

Greg Sandow on the Web

`pages.prodigy.com/gsandow/index.htm`

Greg Sandow's Web site is an extraordinarily wonderful example of a Web portfolio. Greg is a composer and a writer who's well known in music circles. His Web site includes a bio, a resume, and an extensive portfolio of his writings, as well as auditory samples of his compositions. Greg says that his Web portfolio saves him from having to send out samples of his work to potential employers and is a real convenience in that regard. If you want to see a truly superb Web portfolio, I encourage you to explore this site. Figure 12-1 shows just the very beginning of the Web page.

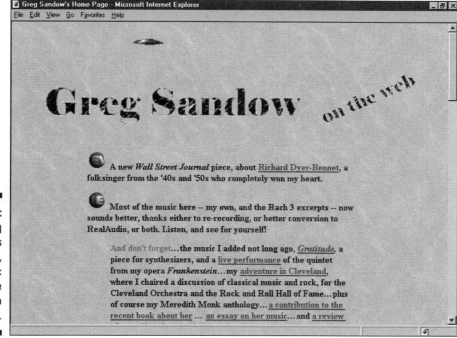

Figure 12-1:
Greg Sandow's Web site, a terrific example of a Web portfolio.

Creating Your Web Page

Web pages are easier to create now than ever before. Super-cheat software that lets you just type in a Web page gives you the ability to whip something up and get it online in less than an hour. (The CD included with this book contains Web page creation software that you can use.)

However, I know that not everyone is willing to create a Web page. That's no problem. Hiring someone to create your Web page and put it online for you is a viable option that shouldn't break your budget. You can get a basic Web site going for somewhere between $50 and $200. More complicated or graphically-heavy sites cost a good deal more.

Your best bet for finding a Web page designer is word of mouth. Do you know someone who has a great Web page? Ask who helped with it. Do you see a terrific Web site online? E-mail the Web site's Webmaster and inquire about the designer. Also, I've had good results with calling local computer clubs and asking for references. If worse comes to worst, you can look up Web designers in the Yellow Pages. My Yellow Pages lists Web designers under "Computers - On-Line Services."

Before you hire any Web page designer, always ask to see the designer's work — online! Also, get a final price quote *in writing* before you agree to any work.

Even if you decide to hire someone to create your Web page for you, you still need to get through Steps 1 through 3 to get a Web site going. Then let your Web page designer take it from there.

Walking through the basic steps of getting your Web page online

Getting a Web page up involves the following steps:

1. **Write your content.**

   Writing your content is a matter of writing your resume and any other textual information that you want on your Web page.

2. **Choose your format.**

   Decide whether you want to put up a simple resume or a more complete Web portfolio.

3. **Collect your art files.**

   Generally, you have to collect the art that you want on your Web site, unless you pay someone to collect or create it for you. If you want to get your own art, you can purchase huge clip art collections for about

$35 at a computer store. I have a fabulous collection of clip art by Broderbund — it contains over 100,000 paintings, photos, and drawings, and it cost less than $50. Please note that the clip art you purchase in such packages is in the public domain, and you are free to use it on your Web pages.

4. **Select a Web page creation tool.**

   If you want to make your own Web page, select the software you want to use to create it (see "Web page creation tools" later in this chapter for details).

5. **Put all your text and art together.**

   Now is the time to fire up your Web page editor (what you use to create the Web page) and put your text and art into the Web page. Each Web page software tool has slightly different instructions for doing so.

6. **Go "live" with your Web page.**

   Going live with your Web page means that you publish it to a *Web server,* the computer that hosts your Web pages. Publishing Web pages varies from slightly frustrating to very easy, depending on who hosts your Web page. The service that I use to host my Web pages makes the process super-simple. You need to ask your Web host provider for exact instructions on how to publish. Be assured, though, that millions of people before you have published Web pages. Generally, the people hosting your Web page will be more than happy to walk you step by step through the process.

If you have further questions about creating a Web site, please refer to Elizabeth Parker's *Home Page Improvement* (IDG Books Worldwide, Inc.) for detailed information about Web pages.

Web page creation tools

Building a Web page doesn't have to be an excruciating affair. *Cheat* software helps you get a Web page up in about an hour. Cheat software is also known as *WYSIWYG* software, because What You See Is What You Get. As you type, you see your Web page as it will look on the Web.

If you're a computer expert, sure, you can enhance your Web page with all the labor-intensive software that I talk about in "Gung-ho graphics software for enthusiasts" later in this chapter. But for most people, a really good bet is to rely on software that takes the fuss out of getting your Web site up.

After all, the point is to get your Web portfolio and resume up on the Web so that you can get a job. Unless you're a Web page designer, you don't need to become one just to get your Web page going.

General Web page creation software

The number of Web page creation tools currently available would make your head spin. Because this isn't a book about creating Web pages, here's a *brief* selection that can help you find your way through the thickets of choices:

- **Claris Home Page:** You can create full-featured Web pages very easily with this powerful WYSIWYG Web page tool. Claris Home Page is a particularly valuable tool for working with graphics and tables.

- **Corel Web.Designer:** I really like Corel Web.Designer — it has 100 templates and an astonishingly rich array of more than 8,000 clip art images. Plus, you can import any of your standard text documents (like a resume) right into one of the templates and be done with your page in about one minute. The drawback is that Corel Web.Designer isn't quite as flexible as Claris Home Page or Microsoft FrontPage.

- **Microsoft FrontPage:** If you want features galore and tons of options, then FrontPage may be a good choice for you — with the caveat that, as of this writing, you need to work on a PC to use it. The main difference between Microsoft FrontPage and Claris Home Page is that FrontPage has more features — you have more tools to make your pages do a song-and-dance routine for you.

- **PageMill 2.0:** PageMill is a sophisticated but easy-to-use WYSIWYG editor for Windows 3.1, Windows 95, and Mac OS. As you type, you see what your finished Web page will look like. For more information, you can check out the CD that came with this book or visit the Adobe site (the makers of PageMill) at www.adobe.com.

A note about building accessible Web pages

Some visually impaired employers are left out of the Web information loop because of Web page design that is not accessible to those with visual disabilities. Because the Web is becoming such an important delivery mode for business information, Web page accessibility is also becoming a *huge* issue. One of the best pages that I found to help explain Web page accessibility is the Starling Access Services page, which you can visit at www.starlingweb.com/acc/actoc.htm.

Meanwhile, here are some quick accessibility tips from the Starling page to help you ensure that *all* employers can access your site:

- Include a text-only option for viewing the Web page.

- Use the full text of the date — for example, January 1, 2000.

- Use vertical links of lists.

- Test your page on a variety of browsers.

- Don't make your words or phrases blink.

Gung-ho graphics software for enthusiasts

Web pages don't have to be boring! Beyond the occasional scanned-in photo or schematic, you can create whirring, twirling, scrolling, flashing, and otherwise Las Vegas–like Web pages.

If a high-profile page appeals to you, you have plenty of tools to choose from. I list a few of the tools here as options for you, just in case you want to create the definitive Web site. But please note that you need to be very comfortable with a computer and have some time to fiddle around and learn the programs. And this stuff takes some time — make no mistake about that!

- ✔ **Macromedia Flash:** Macromedia's Flash program enables you to create quick interactive Web interfaces and animations. You can make scrolling banners and technical drawings and place interactive buttons in pictures with Macromedia Flash. Be forewarned, though: If you've never used Flash before, you may go into learning-curve shock.

- ✔ **Macromedia Director:** Macromedia Director is to Web pages what Microsoft Word is to word processing. Macromedia Director is a very high-end Web page creation tool that you should look into if you're a high-end computer graphics professional or a Web site designer. In fact, if you're trying to get a job as a computer graphic artist and you aren't using Macromedia Director on your Web site, employers may consider that a red flag.

- ✔ **HotDog:** HotDog, a Windows 3.1 and Windows 95 program from Sausage Software, is a "straight" HTML editor, which means that you work directly with HTML tags to create a Web page. This is a great program if you want to get very creative with your Web page and know HTML markup language well. You can find this program on the CD that came with this book. For more information, check out the Sausage Software Web site at www.sausage.com.

- ✔ **3-D Website Builder:** Virtus's 3-D tool is great for creating genuinely three-dimensional Web sites. You can create houses to walk through, gardens to stroll in, and picture galleries to visit. This tool is mainly for creating a physical display of one of your projects. I know of several museums, architects, graphic artists, and scientists using this tool on their Web sites.

- ✔ **Visual Café:** Symantec Visual Café is a useful tool for creating Java applets in a big hurry. (*Java applets* are active parts of Web pages. If you see something highly animated on a Web page, it's probably a Java applet at work.) Visual Café employs a relatively easy interface that shields you from having to enter any nasty Java programming code, but this is still a tool best used only if you're an advanced computer user.

Part IV
Finding and Choosing a Job Online

The 5th Wave   By Rich Tennant

KEG BROWSER

"YEAH, I STARTED THE COMPANY RIGHT AFTER I GRADUATED FROM COLLEGE. HOW'D YOU GUESS?"

In this part . . .

*E*ven if you have the world's best electronic resume, it
doesn't do you much good if you don't know where
to send it! Part IV helps you figure out the best hot spots
to visit in your job search. In these pages, you find out
where the most famous, most helpful, and most user-
friendly online employment sites are hiding.

After you get to an online hot spot, you find out how you
can sail smoothly through the sea of job advertisements
that you find. You discover time-saving tips and tricks
that can help you find the job you've been hoping for —
in a hurry!

And even though it's difficult to think ahead to the results
part of your job search while you're just getting going, I
help you look ahead and prepare for the fruits of your job-
search efforts. (Mindset is everything: Definitely expect
positive results from your job search!)

Chapter 13

Where the Jobs Are: Uncovering the Best of the Best

In This Chapter

▶ Finding the biggest and best online job databases

▶ Discovering rare job searching treasures

▶ Finding your own top search spots

I'm an avid hobbyist runner. Not that I'm fast — believe me, I'm not. But I find running (er, make that plodding along) to be a wonderful way to get outdoors and explore the neighborhood.

In terms of exploring, I'm afraid that I've turned the natural act of running along a neighborhood street into a computer-software love affair. The culprit is a computerized street map program that I found a couple of years ago. It shows me all the streets in the United States. In detail.

Now, my idea of running seems to be just that: an idea. Before I go running, I sit with anticipation at my computer to check out which streets I want to run on, how far it is *exactly* (the program measures that, too), and what kind of terrain I might meet in the vast wilds of Southern California.

In your job search, you need exactly what I have for my running: a compelling and detailed road map. Except that your road map needs to help you navigate the wilds of the online employment databases in cyberspace, among other things!

In this chapter, I give you the zoom-out part of your road map. Here, I give you a big-picture view of the cyberspace employment site terrain so that you know which direction you're heading when you get down to street level.

And just in case you're wondering, your detailed street-level map of the best online sites for job searching is located in the Internet Directory at the back of this book. Now you can explore from your desktop, too! And the CD that came with this book includes links to all the sites mentioned in the directory, so you don't even have to type in the URLs.

Trekking through the Online Job Databases

Online job databases have truly revolutionized job searching. No longer do you have to wonder where you might go to locate job leads; now, the question is how do you possibly know which database to go to?

That's a valid question. After all, at last count, well over 1,300 employment sites were on the Web — and that's a conservative estimate. Where is a person to start looking? Frankly, start here!

At this point in cyberspace development, it's faster and more efficient to let someone else — me, in this case — weed out the field for you. In the following pages, you find a big-picture look at the best-of-the-best places in cyberspace to uncover jobs.

Just in case you aren't quite sure, *online job databases,* also called *online employment sites, Web employment sites,* and *Web job-search sites,* are online repositories for jobs. Some online databases post over 500 new jobs every day.

The Big Seven

"The Big Seven" is a nickname that I coined a while back to describe the monster databases on the Web. These databases are so big, so popular, and so filled with jobs that they stand out as the most prominent denizens of employment cyberspace.

In Chapter 2, I discuss various strategies that you can use to find a job online. The Big Seven are in just about every strategy, simply because of their quality and importance. Be sure to read the detailed descriptions of the Big Seven in the Internet Directory at the back of this book.

Here are the Big Seven and what makes each of them stand out to me, beyond big numbers:

- ✔ **America's Job Bank** (`www.ajb.dni.us/`): A great site for finding state and government jobs
- ✔ **Career Mosaic** (`www.careermosaic.com`): A terrific site for finding technical and other general jobs
- ✔ **CareerPath.com** (`www.careerpath.com/`): One of the best job sites to use when you're relocating

- ✔ **E.span** (`www.espan.com`): A long-standing, stable site that recently has been dramatically renovated and upgraded

- ✔ **Monster Board** (`www.monster.com/`): A terrific place for both new grads and upwardly mobile types to find a wide variety of jobs

- ✔ **Online Career Center** (`www.occ.com`): A high-quality site that's great for seasoned professionals

- ✔ **Yahoo! Classifieds** (`classifieds.yahoo.com/employment.html`): A great place to look for all types of jobs

Treasures off the beaten path: Other general employment sites

Even though the Big Seven are terrific sites, you can't content yourself with visiting only them if you want to spread your net as efficiently and capably as possible. A whole world of general job databases exists. These databases aren't quite as big or as famous as the Big Seven, but the quality of jobs that you can find is terrific.

Also, as I mention in Chapter 2, no one job database has all the jobs. Therefore, try a bunch of them! While I was researching this book, some general job sites really stood out to me as being of particularly high quality. Here are some of my absolute favorites from this category (for a much larger listing, please see the Internet Directory):

- ✔ **The Black Collegian** (`www.black-collegian.com/`): This site impressed me because of its focused content and its high-quality jobs.

- ✔ **CareerCast** (`www.careercast.com/`): CareerCast blew me away because of its extraordinarily good database and high-quality search engine. I'm taking bets that this site goes first-tier and makes the "Big Seven" the "Big Eight."

- ✔ **JobBank USA** (`www.jobbankusa.com/`): I really like the organization of this site, as well as the selection of jobs. A bonus is that this site has a nice tone — it's friendly!

- ✔ **NationJob Network** (`www.nationjob.com/`): NationJob Network stood out to me because of the detailed specialty sites it maintains.

- ✔ **Net-Temps** (`www.net-temps.com/`): I was surprised at this site! I actually bugged the owners to give me a password so that I could explore it from the inside out. I did. And I'm thoroughly impressed. I like the quality of jobs here, as well as the overall tone of the site.

Fabulous specialty or "niche" employment sites

Niche employment sites are the places you want to go when you know *exactly* what kind of job you want, and none other will do. Niche sites exist for nearly every profession. The hallmark of a good niche site is that it focuses on only one type of job or only one industry. For that reason, niche sites tend to have fewer jobs overall, but the jobs are typically a better fit for you if you work in the particular profession that the site covers.

The trick with niche sites is not to get tricked into paying money to look at jobs or post resumes! Be especially alert for cobranding deals. (*Cobranding* is when an employment site has an agreement with another job database. The databases share resumes, jobs, and other data with each other.)

As I hiked through cyber-employment space, I found some real standout specialty sites. Each site I mention here made it because of its extraordinary quality.

- **Attorneys @ Work** (www.attorneysatwork.com): I found this site almost on a fluke! But I was sure glad that I found it. This site is a top-notch site for attorneys. If I were an attorney, I would post my resume here.

- **Adweek Online** (www.adweek.online/): This site is unusual in that it's a site for advertising execs, but it isn't loaded with advertising hype. I was impressed by the quality of jobs that I found here, particularly because advertising isn't the easiest profession to find a job in.

- **Academic Employment Network** (www.academploy.com/): I like this site because it focuses on a much-neglected population — elementary school and high school teachers. For some reason, you could always find job sites for college professors, but other teachers used to get left out in the cold. Not anymore!

- **Cool Works** (www.coolworks.com/showme/): This site stands out because it's extremely unusual. The "cool" in the title refers to the breezes you feel if you take a job that you find at this site; the Cool Works site lists jobs for people who want to work in the great outdoors. I wish that this site had been around when I was in high school and college — working some of the temp jobs you find here would've been a lot of fun.

Geography is destiny at the regional employment sites

Regional employment sites stick to their roots and serve an important purpose in your job search. If you live in a beautiful place and you absolutely don't want to move, then a regional job bank may help you stay put. Regional sites may also help you if you want to relocate to a very specific locale.

Regionals list jobs in only one specific geographical area, as you can surmise. Three years ago, very few regional sites existed. All the career experts wondered openly what the problem was. I guess the job market just took a little while to catch up to the Web.

As I looked over loads of regionals, a couple stood out to me:

- ✔ **Alaska Jobs Center** (`www.ilovealaska.com/alaskajobs/#professional`)**:** This is one of the best regional sites I found. I guess if you're trying to lure employees to a place where it's dark for months at a time, you'd better have a good Web site! This is a good site, and it almost had me thinking about a move.

- ✔ **JobSmart California Job Search Guide** (`jobsmart.org/`)**:** This site gets my vote as one of the most thorough and idealistic sites on the Web. The creator of this site maintains the site as a service for job seekers, not as an advertisement for a particular firm. The site does an amazing job of putting together the very best resources for job seekers. It doesn't miss much in terms of what kind of job-search resources you can find.

Expanding your horizons at international employment sites

International sites abound on the Web. They enable you to look around and dream about jobs in foreign lands without any of the painfully expensive plane tickets that usually accompany such pondering.

Though many international sites are terrific, others ask you for money. Don't do it! You don't need to become a victim of this age-old scam. Don't pay to post your resume or to get job listings. The best international sites give you the goods for free.

Here are a couple of neat (and free) international sites to visit:

- ✔ **EscapeArtist.com (`www.escapeartist.com`):** This is an incredible site, one of the best for really understanding what it's like to work and live overseas. The information that you find here is sound, thorough, and even fun.

- ✔ **Overseas Job Web (`www.overseasjobs.com/do/jobs.cgi/overseas`):** This site stood out to me because of the large number of high-quality jobs that it lists. I always check general international job sites for jobs in Ireland. It's a great test, because there are so few jobs in Ireland. To this site's credit, not only did it list jobs in Ireland, but it listed really good jobs in Ireland.

Finding Your Own Top Job-Search Spots

After you've explored the sites I mention in this chapter, as well as the sites that I mention in the Internet Directory, it's time to do some off-road exploring. Off-road exploring can take you to sites that I didn't have room to cover in this book, as well as to brand-new sites.

Here are some tips to help you keep your direction as you go off-road:

- ✔ **Use meta lists.** Meta lists are giant lists of links. Several very good meta lists can help you keep up-to-date on the latest online job databases. All you have to do is access the meta lists, and you find hundreds of new links to job sites. On my Web site (`www.pamdixon.com`), I keep a list of updated links for the Internet Directory at the back of this book as well as links to job-search meta lists. Other excellent lists include the JobHunt meta list at `www.job-hunt.org/index.html` and the Purdue list at `www.ups.purdue.edu/Student/jobsites.htm`.

- ✔ **Check out college lists.** Quite a number of colleges keep good lists of employment databases and sites for their students. William and Mary (`www.wm.edu/csrv/career/stualum/`), the University of Michigan (`www.umich.edu/~cpp/`), and the University of Minnesota (`www.umn.edu/ohr/ecep`) are three academic institutions that maintain lists. Hundreds more exist. To find college sites, simply perform a keyword search for the name of the college, or look in an index like Yahoo! for the college listing (see Chapter 3 for details on performing these searches if you're not sure how).

- ✔ **Perform your own searches.** Don't be afraid to perform your own independent searches for employment databases. Some career sites aren't even on meta lists! I recommend a Narrow It Down search method for finding new sites (see Chapter 3 for search method details).

Chapter 14

Working the Online Job Databases

*I*once received a holiday gift called a 3-D-O Calendar from a friend. At first, the calendar looked like millions of unrelated black dots printed on paper. But when I looked at the calendar just right, all of a sudden I saw three-dimensional images and messages emerging where only dots had been before. After I got my calendar, I noticed a lot of other 3-D types of calendars, and I always take a moment to "decode" the pictures to see what's hidden in the dots.

Online job databases are a lot like 3-D calendars. In most databases, you find lots and lots of information about jobs, but that information doesn't neces-sarily mean anything to you as a job seeker unless you can decode it. But if you can decode the information, then it becomes meaningful — and perhaps even useful.

When you go job hunting at an online job database, you find that most databases have certain common qualities. You see the same general "floor plan" over and over again, with some variations. If you can get a handle on these common elements, you can learn how to extract the information you need from an online job site very quickly.

In this chapter, I let you in on insider's tips and tricks that save you time, frustration, and disappointment. Along the way, I help you streamline your job database skills to the point that you can pop online, go to a job data-base, extract what you want in a matter of minutes, and then move on to the next job-search item.

Understanding the Opening or Main Page

Most job sites have a "front page" that directs you to every other portion of the site. Ideally, that opening page clearly indicates where you can search for jobs, post resumes, and contact the people who maintain the site.

The opening page typically lets you know how logically the whole site is put together. In Figure 14-1, you see the jobEngine job site — a good example of a well-organized site. The links for job seekers are listed clearly on the left side of the screen, plus you can click on the target icon to get to where you want to go. In one glance, you know that you can search for jobs and post a resume at this site. That's the way it should be.

The following sections give you tips for working successfully with opening pages, because not all of them are as well-organized as jobEngine's.

Take the time to read the entire opening page before you begin clicking on links

Reading through an entire Web page when you want to race off and look for job ads takes enormous discipline, but doing so really saves you hassles in the long run. Some opening pages are so difficult to read that just getting through all the details takes five minutes. But your effort up front is well worth it.

Reading the opening page thoroughly gives you a map of what the employment site can and can't do for you. After reading the opening page, you should know whether you can post your resume, whether the site has an agent (see the section "Using the Push Technology and Job Search Agent Page" for more information about agents), and whether cobranding agreements are in effect. You also find out whether the site is for-pay or free. (Plenty of for-pay sites are out there, waiting to take your money!)

You probably already know my opinion on this, but I'll state it yet one more time: The best job databases are free to the job seeker. Period. No exceptions.

Stick to the basics

While doing research for this book, I looked at more than 1,000 employment databases. I learned quickly that if I went off exploring links, I soon got "lost" in the database. Though exploring employment databases is certainly interesting and informative, you can save yourself a lot of time by sticking to the basics and not wandering around.

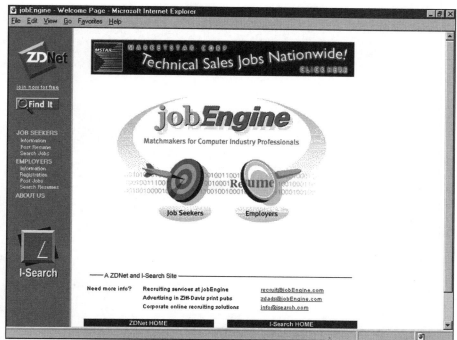

Figure 14-1:
The opening page of jobEngine, a well-organized site.

Spot cobranding and joint agreements

The term *cobranding agreement* means that two or more businesses have teamed up to bring you a job or resume database. A good example of cobranding done the right way is jobEngine (www.jobengine.com), which is a joint venture between I-Search and ZDNet.

Another joint deal between job databases is a *joint agreement* or *alliance*. In an alliance, two or more databases or companies agree to share information, but they don't necessarily agree to cobrand, or promote each other's brand name.

I can't emphasize this critical point enough: *A good database has cobranding agreements and joint agreements stated clearly on the opening page.* The ethical thing to do is to let you, the job seeker, know exactly how the various agreements impact you right up front. In some cases, you won't be impacted at all. In other cases, you may be sending your resume to as many as 15 other databases, none of which you know about.

Figure 14-2 shows a complete list of Career Mosaic alliances. The list is clear, specific, and right on the opening page. This is what you want to see! (In this figure, I scrolled down just a little way to get to the list of alliances.)

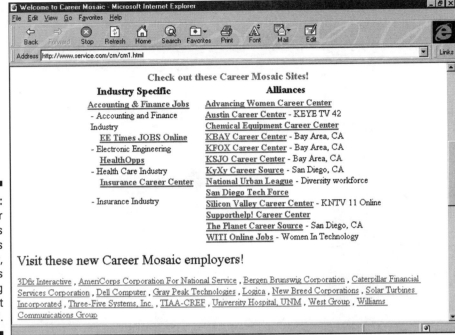

Figure 14-2:
Career
Mosaic lists
its alliances
clearly,
right on its
opening
page, as it
should.

Unfortunately, not all databases disclose cobranding or joint agreements. The problem with this is that you may be sending your resume to one or more companies or databases that you aren't aware of. If even one of the databases you send your resume to is open to the general public, you need to know in advance; otherwise, your resume can be seen by anyone with a Web connection. So always be on the lookout for language about cobranding or joint agreements.

If you see logos posted on a job site that aren't related naturally to that site, consider the logos a tip-off to a cobranding or joint agreement — even if nothing about such an agreement is directly stated. For example, Women's Wire has a Monster Board logo on its site. That's a tip-off that when you search for jobs and post resumes on Women's Wire, you're really searching Monster Board jobs.

Scroll down to see the fine print

Sometimes job seekers don't read the fine print. The reason is that the fine print is typically way at the bottom of a long Web page, and not everyone scrolls to the bottom of every Web page.

On the opening or main page of a job database, however, you really do need to scroll down and see what the fine print tells you. That's where you often find cobranding agreement notices, for-pay notices, and e-mail contact addresses.

Working with the Job-Search Page

The job-search page is the heart of most online job sites. Job-search pages are the interfaces to the job databases and fall into several categories:

- ✔ A keyword search job page
- ✔ A list search job page — the list can be organized by industry, by company, geographically, or chronologically
- ✔ A combination keyword search and list search job page

Figure 14-3 shows a combination keyword search and list search job page at the Black Collegian Web site. You can type in a keyword to look for a job, or you can scroll down the page and click on a list of company names offering jobs. (The actual company names didn't fit on my screen, but they're there!)

Figure 14-3:
A good combination keyword search and list search job page. This one is at the Black Collegian Web site.

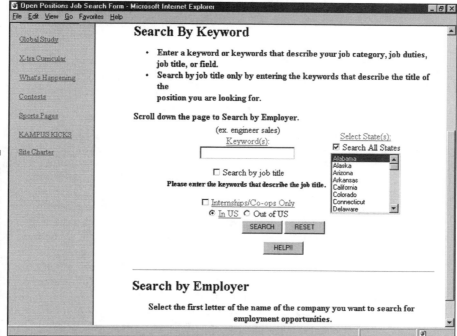

Navigating the seas of jobs

A good job database has far too much information to search simply by looking at its contents all at once. The best job databases would simply overwhelm you with the amount of data that they contain. That's why all the larger databases rely on a search engine to do the hard work of searching for you.

If you read Chapter 3, you know that a *search engine* is a piece of software that uses keywords to extract information from databases. Search engines can be very helpful, but they have their limitations.

- ✔ If you search a poor database with a great search engine, you'll get poor results.

- ✔ If you search a knock-your-socks-off database with a limited search engine, the search engine won't even begin to touch the bottom of the database. It will skim information off the top, leaving you with poor search results.

- ✔ If you have a great search engine paired with a great database, you're in the money.

I've spent a lot of time trying to find the best search engines and the best databases, with good results. But another factor affecting your ability to search job databases, which I haven't mentioned yet, is your ability to use keywords! See the following section for all the details.

Perfect your job-search keywords

Keywords are terms that describe a profession or an industry. They form the base vocabulary of your profession and are used by employers to describe jobs within your industry.

You use keywords in search engines to tell the search engine what you want it to look for. For example, if you're a technical writer, one of the keywords you should use in your job search is *technical writer.* If you're an ironworker, your keywords include *welding, stainless steel,* and *fabricating.*

I can't even begin to tell you how important keywords are in your job search. If you use good keywords, you'll get good results. If you don't use good keywords, you'll get poor search results, even on the best databases.

I make quite a fuss about keywords when I talk to job seekers about online job searching because keywords are the primary way to access job databases. Though some job databases do have nice lists (like the Black Collegian job database), many great job databases don't maintain a single list. CareerCast, pictured in Figure 14-4, is one such site.

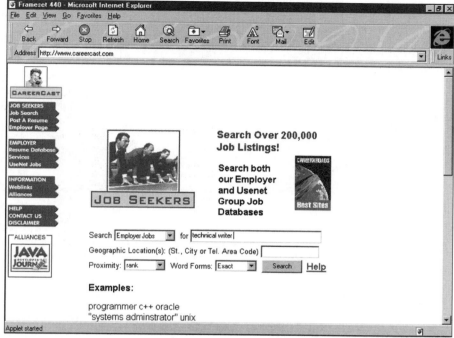

Figure 14-4:
The search
engine
at the
CareerCast
employment
site.

CareerCast looks deceptively simple, doesn't it? But CareerCast actually has one of the best search engines available. Additionally, CareerCast's database is excellent. But to mine and harvest CareerCast's riches, you need to have your keywords in order, or you won't gather a single job treasure.

In Figure 14-4, you may notice that I typed the keyword **technical writer** in the CareerCast search for box. After I typed **technical writer**, I clicked on the Search button and received several hundred matches. The matches were very close to what I wanted because the CareerCast search engine is a good one, and because the CareerCast database is good. But I also used the right keyword.

These tips can help you develop keywords for your job search:

✔ Read job advertisements in local and national papers to see what terms employers are using to describe the jobs you want. Terms that you see frequently are important keywords for you to use.

✔ Scan trade publications online and offline to find industry-related terms. Again, industry-related terms are important keywords.

Find a job like you would a restaurant

If you're still having trouble figuring out how keywords operate, imagine that you're visiting a new city. Now imagine that every restaurant in the city is keyword-searchable, along with all the restaurants' menus. Imagine performing a search for restaurants you enjoy. You can type in **Chinese**, **Italian**, **Thai**, **American**, and **Southwestern**, for starters. Or you can type in price range, location, and specific menu items. If you can think of keywords that describe foods you enjoy, then you can eventually come up with keywords about the profession you work in!

✔ Go to large classifieds databases like CareerPath.com and Yahoo! and scan the job advertisements for terms that employers use to describe jobs. This is another source for keywords in your industry.

✔ Look at online association Web pages and read the content carefully, noting any industry buzzwords for your profession. (More keywords!)

Perfect your list-grazing skills

Grazing a list is easier for some people than others. I know one recruiter who can't stand looking at lists. But me, I love them! It really comes down to personal taste.

No matter what your preferences, grazing a list is simple. Follow these steps:

1. **Open the job list.**

2. **Scan the list quickly, scrolling down the page if you need to.**

   The key is to scan the entire list very quickly.

3. **Choose a category or link and click on it.**

4. **Explore!**

Figure 14-5 shows a good example of a job advertisement list. This list of jobs available in West Palm Beach is found on the Yahoo! Employment Classifieds. If you were looking for a job on the list in Figure 14-5, you would click on the appropriate link and explore your options.

Print up a paper flurry

Some people may disagree with me on this point. However, I've found that this advice is helpful to many job seekers, so I'm passing it along to you.

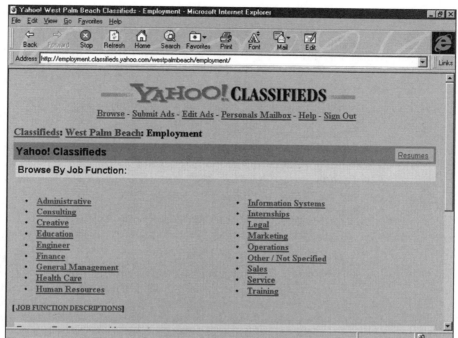

Figure 14-5:
A list of job functions at the Yahoo! Classifieds.

In a traditional job search, you may reply to a dozen or so job advertisements per week at the beginning of a search, and perhaps send out about 20 resumes as "cold calls" to companies or organizations you want to work for. Keeping track of that amount of job-search information isn't burdensome.

But in an online job search, you tend to put your resume on more databases, send your resume to more employers, and reply to more ads. Thanks to the efficiency of the online medium, you can e-mail your resume to 100 employers a day if you want, and thousands more employers may find your resume on a database.

Because an online job search can involve so much more information than a traditional job search, I recommend that, when you see a job advertisement that appeals to you, you print it out right away. You have a record of the job ad, plus you won't have to try to find the job ad again if you lose your place on the Web site or forget where you found the job ad.

I know that the idea of a paperless office is fashionable. During a job search, though, the paperless concept isn't very practical. Try not to feel guilty about making lots of printouts.

If you can, purchase copier or printer paper that has been prepunched for use in three-ring binders. Use your prepunched paper to print out all your job-search info, and you'll be able to pop the printouts right into a job-search notebook without any extra fuss or work. I use this trick all the time with my online research, and believe me, it works organizational miracles!

Scoping out the jobs

Long lists of job advertisements can be as alluring as an ice cream cone on a hot summer day. They all look so darned good! But like ice cream, job advertisements can be sticky business. By asking just a few key questions, you can zoom through long lists of jobs and weed out the good from the bad quickly and easily.

Who is offering the job?

The first thing you need to note about any job advertisement is who is offering the job. If the company that's offering the job is not listed, you need to figure out why. The job may have been hard to fill, so the company passed it on to a third-party recruiter. If so, you should see the complete third-party company or name. If you don't see a full name, that's a red flag.

For example, browsing through Usenet, you see postings that read

```
USA, CA, Sunnyvale - Analog Designer, HEART Advertising
```

This posting is fine. It names a place, names a specific job, and lists a company name. In this case, HEART is a third-party firm that has been contracted to recruit candidates. This ad looks above-board.

Also browsing through Usenet, you come across postings such as the following:

```
C++ Programmers, afinza
```

The C++ Programmers is the generic listing, and afinza is the person who posted the job. It's very likely that afinza has posted a phony job. (I altered the name slightly, but I took this information from a real posting.) You don't see a job title or a company name, nor do you see a specific location for the job. This ad is a blatant attempt to scoop up resumes. (See the "Is this a real job?" section for more information on this subject.)

Does the job advertisement ask you for money?

If you're thinking about responding to a job advertisement that asks you for money, please let me persuade you to forget about that plan. No legitimate employer ever asks a candidate to fork over money to apply for a job. Ignore the requests.

How old are the offers?

Most job postings are updated daily, at least in theory. Thanks to the advent of efficient dating systems, old jobs may be continually updated to look newly opened. This isn't necessarily a problem. Some jobs are indeed hard to fill, and you shouldn't consider it a strike against a company if it hasn't been able to fill a job.

But if you're leery of jobs that have been open for too long, the trick is to track the job by requisition number. Dates may change, but requisition numbers don't. I've gone through databases and found jobs that have been open for more than a year by looking for requisition numbers that have been reposted over and over again.

Not all databases can handle a search by requisition number. But if you can search a database by requisition number, you can find true date information, as long as it hasn't been deleted. Just get a job's requisition number, type the requisition number in the search box, and click on the search button. The database typically pulls up the last few months of the posting history of that particular job.

Of course, you can always try the low-tech way of finding out how long a job has been open: Ask the recruiter or employer who posted the position!

Is this a real job?

Unfortunately, not every job advertisement that is currently online is a real job ad. Let me hasten to say that if you're searching a reliable database, it's much less likely that you'll run into a bum ad. But if you're searching an international database, Usenet, databases that carry Usenet job postings, or databases where posting a job is free, then your chances of running across a phony job ad increase.

When I mention phony ads to job seekers, they always ask me what the point of a phony ad is. The point is to haul in resumes. People used to post phony ads in newspapers, but newspaper advertising has gotten too expensive. So some of that old newspaper traffic has moved to the Web, particularly to Usenet.

Typically, the person who posts a phony ad is a third-party recruiter who is simply trying to find a certain type of candidate. The recruiter may not have a job for you at the moment, but, eventually, he or she probably will. The point is, unless you're going all-out for a job (see the Blowout search method in Chapter 2), you don't want to waste your time with phony ads.

Simply being aware that ads need to be verified is often protection enough. Here are the potential tip-offs to a phony ad:

✔ The job announcement is worded vaguely.

✔ No company name is listed.

✔ No physical address or phone number is listed; you see just an e-mail address or fax number.

✔ No requisition number appears for a job that is also worded vaguely.

✔ When you look at the job ad, you see statements like: "We are offering opportunities with top firms and are accepting resumes from candidates at all levels. Please e-mail your resume to jobs@phony.com or fax it to 800-000-0000. We have thousands of opportunities." These kinds of vague, general statements form the template for phony job ads.

Credible companies offer *specific* jobs in *specific* places. Credible companies also list their names, phone numbers, and physical addresses.

Here's a real-life example of a phony job ad. I pulled this phony ad from Usenet — the only changes I made were to the names and identifying information.

Phony job ad:

> A-Z Company and Associates, a huge search firm, is offering opportunities with top firms, in search of Technology Specialists. We are accepting resumes from candidates at all levels. Please email your resume to atoz@hugesearchfirm.com, or fax it to 800-000-0000. We have 100's of opportunities. Please respond ASAP we guarantee a response.

And here's a real-life example of a genuine ad. Notice the *huge* difference in the level of detail. Again, this is a real job ad, but I altered names and addresses.

Real job ad:

> Work for one of the fastest growing privately held Software Development companies in Chicago. In existence since 1985. Pioneered the Software found in luxury automobiles and Hertz rent-a-cars which have PCs in the car giving turn-by-turn route guidance to the driver. Currently the company is in an incredible growth mode, and it's anticipated that within the next 10 years every new automobile sold in the U.S., Europe, and Asia will have a PC built into it.
>
> Companies such as Microsoft and Intel have demonstrated great interest in making PCs in every car a reality because it opens up a whole new market to sell their products as well.

Still relatively small and young, everyone hired at this point is crucial to the future success of the firm. The environment is casual dress and a pool table and Fuse-ball table are in-house for the times when a break is needed from development. The sky is the limit.

Company offers competitive salary and comprehensive benefits package. Currently looking for career minded individuals with a foundation in C/UNIX. Candidates should have a degree in Computer Science or related field and a minimum of 2-years experience in any of the following: C++, large relational database, GUI tools, or Internet technology. Experience in full life cycle development, or Ph.D. would be a definite plus.

Qualified candidates should submit their resume in confidence to:

Marmot Associates, Attn.: Georgia Turander, 2304 W. Ernest, Suite 65790 Chicago, IL 90610

Using the Push Technology and Job Search Agent Page

Many employment Web sites now offer a corollary way of searching jobs: They let a job search agent do the searching for you. You usually find this dandy feature on its own page.

Essentially, a *job search agent* is a computer program that matches your requests to incoming jobs. The agent then sends the job announcements to your e-mail address, where you can look at the list of jobs at your leisure. (Note that you *do* need an e-mail address to sign up for a job search agent. Chapter 10 gives suggestions for signing up for a free e-mail account.)

The idea sounds great, doesn't it? Job search agents are handy, but no matter what an employment Web site claims, the truth of the matter is that a job search agent is a nice *extra,* a *bonus* search feature. A job search agent simply isn't smart enough to do all your job-search work for you — at least not yet.

Job search agents are great if you're just testing the job-search waters. If you don't need a job right away, then the slow rate of job search agents won't bother you. (Most agents send material once a week.) But if you're really serious about finding a job fast, you're best off visiting a database and conducting various keyword searches.

To give you a feel for job search agents, Figure 14-6 shows the job search agent page of the NationJob employment site. NationJob calls its agent Personal Job Scout, or P.J. Scout for short. It has given P.J. a folksy, friendly flair. P.J. Scout is one of the better job search agents currently available.

To use a job search agent, you need to fill out quite a few forms. Again, that's because you have to tell an agent exactly what to look for. Think of a job search agent like a keyword search that you do in advance. In Figure 14-7, you see a part of the form that you need to fill out to get P.J. Scout set up.

After you fill out and submit your agent form, it takes a while for the jobs to start coming your way. And even after the jobs do start coming your way, I should prepare you in advance: Many job seekers have been very disappointed with the results they got from job search agents.

Job search agents typically don't return enough results for most people, due in part to the fact that agent technology is very young. Poor results are also due to poor agenting techniques. (I can help you with that part! See the "Using agents effectively" section.)

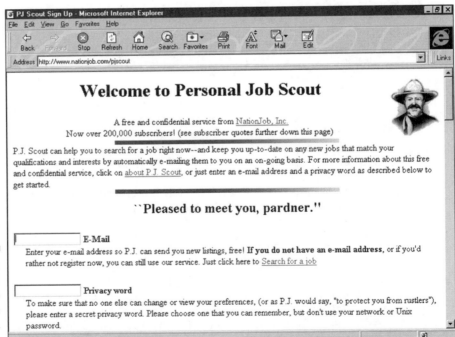

Figure 14-6:
The NationJob job search agent page.

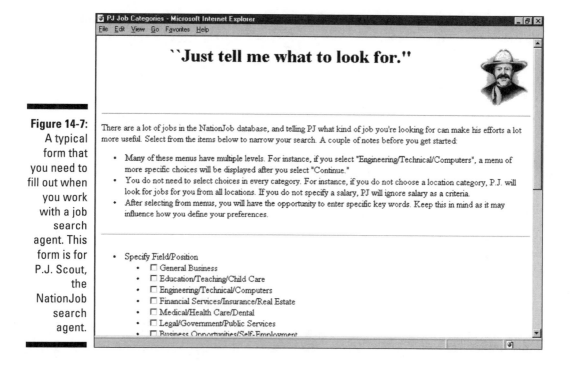

PJ Job Categories - Microsoft Internet Explorer

File Edit View Go Favorites Help

``Just tell me what to look for.''

There are a lot of jobs in the NationJob database, and telling PJ what kind of job you're looking for can make his efforts a lot more useful. Select from the items below to narrow your search. A couple of notes before you get started:

• Many of these menus have multiple levels. For instance, if you select "Engineering/Technical/Computers", a menu of more specific choices will be displayed after you select "Continue."
• You do not need to select choices in every category. For instance, if you do not choose a location category, P.J. will look for jobs for you from all locations. If you do not specify a salary, PJ will ignore salary as a criteria.
• After selecting from menus, you will have the opportunity to enter specific key words. Keep this in mind as it may influence how you define your preferences.

• Specify Field/Position
    • □ General Business
    • □ Education/Teaching/Child Care
    • □ Engineering/Technical/Computers
    • □ Financial Services/Insurance/Real Estate
    • □ Medical/Health Care/Dental
    • □ Legal/Government/Public Services
    • □ Business Opportunities/Self-Employment

Figure 14-7:
A typical form that you need to fill out when you work with a job search agent. This form is for P.J. Scout, the NationJob search agent.

Figure 14-8 shows my search agent results from P.J. Scout. I received 16 pages of over 1,000 job advertisements. (Keep in mind that I requested every single job from the agent.) Note that the job list you see in Figure 14-8 may look slightly different in your e-mail box, depending on what kind of e-mail software you use.

Using agents effectively

If you want to try an agent, here are some tips and suggestions that can help you be as effective as possible:

  ✔ **Search broadly the first time out.** When you set up your job search agent, err on the side of being too broad in scope. Many people, myself included, have received zero jobs from an agent. The problem is either that the employment database isn't all that great or that you have been too specific in your search terms. You can eliminate the too-specific problem by asking for all sorts of jobs to come your way and then narrowing down your selection as you get a feel for how the search agent operates and how good the job database is.

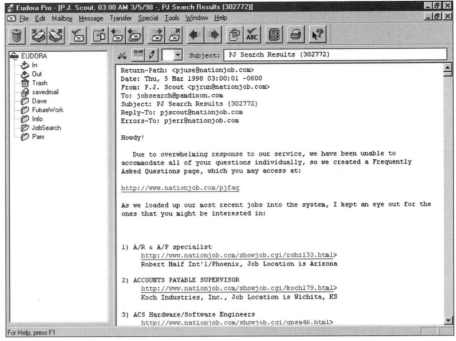

Figure 14-8:
The results
of a P.J.
Scout
agented
search.

✔ **Don't buy into the hype — literally.** You should never have to pay anything to use a job search agent. The best agents are free of charge.

✔ **Revisit your agent and tweak it at least once a month.** You can make an agent better by giving it instructions that tightly match what you want. If you notice that you're getting too few or too many job results from the agent, go back to your agent profile and add or delete a few keywords.

✔ **Understand the downside and upside of job search agents.** Agents are great tools if you're a passive job seeker — that is, if you're just keeping your eye out for a job in case something great comes along. But understand that using an agent is just like going to a job database and performing the same keyword search on the database every time you visit. That may be just what you want. Or maybe one search isn't enough. As long as you know the difference, there's no harm done.

A job search agent reality check

Some employment Web sites are using terms like *push technology, e-mail agents,* and *search agents* interchangeably. Actually, though, the terms aren't interchangeable. I normally wouldn't digress in a book about job searching to discuss details of technical terms such as push technology and search agents. But unfortunately, some employment Web sites are making *outrageous* claims about what they can do for you based on push technology and search agents.

A search agent is a component of a software program (or a piece of hardware) that automates tasks for you. The idea is to take away some of the drudgery of conducting the same tasks over and over again. A job search agent is simply an agent that collects your preferences, compares your preferences to a database, and

then collects what you want from the database and sends you an e-mail message listing the results. That's all there is to it.

Job search agents are meant to serve as a *convenience* to you. They are not revolutionary, nor are they better than you are at searching the database. And job search agents are *especially* not push technology!

In true push technology, a Web site literally pushes data to your computer *screen* (rather than to your e-mail account) via an Internet connection. Typically, you need to download proprietary software to use push technology. Though some job searching and employment Web sites truly do "push" information to you, many more don't. Don't believe everything you read!

Scrolling through the Resume Page

The resume page of an online database, if the database has a resume section, is where you can e-mail or post your resume. Typically, employers access resumes from a completely different page. As a job seeker, your main focus is on creating a resume, whereas employers access resumes to search them. In this section, I discuss only the job seeker's resume page.

Figure 14-9 is an example of an online resume page for job seekers; in this case, it's CareerPath.com's. CareerPath.com has a high-quality, high-confidentiality database where you control your resume at all times, which is explained to you right on the resume page.

In Figure 14-10, I scrolled down CareerPath.com's resume page so that you can see the form you need to fill out in order to post your resume online. Filling out such a form is pretty typical at resume pages. Resume forms can be as short as one page and as long as ten pages; the length depends on the site.

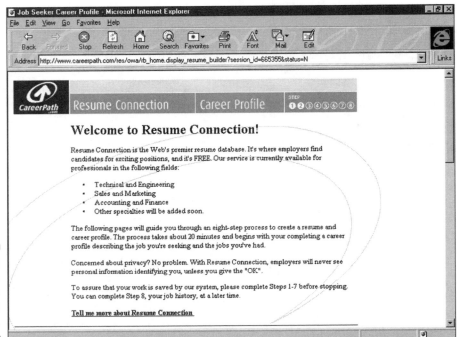

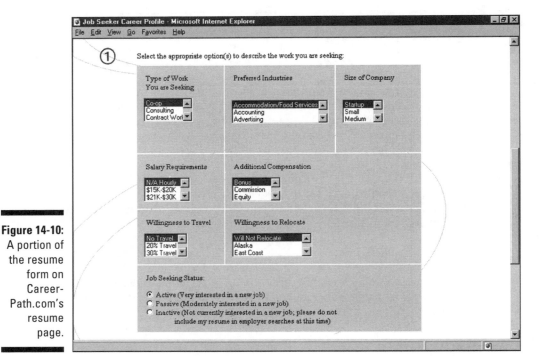

Unfortunately, not all databases seem to be as concerned about your privacy as CareerPath.com is. Resume sections of online employment sites contain *vast* quality differences. Some resume databases are blatantly open to the public; others are very private and afford you complete control of your resume. Currently, there's no rhyme or reason as to which employment sites are private and which aren't. You have to take each site on a case-by-case basis.

Short of calling the people who run the database, your best clue to any resume database is to read the resume page thoroughly. A good employment database explains to you on the resume page all the resume confidentiality and privacy policies. If you see no mention of privacy or explanations about who sees your resume, that's a very bad sign!

Unfortunately, being vigilant about your resume privacy is a lot of work, because there are no standards in the industry yet. You need to go through each database and decide for yourself whether it affords you the level of privacy you need.

Be *very* cautious about where you post your resume. I talked with a job seeker recently who was fired *on the spot* after his boss found his resume online on an open, or public, database. He worked in a sensitive technical area, so his employer had every legal right to let him go. After all, the employer had proof that his employee was looking for a job with a competitor. Don't let this happen to you. Only post your resume where you have complete control over who sees it.

Resume red flags

Chapter 7 includes many examples of how to check on your resume privacy. For now, here are some big warning signs that a resume database should be avoided. If you post to a resume database with any of these signs, know up front that anyone may be able to see your resume:

- ✔ Unclear cobranding agreements
- ✔ Open resume database (anyone can access the database)
- ✔ A registration procedure that anyone could get through
- ✔ No password protection
- ✔ Resume pass-around (your resume may be shared with other databases as part of a joint agreement)

Resume privacy checklist

Before you send your resume anywhere, ask yourself the following questions. Or better yet, ask the site to which you want to send your resume!

- ✔ Is the resume database password-protected? Who has the password? (Hopeful answer: Yes, it is password-protected, and only credible employers have the password.)

- ✔ Which companies see my resume? (You'll need to get a list, which should be available.)

- ✔ Is my resume passed around by those companies? (You'll want to hear a big "no" on this question.)

- ✔ Is my resume shared with another database or group of databases? (Again, you want to hear a resounding "no" to this question.)

- ✔ Does my resume get sent to another database *at any time?* (Sometimes resumes are exchanged as a one-time deal, as opposed to an ongoing sharing arrangement. You want assurance that your resume is never sold at any time or shared, even for one-time deals.)

- ✔ What confidentiality arrangements can I make for my resume information? (Answers will vary.)

- ✔ Is there a cobranding agreement that may influence the privacy of my resume? (You want to hear about all cobranding agreements up front and make a decision based on the information you receive.)

Looking at the Contact Page

The contact page of an employment site is simply the page where the site lists contact information. I personally like to see a phone number and a business address listed in addition to an e-mail address. After all, employment databases are businesses, not private home pages.

To me, it's a warning sign if a database won't disclose its place of business. I've found that if an employment database doesn't list an address, typically it's because the database is being run from an apartment or a basement in someone's house. Though many wonderful businesses can and do start in basements, you may not want to be looking for your dream job in a start-up database site.

Chapter 15

Dealing with the Results of Your Online Job Search

*F*iguring out how to get a job online means a whole lot more than just going online, popping your letter-perfect resume on the Web, and waiting for the phone to ring. Though all those activities are part and parcel of getting a job, an online job search involves a critical follow-up component, and that's what this chapter is all about.

A big part of what has changed about job searching is that the phone has become a critical "back-end" part of the job search. This is *particularly* true of an online job search.

Even if you have a great resume, even if you have put it in all the right spots, and even if you're inundated with 100 phone calls as a result, you still have to "win" the phone calls that you receive in order to land interviews and ultimately get a job.

This chapter steers you through the untamed wilds of what to do *after* you've done all your preliminary online job-search work. When your phone starts ringing, you'll be ready. And when you start "winning" your phone calls and getting lucrative offers, this chapter can help you figure out how to narrow your choices and find the best fit for your future.

Important Preparation Tips for Everyone

Before you post your first resume online or e-mail your first resume to an employer, you want to be thinking ahead to how you're going to handle the phone calls that you receive.

One of the unique aspects of an online job search is the amazing response that just a few simple actions can generate. In a traditional job search, you may send out one or two resumes a day, or even a few per week. That means you get one or two phone calls per week, if that.

But in an online job search, everything moves quickly and tends to get multiplied. Instead of getting one call a week later in response to a resume, you may get 20 calls on the day you put your resume online. Twenty calls a day may sound wonderful right now, but when you're actually fielding the calls, that kind of intensity can be overwhelming. That's why you need to be ready ahead of time.

The following preparation tips will see you safely through a potential onslaught.

Preparatory phone tips

How you handle yourself during phone calls from potential employers can make or break your chances of getting a job. Here are some basic preparations that you can make now as you get your online job search underway:

✔ If you listed your home phone number as a contact number, be sure that you have voice mail or a high-quality answering machine set up to handle the calls. If at all possible, get a messaging system that lets you store at least 30 messages, if not more.

✔ Make sure that your answering machine or voice-mail message sounds professional. If you have a penchant for fun voice messages, hold back during your job search. Settle for a sedate message that simply states your name, your phone number, and when you expect to be available to return calls. A teacher I know lost a job offer because the school that had planned to hire her found her voice mail message unprofessional. (The school had called her to follow up on the final paperwork for the job offer, and then retracted the offer a day later. When my friend asked why, they gave her the news about her message, which she had forgotten all about.)

✔ If you've given out your work number as a contact number, well, that was a mistake. You need to redirect calls to your home number or schedule an off-work time to call people back. Don't take calls during work hours — it's an unfair use of your current employer's time, and the person talking with you will note that.

✔ Get rid of call waiting, at least during your job search. Call waiting may be convenient for you, but it's a horrible distraction and is flat-out annoying to the person on the other end of the line. Get voice mail instead. That way, you won't miss any incoming phone calls.

✔ Write a telephone script for yourself so that you're at ease talking about the important points of your background and experience. Try to anticipate the questions you may receive on the phone, and jot down answers in advance. This preparation can help you enormously when the calls start coming fast and furious.

Preparatory organization tips

You have about three to five phone rings to get organized before you talk to a caller. That gives you an average of five to ten seconds to be settled and ready to roll. Because no one could rescue a pen, paper, resumes, charts, and job announcements from a chaotic heap in that amount of time, it's important for you to be totally organized well in advance of any incoming call.

I can always tell when someone at the other end of the phone line is scrambling and shuffling for information. I bet you can, too. Not only can you hear the papers rustling, but you also can hear the discomfort in the person's voice.

I know that obtaining the self-discipline to get and stay organized may be difficult for you. But it's worth it, particularly in a high-speed online job search.

The following tips have helped even the most disorganized job searchers stay ready for rapid-fire or unexpected phone calls:

✔ Print out every single job advertisement that you respond to. Write the date you sent your resume right on the printout. Also write down the URL of the online database or Web site where you found it. Always write the information in the same place so that you don't have to scout to figure out what you did. The top-right corner is a good choice.

✔ At the top of every job advertisement that you print out, write the contact name and information in red or another very obvious contrasting color. You want to do this so that you aren't skimming the job ad for the person's name when that person calls you. As you wildly search for bits of pertinent information, the person on the other end of the line is talking — and you may miss critical information.

✔ If you sent a resume to a company Web site, print out the appropriate Web page and write on it the date and the name of the person to whom you sent your resume.

✔ If you use several versions of your resume (longer, shorter, more detailed, and so on), place the version of your resume that you used *with* the particular job ad. Staple the two items together!

✔ If you've done extra research on a company that you sent a resume to, place that research with the job advertisement or Web page printout.

✔ Keep all your job advertisements, resumes, and company Web page printouts in a folder next to the phone where you take your screening calls. If you take your calls at more than one phone, consider making a double set of printouts and keeping them by each phone.

✔ Keep a stack of fill-in-the-blank forms ready to use when a screener calls. For every call, fill in your form and file it with the pertinent job ad or Web site printout (see the next section for information about the forms).

✔ Keep the script that you wrote next to the phone (see the "Preparatory phone tips" section earlier in this chapter).

What to Do After the Phone Starts Ringing . . . or Not

As soon as you post your resume online, be prepared for the phone to start ringing within 24 hours. Even if the phone doesn't ring, you need to be ready for it at any time. I talked with a recent college graduate who had to wait a month to get her first phone call. Though she was surprised to get the call, she had prepared for it.

The bottom line is that if you can't "win" the phone calls that you receive, then you won't land a job. In an online job search, recruiters move quickly through online resumes. They pick up the phone and call the people they're interested in. Once.

Here's what you can do to make that call count.

Get as much information as possible from the caller

When the phone rings, the screener usually tries to get as much information as possible from you. The idea is to see how good a fit you are for the position. A screener can be a person working in the human resources department of a company, a third-party recruiter, an in-house recruiter, or, if you're lucky, a hiring vice president or manager. If your resume is red-hot, the caller will push for an interview immediately. Of course, you'll be ready for the questions. But you should also have a few questions of your own to ask, even during the very first phone call from a screener.

Here's a list of basic information to get from your screening phone call:

- **The recruiter's or employer's name:** Remember to note gender in cases of unusual names.

- **Contact information:** Get an e-mail address, phone number, and fax number right away. Don't wait until the end of the phone call, when the screener may have lost interest in you. Nab the info up front so that you can send a follow-up e-mail immediately.

- **The name of the company offering the job:** You may be dealing with a third-party recruiter, so be sure to have the name of the company actually offering the job before you hang up.

- **Salary information:** Sometimes the best time to get salary information out of people is right up front during the screening call. This is particularly true of third-party recruiters, who will almost always give salary information. If you aren't talking to a recruiter, you may want to wait until the caller brings up the salary issue.

- **Relocation information:** Where is the job located? Find out right away if the job involves relocation. If you're willing to relocate, ask about moving expenses.

- **Job title:** Make sure that it's entry-level or senior — whatever you're aiming for. If you're a senior engineer, for example, you don't want to pursue a junior-level job.

- **Job responsibilities:** Pin down this information as tightly as possible. Get specifics.

I recommend that you create a simple form that helps you to collect information every time the phone rings — kind of like a phone message form, except this is a job phone-call form! That way, you won't get flustered during a conversation and hang up without getting the information that you need to make a good decision.

To make a form, just create a fill-in-the-blank form using word-processing software and print out as many forms as you need. Of course, you want to put your forms in a safe place, preferably in your job-search notebook. You'll make your life easier if you print your forms on three-hole-punched paper. You can pop the forms right into a binder so that individual sheets of paper won't stray away into drifts of desk clutter. Your form can look something like this:

Screener's name: _____

Company the screener represents: _____

Screener's position: _____

Contact information: _____

       Phone number: _____

       E-mail address: _____

       Company Web site URL: _____

Calling about what job opportunity: _____

With what company or organization: _____

Location of the job: _____

Salary range (if the screener is a recruiter): _____

Job title: (List specific title as found in the job ad, if available.) _____

Primary job responsibilities: _____

_____

Approximate date the job would begin: _____

Screener's primary area of questioning: _____

_____

I need to follow up on: _____

_____

_____

Make a quick decision based on the facts at hand

After you get on the phone with a screener, you need to decide within a minute or two whether you want to pursue the job opportunity you're discussing. If you hear any information that doesn't sit well with you, then your best bet is to get the recruiter's contact information and politely tell the caller that the opportunity isn't quite right for you. Of course, you can let the recruiter know what type of position would be a better fit.

If, for example, you hear that a job opportunity is in Alaska and you want to work in a warm climate, be honest and up-front about it. Or if a recruiter pitches you a job at a company with which you've had a bad experience, just tell the recruiter that the job isn't the right fit. (Don't say anything negative during a screening phone call.)

On the other hand, if the job you're hearing about is a good fit, immediately push for an interview. You need to be persuasive and quick about it (see "Work to land the interview" for pointers). Keep in mind that, on average, a recruiter has only about three to seven minutes to talk with you.

Work to land the interview

Your number-one priority during a screening call is to land an interview. I can't say it enough: You must "win" the screening call to get a job!

If you did your prep work, then you have your job-search material, such as resumes and Web printouts, by the phone. As soon as you get the call, turn to your information and scan it quickly.

But realize that if you put your resume on a database where many employers can search it, you may get calls from companies to which you haven't specifically sent your resume. When these "cold" calls come in, whip out your phone-screening form and get the information you need right away. Make a quick decision about whether the job is right for you, and then *concentrate on selling yourself to the caller.*

As far as selling yourself, when I asked recruiters for phone-screening advice for job seekers, I got an overwhelming response: "Tell them not to be negative!" Everything that comes out of your mouth during a screening phone call needs to be positive.

If you had a bad experience at your last job, let it go. If you're looking for a job because you hate your current boss, let that information go unrevealed. Were you fired? Don't tell the screener. Get the interview! Say only good things about yourself and your work experiences.

Another tip that can help you steer the call your way is to stay focused on job-related information during your conversation. Ask pertinent questions, sound enthusiastic, and keep the conversation focused on how your current skills match the current job that you and the screener are discussing. Come right out and ask to schedule an interview. Say something like:

- ✔ "This position sounds like a perfect fit. Can we schedule an appointment?"
- ✔ "My background in _____, _____, and _____ sounds like it's just what you're looking for. Can we schedule an appointment to discuss this further?"
- ✔ "The position you've described during our phone conversation is just right for my goals and current skills. Can we schedule an interview?"

Remember, sometimes half the battle is just getting your foot in the door, and sometimes you need to push a little bit to get your foot in there.

Send a follow-up note

In the end, follow-up e-mail is what separates you from the masses. It also makes or breaks your job search. Fortunately, e-mail provides you with a terrific means to follow up unobtrusively on screening phone calls.

In today's corporate culture, calling recruiters and employers is pretty much a no-no. People simply don't have the time to take phone calls from job candidates. Just as the online job search has increased the volume of your responses, the online job search has increased employers' volume of job candidates. So you need to be very careful about how you follow up.

Here's my advice: After you receive a screening phone call, no matter how well or how badly it went, if you still want the job, go ahead and fire off an e-mail immediately. Keep your e-mail very short, to just one or two power paragraphs.

You want to communicate the following ideas in your follow-up e-mail:

- ✔ You listened attentively to the caller.
- ✔ Your skills are just right for the position you discussed.
- ✔ You are an open, flexible, energetic, and warm person who is very capable of working on a team.

Also reaffirm any questions or points the caller seemed particularly interested in. And, as always, follow good e-mail style and etiquette (see Chapter 10).

Dealing with a "no thanks"

Somewhere along the line, you may get a "no thanks" from an employer who has interviewed you or talked to you on the phone. You may not enjoy this advice, but I recommend that you send a polite e-mail follow-up after a rejection. It doesn't have to be long — just a quick note that reaffirms your desire to work with that person in the future.

"Why bother?" you may ask. The reason is simple. The workforce today is extremely mobile. The person who didn't hire you today may hire you tomorrow, at a different company or maybe even at the same company at a different time.

The important thing to know is that people move on, but they do carry their memories of how you responded to a "no thanks" along with them. A follow-up note to a rejection always makes an impression because it's so rare. And an e-mailed note is not intrusive in the least. You have no risk in sending it, not even to your somewhat bruised and battered ego.

If you follow up scrupulously in your job search, you never know what good things may happen. Perhaps the candidate to whom you "lost" the job won't work out. In one or two months, you may get that job offer that you just lost out on. Or another position more closely matching your skills may open up. Your good follow-up notes may well have placed you in first position for new jobs that come along.

The follow-up is just one little e-mail. You have a lot to gain and absolutely nothing to lose. Here are some samples to get you started (for more samples, see Chapter 10):

✔ "I was impressed with the company's emphasis on [name a prime point from the interview, like teamwork, ingenuity, or productivity]. Even though I'm not the right fit for your company right now, I would enjoy working with you in the future."

✔ "Although I was not the right fit for your company at this time, I wanted to reaffirm how much I enjoyed meeting with you and discussing the goals of the company. I admired and enjoyed the corporate structure and culture at [name the company] and still look forward to the possibility of working there sometime in the future."

✔ "I appreciate the time you spent interviewing me and answering my questions about [name the company]. I realize that I wasn't the best fit for the job you just filled, but I'm impressed with the company's [name something about the company you like — vision, mission, goals, and so on]. I hope to work with you in the future."

Dealing with special circumstances

An online job search can turn up results on both ends of the spectrum — that is, too many results or too few. This section gives you some tips to help you deal with both sets of circumstances.

Too many responses

If you have high-level skills in a high-demand industry, you may receive an extraordinary amount of response to your resume posting. Currently, there's a much ballyhooed shortage of certain types of professionals. In fact, some skills are in such high demand that several major U.S. companies (such as Microsoft) have gone before Congress to ask that more foreign workers in certain skill areas be allowed into the country.

Current high-demand skill areas include the following:

✔ Programming skills, particularly in C, C++, Visual Basic, and Java

✔ Database skills, particularly in Oracle, Sybase, Informix, and SAP

✔ Systems administration skills, particularly UNIX and Windows NT

✔ Network skills, particularly Novell and Microsoft NT

✔ Engineering skills, particularly electrical engineers and ASICS designers

If you have expertise in any of the areas I just listed, you may receive an absolutely astonishing response to your online job search. This may be particularly true if you post your resume on an open resume database. I talked to one man who received approximately 24 calls a day for four months because he had posted his resume on Usenet. Needless to say, he was ready to tear his hair out from frustration.

The best way to avoid this frustration is to post only on resume databases where *you* control your resume. But if, for some reason, you want a lot of phone calls, your next-best preparation is to get a dedicated second or third phone line set up for your job search. That way, when you're ready to end your job search, you can immediately end the phone calls, or at least leave the phone calls to your message machine.

If you didn't take any precautions and find yourself getting way too many phone calls, these tips can help you deal effectively with the flow of calls:

✔ Take advantage of the phone calls, at least for a while. You may want to have access to all those recruiters' names and numbers sometime in the future. Your first job is to collect pertinent contact information and store it in your job-search notebook. (You *are* keeping one, right?)

✔ After you collect contact information, ask all the people who call you *where* they found your resume. That way, you can track down your resume and remove it from circulation.

✔ Ask the people who call you to remove your resume from consideration and from their personal databases. This can help you a lot, as some resumes are passed around extensively for about one to three months.

✔ If you have already accepted a job offer, have collected a notebook full of fresh recruiting contacts, and just can't stand any more phone calls, put a message on your voice mail or answering machine stating that you've accepted a position. Give your family and friends an alternate phone number. Your phone calls will subside in about four months.

✔ Above all, be very polite to the recruiters who call you. You never know who you may work with in the future.

Not enough responses

You've done everything correctly. You created a great electronic resume, and you carefully posted it on a dozen employment sites. But it's been a month, and you haven't received a single bite.

Without talking with you individually, I can't tell exactly what has gone awry. But I've talked with a lot of people whose online job searches don't produce results, and I've learned that the problems often break down to a couple of trouble spots.

The big job-search problems typically roost in the following areas:

- ✓ **A resume with references' contact information included:** You may be shocked to learn this, but if you've been including your references' contact information, get it off your resume immediately! A favorite recruiter tactic is to call your references and hire *them*.

  Why? Typically, your references are the people you've worked *for*. That means your references work in the same industry you do but supposedly have a more advanced skill set. Don't unwittingly send recruiters and employers to your references and old bosses!

- ✓ **Insufficient or incorrect keywords:** If you're applying to Fortune 100 and 500 companies, you're probably sending your resume to a resume database system. That means you're at the mercy of your skill with keywords. If you aren't getting bites, it's probably the direct result of your keyword choices. Be sure to read Chapters 5 and 6 for help in this area.

- ✓ **Spelling errors on the resume:** Don't let this happen to you! Have a friend read your resume for spelling errors that you may not have caught. A glaring error almost always lands you on the reject pile.

- ✓ **Missing career objective:** Make sure that you have a concise, clear career objective placed near the top of your resume. Busy recruiters rely on finding a career objective to help fit you into positions. If you don't have a career objective, recruiters can easily pass over your resume in favor of resumes that do contain career objectives. See Chapter 6 for details on writing a career objective.

- ✓ **Missing, mistyped, or misplaced contact information:** For whatever reason, people tend to read and reread their resumes, but not the contact information on their resumes. Watch for typos in your phone number or e-mail address.

  Another possibility is that you've put your contact information in an unusual place — for example, at the end of your resume. If you've placed contact information anywhere but at the top of your resume, move it immediately.

- ✓ **Area code splits:** If you live in a metropolitan area, make sure that your resume doesn't have your old area code listed in the contact information. My area code changes constantly, thanks to area code splitting (area code splitting is when an existing area code is split into two area codes). I can barely keep my business cards updated, and I constantly find documents containing my old area code!

For most people, when they hear a recording stating that your area code has changed, your entire resume seems suspect. The thought is: "If the area code is different, then I bet this resume is out-of-date." Be sure to take care of this small but important change.

✔ **Employment problems:** Beyond any technical problem with your resume, you may have a skill set that isn't in demand anymore. Or you may have job-hopped a bit too much or even gotten fired or spent time in prison. Please refer to Max Messmer's excellent book, *Job Hunting For Dummies*. Also, try Joyce Lain Kennedy's *Resumes For Dummies*. (Both books are published by IDG Books Worldwide, Inc.) I'm not just recommending these books because they're *...For Dummies* books; I've read the books and I like them. Plus, both books contain specific and detailed help for your situation.

The Next Prep Step: Preparing for Your Interview

If you win your screening phone call, you'll be invited to an interview. Hooray! The interview may be over the phone, on a videoconference system, or in person. No matter how the interview takes place, your job is to prepare diligently for your interview.

In Chapter 9, I discuss in detail the ways you can use the Web to prepare for your interview. Here, I want to mention that, while you prepare for interviews, you may still be fielding screening phone calls from recruiters. You don't know how your interviews will turn out, so keep taking the calls until you've accepted an offer.

Several job hunters have told me that they found the process of keeping all the information about recruiters and interviewers organized to be overwhelming. At this point in your job search, keeping a neat chart of who you talk to and about what is crucial. You also want to chart who you sent follow-up notes to and when. Refer to Chapter 2 for strategies that can get you through your job search intact.

Finally! Figuring Out What to Do When the Job Offers Start Rolling In

At long last — the moment you have been working toward and waiting for arrives. You get a job offer. You may even get several job offers. All of a sudden, the golden moment of being offered a job turns into something not quite as shiny and pretty. Now you have to make a decision.

Depending on your decision-making style, making a final decision either will feel great or will make you feel queasy and perhaps physically ill. Neither decision-making style is better than the other; they're just different approaches.

To eliminate job offers, here's a method that I've shared with many people that really helps narrow the field. All you need to do is work through each elimination step very honestly. By the time you reach the end of the steps, you should be much closer to an answer. (But it only works if you're absolutely honest with your answers!)

Ground Zero: How you were treated during the interview

Ground Zero involves your interview experience. As far as I'm concerned, if you detected even a twinge of rudeness during your interview, pass on the opportunity. Think about it: An interview is like a first date. Everyone is on his or her best behavior, or at least that's the way it's supposed to be.

If the people who interviewed you displayed arrogance or impatience, asked potentially discriminating questions, were invasive with your private life, or in any way gave you pause, *cross them off the list.* Just imagine how they may treat you after the "honeymoon."

My husband once went through a tough interview process at a company. Because the job was extremely competitive, he chalked up the tough interviews to the nature of the job. But after he got the job and started working at the company, he realized that the interview style simply reflected the corporate culture. His experience is not at all unusual! You may as well learn from it without having to go through it yourself.

Note: The only exception to this elimination rule is temporary help or contractors. Temporary workers don't count in the Ground Zero evaluation because, as outsiders, they don't represent corporate culture.

Elimination Round One: Fiscal stability

If you had good interview experiences, then look at the company's fiscal stability. If you did your homework for your interviews, you probably already know the answer to this question. (If you didn't check out the company before the interview, read Chapter 9 to get the details on how you can get company backgrounds through online research.)

Assessing whether a merger or a buyout is in the company's future is especially important. Again, check Chapter 9 for details about doing this type of checking online.

Elimination Round Two: Corporate personality

Elimination Round Two is crucial to your long-term success. The brilliant analyst Robert L. Dilenschneider (who wrote the well-known book *Power and Influence*) says that if you don't fit in a particular corporate culture, then you need to get out of it as quickly as possible and find a place where you do fit. The fact of the matter is that if you don't find a good fit, your career will suffer.

It doesn't matter how good you are at what you do. If the fit is off, you'll be passed over for promotions and perhaps laid off — even if you do a good job. You may be viewed as an outsider.

During your interview, have your radar switched to the "on" position for determining corporate personality. Even if you weren't assessing corporate personality during your interview, you can probably remember a good many details that can help you figure it out.

Here are some clues that can help you determine corporate personality:

- ✔ What is the work atmosphere like? Is it laid back, formal, energetic, eccentric, warm, structured?
- ✔ How do the people at your level dress? Does their style match yours, or are the people far more casual or dressy than you?
- ✔ Will you be working in or managing a group, team, or department, or will you be on your own?
- ✔ How many people will you report to on a daily basis?
- ✔ If you're managing, how many people will you be managing?
- ✔ How close of tabs will people keep on you? Will you need to fill out weekly, monthly, or daily reports?
- ✔ How many meetings and what kinds of meetings will you be involved in? Will you meet with your team or with your boss on a regular basis?
- ✔ How much public interface does the job involve? Does the amount of interface suit you?

Elimination Round Three: Salary, training, benefits, and cost of living

Salary is a basic question that most people can figure out pretty quickly. To help you along, the Internet Directory section at the back of this book includes a section called "Interview Preparation." In that section, you can find an entry called the Salary Calculator (www2.homefair.com/calc/ salcalc.html), which you can use to check salaries according to where in the country you want to work. With this online tool, you can quickly see that the high salary you get paid in Alaska may not go very far when you factor in your heating bill!

Also, take training budgets very seriously. With the right training, you can significantly upgrade your resume. Conversely, with a lack of training, you can stagnate. To find out about training budgets, simply ask the interviewer how much money or time is allocated for employee training per year. Usually, you hear an answer like "We send our employees to four classes a year" or "We send key employees to management classes." What you don't want to hear is that the company has no training budget.

Elimination Round Four: Your place in the corporate structure

Don't underestimate Round Four. Some companies are much more open than others to placing you where you want to be and to letting you move around after you get there. For example, I'm most comfortable in an environment where I have room for advancement according to my level of expertise. I simply wouldn't be comfortable working at a job in which I could "see the ceiling."

Determine what you need in terms of movement, either lateral (jumping to a similar position in another department) or vertical (moving up the ladder). Also think about how the job you're considering enhances your resume. If necessary, call the person who interviewed you for clarification on this crucial point. And above all, be honest with yourself.

Elimination Round Five: Personal reconnaissance

If an offer has made it all the way through Round Four, then you need to do some personal reconnaissance — otherwise known as investigative gossip. At this point, you want to hop online and get the buzz about the company that you're considering working for. Believe me, it's out there. All you have to do is tap into it. For details on buzz-tapping techniques, see Chapter 11.

Without ever having stepped foot into any one of dozens of local companies, I can tell you detailed employment gossip about them. I've culled my investigative gossip from former employees, current employees, and interview subjects. My take is that when more than ten trustworthy people are saying the same thing about a company, what they are saying is legitimate "buzz." Buzz can't be taken as fact, but you should weigh it in light of your experiences and the facts you uncover about the company.

Let me give you an example. A good friend of mine recently changed jobs. She had three excellent job offers, and she went through each elimination round. In Round Five, she discovered that *none* of the current employees at one of the companies was happy in the work environment. Whoosh! One of her choices went right off her list. The other two companies had positive buzz but different corporate cultures. Eventually, the deciding factor for my friend was the culture. Happily, her investigative gossip protected her from an unhappy working environment.

Elimination Round Six: Your gut-level feeling

About seven years ago, I became consumed with a question: How does intuition influence the decision-making process? Is it viable? In my research, I came across a book, *Anatomy of Reality: Merging of Intuition and Reason,* written by the famous researcher Jonas Salk. In his book, he detailed how intuition was a primary aspect of how he conducted his scientific research and found the vaccine. It was good to know that among the test tubes, the very human notion of intuition was still a big part of the picture.

As far as your decision about a job, I encourage you to listen to what your own intuition is telling you. If the facts are screaming "yes!" and your intuition is giving you a bellyache and saying "no," you may want to spend a little more time figuring out what's causing the discrepancy.

Unfortunately, I can't offer any specific advice in this area, other than to tell you that intuition is typically a good guide to corporate fit more than anything else. Sometimes, going with a great fit at a smaller company in a less glamorous locale is better than going with an okay fit at a major company in a great location. My instinct is always to go with the very best corporate fit possible.

Part V
The Part of Tens

In this part . . .

Searching for a job that fits your personality and skills ever-so-perfectly takes generous amounts of quality time. Every moment that you invest in your job search is definitely worth it; why not beat the clock whenever you can?

In this part, I help you shave precious time off your job-search efforts by giving you meaty, condensed lists of advice from job hunting insiders. The chapters in this part contain road-tested tips about beating the odds, advice from employers, answers to the most frequently asked questions, and time-wasters to avoid.

With the information you find in this part, you may well find yourself landing a job in no time flat!

Chapter 16

Ten Ways to Improve Your Online Job-Search Odds

- -

- -

Sometimes even the smallest resume enhancements and job-search technique tips can make big differences to employers and recruiters. Recruiters, who see hundreds of resumes a day, have a keen sense for recognizing when a candidate has put forth extra effort.

Make no mistake about it — in a job search, extra effort *counts.* You can bet that going that extra mile will get you farther and boost your odds of landing a good job in a very positive way.

In this chapter, I identify ten terrific things that you can do right away to increase your chances of landing not just any job, but the job you want more than anything else.

Have a Three-Second Resume

I know that you've slaved over your resume, checking and rechecking every point. (At least, I'm hoping that you checked and rechecked everything!) But the annoying truth is that your perfect resume has one last hurdle to clear: the three-second scan test.

Just about any decent headhunter will tell you (usually off the record) that making a decision about an individual resume takes no longer than three seconds.

Three seconds! Time it for yourself. Look at your resume for just three seconds. Count "one thousand one, one thousand two, one thousand three" out loud, and then look away. Now you have a clear picture of the extent of your typical resume exposure.

What are the lessons here?

- ✓ Put your name at the top of the resume — don't bury it at the end or put it in teeny print off in a corner.
- ✓ Include an appropriate, very short career objective under your name.
- ✓ Use concise, headline-style sentences to break up your work experience.
- ✓ Make your resume one page if you can, two pages only if you have to, and three pages *tops*. I must warn you: When you're sending out electronic resumes, you're much better off creating a one-page resume with no frills. After you get the call from an employer, you can send a longer, more detailed resume (which the employer will probably request).

For more information about electronic resumes, refer to Chapters 5, 6, and 7.

Hand-Tailor Each Resume

So you're all set. Your electronic resume is a work of polished perfection. It passes all the tests, even the three-second test (discussed in the preceding section).

Now, to really ensure your chances of landing the job that you have your heart set on, go through and tailor your resume for *one* particular job. No way can one resume fit every single job announcement. Just as a real-life tailor fits clothing to just one person at a time, you need to tailor your resume for just one job at a time if you want the best odds.

Try these strategies:

- ✓ Tweak the wording of your career objective to reflect the exact position you're applying for.
- ✓ Make the language you use in your resume subtly reflect the language of the job posting. Use the same words, or the same types of words.

> ✔ Look at the company Web site — no, *scour* the company Web site —
> for insight into the corporate culture. Then reflect the culture in your
> cover letter and your resume. Is the company casual? Formal? Is the
> company hip or is it staid? Figure it out and use that angle.

I agree that tailoring each resume that you e-mail to a company takes more
time and effort. But if you want to improve your odds, honing your resume
to focus on one job at a time is a great way of winning all bets.

Spell-Check Your Spell Checker

You've heard the advice before: Run your resume, cover letters, e-mail
correspondence, and Web pages through a spell checker before you send
them, post them, or otherwise put them into public view. Well, I have a
better bit of advice for you. Yes, definitely spell-check your documents. But
also spell-check your spell checker.

Not too long ago, I wrote an important letter, which I rigorously read, reread,
and spell-checked. But knowing from experience how easy it is to miss the
most blatant errors, I let the letter sit for a day before I sent it out.

When I returned to the letter the next day, I read it with fresh eyes, and
voilà! I hadn't spelled any words incorrectly, but my spell checker, in its
hyper-helpfulness, had altered a word that I didn't want altered. The new
word didn't make any sense in the sentence. I was, once again, happy that I
had spell-checked my spell checker!

In your job search, don't let an assertive spell checker undo your best
efforts. If you can't wait a day before sending your resumes and other
written job-search correspondence, then have a second person read your
work for errors. No one should lose a good opportunity over a correctly
spelled word that's in the wrong place, but it happens every day.

Be Savvy about Employer Resume Software

If you want to ace the competition, understand that almost every time you
mail your resume to a mid- to large-sized corporation, you're mailing your
resume straight into the digital clutches of a giant resume database.

If you understand certain key points about dealing with employers' internal resume databases, you can radically improve your job-search odds:

- ✔ You must write your resume so that a recruiter searching the resume database can find you. (See Chapter 6 for how-to information.)

- ✔ If you fax your resume to an employer, you significantly decrease your chances of getting your personal information into the database without errors. Faxed resumes are of lower scannable quality than paper resumes and are of much lower quality than e-mailed resumes. (See Chapters 5, 6, and 7 for more information about this topic.)

- ✔ If you mail or fax a heavily *formatted* resume, which means that it contains lots of pretty fonts, fancy layouts, bullets, and graphics, then you won't make it into the resume system without errors, if you make it in at all. This is due to the way resume scanning software works. Again, see Chapter 6 for more information.

- ✔ You need to include every shred of information that a recruiter might possibly request on your *resume,* versus your cover letter. For instance, your skills, recent work experience, and even contact information must also appear on your resume. This is because most resume tracking systems do not store cover letters the same way as resumes! Therefore, spend your energy on your resume first and foremost. Understand that recruiters often read cover letters second, only after they have read your resume.

Be Employed

Please don't be offended by my heading! I know good and well that you're looking for a job; otherwise, you wouldn't be reading this book. But I also know that now more than ever before, employers are more likely to hire someone who already has a job.

If you're currently employed, great! Your biggest job is to find the *right* job to move to. Employers keep telling me that they're looking for someone who is not desperate, someone who is coming to a job because he or she wants the job, not because he or she needs it. Giving an employer the appearance that you're looking for the perfect fit (and not just any old job) is to your advantage.

If you're not employed right now and haven't had the best of luck in your search, take heart. If you need a job pronto, check out temporary staffing options or contract employment. (See the temporary and contract job listing section in the Internet Directory at the back of this book. There, you can find numerous places to start looking for temporary employment.) With a temp job, you'll lose that desperate air in a jiffy. (I talked to one engineer who took three contract jobs over the course of one year while he waited for just the right job to come his way. He found his perfect job, by the way.)

If you're a new college grad, I especially recommend a stint either as an intern or as a temp to help you build your resume while you search for the job you dreamed of while you sweated through four years or more of exams and deadlines. You needn't worry — start getting your name out in the marketplace, and you'll get hired in no time.

Prepare for Phone Interviews — Right Away!

Typically, when your resume generates interest with a prospective employer, you get a phone call from that company. You need to be ready for those phone calls.

Let me warn you — an online job search is typically very effective. You may get far more phone calls than you're expecting. If you apply for 15 different positions, you want to make very sure that you can sound intelligent if you hear from all 15 recruiters in one day.

All too often, employers tell me that otherwise wonderful candidates who looked good on paper failed their phone test. You can better your odds dramatically by preparing yourself for the phone test before the phone ever rings.

Here are some steps you can take to clinch your job-search phone conversations:

1. **Print out every job advertisement that you've responded to.**

2. **Take the time to visit the appropriate company Web site and print out any relevant company information.**

3. **File the job advertisement and company information together in a clearly marked file folder.**

4. **Put the file folders (however many you create) right next to the phone.**

   That way, when an executive calls to check you out, you will be totally on top of things. You can reach right for the company's file and sound as though you've been focusing only on that company for a job.

5. **If you customize your resume for a particular job, make sure that you put a copy of your specially customized resume in the file, too.**

   Be ready to answer interview questions relating to your work goals (see Chapter 9).

As far as general phone etiquette, remember a few basics:

- ✔ Don't talk to potential employers on a cordless phone. You'll crackle in and out and sound less than clear.
- ✔ At all costs, avoid using a speaker phone while conducting phone interviews. Nothing is more annoying to a potential employer.
- ✔ Make sure that your answering machine message sounds professional and cheerful.

Take a Portfolio to the Interview, No Matter What Your Profession

Portfolios are a trend that's catching on big with employers. Portfolios, which are essentially collections of your best work, certainly aren't a new concept — artists and creative types have been using them for decades. But the popularity of portfolios has spread to many professions, from computer science to teaching to public relations to accounting.

Just because you may not have pretty photos or drawings to show off doesn't mean that you can't collect samples of your work, along with glowing letters of recommendation and other kudos.

Make no mistake about it — after you land the interview, a portfolio is a definite odds-enhancer. One clever interview subject put her portfolio on the Web. When the employer asked about her prior work experience, she directed the interviewer to her Web portfolio. She left the interview with the job.

I followed up and asked the employer why he hired the candidate in question. He told me that he liked the idea of a portfolio (it showed initiative). He also liked the fact that the candidate had Web skills (good use of modern technology).

Develop Strong Computer Skills

Computer skills are very important for you to have. Yet merely saying to job candidates, "You need to know how to use a computer," is not terribly helpful. Today's employers *expect* you to have basic computer skills. Word processing, spreadsheet creating, and Web browsing skills are pretty much standard. I'm sorry to say that these basic computer skills just aren't enough to get you ahead anymore.

But you can make yourself stand out with a minimum of effort. Outside the technical professions, few job candidates take the time to be a little better, a little sharper, a little more knowledgeable when it comes to computer skills.

Here are some simple ways that you can make yourself a computer standout, even if you aren't a techie type:

- ✔ **Get to know the relevant software relating to your profession.** Purchase the software or borrow it. Learn how to use it, or at least become familiar with it. For example, if you're a teacher, you want to be familiar with software like HyperStudio, Lesson Planner Deluxe, and Microsoft Publisher. If you're an entry-level account executive, you want to get familiar with productivity management software like My Maillist Manager and Calendar Creator.

  If you aren't sure of what software is available for your profession, go into a mega-computer store (either in person or online) and browse the titles. For example, CompUSA boasts a good selection of products at both its physical stores and at its Web site (www.compusa.com).

- ✔ **Make sure that you know the major Web sites relating to your profession.** Writers, for example, should know the hot news and publishing sites. Financial planners should be familiar with the fastest and best market trading sites. Employers frequently keep their eyes on the key Web sites for their profession — they'll be happy to know that you're familiar with the sites, too. Knowing your profession's main Web sites is like subscribing to your profession's trade publications.

- ✔ **Learn how to create first-rate Web pages.** Creating Web pages is still considered a bonus skill in many professions. Whenever you add a bonus skill to your resume, you become a standout and increase your odds of landing a job. Please refer to Chapter 12 for more advice, and check out the CD that came with this book for software that can help you create Web pages.

On your resume and in your interviews, be sure to show off your extra computer knowledge. By making yourself a computer standout, you dramatically increase your job market value.

Create a Web Site That's a Known Hub for Your Profession

If you want to really boost your odds, then make your Web site count — a lot. I recently interviewed a young man, Chris Brady, who created a primo industry networking site on his Web page. (Here, I mean _networking_ as in making connections with fellow professionals.)

He didn't just put his resume on his Web site; he created a nationally recognized online networking center for the members of his profession to network and exchange war stories.

Since putting up his Web site, Chris has been offered several very lucrative positions and professional opportunities — and he wasn't even job hunting at the time. (You can read more about Chris Brady's Web methods in Chapter 12.)

What can you discover from Chris's success? By all means, take the initiative. If you have a passion for your profession or a special skill that relates to your job, show it off on a Web site — your Web site.

For example, if you're in advertising, you could put up a Web page that links to all the major advertising sites on the Web. You could post daily news clips especially related to advertising. You could also write a weekly column. If all this effort sounds like a lot of work, it is. But that's precisely the point. If you want to get the best jobs, you need to be the standout candidate.

Don't Overlook Low-Profile Companies

Just because a company is small doesn't mean that it doesn't have a lot to offer you! If you choose to work for a small company, you may get the opportunity to do things that you're not allowed to do in a bigger company, such as contribute to decisions about company direction and goals.

Everyone is clamoring to get through the doors of the Fortune 1000. Ease away from the thundering herds, and you give yourself a tactical advantage. Smaller companies with lesser-known names don't get as many applicants, so you have already increased your chances of getting a job.

You can find low-profile companies by checking the Internet Directory at the back of this book.

Chapter 17

The Top Ten Online Job-Search Questions and Answers

. . . .

In This Chapter
▶ Answering questions about online effectiveness
▶ Knowing what to do if you don't have your own computer and e-mail account
▶ Avoiding trouble with your boss
▶ Figuring out what does and doesn't work online
▶ Gauging response time

. . . .

At least half the battle in doing anything well involves asking the right questions, or so I always say.

The drive to ask questions is built into the very fabric of being human. Personally, I like questions — when I ask questions, I get answers. And when other people ask me questions, I learn a lot about what's really important to them.

In choosing the questions to include in this chapter, I relied heavily on job seekers like you. I polled numerous people of all ages and of widely varying technical and professional backgrounds about what questions were on their minds regarding online job searching.

In this chapter, you find my list of the top ten job-search questions that people wanted answers for.

What If I Don't Have My Own Computer?

Anymore, not having a computer isn't a valid excuse for avoiding an online job search. For example, in researching this book, I talked with a recent college grad who found her job by using a busy computer at a public library. She went online for 30-minute intervals just a few times a week, and she managed to find a great job in her field in only a month and a half.

In the event that your local public library doesn't offer Web access, try these other sources for online access:

- ✔ If you're in school, by all means see whether you can use the school computers for job-search purposes.

    You don't even need to be a student in order to use the computers at many schools. For example, I live by a large university; I can waltz into the university library at any time and access the Web for as long as I want.

- ✔ Check with copy centers and office-supply stores. Many stores rent time on the computer for about $10 to $12 per hour.

Employers have come to expect you to figure out how to access a computer. Follow through with the tips I outline here so that you look as up-to-date and competitive as possible.

What If I Don't Have My Own E-Mail Account?

If you don't have e-mail — no problem! At long last, you can get a free *Web-based e-mail* address. Web-based e-mail is completely portable — that is, you can pick up your mail from any computer that has access to the Web. You can send and receive your e-mail from locations like the following:

- ✔ A library computer
- ✔ A public computer at an airport
- ✔ A computer in a coffee shop or cyber café
- ✔ Your friends' computers
- ✔ School computers

Just about the only place you shouldn't be picking up your Web-based e-mail is at work!

Here's how Web-based e-mail works: Instead of being saved on a machine that can be accessed only by certain proprietary software that's set up absolutely perfectly, e-mail messages are stored on the Web. You can access Web-based e-mail from any computer by using a standard Web browser like Netscape Communicator or Internet Explorer.

Hotmail is just one of a handful of Web-based e-mail sites available. I recommend Hotmail, which is completely free because it's heavily supported by advertisers. All you need to do to get an account is to sign up at the Web site, www.hotmail.com.

You needn't let a lack of e-mail be your downfall anymore. And yes, you *absolutely* need your own private e-mail account for your job search!

There Are Sooo Many Job-Search Sites on the Web — Where Do I Start?

The biggest complaint that I hear from job seekers (second only to privacy concerns) is that the Web simply contains too much information. For most people, the information is completely overwhelming and unmanageable.

Take a case in point: If you go to the Yahoo! directory at www.yahoo.com and search for "employment," you can't even *begin* to look at all the listings without getting techno-stressed. (*Techno-stress* is a term I invoke whenever technology gives you an overwhelming amount of information to absorb.)

 Using a *search engine* is even more horrifying. (A search engine looks through general Web pages for information.) I recently searched for the word *employment* on one of my favorite search engines and received over *50 million* hits. Who has time to look through 50 million Web pages? For more information about searching the Web with search engines and directories like Yahoo!, see Chapter 3.

I'll let you in on a major online job-search secret. Ignore — yes, ignore — all those millions of hits and thousands of job sites. Instead, cut a path directly to the following places:

- ✔ Sign up for a few (three is a good number) databases with *job search agents.* A job search agent e-mails job listings to you. For example, the Online Career Center (www.occ.com) has a job search agent.

- ✔ Find one or two job databases that specialize in your profession. If you're a nurse, sign up at a nursing job database. If you're an attorney, sign up at an attorneys-only job database like www.attorneysatwork.com. If you want an electrical engineering job, sign up at a site dedicated just to electrical engineering, such as IEEE (www.ieee.org). Check the Internet Directory section at the back of this book for specialized databases.

- ✔ Locate the Web sites of the newspapers in your area (or in the area you want to move to). Also locate one or two other regional-based job sites. For example, if you live in Wisconsin, visit Wisconsin JobNet at aspweb1.dwd.state.wi.us/jobnet and sign up.

Following the preceding advice can help you clear the thickets of extraneous information out of your way. For your next job-search steps, consult Chapter 2.

How Can I Tell the Good Sites from the Bad?

Always check Web sites for certain key information. If a site doesn't pass the following basic tests, consider the site a dud and move on:

- ✔ **Who is behind the scenes of the site?** Is the backer a reputable, established association, company, state, or educational institution? Job Web sites are big business these days, complete with major, multimillion dollar agreements. Finding out the *who* behind the dollars is in your interest. For example, the very large and well-known Monster Board is owned by TMP, which is a recruitment advertising company.

- ✔ **Does the site list a physical address?** Does the address check out? I use electronic road atlases like Rand McNally's StreetFinder to check out physical addresses. I type in the address and click, and then the software points to the exact location of the business. You may be surprised what you can learn about a site in this manner.

- ✔ **How long has the site been around?** The oldest sites in this business are about four or five years old, so don't expect to hear dates stretching back to 1889. But you do want *some* stability. I like to see a site that has been around for at least six months.

- ✔ **When you call the phone number (it's listed on the Web page, I hope), is the phone connected?** Do you get a hokey recording or a professional-sounding one? Does a live person answer the phone?

- ✔ **When you send e-mail, do you get a speedy, professional response?**

- ✔ **Will the site send you printed material detailing its track record?**

- ✔ **If the site publishes numbers of *hits* (or visits), are those numbers audited by an independent third party?** An independent audit ensures that the claims made by the site are true.

- ✔ **Does the site inform you up front about collaborations and associations with other online job sites?** You must always know where your resume goes and who can access it before you post. And finding such information shouldn't be difficult at all.

- ✔ **Are employers who are currently using the service listed on the site, along with contact information?**

How Long Does an Online Job Search Usually Take?

I talked to many successful job-search candidates in researching this book. Through all the interviews, my best estimate is that the average time for an online job search is about two weeks. Two weeks. Seriously.

However, some exceptions do crop up:

- ✔ If you're in a high-demand profession (anything technical or computer-related), the average time is 24 hours. I'm not kidding.
- ✔ If you're in the field of marketing and public relations, the average time you can expect to spend on an online job search is about a week.
- ✔ If you're a new college grad, the average time is about one and a half months.

One major caveat: If you've been unemployed for a year or more because you out-and-out cannot find a job, online job searching may not serve as a magic career pill for you. Most people who try it, however, eventually have success.

How Can I Tell Whether My Electronic Resume Arrived in One Piece?

If you apply to a large corporation, chances are that the employers are using a *resume tracking system*. (A resume tracking system stores your resume electronically for easy access by the employer.) Most tracking systems notify you via postal mail that your resume arrived and has been put into a database. And of course, if you get a call from an employer who's interested in your resume, you can bet that your resume arrived in good shape.

But other than getting a call from an employer or receiving a notice via postal mail, you probably can't tell whether your electronic resume arrived in one piece. Why? Companies are very cautious about sending e-mail replies to job seekers. Potential employers don't want your boss to know that you're looking for a job. When a company is interested in you, someone there will call you.

If you absolutely must track your resume, try one or both of the following options:

- ✔ Mail a paper follow-up resume.
- ✔ Send a short follow-up e-mail as a confirmation one to two weeks after you send in your resume. State the date you sent your resume, and then ask the e-mail recipient to contact you only if your resume has *not* been received. Most companies are very responsible about following through on this type of notice.

What Happens to My Resume After I Post It on the Web or Send It to a Company?

After you send your resume to a company, your resume is either stored immediately in a large computer database or sent to a key hiring executive's e-mail address. Often, the key executive is a recruiter (in large organizations) or a hiring manager (in smaller organizations). If you're applying to a very small organization, your resume may well go straight to the president of the company.

At that point, quite a few variations can occur, depending on the way an organization is set up. In general, though, you will almost always receive a call from a key executive if the company is interested in setting up an interview with you.

After you send your resume to the Web, on the other hand, your resume is stored digitally in a database. *You* need to take responsibility of what happens to your resume after you post it on the Web. Take a look at Chapters 4 and 7 to discover the best ways to take charge of your resume after it's on the Web.

Will My Boss See My Resume If I Post It Online?

Can your boss discover that you're job hunting by finding your smiling mug (and your resume) posted on HeadHunter.NET? In a word: maybe. It all depends on what kind of resume database you post your resume to. Just a few years ago, I would have advised you not to worry about your boss seeing your resume online. But times have really changed.

With everyone online nowadays, your chances of getting found out by your boss are much greater — but only if you post your resume on an *open* resume board. An open resume board is not password-protected, so absolutely anyone with an Internet connection can access and view your resume.

But a *candidate-controlled* or *password-protected* resume database gives you the option of blocking certain companies from ever accessing your resume. You also decide who gets to see your resume and when. In a candidate-controlled or password-protected database, it's less likely that your boss will see your resume online. You can understand, then, why I advise job seekers to post resumes primarily on candidate-controlled sites.

For further details on keeping your privacy intact online (and working with candidate-controlled and password-protected resume sites), see Chapter 4.

Is It True That Online Job Searching Works Only for Techies?

I hear the same buzz that you do. When online job searching first started to get hot about five years ago, job searching *was* primarily effective for techies. But even five years ago, people working in non-technical professions were also finding great jobs.

It really bothers me when I read misinformed, out-of-date information stating that online job searching either doesn't work very well at all or only works for less than 10 percent of the techies — and less than 1 percent of the general population. When you hear noise like this, ignore it.

The reality is that online job searching is the best way to look for a job. Countless studies and major national polls show that 90 percent of employers now hire an average of 37 percent of their workforce via online methods. And in the high-tech arena, that number climbs even higher, up to 89 percent. Of course, you can interpret polls in many different ways, but still, the numbers are high.

When I began lining up people to interview for this book, I sent out a simple Profnet query for information. (Profnet is a service that sends a professional reporter's or writer's message to about 4,000 people.) The response I got was *unbelievable.* I heard from literally hundreds of employers — and I kept hearing from them! The message was always the same:

> "We are online, we are committed to online recruiting methods, and we are most definitely hiring candidates we find online."

The bottom line is that good job candidates just can't ignore online job searching anymore. The Web has become part and parcel of the general culture. You can't even go to a movie anymore without seeing the movie's Web site displayed right along with the credits. The Web has similarly become completely intertwined in job-search methods and strategies.

Let me relay an insider story to you. While researching this book, I interviewed a brilliant headhunter who spends much of her day on the Web looking for CEOs, CIOs, and other *very* high-level executives. This headhunter places executives and managers in the largest, best-paying companies in the world.

She fully *expects* that if a candidate is worthwhile, the candidate will have Web savvy and a Web presence. This headhunter doesn't post job openings online, but she *does* accept e-mailed resumes. She also scours the Web for candidates who are active online in relevant associations and newsgroups, and she looks for solid Web pages and clear indications that the candidate can conduct the business of a job search via online methods.

If you need more convincing, check out Chapter 1, where I list a variety of poll and survey results relating to online job searching.

What Parts of a Traditional Job Search Transfer Best to an Online Job Search?

Online job searching is not a panacea for all job searching woes. Neither is it ineffectual, as some claim. The truth of the matter is that some areas of job searching lend themselves better than others to an online job search.

The online medium works *extremely* well in the following areas:

- Posting resumes to databases
- E-mailing resumes to companies, either in response to a position announcement or cold calling
- E-mailing follow-up notes to resumes, calls, and interviews
- Researching company information
- Locating sources of further help

In these areas, you really can't beat an online job search for getting in there and helping you to find leads, get information, crack open the hidden job market, and get yourself into the job market.

For most people, though, an online job search really falls down in one area: the ability to forge substantial business relationships — typically known as *networking*. When it comes to networking online, you need to lay your groundwork very carefully.

- Yes, you absolutely can meet great contacts online. And yes, you can find a great deal of one-to-one help online. But in my opinion, much of your highest-quality networking is best done on the phone or in person.
- Online networking works best when you use it in conjunction with traditional networking. That means calling on those you know in real life as well as making connections online.
- Online networking works least well when you use it to cold call "the experts" for help in finding a job. Believe me, as the recipient of many such e-mails, I really need to know that the person e-mailing me either knows me, has met me, knows a friend of mine, or knows even a friend of a friend of a friend of mine. (Or is a reader like you!)

I go into detail about how you can best use the Web and other online media to network with others in Chapter 11.

Chapter 18

Ten Hot Tips from Employers

In This Chapter

▶ How not to irritate and annoy potential employers

▶ The skinny from employers on resumes and cover letters

▶ The right way to show initiative online

*N*o one is perfect, no doubt about it. But while you're searching for a job, you have to at least pretend to be. Perfect, that is. Thankfully, even though you're a mere mortal, you can hold up the image of near-perfection by following through on some simple tips.

Many job seekers I talk to aren't sure what sets a candidate apart in an employer's eye. So, in this chapter, I let loose with the most common things that employers complain about and praise as they scout for candidates. If you can add even a few of the following ideas to your quiver of job-search ammunition, you'll find yourself looking pretty darn good in employers' eyes.

Read My Web Site Content Before You Apply or Interview

When the Web made its debut in the early 1990s, you could find great scientific and government information residing on several thousand Web pages. A few savvy companies maintained Web pages, but those early corporate adopters were the rare exception rather than the rule.

Today's Web contents are a completely different story. Nowadays, business and corporation pages are filling up cyberspace faster than you can say "URL." And you can just about be sure that among the millions of corporate Web sites available, one of them tells the story of a company where you may want to apply for a job or go for an interview.

Because corporate Web pages are a font of information, believe me when I relay to you that employers absolutely *expect* you to read their Web sites very thoroughly before you apply for a job. And before you come for an interview, you should know by heart the corporate philosophy as it's set forth on the corporate Web site.

Employers tell me that they can always tell when applicants or interview subjects have taken the time to familiarize themselves with the parts of the corporate Web site that don't have to do with job listings. Be forewarned: Employers tell me that those candidates who don't make the effort usually don't get hired.

Don't Send Me Attachments!

All the top e-mail programs, including Eudora, Pegasus, and Netscape Communicator, offer you the capability to attach documents to your e-mail messages. All you do is write your message, click on a button, and tell the computer which file you want to send. In your case, you send your resume. (If you have questions about attaching files, see Chapter 10.)

But before you send your resume as an e-mail attachment, let me relay the advice I heard from employers: Don't send attachments!

If you want employers to read your resume, make it as simple as possible for them to do so. Even if *you* are sophisticated and can send and open any kind of e-mail, don't assume that a busy executive looking at over 200 resumes a week is going to open e-mail files that require extra work. The president of a mid-sized firm told me that she simply sets aside resumes that come in as attachments. By the time she gets around to opening the attachments, the candidates who sent their resume in plain text are already well into the interview process.

Also, several executives in high-tech companies told me that they *never* open e-mail attachments from non-company employees. Evidently, high-tech companies are often the target of prankster e-mail viruses.

To ensure that executives read your resume, stick to the basics:

✔ Send your resume in plain-vanilla style. *Plain-vanilla style* means a plain-text or ASCII resume.

✔ Send your resume via e-mail, but paste or type your resume right into the body of your e-mail message. (If you need help creating and sending electronic resumes, see Chapters 5 through 7 for all the details.)

Spell Correctly and Organize Cleanly

I know you already realize that you need to spell everything correctly. But judging from the resumes I see on the Web and from employers' and headhunters' comments, plenty of people don't heed the number-one rule of writing a resume: Get the spelling right.

I listen to a lot of employers in the course of a week. One thing employers frequently tell me is that if a resume has even one small typo, the candidate is automatically passed over.

If spelling is your nemesis, have a friend — or, better yet, two friends — look over your resume to make sure that your spelling is 100 percent perfect.

As soon as you have the spelling perfect, give your resume a once-over for clarity. Also, be sure to double-check for spell checker errors — those little mistakes that spell checkers don't catch. Employers don't require perfect layouts on resumes, but if you can organize your resume into a simple, clear format, then you have a real advantage over your competitors. In Chapter 5, I discuss employer-friendly resume formats in detail.

Keep Electronic Cover Letters to One Paragraph or Less

The cover letter has undergone radical transformation in the age of the Internet. Gone are the days of sculpting a solid page full of tailored, perfect paragraphs serving as a pre-resume appetizer.

When you e-mail a resume, employers want *at most* a quick paragraph at the top of an e-mail message. The paragraph serves as a sort of mini-cover letter. The "cover" paragraph should state who you are, tell what job you're applying or hoping for, and indicate your knowledge of the company. Your resume should follow right on the heels of the cover letter with only a little bit of space between the two.

You may not be aware that nowadays, the cover letter is the dessert instead of the first course! Oddly enough, most employers read electronic cover letters (or should I say paragraphs) only *after* they read the accompanying resumes. So the lesson here is that, if you have wonderful information about your accomplishments, you need to make sure that the information finds its way into your resume first and foremost.

If you're sending a formatted paper resume, by all means take the time to sculpt a perfect cover letter. When you send paper, a good cover letter still counts.

Mail Me a Formatted Paper Resume as a Follow-Up with a Short Note

Surprisingly, many employers, especially those in small to mid-sized companies, appreciate a formatted paper resume follow-up. (A formatted paper resume is a "pretty" resume with all the fonts and layout intact.)

Employers working in the more liberal-arts oriented, creative professions, such as advertising, marketing, and public relations, are especially keen on receiving a formatted paper resume. Sending a formatted paper resume is also important for high-level, high-income executives.

As a first step in your job search, go ahead and e-mail a plain-text electronic resume to a prospective employer. On the same day, send your pretty paper resume flat and unfolded in a large envelope.

Writing a nice cover letter explaining that your paper resume is simply a follow-up to your electronic resume is completely appropriate. Most employers appreciate the opportunity to see how you organize your resume when you have all the fonts, bullets, and spacing at your disposal. And employers tell me over and over again that they look more closely at candidates who display ease working with both paper and electronic resumes.

Don't Call!

I know that employers often list their phone numbers on Web sites and on job ads. But that doesn't mean that the availability of a phone number is an invitation to pick up the phone and make a call. Hold yourself back. Recruiters and hiring managers like to be the ones to call you. Believe me: If a company is interested in you, they will call you.

Sending e-mail, postal mail, and faxes (if specifically requested) is fine. But avoid using the phone to make contact with a potential employer. Calling is one of the fastest ways of scoring a top position on an employer's "Most Annoying People" list.

Keep in Touch Via E-Mail, Even If I Don't Hire You

Perhaps someone with more experience beat you out in the interview. Or perhaps your skill set didn't gel with the position that was open. Whatever the case, don't assume that you didn't get a job because the employer didn't like you or appreciate your value.

If you sent a resume to a company and got a call from someone at the company, make sure to keep in touch with the person who called you. That person liked you enough to call you the first time. Even if you didn't get the job offer the first time, it doesn't mean that you won't ever get an offer.

Hang in there. Have the presence of mind to get the caller's e-mail address when you talk. Send a short, polite e-mail every month or two to indicate that you're still interested in working for the company should the right position become available. Keeping in touch every so often is a strategy that works wonders when you have your heart *set* on a company.

A writer I heard speak at a conference explained how he got one of the top writing staff positions at *People Magazine*. The man sent in well over 200 query letters trying to get his foot in the door. After several *years,* the magazine finally found the right niche for him and hired him. Now, he's a senior writer for *People Magazine.* He hung in there for his ideal job and landed it. You can do the same.

Don't Fax Me a Resume Unless I Specifically Ask for a Fax

With the exception of one major airline I talked with, few employers liked getting faxed resumes. In fact, a fair number of employers, particularly mid-sized companies, told me that they ignore faxed resumes unless the candidate is just incredible. Too often, the resumes don't come through cleanly enough to be scanned into a database.

When in doubt, know that, today, most employers prefer e-mailed resumes hands down. A resume that is e-mailed into the system comes through without any mistakes (usually) and requires no extra effort from the employer.

Faxed resumes, on the other hand, often have to be manually typed into a company's system. Unless you're applying to a company with enough resources to have a staff ready and waiting to retype your resume, avoid faxing your resume.

Be Committed to and Interested in My Company

While watching the horrendous downsizings of the late 1980s, I remember thinking that, eventually, companies would kick themselves for creating a generation of workers who couldn't muster company loyalty. From what I'm seeing, plenty of companies are now paying for their downsizing ways in human terms. Companies just aren't finding those loyal-to-the-death employees in the current workforce anymore. But that very lack seems to have made companies all the more adamant about insisting on company loyalty during the hiring process.

I know — it's incredibly unfair for companies to ask for your undying loyalty before you even sign up. But you need to show an interest in and commitment to a company's goals and vision if you want to get a top job.

Now that you've been forewarned, you can better prepare by familiarizing yourself with a company's overall goals.

- ✔ Make sure that you can comfortably buy into a company's goals before you get too far into the hiring process.
- ✔ Anticipate interview questions like "How do your career goals match our company's long-term objectives?" and be prepared with good answers.

Send Me Your Resume Even If You Don't See a Job Opening

Just because you don't see a job opening that matches your skills on a company's Web site doesn't mean that an opening doesn't exist. Employer after employer told me that they wait to see who really wants to work for them. (See the preceding section about corporate loyalty!) Often, when a job opening is posted, it means that the company needs to hire *very quickly.*

If you find a company or organization that you really want to work for, by all means follow through.

1. **Locate the company's job posting area on the company Web site.**

2. **Send a neat, clean resume with an introductory paragraph that demonstrates a clear interest in and knowledge of the company.**

3. **Explain that, even though you didn't see a job posted that was suitable for you, you are very interested if something suitable does become available.**

4. **If you don't hear from the company in one or two months, send a follow-up e-mail to the contact person to whom you sent your resume.**

   As a safeguard, check the Web page to see whether it lists a new contact person. Perhaps the person who received your resume has left the company, leaving you lost in the shuffle.

To an employer, finding a resume that reveals real interest in the company is the equivalent of finding gold. Be assured that if you have the right skills for the job, when a job does come up, you'll be first on the list.

Note: Some companies do not post job openings at all on their Web sites. In this situation, you're forced to send a "cold call" resume. I recommend that you scour the Web site to make *double sure* that a contact for employment opportunities isn't listed somewhere deep in its recesses. If you find no employment references, call the switchboard operator and ask for the appropriate e-mail address for e-mailing a resume. The point is, you want your resume to have the best possible chance of landing in front of the right person.

Chapter 19

Ten Big-Time Online Goofs That Can Cost You a Job — or Worse

*J*ust about the only thing worse than making a mistake is *not knowing* that you made a mistake.

Many online job seekers I talk to wonder what secret, unwritten rules of the cyber-road they're unknowingly breaking. In this chapter, I discuss the by and large unwritten rules of the online job search. I've collected the most important slip-ups that you can make, so you don't have to go around wondering anymore!

In "real" life, the old saying goes that an ounce of prevention is worth a pound of cure. Things aren't so different online, after all.

Cold-Call E-Mailing the Company President, or Vice President, or . . .

In days of old, mailing a formatted paper resume to a complete stranger at a company was considered resourceful. Times have certainly changed.

Company Web pages are wonderful resources for discovering people to send contact notes or resumes to. In just a few moments, you can hop on a corporate Web site, click your way over to the corporate directory, and look up everyone from the CEO to the entry-level technicians. You can even find e-mail addresses all highlighted and ready for you to click on and send a quick note or resume to. Right? No way.

Even though your e-mail message may be pleasant, and even though you may send the perfect resume to a hiring manager, you should be aware of some new workplace protocols:

✔ If a company has a Web site with an employment area, the employer expects you to read the Web site and *follow the company's directions for employment contact.*

✔ If you e-mail a resume to *anyone* but the appropriate human resources or other listed contact person, you are essentially toast.

✔ Cold-call e-mailing a different person than the contact listed on the Web page makes you look like you skimmed the Web site impatiently. You also look like a person who doesn't want to (or like to) follow directions.

Typically, any e-mail you send that doesn't jive with the directions on the company Web site sets off various intruder alerts and is forwarded to the correct department and person, where staffers make sure that you aren't called for any interviews.

"Why not?" you may ask. The answer is simple. It all comes down to showing a company that you care enough to take time to learn about its processes and needs.

Please note a very important point: Sending a resume to a company even if you don't see a job posted is *perfectly acceptable.* The trick is to follow the company's directions as to whom to send that resume to. (I discuss how to cold-call with your electronic resume in detail in Chapter 7.) You only get into hot water when you send your resume willy-nilly to just anyone you can find listed on any part of an employer's Web site.

If you can't find an appropriate person to send your resume to, take some time to scan Chapters 3 and 11. Through research, you may just find that critical contact person.

But what if you don't find the person, and you don't have a contact name from a job ad? Call! A quick investigative call often can help you locate the right person. Start by asking for human resources; you can almost always find help from someone there.

One additional tip: Call, ask, wait a few days, and then call and ask again. Try to get the name of a second person within the company to talk to. If you get the same name twice, you're in good shape. If you don't, try a few more phone calls to get clarification. People forget a 30-second phone call pretty quickly, so you should be fine if you keep your calls very short and to the point.

Now for a giant caveat: Some Paleolithic companies may not have a Web site. If, in fact, you want to apply to a company that doesn't have a Web site, ignore all the advice I dispensed in the preceding paragraphs. Snail-mail a formatted paper resume and don't even worry about electronic resumes when dealing with that particular company.

Putting Too Much and Too-Detailed Contact Information on Your E-Resume

Looking for a job online is safer now than ever before — that is, if you know what to leave off your resume and you know that you need to post your resume only in high-quality resume databases. The stakes of ignoring basic online security issues have gotten, well, a bit high.

Imagine this scenario: A broke, desperate couple moseys into a public library in Anytown, USA. The couple goes online and noses around a couple of open online resume databases (see the next section in this chapter for more on open resume databases), looking for golden nuggets of personal information. They find the resume of a senior engineer. Great! Good earning potential!

Conveniently for the couple, the engineer listed a home address, a home phone number, a complete record of places of employment with dates, an age, a family background, and a URL for a Web site with more information.

The couple clicks over to the engineer's Web site and finds photos, information about hobbies, and a very detailed *C.V.,* or *curriculum vitae* — a lengthy resume. With the engineer's detailed information in hand, all it takes for the experienced couple is a few phone calls to get the engineer's social security number and other key financial information. And then the couple goes on a spending spree — using the engineer's identity.

Does my scenario sound preposterous and paranoid to you? It shouldn't, because it's happened.

When you're looking for a job, you need to strike a balance between "putting yourself out there," as one job seeker expressed to me, and maintaining privacy.

Fortunately, looking for a job online doesn't have to be unsafe. In Chapter 4, I detail what you can do to protect your resume information and stay out of the hands of ne'er-do-wells while still getting your information into employers' hands.

Meanwhile, the following tips can keep you out of trouble:

- ✔ Be very careful about putting too-specific personal information on any electronic resume. Age, social security number, and home street address are the biggest offenders.

- ✔ Consider cloaking the exact names of the companies that you've worked for. Instead of saying "Ford," you could say "major automobile manufacturer." Interested employers can ask you for a complete resume when they call you.

- ✔ During your job search, modify your Web site to include only business information. Leave off all photos and personal information.

- ✔ Post your electronic resume only on password-protected resume databases. That way, only legitimate employers have access to your resume.

Posting Your Resume on Open Resume Databases

An *open resume database* is one that is not password-protected. Anyone can scour through an open resume database, including your current employer and would-be identity thieves. (See "Putting Too Much and Too-Detailed Contact Information on Your E-Resume" earlier in this chapter.)

I have to admit — I've talked with a number of excellent headhunters who use open resume databases to find good candidates. It's cheaper and easier for headhunters to look for you when they don't have to pay up front for the privilege of doing so.

Considering that there are both good and bad aspects of open posting, my advice is this: If you aren't desperate for a job, post only to resume databases that are password-protected or in some way offer you the capability to control who does and doesn't see your resume. In the Internet Directory at the back of this book, I note which resume databases are open.

But if you're a brand-new college graduate, posting to an open resume database doesn't pose as much of a threat to you. Criminals won't be interested in you because you probably haven't accrued all sorts of cars, houses, and juicy bank accounts yet. And because you don't have a boss yet, you don't have to worry about your boss discovering that you're looking for a job.

But if you are currently employed and can take a little more time for your job search, take the cautious approach and make sure that not just anyone can see your resume. Consider what Bill Warren, president of the Online

Career Center, told me when I asked him about open resume posting: "Sure, post, but only if you don't mind having your resume floating around the Web for two or three years." Enough said!

Paying to Post a Resume

I heard the best line recently. While talking to the president of a major international job search site, I asked his opinion of sites that make you, the job seeker, pay to post a resume. He said, "If you see that a site asks a job seeker to pay to post a resume, it's the first sign of a loser."

This wise man isn't alone in his opinion. I have polled literally hundreds of career insiders on this question and have heard a thunderingly unanimous reply: Don't do it. Paying to post your resume is a waste of your money, with almost no exceptions.

You see, the best resume sites around are the best because the volume of visits from employers and headhunters is huge. You attract big-time traffic only when you have a lot of resumes for employers to see. And you get a lot of resumes only when people can post them for free. If you could peer deeply into the digital recesses of resume databases, you would see quickly and clearly that the very best resume posting sites are absolutely, 100 percent free.

By the way, all the resume databases that I list in the Internet Directory at the end of this book are free for job seekers.

Using Your Work E-Mail in Your Job-Search Efforts

If you've fallen into the trap of using your ever-so-convenient work e-mail address for job searching, reconsider your decision — and quickly! According to just about every employment attorney and online expert I consulted, if you use your work e-mail to look for a job, you can get fired for it. And yes, your boss most definitely has the right to filter and scan all your incoming and outgoing e-mail, at least according to current law.

If you're in a bind and don't currently have a personal e-mail account, I have several recommendations:

> ✔ If you have a computer at home, the answer is simple: Just get a free e-mail account through one of the many free e-mail providers. (Juno is the most popular free e-mail that I know of. Visit www.juno.com for details on signing up.)

✔ If you don't have a computer of your own, sign up for a *Web-based* e-mail account. A Web-based e-mail account is one that you can access from any computer with a standard Web browser like Netscape Communicator or Internet Explorer.

Essentially, Web e-mail is 100 percent portable e-mail. With a Web-based e-mail account, you can use either a library computer or a friend's computer, or you can rent time on a computer at a place like Kinko's. All you need is a connection to the Web.

A completely free Web-based e-mail company that I like is Hotmail. You can sign up for a Hotmail account at `www.hotmail.com`. Just don't check your e-mail at work! (See Chapter 10 for more information about free e-mail.)

Sending a Formatted Resume Via E-Mail

When you hear employers chatting about how convenient and wonderful electronic resumes are, they're referring to *plain-text* electronic resumes. (See Chapter 5 for details on electronic resumes, plain-text and otherwise.)

Plain text means that the resume has been saved as ASCII, or without special fonts, colors, or bullets. When employers receive a plain-text resume, all they have to do is open the e-mail message to read the resume.

On the other hand, if an employer gets a fully formatted electronic resume complete with pretty fonts, bullets, and spacing, the employer has to go through several extra steps to be able to see and read your resume. Based on my interviews, I guarantee that 90 percent of employers ignore formatted electronic resumes — formatted resumes are prettier to look at, but employers just don't want to take the time or the extra effort to do so.

If you aren't sure whether you've been sending out a formatted resume, here are some sure clues:

✔ Did you write a resume using Microsoft Word or Corel WordPerfect (or any other word-processing software) and then save the resume without specifically saving it as ASCII text?

✔ Did your resume have a name like myresume.doc or myresume.wpd?

If you answered yes to either of the preceding questions, then you probably have been sending out a formatted resume.

When you send a resume via e-mail, send only plain text, and put the plain-text resume right in the e-mail message. If you have any questions about how to do so, I walk you through the entire process in Chapter 7.

Flaming Anyone, Anywhere, Anytime

A few months ago, a good friend of mine called me up and asked me to check and see whether a guy she was thinking of going out with was on the Internet. (My friend doesn't have a computer, but she certainly appreciates the Internet!) All I had to go on was a name and an e-mail address.

I opened up one of my favorite search engines and typed in the man's name, and guess what I found? I found my friend's potential date making, er, certain *disparaging* comments to other people online. (He was making comments on Usenet, an area of the Internet that I discuss in Chapter 11.)

I printed out the man's comments and gave them to my friend. When the man asked her out, my friend handed him the printouts and said, "No, thanks. I already know as much about you as I care to."

Employers aren't a whole lot different from me and my friend. They check you out, too. Many companies have even taken the step of hiring in-house Web surfers to search for and research job candidates. Needless to say, any negative comment with your name and e-mail address attached to it is not a positive thing.

Keep in mind that some of the comments that my friend's potential date made were *over a year old.* If you are always posting messages, chatting in chat rooms, and signing Web guest books with comments, make sure that your online conversations are always on the up-and-up and are always *clean* and *positive.*

I cannot say it enough — after you've put written communication on any portion of the Internet or the Web, you *never know* where it may turn up again. Make sure that your words always help you, never hurt you.

Applying for Too Many Jobs at One Site

I know that being ambitious is always a good thing, but there's a limit to how far you should go in trying to land a job. Employers frequently mention to me that when they see an applicant responding to more than three positions at once, a giant, job-offer-stopping red flag goes up.

Employers like to think that you're applying for a position because you're uniquely qualified for it. They also want to think that you're going to stick around for a while because you're committed to the company. And they want to hire someone who isn't desperate for a job.

Simply put, applying to every job available at a company makes you look desperate. It also makes you look a little silly, because most of the applications are funneling into one database or into one person's e-mail account.

I recently talked to an in-house recruiter for a well-known restaurant chain. He told me that even if an applicant qualifies for ten jobs, *he* wants to be the one to decide where to place the applicant. The recruiter in question actually gets insulted when an applicant goes to the restaurant Web site and fires off five or more resumes.

Your best bet is to read through the jobs offered at any given site and then choose just one or *at most* two jobs to apply for.

Putting Silly Information on Your Web Page

Web pages are terrific vehicles for cutting loose with creative graphics, words, and whatever else you can dream up. Even I have a "miscellaneous" page on my Web site, where I list my favorite things. Things, mind you, that have precious little to do with business.

In confessing my weakness for free self-expression, let me strongly encourage you to curb your self-expression while you're job searching. More than one candidate has lost a job opportunity because a potential employer didn't like the contents of the candidate's Web site.

Chapter 12 gives all sorts of tips for creating compelling Web pages that can *enhance* your job search, sometimes dramatically. Meanwhile, here are some basic tips that can keep you out of hot water:

- Remove links to sexually explicit and politically volatile or extreme sites.

- Edit your personal interests and family information to the bare minimum. You don't want your employer to think that you don't have time to do a good job for them because you have so many outside interests.

- Unless you're positively stunning, remove photographs of yourself. And even if you are stunning, consider taking down photos of yourself while you're searching for a job (see Chapter 12 for more information about this point).

- Spell-check your Web pages! You want to look as sharp and competent on your Web page as you do on your resume.

- Clean up stale links and broken graphics.

- Don't forget to add links to professional associations and Web sites related to your profession.

Underestimating the Real-World Impact of an Online Job Search

If you're in a high-demand profession, expect to get a deluge of calls — and I mean a deluge — after you post your resume online. I interviewed hundreds of people for this book, and one of the biggest tips that successful candidates kept telling me is that an online response can be *huge*.

The worst (or best, depending on how you look at it) inundation story I heard was from a "techie" who had computer networking skills, programming skills in three languages, and engineering skills in the area of cellular phone development. He was what recruiters call a "hot lead."

This man posted his resume on a Sunday night. By Monday morning, he had received 73 phone calls requesting interviews. By the end of the week, the pace had *increased*. Within two days, the man in question had accepted a lucrative offer. But he still had to deal with phone calls for the next few weeks.

Even now, months after his initial job posting, he still gets a trickle of phone calls. (Part of the problem is that this man posted his resume on an open, non-password-protected job site. See "Posting Your Resume on Open Resume Databases" earlier in this chapter for more details.)

Here are some tips for handling a phone call deluge:

✔ Add a second phone number and phone line if you have high-demand technical skills. Put only the second phone number on your resume so that you can turn off the flow of calls quickly and permanently when you're done with your job search.

✔ Set up a voice-mail account to handle extra call volume, even if you keep the account for only one month. A standard answering machine can't handle the volume of calls. Most phone companies offer voice-mail — check with your telephone service provider for more information.

✔ When you get a phone call, be prepared to check out the caller. Ask each caller for a Web site address, a physical address, and a phone number.

✔ Have fun feeling like the most important, sought-after person in your neighborhood!

The Job Searching Online For Dummies Internet Directory

*A*s I promised in this book, I don't leave you to fend for yourself in the wilds of cyberspace. This directory is built with you, the job seeker, in mind. Here, in these yellow pages, you find an extensive list of Web resources that you can use to jump-start your job search.

- ✔ **"The Top Job Databases on the Web"** covers a large selection of job sites on the Web, including

  - The top job databases on the Web

  - General job databases

  - High-tech and computer employment sites

  - Advertising, sales, marketing, and PR employment sites

  - Legal sites

  - A sampling of career databases

  - Regional job databases

  - Federal, state, government, and military job databases

  - Nonprofit job databases

  - Diversity employment sites

  - International employment sites

- ✔ **"Company-Related Information"** helps you find company-related information, including corporate doings and finance, lookup tools, and meta lists of companies online.

- ✔ **"Associations Meta Lists"** focuses on helping you find relevant professional associations online.

- ✔ **"Networking Resources"** helps you find online networking resources. I list great networking sites such as Web forums, mailing lists, chat resources, and Usenet tools.

- ✔ **"Job-Search Toolkit"** is where you find resources for your job-search toolkit. Here, I list Web sites that help you find research information for your job search and help you keep up-to-date with the latest trends. I also show you hot search engines, job-search meta lists, sample resumes and cover letters, and interview preparation sites.

- ✔ **"Privacy Resources"** shows you tools that can help you learn more about online privacy.

To use the directory, all you need to do is to browse through it, read the descriptions that appeal to you, and then visit those sites. The CD-ROM included with this book contains a complete bookmark file of all the URLs I list here, which can save you quite a few hours of typing!

I want you to be able to glance though this directory and get a quick sense of what's what. So, where appropriate, I've added teeny little icons, otherwise known as *micons,* to guide your browsings. Here's what each micon means:

★★★★ I use this micon to indicate that a site is particularly valuable for job seekers. Most often, I place the four-star micon on sites that have terrific content.

When a Web site accepts resumes, I use this micon to indicate that to you.

$ This micon indicates that you may be required to pay a fee for services at a site.

Sites marked with the graphics micon are graphics-heavy and may load more slowly than other sites.

This micon alerts you to superb lists of links within a site.

Sites marked with the chat micon feature live chat.

Inevitably, the links in this directory will change. For an update of changed links, please visit my Web site at www.pamdixon.com. If you find stale links in this directory, please drop me an e-mail at Jobsearch@pamdixon.com so that I can keep my list of updates as accurate as possible!

The Top Job Databases on the Web

Cutting a path through the thickets of online job-search databases isn't easy. Hundreds of employment sites actively post all manner of jobs on the Web. And on those sites, tens of thousands of employers, such as federal agencies, technical companies, law firms, investment firms, Fortune 500 companies, sole proprietorships, universities, and even cruise ships, post job advertisements. But the question remains: Just where is everyone posting the top jobs? In this portion of the directory, I help you find the best online hot spots for employment listings.

Note: I tested every job database in this directory with 14 or more keywords. If a database didn't have a keyword search box, I browsed the jobs one by one to see what was available. If you don't know what keywords are, or if you have any questions about using keywords, be sure to go back and read Chapter 14, where I explain keywords and how to use them effectively in job databases. If you can, it's a good idea to decide early in your job search on a dozen or so keywords that you will use when you look online for positions.

The Big Seven

One of the biggest complaints I hear from job seekers who want to use the Web in their job hunt is this: "There's too much information out there!" Well, this section of the directory narrows your search to just seven great job hot spots. Career pros who work as online recruiters have much experience with online job databases, and as such, they really know

what's what. I grilled numerous third-party and corporate recruiters in researching this book. After distilling their ideas and backing everything up with my own research, I compiled a list of what I call "The Big Seven."

The Big Seven are the very top tier of online job databases. Big Seven databases contain the *largest number of job positions,* and, with the exception of two databases, they also boast the most significant and active resume databases available online. In the listing that follows, you find quick thumbnail sketches of each Big Seven database. I highly recommend that you visit and peruse the jobs available at the Big Seven sites.

America's Job Bank

www.ajb.dni.us/

★★
★★

Extraordinary national clearinghouse for jobs: America's Job Bank gets its share of visitors, that's for sure. In one six-month period, AJB received a total of 221,540,100–plus hits on its Web site. That's an incredible number! AJB really is a government site (it gets all its job listings from state public employment agencies). However, before you write off AJB as a fuddy-duddy government site, take a look at the jobs available. I consistently find excellent jobs at this site — it's most definitely worth your time. Concerning resumes, AJB is in the process of putting together a resume service that will be operational within a year. Until the resume service is up, make sure to send your resume directly to the employer listed on any job advertisement that catches your eye.

Career Mosaic

www.careermosaic.com

★★
★★

Major online database with a technical and financial spin: Career Mosaic is the place that many recruiters go to find executive-level candidates and to find candidates who have experience in some facet of the high-tech, engineering, and financial industries. Most of the recruiters I talk with use Career Mosaic actively, and I've learned that recruiters conglomerate in the hot spots. The opening page of Career Mosaic is simple and easy to navigate. For jobs, click on the JOBS button. To post a resume, click on the ResumeCM button. One important note about the resume database: Currently, the resume database requires registration, but it is essentially an open resume database that anyone can look through. That hasn't stopped over 50,000 people from posting resumes, though; I leave it up to you! Just be forewarned that information posted here is openly searchable.

CareerPath.com

www.careerpath.com/

★★
★★

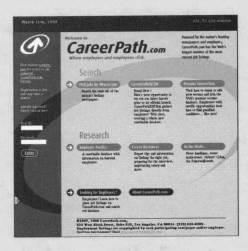

One-stop shopping for newspaper adver-tisements across the nation: CareerPath.com is a site that you can't afford to miss. It contains a private database that allows you complete control over your resume. This site advertises thousands of new positions daily and brings in huge amounts of traffic from employers. CareerPath.com's interface is easy to understand and use, and the site keeps its technology up-to-date — which is pretty darned important. Many of the successful job candidates I interviewed for this book used CareerPath.com as one of their primary databases, with great results. CareerPath.com is best suited for recent college grads or for people who want to relocate.

E.span

www.espan.com

Longtime player in the database game: E.span has big numbers, good job postings, and a new feature that sends listings to you. Your resume is protected in a private database, which is great. When I visited, I found lots of jobs in non-technical and technical areas. E.span is a solid but basic, no-frills site with good volume, and that's why it made this list.

Any recruiter will put E.span in the top tier of job databases. As of this writing, E.span is about to undergo a major renovation. The interface is set to change, as well as the site name. I'll keep you updated on changes at my Web site, www.pamdixon.com.

The Monster Board

www.monster.com/

★★
★★ 🗒

Mega-site popular with recent grads and those under 35: The Monster Board is owned by TMP Worldwide, which is the same company that now owns the Online Career Center. The Monster Board and the Online Career Center are completely different job databases in every way, though. Both databases boast high numbers, both let you post your resume to a password-protected database, both contain great job ads, and both now feature agents that send job listings to your e-mail address. But with its funky graphics, the Monster Board skews younger. I received a lot of mixed reports from recruiters about this site. Some love it, and others think that it's too "young" for the type of executive they're looking for. Essentially, if you're a new grad or are in the first ten years of your career, then Monster Board is an excellent choice for

you. All job seekers can benefit from its excellent set of reference and career tools. In particular, the Employer Profiles link on the opening page is a great resource for researching companies.

Online Career Center

www.occ.com/

★★
★★ 🗒

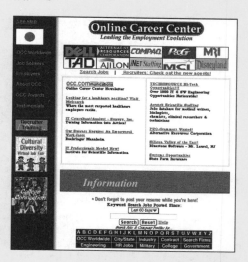

An extraordinarily high-quality online job and resume database: When I wrote my first book about online job searching in 1994, the Online Career Center was already well established; it was one of the first mega-career sites on the Internet. I'm happy to say that in the intervening years, OCC has gotten better and better. Currently, OCC offers what only the best online job databases can: visibility and security. When you post a resume with OCC, rest assured that your resume is really being seen. Plus, you know that your resume is in a password-protected database. Posting a resume and looking at job ads are free. The job ads in OCC are robust, although they tend a bit toward the technical side. OCC recently added an agent that sends job postings to your e-mail address, along with worldwide outposts so that you can search for jobs in several countries, such as Mexico and the Netherlands. A *highly* recommended site, particularly for seasoned professionals and those in sales, marketing, and high-tech industries.

Yahoo! Classifieds

classifieds.yahoo.com/employment.html

★★
★★

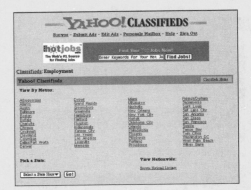

Extraordinary job hub with millions of hits per week: I haven't seen the Yahoo! Classifieds mentioned on many job-search meta lists, and I'm not sure why. But this lack of listings hasn't stopped folks who are actually looking for jobs from using the Yahoo! Classifieds in astonishing numbers. My sense is that the Yahoo! Classifieds will become a major online hub for the job-search process. Why? Because of the numbers, which are what really count in the Web way of doing business. You can view the Yahoo! Classifieds by metropolitan area or by state. After you open the Yahoo! Employment Classifieds page, click on a city you're interested in. The next page contains two links: a link to Job Listings and a link to Resumes. Clicking on the Job Listings link takes you to a page full of links to jobs. You can browse the job listings by company name, job function (like education or finance), or keyword. The depth of job advertisements in Yahoo! is good, and the ads are definitely worth browsing. The resume database, on the other hand, is open as of this writing. This means that if you post your resume to Yahoo!, everyone in the world can, and

probably will, see your resume in all its glory. The manager of the Employment section of Yahoo! assured me that Yahoo! is looking to completely overhaul its current resume system to take care of customers' privacy concerns. But until that overhaul occurs, I recommend that you use Yahoo! for looking at ads — not for posting your resume.

Other Stuff to Check Out

volvo.gslis.utexas.edu/~acadres/jobs/
    index.html
www.black-collegian.com/
www.career.com/
www.careerbuilder.com/

General Job Databases

In this portion of the directory, I tame the chaos that is the mass of general job databases available on the Web. After the Big Seven (the biggest job databases on the Web), you still have *plenty* of general job databases to explore. Unfortunately, many job seekers tell me that they have no idea how to weed their way through what's available on the Web. A big part of the confusion is the general job databases. Sure, everyone understands career-specific databases — databases that hone in on a specialty, like law or medicine. And everyone understands regional databases that clue you in to jobs in just one geographic area. But general job databases — forget it! There are simply too many now, and they all look so much alike.

In this section, you get the lowdown on job databases that you may have seen but haven't taken time to explore. The descriptions I provide enable you to take what's best from these sites and leave the rest, without spending time in each site trying to figure out what's what. And if something is negative or avoidable, I let you know that, too.

Sometimes, mid-sized sites like the ones in this portion of the directory offer exclusives on jobs from certain companies. Other times, these sites offer high-quality, hand-picked jobs.

4Work.com

www.4work.com/

Best for locating internships: I found 4Work.com to have the best of intentions: It includes helpful internship information and emphasizes volunteer work. But the site has its problems. When I conducted my standard 14 keyword tests, I found barely any jobs — and I mean barely any. The keyword that usually brings up the most jobs at any general database, *programmer,* brought up only two jobs on this site — a *very* poor showing for a general national site. If you're interested in this site, I suggest that you have the Job Alert e-mail agent send you notices; that way, you don't have to spend your time trying to find jobs that may be difficult to uncover with keyword searches.

Academe This Week/The Chronicle of Higher Education

chronicle.merit.edu/.ads/.links.html

★ ★
★ ★

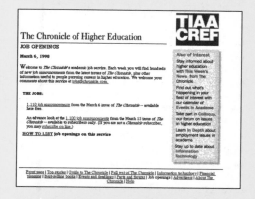

Top spot for academic jobs: The Chronicle of Higher Education's online site lists about 1,200 jobs in higher education

every week. The jobs are of the highest caliber — most of the jobs are faculty and research positions in the humanities, the social sciences, science and technology, professional fields, and administration, with a smattering of openings outside academia. The Web site is very well designed — everything is just a click away. A keyword search netted excellent results, even for non-academic types of jobs. In fact, I found great marketing positions, such as director of marketing and public affairs, associate director of admissions, and, of course, faculty positions teaching marketing.

Best Jobs USA

www.bestjobsusa.com/

★ ★
★ ★

Chaotic Web design and an overload of hype, but some good resources: This is one of those Web sites that's loaded with design that ends up being confusing rather than helpful. Head for safety immediately: Click on the Career Guide link that you find on the left side of the screen. (You really need frames for this site.) Then go to the Best Jobs Database. You can post a job at this site, but the resume posting page was not working when I visited. A good resource to check out is the City Outlines resource, which gives you helpful information about relocation. I had trouble loading this page; I got a "We're Sorry!" message several times.

Black Collegian

www.black-collegian.com/

★ ★
★ ★

I discuss this terrific site in the "Diversity" section later in this directory. Don't miss this site — it's one of the best job-search sites on the Web, well organized and filled with great content. I can't recommend it highly enough.

career.com

www.career.com/

Super-easy to use and not a lot of hype: I've always liked HEART, which is the advertising network that supports this database. Surprisingly enough, the database is not filled with blinking banner ads or flashing menu items screaming for your attention. The Search Jobs link features seven different ways for you to look for jobs: by category, location, keyword, and so on. The jobs at career.com cover a nice range of areas, with an emphasis in computing, engineering, accounting, business development, marketing, and administration. One especially nice feature is that you can search for entry-level jobs as a group — just click on the pertinent option from the Job Search page.

CareerBuilder

www.careerbuilder.com/

Navigation at this solid database site is tricky but worth the effort: If you use a smaller monitor, you need to scroll down to access important features at this site. When you open the URL, click on the Job Search icon. Scrolling down the page, you see a list of companies using CareerBuilder, along with a helpful salary survey, a salary calculator, career advice, and more. When you're ready, click on the Job Search icon. You go to a Job Search page where you can fill out a form asking for such information as the region in which you want to work, salary requirements, and pertinent keywords. I discovered that the search form occasionally returns an error message, probably indicating that the server is down. Try later — that's what I had to do.

CareerCast

www.careercast.com/

★ ★
★ ★

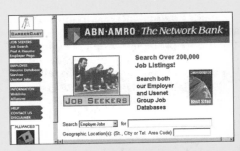

New kid on the job database block: CareerCast has several key items going for it, chiefly a truly decent search engine and a decent number of jobs to search. This site contains more depth than you'd expect from looking at the opening page. You may be put off by the bare-bones appearance, and by the fact that CareerCast presents you with a job-search box immediately (having become used to digging around a Web site to find the job database). After looking at probably thousands of Web sites, I can tell you that finding a search box right on the opening page is an absolute relief. But you can't just pore through lists of jobs at CareerCast; you need to know exactly what you want. Feed the search engine a keyword pertinent to your field and be aware that the CareerCast search engine is smart — you get tight matches to your search query. When I performed searches with my favorite 14 keywords, I got great results. *Programmer* gave me 1,250 matches, *marketing* reaped nearly 3,000 matches, and even the esoteric *forestry* gave me results. This database is rich in the technical and business areas. Resume posting at this site is password-protected and free to job seekers.

CareerCity

www.careercity.com/

Solid, likable general database: CareerCity definitely tries hard, but the site is not completely user-friendly. The layout is clean and simple, and you can easily navigate to the job database and the resume database with just one click. At the Job page, you find several search boxes with pull-down menus. You must specify the job category and location or your search won't work, which can be tedious. I specified a number of jobs in several locations, netting good results. (My search for marketing jobs in the West brought back over 350 jobs, which is great!) Be forewarned that posting your resume with CareerCity entails filling out its resume form — it doesn't accept e-mailed ASCII resumes. CareerCity lets you block specific companies from seeing your resume, but remember: Blocking isn't foolproof! It only works if the person at the company being blocked uses the same e-mail address all the time.

CareerMart

www.careermart.com/

General job database with extraordinarily clever graphics: I discuss CareerMart in the "Career Focus: Advertising, Sales, Marketing, and PR Jobs" section, for the simple reason that CareerMart covers many of these types of jobs. But this solid database is worth a look for generalists, too.

CareerWeb

www.cweb.com/

I discuss this excellent site in the "Career Focus: High-Tech and Computer Jobs" section later in this directory.

College Grad Job Hunter

www.collegegrad.com/

Slow-loading but content-rich site: The College Grad Job Hunter lives up to its name. After the opening page loads, which takes a while, you see a clear menu of options suited to new grads. You can prepare resumes and cover letters, learn about interviewing, view job postings, and even get information about what to do once you land a job. The job postings are appropriately geared toward entry-level positions. A must-see for new grads.

The Internet Job Locator

www.joblocator.com/jobs/

A sleek, smart job database: Despite its '50s look, the whole point of the Internet Job Locator is to keep jobs and job seekers as current as possible. You can sign up to receive only brand-new job postings for 30 days and renew for another 30 days. The Job Locator resume postings are password-protected, but resumes go to all sorts of employers; you won't find much privacy. You can instruct the Job Locator to post your resume instantly to Usenet newsgroups, but don't do so unless you're ready for the consequences of having your resume publicly available! The Internet Locator database relies heavily on jobs that have been posted to Usenet, which is not always a bad thing. I recommend the Jobs by E-mail feature; you can't go wrong when the job openings come to you.

JobBank USA

www.jobbankusa.com/

Clear, helpful search engine: JobBank USA could lay off the hype a bit, but other than that, it's a healthy job database. JobBank USA actually works like a parallel search engine in that it looks through several job databases, newspapers, and other job sources to find jobs matching your keywords, and then compiles a list of jobs for you. I find JobBank helpful as a big-picture search tool. JobScout is an e-mail agent that sends JobBank job listings to your e-mail address. JobBank boasts a nice resume-builder feature that you may find helpful if you're new to writing resumes. But I recommend against posting your resume at this site because you lose control of it after you post it.

JobDirect

www.jobdirect.com/

Hip site for college students: I first learned of JobDirect while browsing PR Newswire, where I read a wild news story about a van that traveled to college campuses to sign students up for a resume and job-matching service. The whole idea at JobDirect is to help students and employers find each other. You submit your resume, and JobDirect matches you up with a job. If you're a new grad or about to be one, you won't hurt yourself by hopping online and submitting your resume to JobDirect. You aren't guaranteed a job by any means, and I don't have

any statistics on success rates (although I tried hard to get them!). View JobDirect as one weapon in your job-finding arsenal.

JobTrak

www.jobtrak.com/

Premier site for selected college students and new grads: JobTrak offers you access to numerous internship opportunities as well as about 3,000 jobs. But your school needs to be a member of JobTrak for you to be able to access the opportunities. Ask your college career office whether you have access to JobTrak.

NationJob Network

www.nationjob.com/

★ ★
★ ★

A complex network of great job listings: Fully mining the depths of NationJob Network takes a while. You can search for a job right from the opening page by clicking on the Search for a Job now link, which is great. You can also sign up for P.J. Scout, one of the ubiquitous e-mail agents that sends jobs to your e-mail address. The value-added part of NationJob comes in the lists of specialized job databases that it maintains. I like NationJob's specialty pages even more than its general search service, which is why you see NationJob referenced so often in this directory. To look at NationJob's specialized job lists, scroll down the opening page and click on the Specialty Pages link. You find a list of specialty job areas such as Accounting, Administrative and Clerical, Advertising,

Education, and dozens more. Click on any of the job specialties displayed to see a list of jobs in that field. Don't miss this must-see site!

Net-Temps

www.net-temps.com/

★★
★★ 🗖

Absolutely giant site for high-quality, high-level temporary, full-time, and part-time jobs: If I could recommend just a few sites for job seekers, this site would make my short list. My keyword searches of this site consistently turn up incredible results. For example, a search on the keyword *programmer* yielded over 6,500 current jobs — and I mean just-within-the-last-few-days kind of current! Don't be fooled by the "temp" part of the site name — Net-Temps covers permanent positions as well as contract and part-time ones. And I love the Net-Temps resume area. Net-Temps doesn't let company personnel departments search the database, so your resume is safe from your boss's eyes. The only people who get to see your resume are Net-Temps members, who are third-party recruiters.

TOPjobs USA

www.topjobsusa.com/

★★
★★

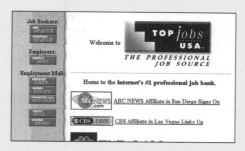

Large database specializing in managerial, technical, and professional job opportunities: TOPjobs USA has been signing on quite a few companies in recent months. Without figures from a third-party auditor,

I don't know how large the actual database is, but even without that information, TOPjobs still warrants a look-see. Click on the Job Search item on the main page, and you land at — you guessed it — the Job Search page. Don't let the large search forms scare you. *Remember:* In general, the larger the search form, the more sophisticated the search engine is, and believe me, you want a good search engine in a big database. I performed all my standard keyword searches on this database and was shocked by the high numbers of results I got. I had to wait about three minutes for my *programmer* search to come up, and when it did, I received thousands of results. The results are even organized geographically, which is a great feature for a lot of job seekers.

Other Stuff to Check Out

solimar1.stanford.edu/
www.americasemployers.com/
www.helpwanted.com/
www.interbiznet.com/
www.ipworld.com/classified/
www.recruiting-links.com

Career Focus: High-Tech and Computer Jobs

This section focuses on jobs for full-on technical professionals. Because this section is specifically for technical professionals, I assume that, if you read the site descriptions in this section, you will understand the acronyms I use, such as AI (artificial intelligence) and DBA (database administrator). In many cases, these sites do not contain hundreds or thousands of jobs; that isn't the point. The point of focused career sites is that they contain fewer jobs that provide a better fit. It's like going to a shoe store that carries only your size of shoes — sure, you'll find fewer shoes than in a big department store. But all the shoes will fit, and a good fit really counts when it comes to enjoying and succeeding in your career.

Advanced Information Systems Group

www.aisg.com/

List of senior and high-level DBA positions: This is not a fancy Web site — when you open the page, all you see is a list of links to jobs. But take a look at the jobs, and you won't care so much about the looks of the list. The number of jobs offered is not incredibly high — I saw several dozen at most — but the jobs are primarily senior-level positions. (*Note:* The positions are in Florida.) A few are six-month contract positions.

Allen Davis & Associates softwarejobs.com

www.softwarejobs.com/

Job listings for SAP, Oracle apps, RDBMS, data warehousing, Windows, Internet, and intranet: softwarejobs.com boasts a simple search interface that is easy to use and encourages browsing. You can search according to your specialty area or by keyword, or you can look at the job postings within the last week. When I viewed the most recent jobs, I found all sorts of great new jobs with six-figure salaries. Examples include positions for C++ software engineers, an Oracle developer (six-month contract position), and a VP of operations with UNIX and system design experience. Worth a visit.

Artificial Intelligence Resources

ai.iit.nrc.ca/ai_point.html

Great AI resources, including links to top AI job databases: The NRC-CNRC Institute for Information Technology hosts and maintains this excellent Web site. After you open the page, scroll down to the AI Employment Opportunities link and click on it. Ignore the grumpy "Please do NOT send me your job ad" message and scroll down the page. The people who maintain this site don't have their own job database (thus the message), but they do link you to the major hot AI job databases, which are exactly what you find at the bottom of the Employment Opportunities page. I found eight plum AI job databases linked from this site. I especially recommend checking out the links to the AI Related Job Posting Archives, Cycorp, and the Santa Fe Institute.

C/C++ Users Journal

www.cplusplusjobs.com/

C jobs all over the world, but especially in the United States: The C/C++ Users Journal sponsors this highly focused resource site for people who love to program in C and C++. The jobs on this site cover every part of the country, and all the jobs appear to be high-quality. I noticed several telecommuting opportunities, so if you're interested in setting up a virtual working environment, I suggest that you give this site a whirl. *Note:* At the bottom of the opening page, you find links to other tech jobs, including COBOL, database, LAN, Lotus Notes, PowerBuilder, and Visual Basic jobs.

CareerWeb

www.careerweb.com/jobs/

General job database that skews toward the technical: CareerWeb features all kinds of jobs, or so it says. However, I found a number of great technical jobs at this site.

The opening page is a bit obnoxious — flashing, annoying ads were plastered over too much of the space when I visited — but if you can get past the ads, the jobs are worth your attention. To use the site, select a job category or enter a keyword and then submit your query. I checked for jobs in networking and found over 1,900 that matched my query, all of them good-looking positions. If you're interested in a position, submit your resume to the contact listed in the job advertisement.

CircuitOnline

www.circuitonline.com/

A service directory and job database for the semiconductor industries: This is the online database of services for all sorts of unpronounceable specialties, such as IC Design, ECAD, EDA, FCC, FIB, gate array, VLSI, optoelectronics, and everything else to do with semiconductors and circuits. The site is nicely designed and easy to navigate; just select a menu category that appeals to you and follow the link. I selected Wafer Foundry and found lists of relevant online magazines, organizations, trade shows, conferences, newsgroups, and other assorted links. To look at the available jobs, scroll to the bottom of the opening page and click on the Classified link, and then type a keyword in the search box and begin your search. I found hundreds of jobs tightly focused to the semiconductor biz. To apply, contact the person listed in the ad. You can also submit your resume to Circuit Online via e-mail. The resume is passed around to recruiters and companies, so you may want to be careful before you fire off your resume to this particular site.

GameJOBS

www.gamejobs.com/

A great listing of jobs for those who want to design in 3-D: This site is hosted by Cyberactive Network, which publishes a number of game-related magazines. It's one of the better sites for finding work in that esoteric area of 3-D animation and heavy-duty computer graphics. To view the jobs, just scroll down the opening page. Some of the links may appear to be bad, but the reality is that most of the home pages listed are among the most graphic-heavy you can possibly imagine. Be patient. On my visit, I found jobs listed from Activision, 3Dfx, AOL, Bally Gaming International, Lucas Arts, Raven Software, and many more. Well worth a browse if you're in this industry niche.

IEEE – USA Job Listing Service

www.ieee.org/jobs.html

★ ★
★ ★

Absolutely top-of-the-line techie site: IEEE (Institute of Electrical and Electronics Engineers) is a well-known organization that helps engineers find and maintain employment. I recommend that you spend time exploring all the rich content available at this site. When you're ready, follow the IEEE-USA Job Listing Service link that you find on the opening page. You find yourself at an easy-to-use job-search site. Just fill in the form that you find and you're all set. I found great jobs at this site, including positions for acoustic, analog, and antenna engineers — even a position for an assistant professor in software engineering. To apply for a job, contact the person listed on the job application. You can view the job listings for free, but to post a resume you must be a member of IEEE.

Java Jobs Online

www.javajobs.com

Hub for Java programmers' resumes and jobs: To see restrained, classic Web page design, check out this site. At the top of the job listing are companies hiring for a number of positions, and below that you find a modest list of individual job openings. The resume-posting area, available from the Resume link on the opening page, takes you to a list of resumes in an open database. You won't find hundreds of listings at this site, but everything is focused on Java, and you find listings that are tightly tailored to a specialty.

Jaye Communications' USjob.network

job.sid.net/

★★ 🖾
★★

A nationwide network of regional high-tech job and resume banks: USjob.network does a good job of collecting regional job information for all facets of high-tech. From the opening page, click on the USjob.network link, click on the Search for Jobs link, choose a state from the pull-down menu, and click on Go. You see three options on the next page — you can submit a resume, search for a job, or delete or modify your resume. The job listings vary, depending on the state you're looking at. I found hundreds of excellent listings. The resume bank allows you to keep your identity private if you want, which I recommend. This site should keep you busy for a long time.

jobEngine

www.jobengine.com

★★ 🖾
★★

One of the best sites for posting your high-tech resume: jobEngine is a fruitful collaboration between Interactive Search, Inc., and ZDNet. Lots of eyes are looking at this site, and it has a very good resume-posting policy, so I recommend that you look for jobs *and* post your resume here. On the opening page, follow the option for Job Seekers. Go ahead and post your resume right away, following the step-by-step instructions. Posting is free, and jobEngine keeps your personal information confidential if you desire. The resume database is password-protected, and the resumes themselves are search-able via a particularly effective search engine. Now, mosey over to the jobs offered section by clicking on the Search Jobs link on the opening page. Fill in the pertinent information in the search form and go for it. One unusual and highly helpful feature of the search engine is that you can look for jobs within a specific radius of a zip code. For example, if you live in San Diego, you can specify jobs a maximum of 60 miles from zip code 92112. I found job ads from Sun Microsystems, Sybase, Wang, USWeb, and other major employers on my visit.

The JobZone

www.internettelephony.com/resources/ frames/jobzone.htm

Job listings for those working in telephony: Although the jobs at this site are in a monster of a list, it's a great site for finding high-level telephony jobs. Just open the URL, and you see a job-search menu right off. You can keyword-search for jobs, or you can view all the jobs. I found jobs for DMS switch technicians in Illinois, switch technicians in Saudi Arabia, senior project engineers in Arizona, Texas, and New York, and construction supervisors in Ohio.

Lucas Arts

www.lucasarts.com

Jobs for computer animators: This is one of the very few company pages in this directory. I found so few general job lists for computer animators that I decided to include this site, the ultimate computer animator's dream. The site has an interesting approach to job listings. From the main page, scroll down and click on the Job Openings link, which is somewhat hard to read (perhaps because it's not the most prominent feature on the page). You may want to read the information about portfolio and demo submission before you do anything else. Then click on the Career Opportunities link and scroll down past the blinking lights until you get to the jobs list. On my visit, I found positions for sound assistants, materials planners, PSX programmers, 3-D programmers, and IS technicians. Please be aware that Lucas Arts stresses high technical ability as well as excellent interpersonal abilities. Requesting and even testing interpersonal skills is a growing trend in high-tech. The days of grumpy super-geeks and rude geniuses are long over! If you want a job at the top, you're going to have to be able to work well with others.

National Center for Supercomputing Applications

www.ncsa.uiuc.edu/General/Jobs/ 00Jobs.html

Help for those who have been seduced by the hum of a supercomputer: After working with supercomputers, nothing else quite compares. I know — I'm afraid I've been hit hard by this particular affliction. I

understand completely if you *must* be near a giant machine, complete with its own plasma field. At the NCSA site, you can try for various jobs that put you in proximity of the powerful digital beasts. During my visit, I found jobs for visualization programmers, a research programmer (specializing in computational biology), a senior project coordinator, a software engineer, and more. Please note: If you're typing in this URL, the 00 characters are zeroes, not the letter O.

The San Jose Mercury News

www.sjmercury.com/

Great source for tech jobs in the Bay Area: After the San Jose Mercury News page loads (which takes a while — it's graphics-heavy), click on the Jobs tab. You find a wealth of technical jobs listed in the classifieds section. For a local newspaper, it has lots of jobs. My test keywords yielded good results here, considering that the site is not a technical job site per se; I found 51 jobs for programmers when I visited. If you simply do not want to relocate and you don't live in the Bay Area, you can always try to talk an employer into a telecommuting position — hey, you never know!

The SenseMedia Surfer

sensemedia.net/getajob

Resume and job listing area for hypermedia professionals: This is a super site for listing your HTML resume as well as surfing for a hypermedia job. Simply scroll down the opening page to access the job listings. The page is organized in a somewhat unconventional way — the jobs are in chart format instead of in a list. No matter. Just click on the opportunities that appeal to you and explore! To post a resume to SenseMedia's open

board, click on the Hypermedia Professionals' Resume Listing link and follow
the appropriate links. Please note that the
resume area can take a lot of time to load.

SuperSite.net/TechJobs

supersite.net/TechJobs/

*A consortium of job banks for high-tech
companies:* SuperSite manages a half
dozen high-tech job banks, including
MacWorld Job Bank, SunWorld Job Bank,
JavaWorld Job Bank, NetscapeWorld Job
Bank, and NCWorld Job Bank. Instead of
listing each job bank separately, I list the
main page for all the banks. I took a look
at the individual job banks, and I recommend that you at least browse them. The
sites are well organized and offer highly
targeted jobs according to the title of the
job bank.

TechJobBank

www.techjobbank.com/

See the entry for "CircuitOnline" earlier in
this section.

Virtual Search

www.vsearch.com/jobs.htm

*Unusually idealistic job site for multimedia
experts:* Virtual Search is all about finding
great multimedia jobs, with an emphasis
on helping people, not hyping themselves. Virtual Search is an executive
search firm, so be prepared to get calls
pretty quickly if you contact them via
e-mail. To see the jobs, click on the
Current Openings tab. You find categories
for engineers, computer artists, designers, marketing, producing, and others. I
found the job descriptions to be very
honest. High-level skills requirements are
noted, and almost all the jobs available in
Virtual Search are for high-level techies.
This one is worth a visit if you're in this
niche.

Westech Virtual Job Fair

www.hightechcareers.com/

★★ ▢

*High-profile site loaded with jobs for those
in high-tech:* One of the keywords I use to
test sites is *programmer,* which shakes
out a whole lot of jobs at most sites. At
the Westech Virtual Job Fair, my *programmer* search yielded 310 matches, which is
a bit low for a site with so much hype.
However, I found an interesting mix of
jobs that I didn't see anywhere else, with
an emphasis on larger, more established
companies. To search this site for a job,
simply type the pertinent keywords in the
search boxes that you see right on the
opening page. The results page is clean
and easy to read. I found jobs for systems
programmers at Visa, HAL Computer
Systems (a Fujitsu Company), SAIC,
California Insurance Group, Federal
Express, Hewlett Packard, and Honeywell-
Measurex. As for resumes, you can post
one with your personal information
blocked out. If you post your full information, be aware that the database is open
to any employer who registers.

ZDNet Jobs

www.zdnet.com/cc/jobs/jobs.html

★★ ▢

Very large database of high-tech jobs: At
the ZDNet job database, you can search
for jobs or post your resume. To post
your resume, you will be zipped right
over to jobEngine (see the entry in this
section under "jobEngine"). If you want to
see jobs, again, you will be zipped right
over to the jobEngine database. I list the
ZDNet database separately because so
many people know of ZDNet.

Other Stuff to Check Out

infotech.jobs-careers.com/
ws3.scripting.com/ads/
www.atlanta.computerjobs.com
www.chicago.computerjobs.com
www.computerjobs.com/
www.computerwork.com/
www.dynamichost.com/jobs/
www.engineerweb.com/
www.hotjobs.com
www.interdev.com/main.html
www.mas-jobs.com
www.ntes.com
www.recruitersonline.com/
www.scitechjobs.com/
www.se-tech.com
www.siliconvalleyjobs.com
www.texas.computerjobs.com
www.tjobs.com/

Career Focus: Advertising, Sales, Marketing, and PR Jobs

At the beginning of this directory, you find a section detailing the Big Seven, or the biggest job databases on the Web. To find the *most* jobs in sales, marketing, advertising, and public relations, it's important to browse those giant job listings. Of the Big Seven, the Monster Board, Yahoo! Classifieds, CareerPath.com, and E.span have the most jobs in sales, marketing, and so on. But companies advertising jobs on the Big Seven tend to have lots of money for job advertising, and you see the same large companies over and over again. Effectively, that means that browsing the Big Seven taps only a small portion of the available jobs. To get leads on small and mid-sized companies, try specialty job databases dedicated to posting jobs in your profession. The small databases usually charge lower fees and enable you

to access offerings from smaller companies. The small databases that I list in the following section lead you to fewer jobs, but to jobs that you may not see anywhere else.

Advertising Age Job Bank

www.adage.com/

Advertising Age offers jobs in conjunction with the Monster Board. Please see the Monster Board listing in "The Big Seven" section of this directory.

Adweek Online

www.adweek.com

★★
★★

Great resource for advertising, marketing, and PR pros: If you're in advertising, marketing, or public relations, I hope that you're already well aware of this site. If you're not, I'm happy to point it out to you. Open the main page — which is packed with news quips, features, and interviews with key players — scroll down to the Help Wanted link at the bottom of the page. The Help Wanted page is just a simple list of job categories, like Marketing/Brand Management, Advertising/PR Account Management, and so on. Jobs are posted weekly, so you won't encounter stale job ads. I was very impressed with the number and quality of the jobs at this site. A sampling of the jobs I found includes director of marketing in Atlanta, promotion assistant for ABC Sports in New York City (how fun!), and director of database marketing in

La Jolla, California. To apply for a position, send your resume directly to the person listed in the advertisement.

CareerMart

www.careermart.com/

General job board, but with good sales, advertising, and marketing ads: CareerMart has a fresh-out-of-college feel to it, plus it has *the* most innovative and creative graphic design of a job database. On the home page, you see a three-dimensional representation of a career mart, complete with a noisy crowd and a "resume bank." Click on the graphic or on the text links to enter the career mart. As for job searching, you can use a variety of criteria, such as the region in which you want to look. I found a good supply of marketing jobs at this site, including positions for a product supply analyst, a general manager, and a project manager. The resume bank is password-protected, but you need to ensure confidentiality on your own. This site is worth keeping an eye on, as it's the type of site that may grow much larger.

Direct Marketing World

www.dmworld.com/

An online info center for the direct marketing industry: This niche site may prove helpful if you're looking for a job in direct marketing. The site boasts about 200 new jobs per month and about the same number of resumes. After you open the site, click on the DM World Job Center link at the top of the page. Then scroll down to the Search for Jobs link or the Post a Resume link. The job-search page supplies you with a basic search engine, or you can view all the posted jobs, as I did. A percentage of the job ads were indeed for marketing positions, but a few technical jobs were on the list, too. The

resume database is open, and I found a number of excellent resumes (so good that I use one in this book, with permission), so feel free to look through the resumes for ideas. This site would greatly benefit from a tighter focus on the marketing niche, but you can still get a lucky break here by diligently checking back for the occasional gem.

Marketing Classifieds

www.marketingjobs.com

Somewhat unfriendly interface, but delivers targeted jobs: The Marketing Classifieds page makes several errors in attracting job seekers. Mainly, you really have to know what you're looking for, and getting where you want to go takes a lot of clicking. Plus, you have to click through a long trail to actually get to the jobs. From the opening page, click on the Job Listings link, which takes you to the Search the Jobs Database link. Click on that, and you finally get a single search box with no frills or thrills. Type in a keyword and hope beyond hope that the very basic search engine finds what you want. (I entered the keyword *marketing* and received a page or two of jobs.) Clicking on any position gives you a detailed description of the position, followed by contact information, which you use to contact employers directly. You can post a resume at this site, too. The resumes are password-protected, but you have to make sure that your information is confidential. The site, like most sites these days, features an e-mail service that e-mails jobs to you.

NationJob Network Marketing and Sales Jobs Page

www.nationjob.com/marketing

Many leads for sales positions: This page opens with a long, basic list of jobs. Just scroll down to view all of them. You can sign up for NationJob's e-mail agent to get jobs matching your criteria sent to your e-mail box. On my visit, I found all sorts of positions for account executives and marketing specialists. Intermingled in the jobs were some unusual opportunities, to say the least. I found an opening for a carcass trainee, for example — actually a decent-paying job at a Fortune 100 company. (After training, you sell meat!) This site is worth a look.

Retail Jobnet

www.retailjobnet.com/

$

An unpretentious site that gets the job done: I'm not thrilled that this site charges you to post resumes, but I do like the job announcements that you can find here. Click on the "Start Your Career Search Here!" menu option and go to a full-featured search engine, where you can specify which metro area you want to work in, what position title you want, and more. I specified the position of advertising manager anywhere and netted nice results. The position results are delivered to you in a user-friendly chart that tells you the position title, company, location, and reference number; you can view a detailed job description if you want. Each job description contains contact information to follow up on. You can also have Retail Jobnet e-mail position announcements to you.

Other Stuff to Check Out

www.ama.org/
www.clickit.com/execunet/
www.commarts.com
www.dwr.www.com.au/advertising/
    adve_main.html
www.halcyon.com/mcoles/awc/
www.marketingtools.com
www.popjobs.com/
www.prsa.org/
www.publicity.com
www.realbank.com/
www.shsinc.com

Career Focus: Legal Jobs

If you are a practicing attorney or planning to be one soon, this section of the directory is for you. I found a number of extremely compelling job databases dedicated to the legal arts. In fact, one of the databases, Attorneys @ Work, is one of my ten favorite job databases on the Web because of its high quality and its excellent resume-privacy policies. If you are a paralegal or work in another support capacity, then by all means check out this section. A number of the legal arts databases also contain opportunities for administrative experts.

Attorneys @ Work

www.attorneysatwork.com

★★ ★★

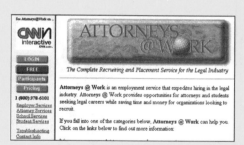

One of the best job databases on the Web: I was very impressed with the folks at Attorneys @ Work when I interviewed them for this book. They really know what they're doing, and the CEO is a savvy, experienced business professional. Moreover, more than 300 of the nation's leading law firms have signed up to offer jobs on this site. I personally know several people who have used the job services at this site, all with excellent results. Though the home page doesn't boast killer graphics, the high-level jobs consistently available, combined with the ability to control your resume from start to finish with complete confidentiality, is impressive. The only reason I didn't include this site in the Big Seven list is that it focuses on the legal profession and as such cannot appeal to the widest range of job seekers.

Department of Justice Attorney Vacancies

www.usdoj.gov/careers/oapm/jobs/

Selected attorney vacancies for experienced attorneys: This no-frills Web page provides a quick list of openings at the Department of Justice. On the opening page, a simple list of links takes you to job listings, available via the Selected Attorney Vacancies link. New grads can link to information about the DOJ's summer law intern program. Worth a look-see.

FindLaw

www.findlaw.com

★★
★★

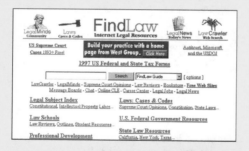

The best source of Internet legal resources: Okay, FindLaw is not technically just a job database. However, it contains great job listings and is an extraordinary legal resource that absolutely will help you in your job search. Opening the FindLaw page lands you at a clean-looking menu. Scan the links to legal data and be grateful that some soul took the time to

collect all those links for you! Then click on the Employment link under the Professional Development heading and scroll down the Employment page to see link after link to job listings all over the Web. On my visit, I looked carefully at the listings in the FindLaw job database and found openings for attorneys, summer clerks, law librarians, paralegals, and legal secretaries. The jobs are listed by state, and not every state contains a listing, but despite the smaller number of jobs, the FindLaw database is worthy of a browse. This site is about quality, not quantity.

Law Employment Center

www.lawjobs.com

★★ 🔗
★★

Hundreds of jobs from the National Law Journal, New York Law Journal, *and others:* The opening page of the Law Employment Center is loaded with distracting links for the legal job seeker — links to legal recruiters and articles on employment trends, an index to the nation's largest law firms, and, of course, access to the Law Employment Center's Legal Job Listings. Click on the Legal Job Listings Link on the opening page to browse jobs by category or region, or do as I did and look at all the jobs at once. I found hundreds of high-quality listings for attorneys in every imaginable specialty, from patent to merger negotiations to antitrust to securities. If you're interested in a position, use the contact information listed in the job ad to respond directly to the employer.

Other Stuff to Check Out

seamless.com/jobs/index.html
www.lawforum.net/employ.htm
www.nationjob.com/legal
www.voicenet.com/~dhumes/

Career Focus: A Sampling of Career-Focused Databases

In this section, I share a collection of truly helpful databases dedicated to a single career focus. For example, I include a database listing jobs for police officers and another listing positions for mathematicians. The list is alphabetical, so to find a particular discipline, look through the list and read the first line of the description — I tell you right up front who the database is for. Also, the list is arbitrary; I chose databases that provide a high level of excellent content. I hope that one of them fits your area of specialty!

Academic Employment Network

www.academploy.com/

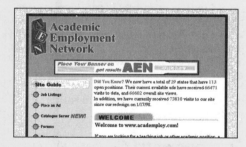

Jobs for teachers at all levels: I found jobs at this well-organized, easy-to-follow site asking for deans of well-known business schools as well as for elementary school math teachers. You won't find hundreds of jobs at this site, but the jobs that are available are of a very high caliber. Very much worth a visit.

American Mathematical Society

www.ams.org/

Jobs for high-level mathematicians: This clean, well-organized site is the official site of the American Mathematical Society. For jobs, just click on the Employment and Careers option. Follow the directions you find at the page, and you end up at a lengthy list of high-level mathematics jobs, from university research positions to industrial statisticians.

Aviation-Aerospace Jobs

www.nationjob.com/aviation

Jobs for aviators, aerospace experts, and support personnel: This database is part of the NationJob Network of specialized job databases. The NationJob databases don't always get all the right "takers" in an industry, but this database is the definitive hot spot — it's very, very good. Just scroll down the page to find jobs from entry-level technicians to aircraft dispatchers to pilots. A great site; don't miss it if you work in this field.

The Blue Line

www.theblueline.com/

★ ★
★ ★

Jobs for law enforcement professionals: This fabulous site is well maintained and hosts high-quality jobs. When I visited, I found nationwide job listings for police officers and dispatchers, firefighters, paramedics, and even a listing from the Department of Justice for a special agent. You should definitely visit this site if you work in this profession. The site also has a feature that e-mails you new job listings.

CFO Jobs

www.cfonet.com/html/cfojobs.html

Listings for CFO positions: I found a modest but interesting listing of CFO (chief financial officer) positions at this site. For example, I found a listing for CFO positions in a well-known restaurant chain and a Silicon Valley multimillion-dollar company, and a region controller in Latin America. This is an excellent corollary site to keep on your visit list.

Chemistry Job Hunting Guide

chemistry.mond.org/

High-level chemistry jobs: Chemistry & Industry Magazine officially hosts this rich site filled with chemistry resources and jobs. Clicking on the Job Search link takes you to the Job Search page, where you can subscribe to receive e-mail updates of new jobs, search the job database, or read up on job hunting tips for chemists. You need to select which specific type of chemistry job you're interested in, such as analytical, inorganic, or chemical, to search the database. You can also use the search engine and search by company name.

Cool Works

www.coolworks.com/showme/

Jobs at resorts, at national parks, on ranches, on cruises, and at camps: The whole idea behind Cool Works is to show you where the jobs are in the most beautiful locations in the world. Do you want to spend the summer in Yosemite?

Do you want to feel the soft breezes of the Bahamas every day? Do you want to sweat it out on a cattle ranch? Then this is the site to visit! You find links to jobs in all the locations I just mentioned, plus many more that I didn't. If you want to play for a while instead of doing "real" work, don't miss this site.

Editor and Publisher Classifieds

epclassifieds.com/EPM/home.html

Positions in news media, newspapers, and publishing: This site is a great repository for all sorts of positions that are typically very difficult to find out about via word of mouth because editing and publishing positions fill so quickly. Clicking on the Employment link on the main page brings you to a search engine. I recommend using the pull-down menu provided to select a category to view. Like most focused sites, Editor and Publisher Classifieds doesn't boast high numbers (although I found over 100 editorial jobs), but it does provide high-quality jobs at mid-sized organizations, with some positions at larger and smaller companies mixed in. For example, I found a position advertised for a producer to manage the science section of ABCNews.com, a major gig. A page designer was at the top of the *Seattle Times'* wish list, as was a business editor for the *Arkansas Democrat-Gazette*, both being lower-profile in terms of circulation but high-profile in terms of professional standards.

Environmental Careers World

environmental-jobs.com/

★★
★★

Jobs for environmentalists and related professions: I am continually impressed by this site — from the clear directions to the blissful absence of hype. The job bank attracts great postings, evidenced by the lengthy list of high-quality jobs available.

On my visit, I found openings for botanists at the Missouri Department of Conservation, risk assessment specialists and a summer field research assistant in Alaska, a vertebrate evolutionary biologist for Sonoma State University, and much more. To apply for a job, contact the person listed on the job advertisement.

Library JobSearch

carousel.lis.uiuc.edu/~jobs/

Jobs in information science, from information brokers to reference librarians to library directors: This site is in the form of a simple list of jobs. But don't let the simplicity fool you — the site rounds up some of the best jobs around in library science. Typically, you find hundreds of jobs. I found openings for children's librarians, government documents librarians, catalogers, fine arts librarians, and even a library professor.

Medsearch

www.medsearch.com

Careers in healthcare and medicine: Medsearch is associated with the Online Career Center. It's a significant, nationwide medical jobs database, home to thousands of healthcare jobs. The easiest way to access the jobs is to click on the pull-down menu at the top of the opening page and select the type of job you want to see — for example, Allied Health, Nursing, Pharmaceuticals, and so on. I chose to view the nursing jobs. The site returned almost 600 newly posted nursing jobs, ranging from intensive care nurse manager to certified nurses' assistants. You can post your resume safely at this site — resumes are password-protected — and you can select a confidentiality option. This site is well worth a visit.

Newspaper Mania Job Central

www.club.innet.be/~year0230/jobs.htm

Jobs in the print and broadcast media: If you're interested in journalism, writing, or broadcast jobs, this is a good site to bookmark and visit. The organization is a bit messy, so just scroll down the page until you find the job area you're looking for. This site is a good starting point for turning up jobs that are very, very hard to find. Be sure to look at the National Diversity Journalism Job Bank (www.newsjobs.com/), to which you find a link at this site.

Online Sports Career Center

www.onlinesports.com/pages/
    CareerCenter.html

Sports- and recreation-related jobs: This straightforward site lets you post resumes in an open resume database for free and easily view a range of sports jobs. I found job listings for an assistant professor in sport administration, sales positions in athletic retail, physical education professors, an adult baseball league president, and more. I noticed many professorships in athletic areas, too.

Optics.org Employment Center

optics.org/employment/

The definitive job database for optics and photonics professionals: Optics' database looks better than ever. You can post your resume and, of course, search the position openings. This very reliable database has been online since at least 1994, and it consistently houses the best optics jobs.

Physics World Jobs Online

www.ioppublishing.com/cgi-bin/Jobs/main

Physics jobs: Just click on the Current Vacancies link, and you head to a world of post-doctoral fellowships in subjects like condensed matter theory and optical design, Ph.D. student researcher positions, quantitative analyst positions, and other challenging opportunities. Jobs are worldwide, with about 50 new positions typically on tap.

Science Professional Network

recruit.sciencemag.org/

Jobs and career resources for high-level scientists: And I do mean high-level. You find many positions targeted to all sorts of sciences listed here, but you'd better be qualified. I found jobs for molecular biologists, physicists, quantitative chemists, botanists, and molecular cytogeneticists, to name but a few. You can post your resume for free if you plan to attend one or more *Science Magazine*-sponsored career fairs.

Social Work and Social Services Jobs Online

gwbweb.wustl.edu

★ ★ 🔗
★ ★

Extraordinary resources for social workers and psychologists: This site, hosted by the George Warren Brown School of Social Work, is not a job database site. Rather, it's quite literally the most comprehensive collection of links to every imaginable area of social service: affirmative action, addiction, adoption, counseling, disaster relief, death and dying, suicidology, welfare, obsessive-compulsive disorder, learning disorders, and so much more. This is a prime site for researching in your field and for finding links to relevant hiring associations and organizations.

Women's Wear Daily

www.wwd.com/classified/class.htm

Fashion jobs for designers, seamstresses, and fit models: Women's Wear Daily contains a great classifieds section that lists insider's jobs from entry to about mid-level, with a few high-level positions. On my visit, I found jobs for a Vera Wang fit model, a textile artist, seamstresses, patternmakers, and other positions within the fashion industry.

Other Stuff to Check Out

www.authorlink.com/jobavail.html
www.daily.umn.edu/~mckinney
ns2.faseb.org/careers/
www.mandy.com/
www.musicjobs.com/
www.newsjobs.com/
www.ohayosensei.com/~ohayo/
www.ua.ac.be/TourWeb/MWT/mwtjob.html

Regional Job-Search Meta Sites

Due to space considerations, I am able to list only a portion of the regional job databases available. However, four meta lists currently on the Internet offer giant lists of regionally oriented links and information. The four resources that you find in this section are of great value if you're trying to relocate or you want to look for jobs only in your region. Please be aware that regional job databases change URLs and close more quickly than other types of job databases.

CareerPath.com

www.careerpath.com

Search regional newspapers for jobs: CareerPath.com is a "Big Seven" job-search site, but beyond that, you may find regional information pertinent to your job search here. CareerPath.com is an online repository for newspaper job advertisements from dozens of newspapers across the United States. If you're living in a cold northerly state and you want to move to Florida, for example, you can select just the Florida newspapers to search. I spoke to several recent college graduates who used CareerPath.com for relocating to another part of the country — it worked well for them, and it can for you, too.

Job Resources by US Region

www.wm.edu/csrv/career/stualum/ jregion.html

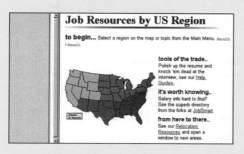

An incredible list of resources from the career offices of the College of William and Mary: The William and Mary Job Resources Web site is extraordinary in its depth and breadth. The site features a clickable map that makes it simple for you to search through mountains of

information quickly. Click on an area of the country that you want to explore, and the site takes you to long lists of pertinent regional information. The best feature of this site is that it includes even the smallest regional resources, so you can investigate every possible avenue. For less populous states, like Alaska, the smaller resources sometimes end up containing the best job leads.

Purdue's Job Listings for Specific Geographical Areas

www.ups.purdue.edu/Student/ geograph.htm

Detailed, state-by-state listings: The Purdue list of regional job databases is organized by state as opposed to region. This setup makes for slower searching, but the interface is simple enough. Simply open the URL and scroll down the page. You see a monster list of states. The Purdue list does not contain as many resources as the William and Mary list, but it's an excellent geographically oriented resource.

Yahoo! Metros

www.yahoo.com

Robust index to various metropolitan areas in the United States: Yahoo! Metros are distinct Yahoo! indexes for 13 major metropolitan hubs and cities in the United States. Currently, each of the following cities has a Yahoo! Metro: Austin, Atlanta, Boston, Chicago, Dallas, Fort Worth, Los Angeles, Miami, Minneapolis/St. Paul, New York, San Francisco Bay Area, Seattle, and Washington, D.C. Each Yahoo! Metro contains rich regional information, including an absolutely terrific list of local job databases available nowhere else (that I could find, at least). To reach the Yahoo! Metros, go to the Yahoo! index at www.yahoo.com. Scroll to the bottom of the page to see the complete listing of Yahoo! Metros. I highly recommend a visit. Also, don't forget the Yahoo! Classifieds, which I mention in "The Big Seven" list of major job resources.

Regional Job Databases: West — Southwest

In this section, I review the top sites that help you find a job in the western and southwestern portions of the United States.

Alaska Jobs Center

www.ilovealaska.com/alaskajobs/
   #professional

★★
★★

Jobs and employment resources in Alaska: This site is a one-stop shop for jobs in Alaska, from seasonal work to fishing gigs to office jobs. The page is maintained as a complete hub for the state of Alaska in terms of employment in the private and public sectors. The bottom line is that if there's employment in Alaska, it's likely that this page will link you to it if the resource is online. The page is broken down into clear categories and is organized well. There's even a link to national parks, should you want to compete with the grizzly bears! This is a great resource if you want to hone in on a job in Alaska.

Bay Area Jobs

www.sonic.net/~allan/ba_jobs.html

Jobs in the Bay Area: This classic and well-established job database essentially gives you two options: You can visit the employment sections of local companies'

home pages, or you can browse the local job databases and the local online employment classifieds. If you're interested in getting work in the Bay Area, plan to spend some time at this treasure of a site.

Colorado Online Job Connection

www.peakweb.com/openings.html

Jobs throughout the state of Colorado, with a smattering of jobs in Austin and Dallas, Texas: This neat, clean site collects jobs in all occupational areas. The jobs are organized by location — that is, jobs in the Boulder area, in Denver and vicinity, and in Austin and Dallas. Many jobs are technically oriented, but there are jobs for healthcare workers, administrative personnel, and salespeople, too. The mix of jobs changes frequently, so check back regularly.

Desert Links

www.desert.net/disk$ebony/tw/www/
   links/All/index.htmlx

Links for Arizona and New Mexico: This site is not a job database per se. The site is set up as an easy-to-use directory of links to businesses, newspaper classifieds, and a few job databases in these two states. To access online newspaper employment classifieds, click on the News and Media link. To find company home pages, click on the Business link and explore. Also helpful is the Government link, which takes you to various city government listings.

Employment Washington Seattle

Members.aol.com/gwattier/
   washjob.htm

Great links for jobs in the state of Washington: This site is essentially a list of links to all sorts of employment resources. After you open the main page, scroll down to the table of contents. From there, you can browse employers' Web pages; school, college, and university Web pages; government Web pages; and links to local headhunters and temporary employment agencies. Well worth a look!

JobSmart California Job Search Guide

jobsmart.org/

★★
★★

The best site for finding a job in California: JobSmart is an extremely well-organized, well-designed site. Open the main page and you'll wish that everyone took employment Web site lessons from the folks who manage this site. You find information about getting ready for work and then getting work. In the getting work category, JobSmart lists local jobs, job fairs, job hotlines, and basically every scrap of job-related information you can find online. The information is grouped into three regional hubs: San Francisco, Los Angeles, and Sacramento. This great site is well worth visiting. *Note:* Another Web site has a very similar name, jobsmart.com, but it's an advertisement for a book. This site is jobsmart.org!

Montana Job Service

jsd.dli.mt.gov

Job listings in Montana: This straightforward site simply lists links for you to follow, and good links at that. At the opening page, scroll down to the Job Search Options heading. Explore the links there, and you'll find everything you need to get a job in Big Sky Country.

Oregon OnLine

www.state.or.us/

Jobs in Oregon: A contender for a prettiest background picture award with its opening picture of lovely Crater Lake, this site links you to government, community, commerce, and education. To view the government job listings, click on the Government link and scroll down to the State of Oregon Job Listings link. You're all set from there. To find private sector jobs, click on the Commerce link; you land at a page titled Economic Resources. Scanning the page, you see a healthy section called Job Opportunities that boasts extensive links to Oregon job databases and employment resources.

TOPjobs USA by DiSX

www.topjobsusa.com/

National job database with listings primarily in the Western U.S.: Although TOPjobs USA is a national database, every time I check it I find listings clustered in the states of California, Nevada, Colorado, Washington, Oregon, Utah, Arizona, and Texas. The database is a good, solid one, with many jobs to offer. The search results are organized geographically by state and city, so picking your job-search area is a simple task.

Other Stuff to Check Out

austin.yahoo.com
dfw.yahoo.com
la.yahoo.com
seattle.yahoo.com
sfbay.yahoo.com

www.dfwjobs.com/
www.htdc.org/joblink.html
www.intex.net/jobbs/dpjobb.html
www.pdxjobs.com/
www.socalbio.org/classified/jobs.htm

Regional Job Databases: Midwest

The following Web sites are high-quality sites that help you search for jobs in the Midwest.

ATN Net

www.atn.net/careerzone

Jobs in McHenry County, Illinois: ATN is a tidy, nicely managed site that does just what it says — it helps you find local jobs. I found good jobs covering a wide range of career areas at this site. All the jobs are local, with a few jobs in neighboring counties. You can also post your resume here. (McHenry County, by the way, is near Chicago.)

Chicago Computer Jobs Store

www.chicago.computerjobs.com/

Computer jobs in Chicago: If you want a job in a technical field and you want to work in Chicago, this is a great place to cyber-visit. The site is clearly laid out, so you won't have any trouble getting to the job-search area. The site lists a fair number of jobs — I found about 800 when I visited. You'll appreciate the great layout of the job-search area — you can click easily through the type of job you want without having to perform a keyword search.

Minnesota's Job Bank

www.des.state.mn.us/jobs/

A fantastic example of a great regional job database: If you want a job in Minnesota, you're in luck. Minnesota's Job Bank is a well-organized site that leads you to varied jobs throughout the state. At the opening page, select the MN Job Bank link. You head right to the Employment Opportunities and Information Page, where you can search job titles by keyword, occupation, or job number. This page also links to all the Minnesota State Employment Service Web sites. Because this job bank is well cared for, keyword searches turn up a good number of jobs. My search on the keyword *computer* turned up 69 jobs, which is great for a regional job bank. To post your resume, click on the ResumeBuilder link.

Missouri Works

www.works.state.mo.us/mw2a.htm

Jobs in Missouri: The Missouri Works site, sponsored by the state of Missouri, does a good job of making job information readily accessible. Just open the main page and click on the Search Missouri Jobs tab to conduct a statewide job search. Use the clickable map to explore jobs in a particular part of Missouri. Additional services available from the job-search area include links to education and law enforcement jobs.

Nebraska Job Service

www.dol.state.ne.us/jobserv.htm

Jobs in Nebraska: This plain site takes you to job listings for the state of Nebraska. Jobs are searchable by keyword, occupation, and job number. A keyword search on *computer* at this site brought back 16 jobs, which is a fair number considering the overall population of Nebraska.

North Dakota Job Service

nd.jobsearch.org/

Jobs in North Dakota: This no-frills site lets you explore the jobs currently available in North Dakota. At the main page, click on the Keyword Search link to search jobs by keyword. Or you can search jobs by looking at a menu of occupations. Click on the Menu Search link if a menu browse is your style. When I performed a keyword test at this site, I uncovered 12 computer jobs and a smattering of jobs in other fields.

South Dakota Department of Labor

sd.jobsearch.org/

Jobs in South Dakota: Although it is a rural state, South Dakota is fully wired into the online job search. From this basic job-search site maintained by South Dakota's Department of Labor, you can search jobs statewide. The search interface is straightforward: You can search by keyword, occupation, or job number. My keyword search on various occupations turned up a lot of support, sales, and service jobs. I also found academic jobs posted on this site.

Wisconsin JobNet Job Search

Badger.state.wi.us/agencies/dilhr

Jobs in Wisconsin: This Web site is managed by the Wisconsin department of Industry, Labor, and Human Relations. The resources at this site are plentiful, but you need to scroll through about four screens of the opening page to before you can click on the Job Openings heading. Click on the JobNet link, and you head right to the job-search area. When I perused the database, I found about 12,000 jobs scattered in most career areas. One feature unique to Wisconsin is the inclusion of farming and heavy farm machinery operating jobs. (I found over 200 jobs in the farming category on my visit!) A solid site that's well worth a visit.

Work Avenue.com

www.starnews.workavenue.com/ index.html

Jobs in Indianapolis: The *Indianapolis Star and News* hosts this nicely designed site. At the opening page, click on the Jobseekers Way link at the top of the page to view profiles of companies located in the Indianapolis area, or to look at the jobs offered. To check out the jobs, click on the Great Jobs link. You can look for jobs by city, job category, or keyword. In the computer category, I found 90 job listings for all parts of Indianapolis. In marketing and sales, I found 19 job listings, all of good quality. To post your resume at Work Avenue, click on the Resume option on the opening page. You get a lengthy form to fill out with space at the bottom to specify your resume status and desired level of confidentiality.

Other Stuff to Check Out

fnalpubs.fnal.gov/employ/jobs.html
members.tripod.com/~Jablon/assess.html
minn.yahoo.com
www.careerlink.org/
www.careermosaic.com/cm/ups/ups8.html
www.umn.edu/ohr/employ.html

Regional Job Databases: Northeast – Mid-Atlantic

Here you find a selection of job databases that can lead you to a position working in the northeastern or mid-Atlantic portion of the United States.

100 Careers in Wall Street

www.globalvillager.com/villager/
WSC.html

★ ★
★ ★

For those who want to work in the heart of New York City: The 100 Careers in Wall Street site lists financial jobs, as you would imagine, but it also lists technical and general business jobs. I always enjoy browsing this site because the jobs are typically very high-level and high-paying. For example, on my most recent visit, I found a slew of offerings, such as *Director of Marketing at prestigious brokerage firm, graduate degree required, to 100K plus bonus.* The quality of the jobs you find here is absolutely terrific — just be prepared for a detailed phone interview if you send in your resume.

Boston Job Bank

www.bostonjobs.com/

Jobs in Boston: This site is quick to the punch. Open the URL and you get to search for jobs right away. Just fill in the search box and you're in. (Why, oh, why don't more job sites let you search right away like this one does?) On my visit, I found a good mix of high-level jobs, such as corporate controller, along with entry-level and professional positions, such as staff accountant and executive assistant. A good, quick way to start looking for a job in Boston.

Henrico County Employment

www.co.henrico.va.us/personnel/rec/
howapply.html

Jobs in Henrico County, Virginia: Before you chuckle at the inclusion of such a home-grown site, let me explain that Henrico County is huge and has over 400 types of jobs available. You can print out an online application form or send an e-mail message requesting applications.

New York's Job Bank

www.labor.state.ny.us/job.search.html

Jobs throughout New York State: After you open the main page, you find three options for looking at job postings: You can search via a menu, via keywords, or by occupational code. Using my trusty keyword tests, I checked this board from top to bottom and netted solid results. Using the keyword *computer,* I found more than 100 matches, which is a good number for a statewide job service. Most of the jobs were located in Albany, Binghamton, Buffalo, Syracuse, and Rochester.

PhillyWorks

www.slipps.com/phillyworks/

Jobs in Philadelphia and surrounding areas: This great little site links you to local search firms, companies, classified advertisements, and, of course, job listings. I recommend deciding up front whether you want to work in a technical or a non-technical company, because that's how the site divides jobs. If you want to work in a tech company, click on the Information Tech/CIS link or on the Other Tech Link. If not, click on the Nontech link. Each link takes you to an expansive list of job resources. By the way, this site lists links to Delaware jobs, as well as to a few jobs in New Jersey.

Washington D.C. Resumail Network

www.washingtondc.resumail.com/
index.html

Jobs in the Washington, D.C. area: Despite the high-intensity graphical interface (which takes a while to load, so be patient), this site lists only a modest number of jobs. Never mind, though, because on a regional board, you're looking for the right job in the right place, and this site supplies great possibilities. From the opening screen, look for the Job Categories item. Use the pull-down menu to choose the career area you want, select the type of position you want (full-time, part-time, and so on), and start your search. The results page gives you all the contact information you need. Resumail's resume-posting service sends your resume everywhere — you really lose control of it. If you don't mind your resume getting into your boss's hands, then the Resumail service will not be a liability for you.

Other Stuff to Check Out

boston.yahoo.com
dc.yahoo.com
ftp.std.com/NE/boseconomy.html
ny.yahoo.com
www.nynma.org/jobs.cfm
www.somerset-hills.com/ymca/prog/
prog_career.html

Regional Job Databases: South – Southeast

In this section, you find a selection of the top regional databases in the south and southeastern United States.

Atlanta ComputerJobs Store

www.atlanta.computerjobs.com/

Computer jobs in Atlanta and vicinity: This site is great for anyone who wants to work in one of the most beautiful cities in the country. Atlanta is a pretty wired city, so you can typically expect to find about 3,000 recent computer jobs listed here. In addition to job listings, you can access numerous company profiles from this site.

The Charlotte's Web JobPage

www.charweb.org/job/jobpage.html

The Charlotte's Web JobPage

Gobs and Gobs (and Gobs) of Jobs!!

(Jump Down)

These pages contains links to state and local job listings as well as links to job banks around the country. There is also information to help you in your job search. If you find a job through one of these listings, we'd love to hear about it, please feel free to leave a comment. If you know of a job bank or resource that you don't see here, please let me know. Also, please understand that while I maintain this page, **I'm a computer consultant, by trade, not a recruiter!**

Jobs in North Carolina and some in South Carolina: This site is a rarity on the Web. It is maintained by a computer consultant, Robbi Meador, who has nothing to sell to you and is not recruiting for anyone. Amazing! The site is just a generous listing of job opportunities in the Carolinas. Scrolling down the main page, you find links to local job postings, government agency postings, North and South Carolina companies, and online classifieds. This is a terrific resource, especially amazing in light of the fact that it's a non-commercial site. Bravo!

Commonwealth of Kentucky

www.state.ky.us/

Jobs in Kentucky: This site is essentially a state government information hub, but you can, by careful clicking, find job information, too. At the opening page, you may be distracted by the race horse video, but scroll past it, and you eventually get to a link called Jobs in Kentucky.

You land at a comparatively sedate page where you can click on the Job Search tab. Finally, you find links to Kentucky's Job Bank, ky.jobsearch.org, and the Kentucky Personnel Cabinet, pershome.htm.

Welcome to The Career Spot

www.careerspot.com/

Jobs in South Florida: If working in a tropical climate suits you, then by all means meander to this Web site. At the opening page, you find all sorts of job resources: company profiles, an overview of the South Florida economy and area, and, of course, a job listing. To get to the jobs, click on the Job link. At the Job Search page, choose a category to search in — for example, computer, financial, technical (which turned up 275 listings), clerical, or sales. Click on Search and you're all set to get your list of job opportunities. I found a lot of jobs in various categories at this site.

Other Stuff to Check Out

atlanta.yahoo.com
miami.yahoo.com
www.esc.state.nc.us/jis/index.html
www.mindspring.com/~exchange/jobbank/
    ga/jobs.html
www.mriky.com/
www.state.sc.us/jobopps.html
www.state.tn.us/

Federal, State, Government, and Military Sites

Finding information relating to the federal government used to be like poking through an enormous paper maze. Now, however, quite a bit of federal information is handily posted on the Web. I'm happy to report that the federal government not only posts tons of general information on the Web but also does a superb job of posting great *job* information. In fact, some of the job resources I list in this section contain the highest number of jobs per database in cyberspace.

Even if you've never considered perusing federal job databases for opportunities before, I encourage you to give it a whirl. Anymore, such a wide variety of state-level and civilian opportunities are posted in federal databases that you can pick from literally 10,000 jobs for which you qualify.

In this section, you find a selection of the best and the biggest federal, state, government, and military databases.

Air Force Link

www.af.mil/sites/sites_com.html

The official Web site of the United States Air Force: Given that my brother is an Air Force pilot, I couldn't very well leave the Air Force off this list! Sibling concerns aside, the Air Force site has a well-thought-out career page, which includes job listings and pay charts for officers, civilians, and enlisted personnel. To get to the career page, simply click on the Career link on the opening page. If you're interested in a position, send an e-mail message or your resume to the contact person listed. (I checked — the job announcements always list an e-mail contact.)

American Federal Jobs Digest

www.jobsfed.com/

Massive listing of federal jobs: American Federal Jobs is a giant listing of — you guessed it — federal job opportunities. What makes this site worth a visit is that you can easily find the most *recent* job listings. On the opening page, you find a link to Today's Live Jobs. (No, you won't find a corresponding link to dead jobs. . . .)

The day I visited, I found well over 5,000 new jobs listed. I also like the way the site organizes job opportunities by occupation — no fussing with a search engine or wading through long lists. You can make your resume available for electronic search by federal employers, but I urge you to read all the fine print before you do so. As of this writing, an option box to submit your resume to non-federal employers is automatically checked. Talk about having zero control of your resume! If you post your resume, I recommend that you uncheck this box. (The box is obvious when you're viewing the page.)

Army Recruiting Web Site

www.goarmy.com

Being all you can be, online: If you visit this site, you may as well spend a few minutes looking around at the non-job offerings. You can download screen savers, find out about all sorts of Army doings, and, in general, get a good feel for what the Army is all about. The site practically oozes teamwork and tough-minded leadership. Job seekers can find links to various jobs (including jobs playing musical instruments in the Army band) as well as some pretty nifty enlistment incentives. If you don't want to go Army, you'd better not visit this site, because it's pretty convincing, and you'll find lots of job opportunities.

FedWorld

www.fedworld.gov/jobs/jobsearch.html

★★
★★

Major repository for business and technology-related federal jobs: FedWorld is a conglomerate of 20 federal job databases. The site is managed by the National Technical Information Service Technology Administration, which is a part of the U.S. Department of Commerce. The whole point of FedWorld's database is to make federal job searching simple. If you wonder what the big difference between FedWorld and Fjobs (see the next listing)

is, wonder no longer. After checking out the services, I can tell you that even though both databases provide extensive government job offerings, the jobs that are offered are not identical. Also, FedWorld allows you to search by using a search engine, whereas Fjobs uses a menu approach. Which site you use to find massive numbers of federal jobs is essentially a matter of preference. Your best bet is to try both and then settle with the site that you're most comfortable with.

Fjobs (also known as USA Jobs)

www.usajobs.opm.gov/

★★
★★

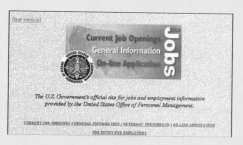

The U.S. government's official site for jobs and employment information: Fjobs is an extraordinary site put together by the U.S. Office of Personnel Management. It is extremely well designed, well organized, and easy to use. Click on the Current Job Openings link on the opening page to find a beautiful menu of six job areas: Professional Career, Entry Level Professional, Senior Executive, Summer, Clerical and Technician, and Trades and Labor. If the menu doesn't appeal to you, you can look at jobs alphabetically or by series. (*Series* is government-speak for level of position that pays a specified amount — for example, GS-13 is a Government Series 13 job. The government pay structure is extremely rigid and strictly predetermined, and it ranges from GS-1 to GS-15, with GS-15 being the highest-paying level.) I found thousands of jobs at this site, including positions for archeologists, park rangers, statisticians, loan clerks, firefighters, and a whole lot more. If you wish, you can apply for a job at this site, but the application process is somewhat complicated. Send an e-mail to the contact name given (and one *is* given!) if you get lost in the application process.

The Internet Job Source

www.statejobs.com

A giant collection of links to state and federal job opportunities: The Internet Job Source definitely doesn't win points for Web page design. But within the confusing layout, you find a collection of helpful links. On the opening page, scroll down to the links to Jobs by State and Federal Jobs. The Jobs by State page lists sources for private and government jobs. Each link on the list leads to dozens of job announcements. Think about it — running a state requires many levels of workers, from janitorial to clerical to travel representatives. You certainly have your pick of jobs. To follow the Federal Jobs link from the opening page, click on the link and scroll down to the list of jobs at individual federal agencies — actually one of the high points of this site. The list contains links to more federal agencies than you probably knew existed. Take a look at this list, if only to get ideas about what kinds of jobs are available.

Jobs in Government

www.jobsingovernment.com/

A site that pushes private-sector and government jobs your way: If you're interested in having state and federal jobs come to you, this site uses push technology to send pertinent job information to your e-mail address. You register by selecting a set of criteria for the jobs you want to see and then entering your name and a password of your choice. After you start getting e-mailed job announcements, you can reply to individual employers (via e-mail) if you choose to.

Navy Opportunities

www.navyjobs.com

Official site for finding seaworthy work: Wow! Who said that military Web sites have to be boring? This site packs a visual punch with its great graphics and snazzy, well-designed layout. Beyond layout, Navy Opportunities surprises you with great opportunities in healthcare as well as in high-tech and scientific areas. If you're at all inclined to sign up, by all means visit this site.

USA Jobs (also known as Fjobs)

www.usajobs.opm.gov/

See the entry for "Fjobs" earlier in this section.

Other Stuff to Check Out

helix.nih.gov:8001/jobs/
jobs.faa.gov/
www.dol.gov:8001/vacancy.nsf/
    ?Opendatabase
www.dot.gov
www.nps.gov
www.nsf.gov
www.peacecorps.gov/
www.sec.gov
www.si.edu
www.state.gov
www.usdoj.gov/careers/careers.html
www.usgs.gov
www.usmc.mil

Nonprofit Sites

If working in the arts and humanities makes your heart beat faster, then this section is a bonanza of information tailored just for you. Just a few years ago, finding good nonprofit information depended on word-of-mouth advice from experienced insiders. Nonprofits, in general, don't have plush advertising budgets that land them in the Sunday classifieds section. But with the advent of the ultimate bulletin board, the Web, nonprofits finally have an inexpensive way of getting the good word out. Now, finding good nonprofit information and jobs is as simple as logging on to the Web and checking out the following organizations.

Action Without Borders

www.idealist.org/

★★
★★

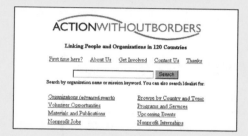

Extraordinary nonprofit site with an excellent job database: The front page of the Action Without Borders site claims to link people and organizations in 120 countries. It does. And in the process, the site provides an excellent, if not the hands-down best, nonprofit job database, plus access to a free weekly e-mail newsletter, a directory of nonprofit internships, and plenty of general nonprofit resource links. A clear menu on the front page lists the nonprofit jobs area. This site has a rich, full job database and an equally rich search engine. You can browse all jobs in the United States and worldwide, or you can search by job description or area of focus, like youth counselor (description) or children and youth (area of focus). I located splendid nonprofit jobs at this site — examples include a director of development for the Society for the Prevention of Cruelty to Animals, a proposal writer, a juvenile case coordinator, a rural finance specialist, and freelance instructors.

Internet Nonprofit Center

www.nonprofits.org/

Meta-site for finding nonprofit organizations: The Internet Nonprofit Center is not a job database per se. What you gain from visiting this site is immediate access to almost every nonprofit organization in the United States and many abroad. If you have a target organization in mind, chances are high that you can find the organization via this site. A nice feature is the mapping utility, called the Nonprofit Locator, which can find over a million tax-exempt organizations for you. After you find an organization, you see all the pertinent information, such as income, assets, and contact name. A nifty map feature blasts you to the exact location of the organization. That way, before you apply for that job advertised in Grapevine, Texas, or Whitefish, Montana, you know exactly what you're getting into.

Nonprofit Career Network

www.nonprofitcareer.com/

$

Large, well-organized site with high-quality nonprofit job listings and job fair information: The Nonprofit Career Network aims to be a one-stop resource (or shall I say one-click resource?) for individuals working in the nonprofit sector. The best resources at this site include the job fair info and the job database. The site's front page offers a clear menu of easy-to-follow links. Job fair information is free of charge and is organized by month. The job center takes you to a nice menu of links covering resumes, membership, and national job listings. Note that in order to post your resume, you get to pay a hefty $40 fee. But looking at the great list of jobs available is completely free. The job listing area has a nice search engine that you can use to search by job type or regional preference. The list of excellent jobs typically hovers between 100 and 200. Some of the jobs I encountered on my visit included chief financial officer for Bushnell, bookkeeper for the Leukemia Society of America, and director of libraries for the Foundation Center in New York — some of the best nonprofit employers out there.

Opportunity NOCs

www.tmcenter.org/

$

Nationwide job listings for paid positions in the arts and humanities: NOC stands for Nonprofit Organization Classifieds. The NOC classifieds cover jobs in six regions: Atlanta, Boston, Dallas, Los Angeles, Philadelphia, and San Francisco. You can view job excellent job listings from the Web site, but be aware that to view the most recent listings, you need to subscribe to a low-cost newsletter. (As of this writing, a subscription cost between $10 and $24, depending on the region.) If you're interested in nonprofit employment, Opportunity NOCs is well worth a visit, and really, you can get what you need without purchasing the subscription.

Philanthropy Journal Online

Jobs.pj.org

Nonprofit jobs from around the nation in an easy-to-view format: The Philanthropy Journal Online's job-search page takes some time to download, because what you see when the page finishes is a colorful, clickable map linking to nonprofit jobs by region. You can also view jobs by category. You won't find thousands of jobs listed, but the jobs you do find are of the highest quality. For example, I found listings for a development officer at the Columbia University

School of Law and for an executive director of United Way. If you get tired of looking at job listings, you can subscribe to the *Philanthropy Journal Alert,* a free e-mail newsletter that keeps you up-to-date on nonprofit issues.

Other Stuff to Check Out

Libertynet.org/~zelson/vol.html
www.clark.net/pub/pwalker
www.eskimo.com/~pbarber
www.idealist.org
www.philanthropy-journal.org/

Diversity Sites

Sure, I could have put any of the Web sites listed in this diversity section in the general listings section of this directory. However, some job resources are so compelling that I want to list them separately to be sure that you can find them easily. I'm impressed by the dedication and extra effort that each site in this section has clearly put into designing and maintaining job-related Web pages. Many employers are looking for ways to connect with specific diverse job candidates, and diversity-oriented Web sites are a perfect vehicle for doing just that. Diversity sites are particularly valuable tools if you want to be sure that you're applying to an organization or company that will roll out a big welcome mat for you.

ASPIRE Online

www.indiana.edu/~aspire/

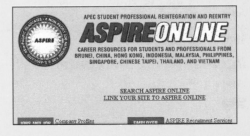

Superb job database and career resources for individuals from Brunei, China, Indonesia, Malaysia, Philippines, Singapore, Chinese Taipei, Thailand, and Vietnam: ASPIRE Online is a nonprofit job network for Asia-Pacific graduates. ASPIRE grants enormous gifts to visitors, including lists of job announcements, company profiles, a free newsletter, articles, recruitment services, and a private resume database. The job announcement list looks deceptively short, filling only two pages. But follow any link and you find gold mines of jobs. The jobs are of the highest caliber, most requiring a minimum of a bachelor's degree, with some requiring master's degrees on up. The resume database, called the Asia-Pacific Job Seeker's Database, lets you enter your resume information online. You can block your identifying information to keep your resume confidential.

The Black Collegian Online

www.black-collegian.com/

★★ ★★

Content-rich career site for students and professionals of color: The Black Collegian Web site is the electronic version of the national career magazine of the same name. In addition to the extraordinary career resources and articles at this site, you have access to huge job and resume databases. The job database is a bit tricky to find; you need to look under the Site Sponsor link, which is clearly noted on the front page menu. At the bottom of Site Sponsor page, click on the Jobs link. Finally, you have access to the Open

Positions Database, where you can uncover your dream opportunity, searching the thousands of job opportunities at this four-star site by either keyword or employer. Posting your resume is free, and you can request that your information remain confidential. One of the hallmarks of a strong resume database is that employers actually look at it. Let's just say that if you're a person of color, you will get a lot of employer interest if you post your resume here.

LatinoWeb

www.latinoweb.com/allusers.html

A virtual information center of Latino resources: LatinoWeb offers plenty of Latino resources for your job search. You can register for free e-mail, sign up for a free LatinoWeb home page, peruse Latino-related publications, and, yes, browse jobs. The job listings at LatinoWeb are not the best organized — they're listed alphabetically in a monster list that continues for pages and pages. However, I've talked with some of the companies listing jobs on LatinoWeb, and the jobs you see are the real thing. Employers told me that they list jobs on LatinoWeb because they absolutely want to recruit Latinos. If you're Latino, make sure to mention that you found the job listing via LatinoWeb when you apply, and your chances are very good.

Saludos Web

www.saludos.com

★★ ★★

Dedicated to promoting Latino careers and education: Saludos Web doesn't blow you away with graphics, but it does get your attention with great content. The site practically vibrates with good intentions, and it does a great job of providing Latino job seekers with general career information, as well as compelling job advertisements and a resume database, which Saludos Web calls a *resume pool.* Please note that resumes in the resume pool are open for all to see and browse. When I visited the job listings at this site, I was impressed by the dedication of the employers to recruiting Latino candidates. Jobs are arranged by state, job field, and company. You don't find overwhelming numbers of jobs here, but you do find high-quality jobs.

Women's Wire

Womenswire.com/work/?wcicareer

Colorful, information-packed site about women and careers: Are you interested in chatting with other frustrated job seekers? Do you want to read up on the best companies for women to work for in the United States? Then Women's Wire is a superb Web water cooler to drop in on. The site is organized nicely, with all the links and information you need contained on one concise opening page. The job database is "powered by" Monster Board, or so says the site. (See the Monster Board entry in "The Big Seven" section earlier in this directory.) When you search the job listings, you really are searching the Monster Board listings, not listings unique to Women's Wire. Similarly, the resume section of Women's Wire uses Monster Board technology to post resumes. Still, the chat feature of Women's Wire makes the site worth a visit.

Other Stuff to Check Out

findjob.womenconnect.com/
www.diversitycareers.com/
www.fortyplus.org
www.minorities-jb.com/
www.narf.org
www.nsbe.org
www.rici.com/acw/index.html

International Job Databases

So it's too snowy in the winter, too humid and buggy in the summer, and you're *really* ready for a change. If you want to, you can easily use the Web sites in this section to dramatically alter your surroundings by landing a job in a different country. Let me forewarn you, though — many people I know who have taken overseas jobs have bemoaned their decisions within a few short months of landing on purportedly greener pastures overseas. But if you really want to pursue a job in another country, this list should prove a valuable starting place.

Important note of warning for all job seekers: If any international site asks you to pay up front for a list of jobs or asks you to in any way let loose with some of your hard-earned cash, run, don't walk, away from that Web site. So many international job scams exist that I can't begin to keep track of them all. Keep your money in the bank, and you'll be fine.

One further word of warning before you begin your forays: I've noticed that international URLs tend to change frequently. I keep an updated list of the links in this directory, including the international links, at my Web site, www.pamdixon.com.

Tip: If you come across a Web page in Italian, German, Spanish, French, or Portuguese, you can use the free AltaVista translation service to un-scramble the text. Just go to the AltaVista search engine at www.altavista.digital.com/ and click on the Translations tab. In the translation box, type the URL of the page you want translated, and then choose the translation you desire from the pull-down menu. Try it — it works like a charm!

Please note that the translation occurs essentially before your eyes and may take a few moments, so be patient. Also, the translator takes a little more effort to use with frames, and some phrases do not translate well, but you should get enough to be able to understand what's going on. (*Frames* are a design feature that some Web page designers like to use. Frames break Web pages into separate "frames" or subpages within a page.)

Asian Career Web

www.rici.com/acw/

$

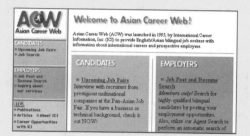

Jobs for English/Asian bilinguals: Asian Career Web is a service of International Career Information, Inc. Its mission is to assist multinational corporations in recruiting bilingual employees. Though many of ICI's services carry a price tag, searching the employment opportunities is free. When you click on the Job Search option on the main page, you see an applicant registration page. Click on the Register Now button to go to a long form that you need to fill in — this site uses e-mail to send you job listings matching your qualifications. After completing the form, you're greeted with a pitch to send in money for a job fair. Doing so is not required. Simply click on Register, and your information is stored on the site's database. I had a lot of trouble performing the registration at this site. If you have problems, send an e-mail to the contact e-mail address listed at the bottom of the page. The person handling the e-mail will help you get registered.

Bolsa de Trabajo

www.infosel.com.mx/BolsaDeTrabajo/

$

Job-search tool for people who want to work in Mexico: Bolsa de Trabajo is a well-organized site that brings job candidates and employers together. The site translates well, so you should have no difficulty navigating or understanding it. (See the introduction of this section for help with online translation.) The Profesionista link takes you to job opportunities in Mexico. I found excellent opportunities, from agricultural to veterinarian, listed at the site. *Please be aware that this is a commercial site* — you can view a sample of listings, but you have to pay to see them all. My suggestion is to browse the freebies and move on.

Byron Employment Australia

Employment.byron.com.au/

A near-comprehensive listing of positions around Australia and the UK: This well-designed site has many jobs posted in a wide variety of occupations. On the opening page, you see all sorts of links, each pertaining to an occupation. Click on the category that interests you, and you go straight to a robust list of jobs that's updated weekly. Each job lists a contact name and relevant contact information. Scrolling down the opening page, you find a helpful set of links leading to other Australian job databases.

CareerChina

www.globalvillager.com/villager/
   CC.html

Database of jobs primarily in China, Singapore, and Hong Kong: CareerChina is a simple job database where you find jobs sorted by date of posting and that's about it. The jobs are primarily in the IT area — I noticed postings for Oracle DBAs, UNIX system administrators, and software engineers. Each job posting contains contact information; CareerChina does not maintain a resume database, so the site asks you to send your resumes individually to employers.

EscapeArtist.com

www.escapeartist.com

★★
★★

Over 3,500 pages of resources for expatriates and those who wish to be but aren't yet: EscapeArtist has a fun, hip name, but the Web site is all business in terms of content. You find a wealth of resources here — everything from offshore banks to global real estate to detailed information on "escaping from America." This site provides information about areas pretty much ignored by other Web sites, such as the Caribbean and smaller European countries. To search for job information, click on the Jobs Overseas link, located on the opening page. Click on the country you're interested in from the lengthy list, and you see a comprehensive (or very near to it) list of links to job databases in that country. When I looked at Canada's page, I found over 20 links to databases. This is a prime resource if you want to work overseas.

Hong Kong Jobs

www.hkjobs.com/

Web site dedicated to providing recruitment information in Hong Kong: This site is a little difficult to navigate, but it boasts plenty of solid content to compensate for the difficulty you encounter. The site is busy — it's accessed approximately 19,000 times per day, which is a considerable number for an international job database. You can submit your resume for free, and you can even have someone review it for you. When I checked, I found a healthy number of openings, many in technology-related fields, as you might expect from Hong Kong (it's one of the most wired cities in the world).

Intermediar

www.bpa.nl/intermediair/

Premium job bank for positions in the Netherlands: This site has major corporate sponsorship and lots of compelling jobs listed. There isn't a word of English on the site, so you have to be pretty serious about working in the Netherlands (or be very good at interpreting icons) to look here. Job postings are available from the Vacatures link, and you can post resumes from the Reactie Aan de Redactie link. (*Note:* The submit buttons read "verstuur" at this site.)

International Computer Professional Associates

www.icpa.com/

Worldwide recruitment of computer professionals: The emphasis at this nicely designed site is on attracting candidates in the technology, marketing, and finance fields for jobs in the Pacific Rim. At the site, you find job listings, a contact name to send ASCII resumes to, and links to articles about Asia. I should issue a warning, though: If you're a high-level IT specialist and send in your resume, be prepared to start interviewing *immediately*. This site is well trafficked.

JobNet Australia

www.jobnet.com.au/index.html

★★
★★

Major recruitment agency hub for Australia and New Zealand: This nicely maintained site has a healthy database of jobs, plus an e-mail agent that sends you jobs that match your criteria. The jobs are updated daily and are mainly in the area of IT management and other technology-related careers. I found over 4,000 jobs listed. A sampling from my visit includes Novell engineer, senior business analyst, Oracle DBA, Visual Basic developer, and UNIX system administrator.

JobOnline

www.tin.it/jobonline/

Non perdere tempo — don't lose any time! Modest repository of jobs in Italy: This site, written in Italian, gives you a modest but high-quality listing of jobs available in Italy. At this site, you always need to scroll to the bottom of pages to see the job listings. At the opening page, scroll down to see a list of links to the other pages of the site. Typically, the list is short. I recommend that you translate this page unless your Italian is spectacular. (See the introduction to this section for translation details.) Click on the Job Network link, which after translation actually reads "the offered ones of Lavoro." (Just look for the word *Lavoro* on the list, click on the link, and you're all set.) At the Job Network page, again, scroll down to see the jobs; you find a good description of each job along with an e-mail contact.

Jobs.cz

www.jobs.cz/

Jobs in Czechoslovakia: This site offers jobs, and the design of the site is just dandy. To see a list of jobs, click on the Volna Mista link. To send e-mail, click on the Minite Zamistnani link. Sorry, folks — I don't have a Czech translator, and that's about all I could figure out! My gut tells me, though, that this is a good site. I found a robust list of jobs for administrative, marketing, technical, finance, and telecommunications professionals.

JobSite

www.jobsite.co.uk/

Excellent database for UK jobs: I found over 3,000 jobs posted at this site. Most of the jobs are located within the United Kingdom, and all are very recently posted. I found jobs in the following areas on my visit: IT, networking, engineering, accounting, sales, marketing, secretarial, management and executive, and legal. You also can sign up to have jobs matching your criteria e-mailed to you.

Malaysia Online

www.mol.com/recruit/default.htm

Straightforward listing of jobs in Malaysia: This site is thankfully written in English, so you won't have any trouble reading the basic text. The opening page contains a simple list of jobs available. I found jobs offered primarily in the technology and sales areas. To the left of the opening page, you find a menu with links to a resume depot, company profiles, contact information, and a mailing list. The English at this site is ever so slightly off, so you may need to read between a few grammatical errors.

Overseas Jobs Web

www.overseasjobs.com/do/jobs.cgi/ overseas

★★
★★

International jobs super-site: This easy-to-navigate site lists jobs by category, which is an unusual departure from most overseas job meta-databases, which typically list jobs by country. You find about 40 categories of job types, like arts and design, medical, construction, retail, sport, seasonal, hotel, and information technology, to name just a few. In the medical category, I found over a dozen jobs. One was for a product development manager for a scientific company located in Galway, Ireland. Another was for a controller in Shanghai, China. You certainly won't be bored as you cruise the jobs at this site! The site welcomes your ASCII or Web resume for posting.

NetJobs

www.netjobs.com/

$

An extensive site for jobs in Canada: This is a rather loud, flashy kind of site that toots its own horn. Nevertheless, it's a great place for looking at jobs based in Canada, particularly high-tech jobs. When you get to the job-search page, available from the opening page, you can search jobs by category, company, location, or date of posting. The company roster is primarily technical, so the jobs offered tend to follow suit. I did find some excellent academically oriented jobs in the mix, though. You can post your resume at NetJobs, but it costs you. (I do not advocate paying to post your resume, but the choice is yours.)

Platsbanken

Jobb.amv.se/

Jobs in Sweden: A simple, lovely site written in Swedish. The links are simple to follow and understand (even though they're in Swedish!). To look at jobs and get the contact information you need, follow the Heta Jobb, Tillfalliga Jobb, or Sommarjobb link. Each link takes you to pages of positions offered.

Russian and Eastern European Institute Employment and Funding Opportunities

www.indiana.edu/~reeiweb/
indemp.html

Great site for finding opportunities in Eastern Europe: Although this site is hosted by Indiana University, it really is a job database for Eastern European positions. On the opening page, click on the Non-Academic positions link. I found positions for a Polish agronomist, an editor at *Russian Magazine,* a public information specialist in Mongolia, and about a dozen others. Some jobs for U.S. positions are intermixed in the list.

Other Stuff to Check Out

Overseasdigest.com/scams.htm
www.careerkey.com/
www.duke.edu/~lpmaskel/intl_hrefs.html
www.jobs.edunet.com/
www.ohayosensei.com/
www.pricejam.com/
www.tkointl.com/
www.webphilippines.com/

Company-Related Information

It's no secret that company information is abundant on the Web. At this point, most job seekers are wise to the technique of scouring company home pages for employment and other pertinent information. But you may not realize the depth of information you can uncover about the financial aspect of companies, both public and private. Several critical research tools now exist on the Web, including the *Hoover's Handbook* of company profiles and the Securities and Exchange Commission's famed EDGAR database. With just these two resources, it's likely that you can access the best company information right from your desktop without ever venturing further.

Fortunately, though, you don't have to settle for just a few great tools. In this portion of the directory, I steer you toward information about the most relevant, current, and important sources of company information on the Web. Many of the sources described here have achieved a sort of digital fame in the business world — being on top of the newest business tools is never a bad thing, particularly for job seekers!

Mega-Lists of Company Web Pages and Profiles

Before you apply to any company, and especially before you interview with a company, it only makes sense to research the company *first.* The Web has made it spectacularly easy to find information that used to be quite difficult and tedious to uncover. Consider yourself lucky, and hop onto some of the Web sites that follow. You'll find giant lists filled with company Web page addresses and detailed company profiles.

BizWeb Business Guide to the Web

www.bizweb.com/

A Web business guide to more than 30,500 companies: The BizWeb Guide to the Web isn't the best-looking site I've ever seen, but it's functional and easy to use. You see a long list of links after you open the

URL. You can use a simple search engine to narrow your choices, but I discovered that browsing through the lengthy list of companies is actually faster. For example, the Media category contains 190-plus links and profiles, further broken down into Guides, Movies, Radio, Television, and a Miscellaneous section. I found a stunning array of companies listed, including Disney, Viacom, Warner Brothers, and Blockbuster Online Services. Clicking on any business sends you to a corporate profile. At the end of the profile is a contact name, an e-mail address, mailing information, and links to the relevant home page.

Business Wire's Corporate Profiles

www.businesswire.com/cnn.shtml

★★
★★

Focused list of high-level companies: Business Wire (BW) doesn't boast tens of thousands of entries on its company profile list, but it's worth looking at anyhow. For each company listed in Business Wire's profile area, you find a company profile, a stock quote, a link to the company home page, and a link to an EDGAR search. BW is one of the best places to find targeted, free company information on the Web.

Companies Online

www.companiesonline.com/

Free service with a fantastic search engine: Companies Online is a great meta-site to visit if you want to keyword-search for companies. It's one of the few meta-company lists that lets you search by name, state, ticker symbol, industry, city, and URL. If you really want to look for companies by category, you can do that, too, but the search is time-consuming due to the way the page is set up. One word of warning: You can find the com-pany Web pages, but you don't get any-thing extra. Plus, you get a pitch to pur-chase a Dun & Bradstreet report for $20.

Forbes 200 Best Small Companies in America

www.forbes.com/tool/toolbox/200best/

A richly detailed site covering the best of the small fries: The Forbes 200 site opens to a clean page that gives you the information you want right away. You can view detailed information about the 200 best small companies in the United States by using several methods. You can view companies alphabetically, by sales, by profits, by market value, or by five-year averages. If, after viewing a company's information at this site, you can't make a decision about it, don't blame the quality of the information! Just a few companies you find detailed here: Clarcor, Dallas Semiconductor, St. John Knits, and McAfee Associates.

Fortune

www.pathfinder.com/ @@AkhD8AYAGDfOvrfz/fortune/

A great magazine with a lousy URL: Fortunately, you can use the links on the CD-ROM included in this book to avoid typing in Fortune's ridiculous URL. Some

very helpful resources await you after you make it through the digital doorway. The opening page of Fortune lists America's most admired companies; also available is the famous Fortune 500 index of America's top-earning companies. At the Fortune 500 index, you can check out the CEOs, earnings, and all sorts of other information about the companies listed. The Global 500 index, a list detailing the top 500 companies in the world, is a must-see resource for international job seekers.

JobSafari

www.jobsafari.com

★★
★★

A large index of companies that have information on the Internet: This site screams at you in blaring red and yellow, so be forewarned. After your eyes adjust, take a look at the resources available here. Two links of special note to job seekers are the ones right at the top of the page: Browse Companies by Alphabet and Browse Companies by Location. If you browse alphabetically, don't be deceived by the first short lists you see — the site managers like to keep their Web pages short, so you click through the pages of the site much like you turn the pages of a book. Describing the site is difficult because it contains so many resources. But if you're looking for a specific company, try JobSafari. You'll probably find the company there.

The Inc. 500

www.inc.com/500/

A superior Web site for finding the fastest-growing companies: Inc. Online has its act together. The site has a nice, simple interface, a URL that's simple to remember, and rich content. You can click immediately through to Inc.'s list of 500 fastest-growing companies, or look through the detailed company spotlights that Inc. provides. I viewed the entire list of Inc. 500 companies — you may be interested to hear the top three: Optiva Corp. in Bellevue, Washington; Duke & Company Inc., in New York City; and Natural Gas Transmission Services, Inc., in Dallas, Texas.

The Web 100

www.w100.com/

The Web's answer to Inc. *and* Fortune: The Web 100 tracks the largest American and global companies based on revenue, cross-referencing its rankings with the Fortune 500 and the Global 500 rankings for comparison. An interesting statistic I found on this site is that in June 1995, barely 20 percent of the Fortune 500 companies had Web sites. Now, nearly 100 percent of the largest corporations have Web sites. That sure didn't take long, did it? When you settle in to look at the Web 100 sites, you find a pleasant, tabbed mini-menu for each company. The General Motors tab, for example, contains links to a stock quote, a Hoover's company capsule, and related sites. You can also link directly to the company's home page. This is a well-maintained and well-organized site.

Other Stuff to Check Out

www.americasemployers.com/
www.careerexposure.com/
www.infospaceinc.com/
www.job-hunt.org/companies.shtml

Corporate Doings, Finance, and News

You can find much company gossip by using Business Wire and the other online publications I list elsewhere in this directory. But gossip takes you only so far. At some point in your job search, you're going to want to find out *exactly* how much the company you may be working for is worth. You'll also want to check stock quotes to see whether that stock-matching benefit plan is worth as much as your potential employer says it is.

This list is a collection of the best company-oriented financial links on the Web. If you want to find out about a company, you can follow the links you find here to get all the nitty-gritty information you need.

American Stock Exchange

www.amex.com/

Get company financial information from the source: The American Stock Exchange is the ultimate source for stock information on the Web. The only problem is that the Wall Street bankers in their smart Armani suits tend to keep this site extremely busy. If you're into staying up all night or getting up well before the crack of dawn, you may be able to get through. Otherwise, try one of the other sites listed in this section.

Better Business Bureau Online

www.bbb.org/

A place you should visit before you need to: I include the wonderful BBB site to help you steer clear of any scams you may run across on the Web. The BBB site possesses a neat and tidy opening page.

Follow the Alerts link to read about recent and past business scam attempts. Many of the scams involve duping consumers, but not all. I found an alert from November 1997 about employee leasing scams. You could easily fall prey to the slick scheme that one company had going — unless, that is, you were an attorney and knew the fine points of employment law. Because the BBB site is so readily available, save yourself the heartache and check to make sure that the people you may work for have only good news on file with the BBB.

EDGAR Database of Corporate Information

www.sec.gov/edgarhp.htm

★★
★★

One of the most useful corporate tools on the Web: If you haven't heard about EDGAR, let me fill you in. EDGAR stands for the Electronic Data Gathering, Analysis, and Retrieval system. The Securities and Exchange Commission uses EDGAR to increase the efficiency and fairness of the securities market and the economy by making time-sensitive corporate information widely available. (Quickly available, too. EDGAR posts information within 24 hours of receipt.) As of May 1996, companies are required to make electronic filings with EDGAR. Prior to that date, though, information is spotty. The EDGAR database page greets you with a simple menu of links. If you haven't used EDGAR before, I strongly suggest that you read the Important Information About EDGAR before you go

searching. You can begin searching EDGAR by clicking on the Search link, available from the opening page. I searched EDGAR for information about SUN Microsystems and perused intimate details of the company's financial activities, liabilities, and assets. I found out, down to the last cent, what the stockholders' equity is, how much is due in accounts payable, and a whole lot more — the report weighed in at 19 pages. So if you *really* want to find out about a company, always check for its SEC filings in the EDGAR database — everyone else does!

Hoover's Online

www.hoovers.com/

★★
★★

Free searching for detailed company information: Hoover's is regarded as the definitive source for online company profiles. Most Web sites featuring company profiles typically link straight to Hoover's. Look for the Hoover's Power Searching boxes right in the middle of the opening page. There, you can search by company name, ticker symbol, keyword, or industry. After you begin your search by industry, you first read an industry snapshot. I chose to search the movies and music industry and got four pages full of information that included links to companies and relevant associations. After I went into the company listings, I found a list of links to companies like Sony, Dolby Laboratories, and Muzak, Inc. I was interested to see just how profitable Muzak is, with its ubiquitous product, and learned that it's a multimillion-dollar company with 751 employees. I now know the CEO's name, as well as who the other key company people are. A link to the Muzak home page was listed, as were Muzak's top three competitors. I think it's fair to say that if you have a Web hookup, you have no reason not to know everything there is to know about a company.

Securities and Exchange Commission

www.jobweb.org/sec.htm

A workable interface for perusing SEC filings: You can see any publicly traded company's annual or quarterly reports from the JobWeb mirror site. (A *mirror site* is one that's duplicated exactly on another Web site.) You do need to know the company name to enter it, though, before you can make use of the site. To find the SEC filing, type the company name in the search box, select a date range from the menu, and submit your choices. It's that simple.

Other Stuff to Check Out

> osei.sable.com/public/cgi/
>   as_web.exe?bbd.ask +F
> www.fastcompany.com/
> www.irs.ustreas.gov/plain/tax_stats/soi/
>   ex_imf.html
> www.jobtrak.com/jobsearch_docs/
>   employer_lists.html
> www.wsrn.com/home/
>   companyResearch.html

Tools for Looking Up Companies

You may know exactly which company you want to work for, but you just can't figure out the company's street address, fax number, or URL. In this situation, help is only a URL away. Currently, three excellent online Yellow Pages provide online national databases of contact information for over 16 million companies. In this list, you find all three.

BigBook

www.bigbook.com

Find companies anywhere in the United States: BigBook is essentially an online

Yellow Pages. You can easily search for any of the 16 million businesses listed in the various Yellow Pages across the U.S. If you have ever trudged to a local library to accomplish this task, you will really appreciate having all the nationwide Yellow Pages at your fingertips! To use the Yellow Pages, simply bring up the BigBook page. You see a search box. Type in a business name, if you know it, or browse through categories to find the name that's eluding you. A nice extra is a map showing driving directions to the company you're searching.

Big Yellow

www1.bigyellow.com/

The "official" Yellow Pages on the Web: Are you detecting a little bit of sibling rivalry? You're not alone. Currently, the mad dash on the Web is for your Yellow Page business, which is good for consumers — currently, you have two great Yellow Page services to choose from. It just so happens that Big Yellow is the official Yellow Pages, but other than being official, you won't notice a whole lot of difference between Big Yellow and BigBook. Big Yellow has about the same number of business listings, 16 million, and uses about the same kind of interface.

GTE Superpages

superpages.gte.net/

Yet another Yellow Pages tool, but with a difference: Yet a third Yellow Pages tool made it into this directory because the GTE Yellow Pages let you search in a more detailed manner — and, best of all, you can search by distance. So if you want to find all the law firms in a 50-mile radius of a certain city, you can easily do just that with the GTE Superpages. This feature alone makes this site worth a visit.

Other Stuff to Check Out

> www.infospaceinc.com
> www.linkstar.com
> www.netpart.com/search.html
> www.zip2.com

Associations Meta Lists

Finding an association to shepherd you through the job-search process is sometimes the best thing you can do as a job seeker. Associations exist for every imaginable discipline and field of inquiry, and they are by and large your best bets for picking up networking contacts. In the following list, you find giant meta lists of associations. If you can't find an association related to your discipline in the following lists, then it's likely that the association isn't on the Web yet! Happy hunting.

Associations and Societies

www.ntu.edu.sg/home/ctng/assoc.htm

★★
★★

Meta list of pretty much every association out there: Leave it to an industrious student — in this case, Ng Chay Tuan of Nanyang Technological University — to put together an astonishing list of associations on the Web. I can't even begin to tell you how many associations are listed on the site — easily thousands. The associations are broken down into very specific categories, like trade and commerce, broadcast media, industrial relations, and so on. Every link I've tried so far has been good. I highly recommend this site to all job seekers.

Associations of Interest to Government and the Public Sector

www.jobsingovernment.com/resource/
associations.htm

A meta list of associations: You can find all sorts of associations at this site; some are definitely government and military oriented, but many more are not. The many associations to which this list links are rare and hard to find, so the site is a good one to browse. On my visit, I found the California Forestry Association, the National Black Police Association, and the National Court Reporters Association, among hundreds of others.

LinkMonster

207.124.99.40/index.html

Directory with great links to organizations: LinkMonster is a full-fledged directory, and it contains thousands of links to associations on the Web. Open the site and click on the Organizations link. You see a new page listing 5,400–plus links to associations worldwide. Not every link is the best choice for you, so you can use the LinkMonster search engine to narrow down your selection. It's a great list to have at your disposal as you look for professional associations.

Professional Associations, by Catapult

www.jobweb.org/catapult/assoc.htm

Short list of employment-related associations: The Catapult list of associations is short, but it focuses on the employment and career fields. The National Association of Colleges and Employers and the Society for Human Resource Management are the two key associations on the list — don't miss them.

University of Waterloo Scholarly Societies Project

**www.lib.uwaterloo.ca/society/
   overview.html**

★★
★★

Resources listing over 1,500 scholarly societies: This database is a real find for everyone, but especially for those working in education, the sciences, or any facet of academia. In addition to the Web pages of scholarly societies, you can access the full-text archives of about 150 newsletters. A sampling of the societies I found includes the American Welding Society, the Archaeological Institute of America, the Portland Cement Association, the International Bee Research Association, and the International Brain Research Organization. You can see from just my small sample that not all the associations are dedicated to strictly scholarly endeavors, which makes this list an even more valuable resource.

Virtual Community of Associations

www.vcanet.org/

A healthy, varied list of organizations: If you have poor luck finding associations relevant to your job search on the other association sites, give this site a try. The Virtual Community of Associations doesn't have a business or scholarly bias and tends to list a wider variety of associations than other sites. Some of the associations I found are the Society of American Florists, the American Corporate Counsel Association, the Association for Multimedia Communications, and the Endocrine Society. As you can see, the associations really run the gamut at this site.

Women's Connection Online

www.womenconnect.com/organizations/

A sizable list of links to organizations for women: Sorry, guys, but I couldn't find a men's association list. Meanwhile, ladies, you have quite a nice list of association links to peruse. You can find all sort of associations, such as the American Business Women's Association, the League of Women Voters, and Women in Advertising and Marketing.

Yahoo! Professional Organizations

**www.yahoo.com/Economy/
   Organizations/Professional/**

Business-oriented list of associations: You can search for associations at the Yahoo! site in two ways. You can go to the page I list here and browse through the hundreds of links — you may find your association if you're in an even remotely business-related field — or you can burrow into the category closest to your profession and search for relevant professional associations. Either way, this list of associations is compelling. The computers and Internet area also holds a significant listing of professional organizations.

You'll discover a few dozen associations, such as the Association of Online Professionals and the Network Professional Association.

Other Stuff to Check Out

envirolink.org/orgs/index.html
www.ai.mit.edu/people/ellens/non.html
www.igc.apc.org/index.html
www.macronet.org/macronet/where.html
www.open.gov.uk/index/orgindex.htm
www.techexpo.com/tech_soc.html

Networking Resources

The Web is a terrific place to expand your networking contacts. Using the Web as your schmooze tool, you can join discussions, ask questions, meet new people you otherwise never would have come in contact with, and in general extend your job-search horizons.

Web networking falls into two main areas: mailing lists and discussions. You can sign up for a mailing list and get messages sent to your e-mail address. You can also participate in online discussions, either by posting a message and checking back or by "chatting" live. Of course, all this online networking does not come without its own set of rules and tools. In the first part of this section of the directory, you find the tools and information you need to move your networking abilities up to the top tier. The next portions detail actual places to put your networking knowledge to good use.

General Networking Resources and Tools

In this section, you find online tools to help you locate real people. You also find tools to help make your digital networking contact pleasant and non-offensive — a real must for every job seeker, and every person, for that matter.

555-1212

www.555-1212.com/

Quick lookup of phone numbers anywhere in the U.S. and Canada: After you open the 555-1212 Web site, click on the geographic area you want to search on the clickable map. You zip over to a Yellow Pages–type search interface that lets you continue your search for phone numbers by business name, city, or state. A simple tool for saving yourself a trip to the library to look at Yellow Pages for other states.

Claris Guide to E-Mail Etiquette

www.claris.com/products/claris/emailer/ eguide/index.html

Make your e-mail count: Claris has put together a thorough but concise guide to e-mail etiquette. In this document, you find a list of do's and don'ts, as well as a great list of emoticons like :& (which means tongue-tied). You also find a list of commonly used e-mail abbreviations. Even if you think that you have the most refined e-mail style, I suggest checking out this document.

Hotmail

www.hotmail.com

Most widely used, free, Web-based e-mail: Hotmail is a service from Microsoft that offers you free e-mail hosted on the Web. I have a Hotmail account and use it whenever I travel. With a Web-based e-mail account, you can check your e-mail from any computer that's hooked up to the Web. You need to sign up, though, and the sign-up process is somewhat lengthy — you have to fork over some detailed information to feed the advertisers that support the site.

Juno

www.juno.com/

Home of the classic free e-mail accounts that you've heard so much about: Juno was one of the first companies to tap into the free e-mail market. Juno offers free e-mail, but in order to use it, you need to download and install the free Juno software, which is a fairly simple process. Please note that Juno e-mail is not Web-based — it only works from computers that have the Juno software. Juno is best for job seekers who have a computer but don't have an e-mail account yet.

Netiquette Home Page

www.albion.com/netiquette/index.html

All the do's and don'ts fit to print: So you want to make a good impression on the Net. Well, then, make this site a must-see on your cyber-travels. On the opening page, you find links to the core rules of netiquette, as well as a great netiquette quiz. The information at this site is super. If, after perusing the site, you're still feeling insecure about how to put your best digital self forward, you can sign up for the official netiquette mailing list and ask more detailed questions.

Other Stuff to Check Out

email.lycos.com/member/login.page
mailexcite.com/
www.mcp.com/

Usenet Newsgroups, Mailing Lists, and Web Forums

Usenet newsgroups, also commonly known as *discussion groups, newsgroups,* or simply *Usenet,* have been around for a long time. Usenet is essentially a massive collection of places to post messages relating to a particular topic. Happily, Usenet is home to compelling job resource information, particularly notices of jobs offered. Mailing lists, sometimes referred to as *listservs,* can also be helpful for job seekers. In using a mailing list, you subscribe to an e-mail address, and messages and information come to you. In this section, I list the very best sites for tapping into discussion groups and mailing lists.

But there's more. I also list good sites for tapping into a relatively new phenomenon, *Web forums,* which have recently become widely popular. Web forums are essentially message boards on Web pages. If you have questions about what Usenet, mailing lists, or Web forums are, either peruse the sites listed here or check out Chapter 11 for more detailed information.

Career Mosaic Usenet Search

www.careermosaic.com/cm/cm36.html

Well-organized place to browse the job-related Usenet groups: Career Mosaic (CM) is best known for its resume-posting and job-listing services. But CM also boasts a great Usenet area that's conveniently organized with job seekers in mind. You can find well over 60,000 job postings daily on the Usenet jobs groups. Mind you, not all the jobs are good ones, and a portion of the postings are repeat listings — double or triple postings of the same job. Also, you find an enormous amount of headhunter and third-party recruiter traffic on Usenet. All that aside, to use the CM Usenet Search site, simply fill out the search engine box with the keywords you want and then indicate the state you want to look in. When I searched for accounting positions in New York, I received a list of over 100 job postings. (A few were repeat postings, but still, many jobs were active posts.)

CyberFiber Newsgroups

www.cyberfiber.com/news/

★★
★★

Truly the most comprehensive Usenet directory: I know, you probably haven't heard of CyberFiber. Lots of techie insiders know about CyberFiber, though, and for good reason. At the CyberFiber opening page, you find a search engine and an extremely well-organized menu of newsgroups. I like to browse the menu because it's so simple and clear. Your best use of CyberFiber is to find newsgroups pertaining to your career

area. CyberFiber is also a good way to double-check offerings from other newsgroup sites. I have found that CyberFiber tends to offer far more complete coverage of Usenet groups than other Usenet search sites, so don't be surprised if you find brand-new groups at this site.

Deja News

www.dejanews.com

Great search engine for finding any newsgroup on any topic: Deja News has become the search engine that most people use when looking for relevant newsgroups. If you're looking strictly for job postings, I suggest using the Career Mosaic site or the Yahoo! site listed elsewhere in this section. However, to strike up a conversation with a peer working in your profession, I suggest that you use the Deja News search engine to perform a keyword search. For example, if you're a public relations specialist, type the keyword *PR, public relations,* or *marketing* in the search box. Deja News immediately returns a list of discussions in Usenet groups containing those words. You won't find job offers, but you will find all sorts of professionals chatting about their gripes, kudos, and places of employment. Great job reconnaissance!

Liszt Select

www.liszt.com

★★
★★

The ultimate mailing list directory: Liszt is a great tool that allows you to search through 84,000–plus mailing lists, and through newsgroups. On the opening page, you find a blissfully clear menu of options. To search for job-related mailing lists, just type *job, jobs, employment, work, career,* or any other job-related keyword in the search box you see. Or if you're feeling adventurous, you can browse the mailing lists by category and topic and find direct links to job mailing lists. When I checked for job lists, I found plenty to choose from, generated by groups like the International Career and Employment Network. Use Liszt Select to find lists pertaining to your specific area of expertise by typing in the keywords of your employment field.

Reference.COM

www.reference.com

★★
★★

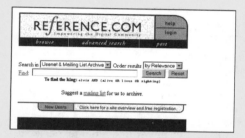

The best site for finding and understanding Web forums: Although you can search through newsgroups and mailing lists via Reference.COM, it really is best used to access Web forums. The newest techno-trend, Web forums, are just now springing up, and Reference.COM is one of the best places to master this phenomenon. The opening page is organized clearly — you can query the search engine or delve into a tabbed menu. What I like about Web forums is that they are sparsely popu-lated (at least right now — although, with 25,000 forums already, this may not last long). What that means for you is that you don't get lost in the crowd, and you have a chance to develop true networking contacts for your job search. (For more on Web forums, please see the introduc-tion to this section.)

Yahoo! Metros

www.yahoo.com

Find job-related Web forums for 12 U.S. cities: If you like the idea of posting messages on the Web, by all means check

out the Yahoo! Metro Web forums. After the Yahoo! Opening page loads, scroll to the bottom and check out the listings for Yahoo! Metros — regionally oriented Web sites, each containing information tailored to a specific city. Currently, Yahoo! Metros are available for Atlanta, Austin, Boston, Chicago, Dallas/Fort Worth, Los Angeles, Miami, Minneapolis/ St. Paul, New York, San Francisco Bay Area, Seattle, and Washington, D.C. Click on a city you're interested in, and the opening page gives you a colorful menu of options. To access Web forums, choose Messages, and you link directly to the message boards (or Web forums) for that city. If you want to find every available job resource for the area, enter the keyword *job* in the search box at the top of the opening page, and you get a list of job options.

Yahoo! Usenet Job List

www.yahoo.com/Business_and_Economy/ Employment/Jobs/Usenet

A good place to overview Usenet job groups: The Yahoo! Usenet list is great for scrolling through and viewing the various job-related groups. You can look at bionet.jobs, which is a listing of scientific job opportunities. Or you can check out nm.jobs to see jobs offered in New Mexico. Some people prefer to see a complete list of items as opposed to using a search engine to search the same list. At the Yahoo! site, you can look at a list.

Other Stuff to Check Out

www.careercast.com
www.careermag.com/forums/index.html
www.excite.com/reference/usenet.html
www.forumone.com
www.ipa.com/newsgroups.html

Chat Resources

If "talking" live is what makes you happiest, then you owe it to yourself to explore chatting resources on the Web. A few years ago, chatting was a difficult proposition that required special technical skills. Now, though, if you have a recent version of a Web browser like Netscape Communicator or Internet Explorer, usually all you have to do is visit the Web site and start chatting.

If you haven't chatted online before, you should know that chatting enables you to type a message and transmit it immediately to a chat area. Others chatting in the same area see your message right away and can respond (or not). It's a lot like live e-mail, if you can imagine that. Many chat areas are plagued with nasty language and unfocused discussions. The chat areas I list here are among the best on the Web and can prove of networking value to job seekers. Each chat area gives complete instructions for getting set up to participate in chat sessions.

The Globe

www.theglobe.com/chat

Great metro sites to chat in: I like the Globe for the power it gives you to access people in specific cities. This feature is especially helpful for networking your way into a regional job. The Globe contains chat rooms for New York, Los Angeles, San Francisco, Chicago, and Atlanta (stateside), and London, Madrid, Paris, Rome, and Sydney (overseas). The rooms for each city fill up primarily during the evening hours. Much of the talk is not related to jobs, but chatters are amenable to helping job seekers, provided that you're polite and you understand how to chat correctly. (See the chat guidelines listed in the "General Networking Resources and Tools" section in this part of the directory.)

Talk City

www.talkcity.com/

★★
★★

The best business chatting on the Web: Talk City is hands-down my favorite pick for job seekers trying to forge networking contacts. The tone is professional, and the people who manage Talk City work very hard to maintain high standards of conduct. I've never had a bad experience on Talk City — in fact, I've even done author chats with good success. The first time you visit Talk City, it takes your browser a good long time to download the Java software. (You don't have to do anything; your browser downloads the correct items automatically.) On subsequent visits, the opening page pops right up. Good categories for job seekers to investigate include People and Connecting, Business and Professional, and Computers and Technology.

Ultimate Chatlist

www.chatlist.com

Well-organized, upbeat chat site: I didn't find any chats related specifically to jobs at this site, but I did find some chat groups related to business topics. Your best bet is to use the search engine on the opening page to find groups pertaining to your interests.

Yack!

www.yack.com/

Best spot for finding serious and generally very high-quality chatting: Despite its hip-sounding name, Yack! is actually a heavy-duty, serious chat site. Yack! lists the daily high-quality chats set for specific times. For example, on my most recent visit to Yack!, I found chats scheduled with Alfred R. Berkeley III (president of the NASDAQ stock market), a CNN News Chat, career counselor Dave Dolak, and Fred Thomas, president of the Service Corps of Retired Executives. (He has incredible job contacts, by the way.) The chats pertain primarily to topical areas like science, computers, economics, and business. Yack! lets you know which chats are Java-based and which require down-loading of software. (Most chats are Java-based, which means that you don't have to download anything if you're using the most recent version of Internet Explorer or Netscape Communicator.) Yack! is a great place for job seekers to schmooze.

Other Stuff to Check Out

chat.yahoo.com/
iseek.com/infoage/pressbox.html
pages.wbs.net/
www.activeworlds.com
www.tribal.com/Products.htm

Job-Search Toolkit

Have you ever wondered what it would be like to conduct a job search and do everything right from start to finish? Most job seekers have a little tickle at the backs of their minds, whispering insinuating comments like "I could've found a better job if I'd started looking sooner" or "I'm accepting a job I don't like, but it's only temporary. I'll do better next time." Well, this time is your next time! Banish those worries and nagging thoughts. Instead, take advantage of the tremendous resources available to you via the Web. I'm not just hyping the use of the Web — the Web really can make your job search easier, better, and faster.

And easier, better, and faster is what the job-search toolkit is all about. In this section of the directory, you find great information-gathering tools, help for creating Web pages, giant lists of job-related information, resume samples and help, interviewing tips, Web resources that help you stay sharp and current, and information about protecting your online privacy during your digital job search.

Hot Search Engines

With Web content mushrooming, you need something that helps you weed through all those millions of Web pages. Enter search engines. Seven years ago, no one knew what a search engine was. Now, search engines are big business. The people who own search engines operate their businesses like major multimillion-dollar corporations — because they are! For your purposes, it serves you well to try out all the search engines on this list and choose at least three to use as your primary search engines. Always use a good cross-section of search engines when you're looking for Web content — as you'll discover, search engines vary widely in quality, number of pages they index, and search methods. This list is a great starting point for checking out the top search engines currently available.

All-in-One

www.albany.net/allinone/

Searchable meta list of just about every search engine: The All-in-One page is a wonderfully simple list of search engines. It's easy to use, too — all you do is type a search term right on the All-in-One page to begin your search. You can work your way right down All-in-One's extensive list of search engines in your quest for data gold. This is an especially good site if you're trying to find rare or unusual search engines. If a search engine is available, it likely is listed on this page.

AltaVista

www.altavista.digital.com/

Internet favorite: AltaVista, a search engine sponsored by Digital Corporation, is one of the old-timers — it's been around about as long as the Web has. The AltaVista search interface changed recently to include handy search tabs on the menu. Menu tab options include signing up for free e-mail, searching for people, searching for businesses, browsing by subject, and seeing the Web in translation. You also have the option of searching Usenet newsgroups via the search interface. If you haven't used AltaVista before, you'll be interested to know that you can search the Web by phrase, by title, by domain name, within date ranges, and for pictures. AltaVista is a great search engine for digging up information — it's one of my favorite search engines.

Excite

www.excite.com/

Essentially free online service: Excite has become very ambitious with its site. Actually, the search engine portion of the Excite site is pretty much the same as it has been for a while. You can perform a keyword search or go into more depth with a power search. The power search boasts a powerful, finely tuned (and expensive) search capability. The power search page may put you off if you've never used it before — you see all sorts of search options to fill out. But believe me, using the power search nets you incredibly tight results for the Web. Another feature you can't help but notice on Excite is the enormous variety of links to what Excite calls "channels." Essentially, you browse information by topic, just in case you don't want to fuss with a search engine. The information is well organized and easy to access.

HotBot

www.hotbot.com

Well-respected search engine with advanced features: HotBot has a funny name, but it does a seriously great job of retrieving information. As is the trend among search engines, you can browse a subject list at the HotBot site or use the search engine. The HotBot technology is very sound — you should try the SuperSearch feature. You see a page full of search options, but go ahead and fill out the options if you want really good search results.

Infoseek

www.infoseek.com

Sleek, easy-to-use search engine: Infoseek enables you to spend a minimum of time worrying about the mechanics of searching. On the opening page, you can browse by channel (or category) or use the search engine. The search engine lets you specify what you want to look for — Web search engines and directories, news, companies, or newsgroups — an option that can save you a lot of time right from the beginning.

The Internet Sleuth

www.isleuth.com

Multiple topical search engines: The Internet Sleuth has the capacity to search in multiple databases at once, and within a range of topics. You use a set of menu options to choose the databases you want to search. For example, you can search simultaneously in AltaVista, Excite, Infoseek, and Yahoo!. Because multiple searches can be time hogs, you also specify how long you're willing to wait for results. You can wait between ten seconds and one full minute, depending on how patient you are. Scrolling down the page, you find all sorts of other things you can search for, like software, business and financial information, and news. This great search engine is loaded with features, so give yourself time to get used to the enormous amount of search capacity you have!

Lycos

www.lycos.com/

Simple searches: Lycos has undergone extensive changes over the years, and it's now pitching itself as "your personal Internet guide." Indeed, the emphasis at the site is on the Web Guide directory. The search engine, however, is pretty basic, with few bells and whistles. (You have to visit HotBot, Excite, or AltaVista for that.) Many beginners appreciate the lack of fuss at Lycos. If you like pared-down searching, Lycos is a good place to try.

ProFusion

www.designlab.ukans.edu/profusion/

Search engine loaded with options and extras: ProFusion is not currently a super well-known search interface, but that doesn't stop it from being a *great* search interface. The search area of ProFusion is larger than most search utilities. You see more boxes and options right up front. Don't let them scare you away. The ProFusion search box offers you the capability to search in several modes, by phrase or by keyword. You can search the Web or Usenet and have your results delivered with or without a summary. A list of nine search engines stands at the ready, all simultaneously. There's so much clutter on search engine sites anymore that a clean, noncommercial site like ProFusion is a relief.

Other Stuff to Check Out

www.dogpile.com
www.inference.com/ifind/
www.metacrawler.com
www.webcrawler.com

General Research Information and Tools

The tools in this section don't relate specifically to job searching. They can, however, help you uncover information on the Web faster than most people can — even if they're using the sturdiest, best search engine. Use the tools you find here to dig for information about your profession, prepare for interviews, check your spelling, and more.

The Argus Clearinghouse

www.clearinghouse.net/

A collection of Internet resource guides: The Clearinghouse for Subject-Oriented Internet Resource Guides showed you every possible Internet resource dealing with all sorts of topics, from the general to the extremely esoteric. Now, the Clearinghouse Guides have been renamed and moved to this location. The same content-rich guides are still in place, but they're updated and organized more effectively. You can find guides for all areas, with a long list of subcategories in each topic. For example, the art category contains subcategory listings of architecture, cinema, dance, design, and on and on. Each guide takes you directly to Internet resources appropriate to the topic.

The History Archives

www.thehistorynet.com/

Where history lives on the Web: You must be wondering why on earth I included a history site in a book about job searching. It's simple: You would be shocked to hear how many applicants get nailed with history questions in interviews and pre-hire exams, all as a way of testing general knowledge. I'll never, ever forget a critical interview that I had about eight years ago while aiming for a fellowship at a major university. I got through all the standard questions I was expecting, and then out of the blue came the type of question that every job seeker dreads: "How does early American history specifically relate to what you do in your daily professional life?" I answered the question, but I sweat bullets for weeks wondering whether my answer was stupid. (I got the fellowship, by the way.) An occasional scan of this historical Web site can't hurt you.

HotSheet

www.hotsheet.com

★ ★
★ ★

The easiest way to the best of the Web: I can't remember how I found HotSheet originally, but now I visit HotSheet at least once a day. Why? On one Web page, you find the best links to an enormous array of categories. I tend to use HotSheet as a sort of standard bookmark list. My bookmark list is so overgrown and unwieldy, sometimes it just makes more sense to pop over to HotSheet and get to where I want to go. HotSheet links to 18 categories, and there's not one bad link in the bunch. Consider it a best-of-the-best list that's easy to use.

LookSmart

www.looksmart.com

A short page for exploring 16,000–plus topics: The value of LookSmart for job seekers is that you can open the page, jump to a category about which you need information, and get right to the information you need. LookSmart is not the most comprehensive directory on the Web — its charm is that it's selective and small. It's fast, too — give it a try if you tend to get overwhelmed when you see page after page of links.

OneLook Dictionaries

www.onelook.com

Search 220 dictionaries at one time: Everyone can use a good dictionary — especially job seekers, who have to put forth perfect documents. The OneLook opening page presents you with a simple search box. Just enter the word as best you can spell it, and OneLook looks it up for you. You can search for spelling, meaning, pronunciation, and acronyms. This tool is handy — I keep it at the top of my bookmark list.

Pitsco's Ask an Expert

www.askanexpert.com/askanexpert/

A directory of links to people who have volunteered their time to answer your questions: Chivalry and brotherhood are alive and well in some corners of this universe, especially the corner defined by this parcel of Web real estate. You really can submit a question to an expert and get it answered, even a job-search question. If you have an honest question — perhaps an interview question that you know will be tough or a question about a particular field of study — come to this Web site and ask away. You need to follow a pretty specific set of instructions to ask your question, but everything is spelled out clearly on the Web site.

Ready Reference

www.ipl.org/ref/RR/

Collection of extremely high-quality Internet resources on various topics: The folks at the Internet Public Library host and maintain this plain-looking site. Scroll down the entire opening page to look at the tools and information available to you. Use Ready Reference when you need a sure thing. If you're prepping for an interview and you work in engineering, for example, Ready Reference can lead you to the best documents in your field. You won't find the most documents, just the ones with the most content.

Research-It!

www.itools.com/research-it/ research-it.html

The best site for general reference tools, all on one page: If you want to look up a computing word, look up a pronunciation, or translate from one language to another, Research-It! can help you. If you want to search for people, streets, and telephone numbers, Research-It! can help you with those tasks, too. If you want the latest stock quotes and currency exchanges, pop right over to this great little Web site. Research-It! is one of those sites that doesn't change much; I've been poking around in it for two years now, and it's always up and ready to go, looking pretty much the same. When you depend on a Web tool for quick retrieval of information, stability is pretty important, and this is a site you can count on.

Other Stuff to Check Out

www.northernlight.com
www.linkmonster.com
thehugelist.com
www.stpt.com/
www.mckinley.com/

Tools and Publications for Keeping Up-to-Date

You know that sinking, morale-shriveling feeling that you're hopelessly behind the times. You see words on the Web that you have no clue about, and you just had an interview with someone who seemed to know every detail of the latest scandal. Small talk can be a big effort if you don't have the latest gossip stored in your mind and ready to trip off of your tongue. In this section, I list tools that are great at keeping you up-to-date and with-it, no matter what your profession. To catch up on your computer lingo, be sure to look at some of the computer sites that I list.

Business Wire

www.businesswire.com/

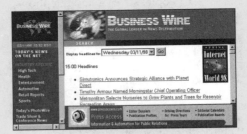

Up-to-the-minute news about corporations: I currently work with an editor who always quizzes me about happenings in the technology world. He expects me to know the latest stock prices of several top companies, the latest mergers and acquisitions, and who has moved to what company. Without Business Wire, I couldn't keep up with the information he expects me to know. But with the help of one of my favorite sites on the Web, I can pick up every scrap of information that I need in minutes. For your job search, I strongly recommend that you log onto Business Wire to scan the headlines pertaining to the industry in which you work. The site is a bit graphics-heavy and is sometimes slow, but navigation is clear and simple. The industries that BW covers are high-tech, health, entertainment, automotive, and retail. Additionally, you can view up-to-the-minute corporate IPOs (initial public offerings) and corporate profiles. BW is well worth scanning!

CNET.COM

www.cnet.com/

The ultimate computer news and information site: If you've never seen CNET before, I highly recommend that you take a quick peek at the site. CNET is a lot like a small city: It flashes, stays up all night, is filled with stories, and contains more information than you can absorb in one glance. For job seekers, the relevance of the site is to get a hold of definitive technology news. I can't think of any profession where it's all right to be behind the curve about technology anymore. You may be overcome by the incredibly loud yellow background of CNET's opening page. Do your best to get over it, though, because the content is great. A sampling includes software reviews, feature stories about marketing on the Web, and lots of free software to download.

Cnews Home Page

www.canoe.com/CNEWS/home.html

Canadian news source on the Web: If you live in Canada or in one of the northern-most states, you'll appreciate this source for in-depth Canadian news. You find top stories, pictures, lots of politics, technology news, corporate news, and special columns. If you're a Canadian citizen, you'll appreciate the in-depth coverage you find here. If you're a U.S. citizen, you can still benefit from visiting the site — it's an excellent tool for getting a different perspective on U.S. news.

Daily News Current

www.newscurrent.com/

An independent daily newspaper for the time-impaired: Browsing this site is a quick way to catch up on the day's headlines, particularly for those living in the Pacific time zone (where the newspaper is physically located). The page opens with a tightly written feature story, followed by bulleted lists of the day's top breaking news and then the week's top news. The writers grab information from the Web and from other traditional sources. I like the bristly quality to this site — it captures the briny reporter feel of the newsroom of a major newspaper.

Drudge Report

www.drudgereport.com

Incredible links to all the major wire services in the world and most political columnists in the United States: Matt Drudge, the creator of the Drudge Report, has a track record of breaking crucial political stories before *The Washington Post* or any other news organization. The site is a worthwhile visit — if you can get in, that is. Let me put it this way: The Drudge Report, on the day of my last visit, had 24,000 hits from the White House domain name and over 300,000 hits from everyone else. What you as a job seeker can gain from this site is easy access to the wire services and an update on political news, in case you need to be up on that kind of thing.

Electric Library

www.elibrary.com

Commercial source of magazine, map, book, and newspaper content: I list elibrary here because you can sign up for a free 30-day subscription. You can search for topics related to your job, get up-to-date, and hopefully get a job before your subscription runs out! I find that much of what you can get on elibrary you can dig up on your own. The only problem is the

digging — when you're conducting a job search, you don't want to spend your time tracking down resources on the Web. Give elibrary a whirl; just remember that you have 30 days before you turn into a pumpkin, so to speak.

Galaxy

lmc.einet.net/galaxy.html

The professional's guide to Internet information: Galaxy is a huge directory of online resources that has been refined and filtered with professionals in mind. As you see from the opening page, Galaxy is clustered into topical areas that you can scan. Areas include business and commerce, engineering and technology, government, humanities, law, medicine, reference, science, and social sciences. If you wish, you can use Galaxy's search engine to winnow down the vast amount of information into bite-sized chunks. For you as a job seeker, a benefit of using Galaxy is that you can find high-quality information related to your field. I use Galaxy whenever I need to cut through the Web clutter and get quick information.

Inc. Online

www.inc.com/

The online version of the paper magazine: If you can stand the annoyingly heavy graphics, Inc. is a good bet for job seekers in business-related careers. In addition to articles and conference information, a helpful feature is the Inc. Online Newsletter, to which you can subscribe from the site. The newsletter comes to you, and you don't have to wait five minutes for the graphics to download.

NetLingo: The Internet Language Dictionary

www.netlingo.com

An online dictionary of emerging technology vocabulary: This is a great site for catching up on the latest World Wide Web terminology, as well as general computer technology terms in current use. If you work in a technology-related profession, you can use NetLingo to enhance the keywords on your resume. If you're in marketing, advertising, financial advising, or any other profession where keeping up is required, you can browse the list and click on any term you don't want to ask about for fear of looking uncool. A sampler of terms I found on a recent visit to this site include *anti-aliasing, cable modem, cache, click rate, clickstream, cornea gumbo, fire off, hacker,* and *GIF.*

Total News

www.totalnews.com/

Links to the top national news sites on the Web from one easy interface: The main page of this site takes a while to open, but it's well worth the wait. The primary benefit of this site is that it enables you to link quickly to other news organizations, such as Fox News, MSNBC, CBS, ABC, NPR, and CNN Interactive.

Utne Lens

www.utne.com/lens/lens.html

Online version of the Utne Reader, *with some twists:* The *Utne Reader* is a philosophical, thought-provoking, highly literary magazine. The Utne Lens has a lot in common with its paper sister. As a job seeker, you can use the Utne Lens to get

good quips, information about the latest trends, and a whole lot of topics to talk about when you need to charm 'em in a social or networking situation. Studies show over and over that it's how well you talk that gets you the job.

Weekly Wire

weeklywire.com/newsstand/

Alternative abundance in a pithy package: The Weekly Wire Web site delivers prickly stories with punch. But even better for job seekers is the listing of 100–plus alternative newsweeklies, such as the *Boulder Weekly,* the *San Diego Reader,* the *Austin Chronicle,* the *Chicago Reader,* and the *Village Voice.* Alternative newsweeklies are great places to pick up on what's really happening in a city. Checking out a newsweekly is especially helpful if you're relocating or prepping for an interview in an unfamiliar place. Many newsweeklies list jobs, too. The link listed here takes you directly to the list of alternative weeklies. Scroll down the page to find the Home link. At the Weekly Wire main page, you find feature stories culled from a half dozen or so newsweeklies nationwide.

Other Stuff to Check Out

pathfinder.com/News/
www.jou.ufl.edu/commres/webjou.htm
www.fednews.com
www.ecola.com/news/
www.www.usnews.com/
www.businesslife.com/

Web Page Help and Tools

Now that you've been surfing the Web for a while, looking for that perfect job, you must be all set to get going on your own Web page, right? Well, with so many free Web pages available nowadays, people just about expect you to have some kind of Web page. And if you're a job seeker, putting your resume on your Web page makes a lot of sense. If the thought of getting a Web page up horrifies you, however, then check out the beginner's tools in this list. And if you already have a Web page but want to dress your page for success, I list resources for you, too.

Builder.com

www.cnet.com/Content/Builder

Terrific site for intermediate and advanced Web site builders: CNET's Builder page is a major repository for Web knowledge. If you're a beginner, you may find it intimidating even to look at this site. Never fear. Bookmark the site and come back when you're feeling more confident. If you have some Web skills under your belt, this site gives you intermediate and advanced information about Web graphics, tracking traffic, and using cookies on your site, as well as adding video, live chat, and other advanced tools, plus Java basics.

HTML Goodies

www.htmlgoodies.com/

★ ★
★ ★

Everything you could ever want to know about HTML, organized into tutorials: This is a super-stop for anyone who wants to get going on a Web site. This site is one of the top 1,000 sites on the Web, and with good reason. All sorts of freebies are readily downloadable. I found over 250 JavaScripts and 400 free images on my visit. For job seekers in a hurry, the tutorials and question-and-answer section can't be beat.

Java Boutique

Javaboutique.internet.com

Applets galore for advanced users: If you know your way around Java and want to add snazzy applets to your Web site, definitely make time for a stop at the Java Boutique. The best links are Java News, the latest additions, and a great help guide on using applets.

Reallybig.com

reallybig.com/

Massive resource for Web builders: If you want free clip art and good marketing advice for your Web page, don't miss this site. You can download backgrounds, textures, bullets, buttons, icons, and photographs. The site boasts excellent instructions on promoting your Web page and increasing your hit count.

WebReference

www.webreference.com

★ ★
★ ★

Content-rich site for Web page builders: Much of the material on the WebReference site is best suited for intermediate-level Web page builders, but it includes great tools for beginners, too. When I visited this site, I even found resources specifically designed to help job seekers send resumes more effectively over the Web. The best links for beginners include the How-To and News links.

WebStep TOP 100

www.mmgco.com/top100.html

Tool for listing your Web site with the top 100 search engines and databases: The WebStep TOP 100 page does not submit your Web page information to search engines and databases for you, but it does provide a handy set of links for you to jump from as you get the good word out. I have to warn you: Submitting your Web page information is vital if you want to be found, but it's a tedious task.

Other Stuff to Check Out

www.ncsa.uiuc.edu/General/Internet/
WWW/HTMLPrimer.html
Members.aol.com/pixelpen/index.html
www.imagiware.com/RxHTML/
www.whatis.com/
www.majon.com/majon.html
www.virtualpromote.com

General Career Resources

General career resources include those sites that dedicate themselves to helping job seekers. The sites listed here are filled with advice for interviewing and choosing the right career, plus all sorts of accumulated career wisdom from columnists and career counselors. Take advantage of other people's hard work in putting together these sites — the ones I list are well researched and quite helpful.

Bureau of Labor Statistics

stats.bls.gov/

The most complete and accurate data about jobs and careers: Thousands of journalists and authors use the Bureau of Labor Statistics (BLS) as their primary reporting source. Simply put, no one can fund career and job research at the level the federal government can. To get to the site, just open the main page, which is easy to work with. You can access data, economic info at a glance, surveys, publications and research papers,

regional information, and a search engine. I suggest that you go right for the information jugular: the Publications & Research Papers area. At the Publications area, please investigate the Occupational Outlook Handbook, the *single most important publication in all of career literature* — I kid you not. A busy horde of researchers grind away daily to compile an incredible mound of data for you, the faithful taxpayer. Take advantage of it! In particular, I recommend using the easy link to the occupational clusters, which detail exactly what pay, benefits, and working conditions you can expect and project long- and short-term success rates for each job. If you want to find a high-demand, high-paying occupation, this is the ultimate source of information.

CAREERMagazine

www.careermag.com

Chatty, good-looking place to find detailed career information: CAREERMagazine has the distinction of being one of the top 1,000 sites on the Web. That's a difficult distinction to earn these days, particularly with a new Web site going up every half minute or so. You may have a bit of trouble adjusting to the busy graphics at this site — it's designed to look like a newspaper, but it doesn't always come off as well organized as it could. Nevertheless, I think that you'll enjoy the content. CAREERMagazine lists job openings and a resume bank, but it also boasts all sorts of free articles and columns of value to job seekers. Additional goodies include relocation resources, a recruiter directory, and links to job fairs. I check this site every now and then to catch up with what online career columnists are saying. During my last visit, I found a feature article about what it's really like to work in Paris. The author discovered that few Americans enjoy the Parisian lifestyle after they get there. You can't hurt yourself by taking a few moments to read the columns that you find at CAREERMagazine!

College Grad Job Hunter

www.collegegrad.com/

★★
★★

Heavy-duty career-related content, all free: Don't let the name of this site discourage you from looking at it if you happen to be long-graduated — I highly recommend it to all job seekers. You find absolutely terrific information about preparing your resume, preparing for interviews, and looking for a job. You can access a Web forum to share ideas, and a detailed, content-rich e-zine (electronic magazine) is at your disposal. Be sure to take a look at the free Web-based career book available at this site, written by the site's maintainers.

JobWeb

www.jobweb.org/

Links job seekers with job-search information: JobWeb is maintained by the National Association of Colleges and Employers (NACE). Choose the Career Planning links to find information about conducting your job search and choosing a career. But some of my favorite resources at this site are located in the resource-rich Career Library, where you can find a host of online periodicals, including *Arts Education, AskERIC,* the *Broadcasting Link, Career Manager,* and *Campus Newspapers on the Internet.* If you're a teacher, you'll like the database of U.S. school districts available at this site, and if you're interested in pursuing more education, you can find excellent resources and tips right on JobWeb.

The WorkSite.com

www.theworksite.com/

Well-organized site with plenty of career tips and advice: This site has a commercial edge to it, but if you can get past that, you can find good content here. The best career resources are located in the section labeled Career Resources, fittingly enough. I especially like the career tips covering interviewing and writing resumes and cover letters. You can ignore some of the resume advice, but definitely take a look at the article on savvy interviewing via telephone. (Remember, an employer who's interested in you will call you rather than send you a letter.) Another good resource is the Corporate Channel section of the site. There, you can find resources for researching companies, a real must before you apply or interview.

Other Stuff to Check Out

cx.bridges.com/
www.jobtrak.com/forum/
cis.uoregon.edu/
www.emory.edu/CAREER/index.html
www.rpi.edu/dept/cdc/
www.jobweb.org/catapult/disabled.htm
www.jobweb.org/catapult/career_info.htm
www.collegegrad.com/
www.umanitoba.ca/counselling/
    careers.html
www.ipa.com/

Job-Search Meta Lists

If you can imagine 50 pages filled with online job resources, then this section will make you very happy. Now, I know that this directory forms its own meta list. (I maintain updates of the links in this directory on my Web site, by the way, which is www.pamdixon.com.) However, I'm of the opinion that you're always better off choosing at least three meta lists and working through each one. Why? Because everyone is human — you have your biases, just as creators of the meta lists have theirs. If you use three lists, you're pretty much assured of getting a good cross-section of the job searching sites you don't want to miss. Also, everyone has a particular way of organizing information. Work to find the blend of content and organization you're most comfortable with.

88K

www.mcs.net/~88k/free/

Free resume submission clearinghouse: I know it sounds really stupid, but a Submit-o-Matic page at the 88K site lets you send one resume to seven databases. When you start e-mailing your resume, you come to understand exactly what a helpful service the Submit-o-Matic is. In addition to the submission tool, you find a healthy list of links to all the top online job databases.

Bay Area Jobs

www.sonic.net/~allan/ba_jobs.html

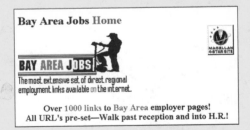

More than 1,000 links to Bay Area employers: Bay Area Jobs has evolved into a premium meta list, surpassing every other regional list I know of. The reason I didn't include Bay Area Jobs in the regional section of this directory is that the list is extensive enough to qualify as a

bona fide meta list. From the opening page, scroll down to the selection of links. You can view the resources by region or by type of resource. Examples of the compelling information you find include links to every Bay Area newspaper imaginable, including alternative papers; links to Bay Area recruitment agencies; and, of course, many direct links to employers.

Business Job Finder

www.cob.ohio-state.edu/dept/fin/ osujobs.htm

Everything you want to know about careers in business: This well-organized site does a great job of providing a giant list of resources targeted to specific business professions. All you need to do to access the information is scroll down the page and click on the area that interests you, such as commercial banking, corporate finance, insurance, management consulting, or strategic planning. Included at this site is an excellent listing of links to major job-search sites, such as the Online Career Center and the Monster Board.

Galaxy Employment Opportunities and Job Postings

galaxy.einet.net/GJ/employment.html

Listing of job searching links with an emphasis on academic information: Though you can find all sorts of employment links on the Galaxy meta site, Galaxy boasts an especially helpful collection of links to jobs in the academic world. For example, on my last visit, I found links to the Academic Position Network, the MIT Personnel Office (along with many other university listings), BIONET, and more.

Job Search and Employment Opportunities: Best Bets from the Net

www.lib.umich.edu/chdocs/employment/

Best-of-the-best short list for people who think that less is more: This site is the University of Michigan's answer to all the super-sized meta lists on the Web. This list, though still a meta list, covers only a few listings in each job-search area. The areas that the list covers are academia/education, humanities and social sciences, science and technology, business and government, and career development resources. If you're overwhelmed by big lists, then this may prove to be a good starting point for you.

JobHunt

www.job-hunt.org/index.html

★★ ☆
★★

My favorite meta list of online job-search resources and services: I have always loved JobHunt — it's always up-to-date, and it's tremendously well organized and thorough. Dane Spearing, who maintains this list, does an aggressive update on the list. I almost never find a bad link. Plus, I tend to agree with Spearing's categorizations and opinions of particular resources. A good link to start with is the New Items link, which takes you to items less than a week old. You can find the newest job databases, no matter how obscure. But your time is best spent following the Outstanding Job Resources link — an extraordinary collection that encompasses the best sites from every corner of the Web (and then some). *Note:* You can find a great list of links to company home pages at this Web site.

Overseas Job Web

www.overseasjobs.com/resources/
   jobs.html

Over 700 international job-search resources: If you want one-stop shopping for an international job, try the Overseas Job Web first. After the opening page loads, click on the Job Resources option. You reach a page linking you to career resources organized by country, which is a great way to conduct an international job search. The site does a great job of including the smaller, harder-to-find resources that many meta lists overlook, simply because maintaining links to international sites can be very time-consuming. You can also find immigration information at this site.

Purdue's Internet Sites for Job Seekers and Employers

www.ups.purdue.edu/Student/
   jobsites.htm

★★ ☆
★★

Granddaddy of all job lists on the Internet: I'm not the only person who believes that this site is the hands-down-best Internet job-search meta list. You could easily spend weeks exploring the links. You must experience this site for yourself to fully grasp its richness, depth, and excellent research. When you open the site, the design doesn't blow you away. You see a gray page with black type, a few yellow banners, and then lots and lots of links, each with a good description. The beauty of this site is in the content and organization. I recommend that you begin by looking at the Outstanding Job Resources. This best-of-the-best list does not contain a single dud or piece of bad advice. You can visit general job searching sites, international sites, classified ads, newsgroups, resume services, federal government job listings, and job listings for various geographical areas. The site is actively maintained, so the number of stale links is minimal.

Other Stuff to Check Out

www.dbm.com/jobguide/
www.emory.edu/CAREER/index.html
www.yahoo.com/yahoo/Business/
Employment/Jobs/
www.jobweb.org/catapult/catapult.htm

International Job-Search Tools and Resources

If you're interested in looking far and away for your next job, this short but rich selection of sites can help you on your journey. The sites in this section are not job databases; rather, they provide all the corollary information you need when considering overseas employment.

BBB Overseas Job Scams

Overseasdigest.com/scams.htm

Great advice for avoiding getting fleeced: The Council of Better Business Bureaus put together this short but extremely helpful reality check. Evidently, not all job databases are on the up and up, as evidenced by some of the advice proffered in the article on the BBB Overseas Job Scams Web page. My advice: Read this article before you do anything else!

Best Bets for Work Abroad

www.uci.edu/~cie/iop/work.html

Great advice for new grads with a thirst for overseas adventure: The University of California, Irvine, has collected a short list of helpful international information. You can find out about short- and long-term work programs, find out how to get a work permit, get advice on turning a short-term overseas experience into long-term employment, and get a great overview of working abroad. The information

is geared to students who are about to graduate, but I found it pertinent for all job seekers hoping to work overseas.

The Canadian Guide to Working and Living Overseas

www.workingoverseas.com/~issi/

★ ★
★ ★

Well-known guide that's useful for all: The Canadian Guide is actually a 1,000-page book. But the author, Jean-Marc Hachey, has placed real treasures from the book online. Click on the Tips from the Author link on the opening page. The author offers great free advice in the areas of myths about living overseas, preparing an international resume, and phone techniques for finding international work. The link with the most content is the one about the myths and realities of living and working overseas. Great information — well worth a visit. Just one word of warning: You get a pitch for the book on every single page you visit!

Duke University's International Resources on the Internet

www.duke.edu/~lpmaskel/intl_hrefs.html

Lots of links for those lusting for a change of place: The opening page of the Duke site probably won't impress you — it's just a short list of links. Deceptively short! Click on any of the opening page links and you land at pages full of links that took a great deal of research to compile. You find a wealth of international job resources, international career resources (incredibly good information), and even top-notch travel information. Very much worth a visit.

Living Abroad Overseas Digest Online

Overseasdigest.com/expat1.htm

Free e-mail newsletter covering all aspects of going overseas to work: Signing up for this newsletter brings you information about planning your time abroad, finding an overseas job, arranging for your children's education, dealing with legal matters, and a lot more.

Overseas Jobs Web

www.overseasjobs.com/resources/ jobs.html

See the review of this site under "International Job Databases," earlier in this directory.

Other Stuff to Check Out

www.istc.umn.edu/Work/work-search.html
www.immlaw.com
www.xmission.com/index.html

Sample Resumes

I spend a lot of time in this book discussing why you need to be careful about where you post your resumes. Why? Because posting your resume on an open resume database allows absolutely anyone with a Web connection to see it. Some brave souls don't seem to mind the exposure, and they give you a great opportunity to see what you like and don't like in a resume. In the following section, I list a selection of open resume databases for you to peruse. Perform a scan test on the resumes you see — does the resume catch your eye? If so, why; if not, why not? I anticipate that in the next few years, there will be fewer and fewer open resume databases due to privacy issues. So scan while you can!

The Job Resource

solimar1.stanford.edu/prospects/ search.html

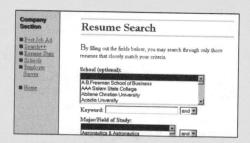

Terrific site for browsing resumes of new graduates: The Job Resource site is great if you're a new grad looking for ideas about how to put your resume together. From the opening page, click on the Resume Search link. Then use the search engines to search for resumes. After you search, you're presented with mini-resumes, each resume having a number assigned to it. To see the entire resume, just click on the number. All the contact and personal information is unavailable, which is fine. All you really want are ideas, so the lack of phone numbers and whatnot shouldn't slow you down one bit.

Resumes on the Web

www.resweb.com/

Simple resume surfing via the Web: If you're stuck and you just can't seem to find the right model for your resume, definitely take a peek at this site. You can search resumes by keyword, or you can look at a resume index categorized by profession. So if you specialize in marketing, click on Marketing. The resumes available in the marketing area open in a list for you to view. Resumes on the Web does not contain thousands of resumes, but the resumes I have seen at this site are generally well designed and have good content. Quality versus quantity is the rule here. *Note:* You can view the resumes for free here, but you have to pay to post your resume, something I strongly discourage.

Yahoo! Classifieds

classifieds.yahoo.com/employment.html

★★ ★★ 🔗

Giant open resume database: The Yahoo! Classifieds is an enormous list of classified advertisements for jobs. You can view the classifieds by metro area. After you go to the metro area of your choice, you find two links: one for job postings and the other for resumes. Click on the resume link for immediate access to resumes in Yahoo!'s open resume database. I talked with Yahoo! about its resume database, and by its figures, thousands of resumes are available. To view resumes of people in your profession, browse the classifieds by national listings. (A link to national listings is available on the Yahoo! Classifieds opening page.) When you view the classifieds nationally, Yahoo! breaks the list of resumes and job postings into topics. For example, you can view listings for computers, business, and so on. Within each category, you find links to job postings and resumes. Read to your heart's content!

Other Stuff to Check Out

www.umn.edu/ohr/ecep/resume/step6.htm
ucsee.eecs.berkeley.edu/resumes/
  resume.html
www.globalvillager.com/villager/csc.html
www.bloomberg.com/fun/jobs.html

Resume and Cover Letter Tools and Help

When it comes down to it, a resume is a piece of paper or an electronic document on which you list your accomplishments and work history. And you hope that your resume accurately reflects you. In this section of the directory, you find tools to help you look your best on the electronic or printed page, ranging from grammar help to resume tips. I even include a resume posting site so that you can spread the good word about your skills once you have a great resume in hand.

11 Rules of Writing

kbidesign.cnchost.com/writing.shtml

Write it right: If you're even the least bit unsure of your grammar, then by all means visit the Rules of Writing page. Here you discover how your cover letter and resume may be busting up grammar rules left and right. Great content in an concise, easy-to-access format.

BridgePath

www.bridgepath.com/getajob/
  index.html

Apply to multiple companies simultaneously: You can save yourself all sorts of e-mailing time by using BridgePath. After the graphics-heavy page finally opens, scroll down to the Features heading and click on the link to ResumePath. ResumePath is a nifty little area that lets you choose up to 30 (out of a total of 200) companies to send your resume to simultaneously. Of course, you can always make a repeat visit and send a resume to another 30 companies. You need a valid e-mail address to use this service, and I suggest that you have an ASCII resume all set to copy and paste into the form that the site provides.

Creating Your Resume, by Resumix

www.resumix.com/resume/
  resumeindex.html

Everything you need to know about scannable resumes: If you've been putting off learning about scannable resumes, visit this site as soon as possible. Resumix is one of the big players in the resume database industry. If you're applying to a Fortune 100 company, your resume has high chances of a face-to-face meeting with Resumix software. (Larger companies with high volume have embraced resume tracking software like Resumix.) Take advice from the ultimate source! On the Creating Your Resume page, Resumix offers a link to a great article on preparing the ideal scannable resume. The advice the article offers is the soundest in the business. Other helpful articles include a general resume advice article by nationally syndicated careers columnist Joyce Lain Kennedy.

Golden Triangle Online

www.golden.net HOMEPAGE

Treasure chest of resume help: This site links to the best articles on the Web about resume and cover letter creation. The sites and articles are rated and reviewed, so you don't have to waste your time reading bad resume advice.

Resumania

www.umn.edu/ohr/ecep/resume

★ ★
★ ★

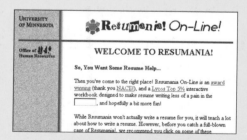

Interactive workbook designed to make resume writing less of a pain: On the Resumania Web site, you find all sorts of interactive workbooks that walk you through the entire resume creation process. I can't say enough good things about this site, maintained by one of my favorite universities, the University of

Minnesota. To use the site, just scroll to the bottom of the opening page and start at Step 1. I guarantee that you won't be sorry for investing a few minutes of your time at this site. The one recommendation I do have is that you be very careful to print out the results of your work! This site doesn't save your work for you. Consider this fantastic site a must-see in your job-search process. (A bonus: Great resume samples are available at Step 6!)

Top Ten Technical Resume Writing Tips

www.taos.com/working/tips.html

Even the score with your friends in artsy professions: Have you ever noticed just how difficult it is to describe computer terms gracefully? "15 years experience with C++, Visual Basic, UNIX, and SAP databases" is hardly poetic. Nevertheless, the helpful tips on this page can get your resume into a more readable state. The advice is tailored specifically to those working in highly technical or scientific fields, with a special emphasis on computer science.

Other Stuff to Check Out

www.damngood.com
www.mcs.net/~88k/free/
www.canisius.edu
www.bio.com/ResumeDissected.html

Interview Preparation

Resume help abounds on the Web, but interview help does not. I guess people think that it's smooth sailing once you get the interview. Well, anyone who has had even one interview knows better than that. I didn't find an overwhelming number of resources, but the material I found is high-quality. Following is a selection of Web sites that can help you prepare for the big day.

CDP Interviewing Tips

130.91.160.224/alumint.htm

Superb interview advice: Finally, an interview prep page that talks about the law! From this simple page of links, you find a thorough chart/article about unlawful interview questions. Along with the unlawful questions, the article makes you aware of the questions that you may think are unlawful but really are not. From the opening page, you also find solid advice on interview preparation, sample interviews, and a host of sample questions that employers are likely to ask you.

Dynastaff Interviewing Tips

www.dynastaff.com/tips.htm

Just about everything you need to know to get ready for your interviews: Dynastaff has created a terrific site. On a clear opening page menu, you find links to information about dressing for success, standard interview questions, tough questions to prep for, a look at why qualified people don't get hired, and advice on how to close the interview. The content at this Web site is rock-solid and complete. For example, this Web site offers one of the best answers I've seen to the common no-win question, "What salary are you looking for?"

The Salary Calculator

www2.homefair.com/calc/salcalc.html

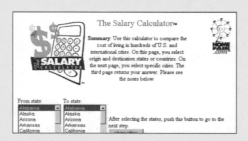

Figure out how to price yourself: Nothing is quite as horrible as pricing yourself out of the market, especially when you really want the job. All too often, candidates win the interview but lose the job offer because they unwittingly price themselves out of the market. Save yourself from this error by checking out this great Web site. Here, you can compare the salaries of your current location to salaries where you want to move. This great tool is simple to use. The only thing you have to lose is a job offer, so give it a try, particularly if you're looking to relocate.

World's Biggest Job Interview Questions Bank

www.sunfeatures.com/~jlk

1,001 job interview questions from Joyce Lain Kennedy: If you want to rehearse interview questions, here's your ultimate opportunity. I highly recommend a visit. You need to work a little bit to get to the questions, but it's worth the effort. At the opening page, click on Joyce's Books. After the page opens, click on Job Interviews For Dummies; then scroll down and click on the Job Interviews For Dummies link. You go directly to the 1,001 interview questions, and you also have access to a sample chapter from Kennedy's best-selling book *Job Interviews For Dummies* (IDG Books Worldwide, Inc.).

Other Stuff to Check Out

www.collegegrad.com/intv/
www.isdn.net/nis/
www.datamasters.com/dm/survey.html
db.dummies.com/cgi/
     fill_out_template.pl?book:1-56884-859-
     5:bookDummies+Press::u2708740234376

Privacy Resources

Forgetting about privacy is so easy when you're browsing around on the Web. It all seems so simple: Just cruise to a Web site, get the information you want, upload your resume to employers, and then turn off your computer and go on to the next thing. If only it were that simple! Privacy has become a huge issue for everyone, especially for job seekers. Five years ago, job searching online was a value-added novelty. Now, employers downright expect you to be looking for a job via online technology. Because online job searching has become a primary way to look for a job, privacy issues have become much more important. I detail those issues in Chapter 4 of this book. The following list covers the most important online privacy information currently available. You needn't get paranoid about privacy — just get informed. These Web resources go a long way toward filling up your privacy knowledge banks.

EFFweb

www.eff.org/

★★
★★

Digital home of the famed Electronic Frontier Foundation: The Electronic Frontier Foundation is a relatively high-profile nonprofit organization working to ensure that civil liberties reign freely yet appropriately in cyberspace. I have a soft spot for EFF because it was one of the first organizations to aggressively work toward bringing Internet access to underprivileged kids. EFF is also active in online privacy rights issues. On the EFF main page, you find links to free speech, encryption, privacy, and intellectual property. EFF does a great job of acting as a hub for the latest information in all four areas. For information about privacy concerns and your job search, follow the Privacy link. From there, you can browse all sorts of privacy-related information, like the latest congressional legislation on electronic privacy, workplace privacy rights and e-mail, and much more.

Electronic Privacy Information Center (EPIC)

www.epic.org/

Extraordinary online guide to privacy resources: EPIC is dedicated to defending your rights in cyberspace — strenuously. EPIC is a high-profile, internationally connected group, active in the U.S. congressional legislation. I want to steer you toward the tremendous collection of privacy resources that EPIC has put together. On the opening page, click on Resources. Then click on EPIC's Online Guide to Privacy Resources. The list of links that you see is formidable, and easily the most comprehensive available. Many international privacy resources are available, which is helpful if you're interested in working overseas.

Privacy International Home Page

www.privacy.org/pi/

Hard-core privacy site with good information for international job-seekers: This site may be a bit too militant for you — so be forewarned! However, if you either live abroad or plan to work abroad in the near future, this site is a must-visit. The reason? Except in France, privacy rights are still somewhat lagging in other foreign countries. Be very aware of the differences in laws before you make any employment agreements! This site can help you figure out what you can tolerate. A good section to peruse is the Country Reports section, which gives privacy information by country. Find the Country Reports by scrolling down to the bottom of the opening page.

Privacy Rights Clearinghouse

www.privacyrights.org/

★★
★★   ∞

Terrific selection of free online brochures dealing with privacy and the workplace: The Privacy Rights Clearinghouse houses a *very* useful set of brochures for job seekers. I recommend that you check out the link to Fact Sheets (at the top of the opening page) as soon as you visit this site. The fact sheets most relevant to a job search include *Privacy Survival Guide, How Private is My Credit Report?, Employee Monitoring, Job Seeker's Guide to Employment Background Checks, Coping with Identity Theft*, and *Privacy in Cyberspace*. I particularly recommend the brochure on background checks, as companies are doing these more and more, much to my and everyone else's dismay. (Some of the background checks that companies are performing simply go too far, in my opinion.) The site also has a good selection of general privacy links. To see the link collection, click on Privacy Links, an option you see on the site's opening page.

Project OPEN

www.isa.net/project-open/

Helping you get the most out of going online: Project OPEN is one of the many projects of the Online Public Education Network, which has as its mission statement "Making the Net Work for You." On the opening page, you see a link to Privacy. Follow it and you find a modest but very helpful section on how to essentially hang a polite "Do Not Disturb" sign on your electronic doorknob. You also can find excellent information about putting a stop to those annoying junk-mail messages that you've probably been getting in your e-mail box.

Truste

www.truste.org/

Bridging information desires of commercial Web sites with privacy concerns of Web users: The whole reason that Truste exists is to build consumer confidence in the Web. I still hesitate every time a Web site asks me to disclose personal information. Unfortunately, with employers encouraging the growing popularity of online job searching, you pretty much have to disclose all sorts of personal information online. The Truste Web site really helps by deflating certain persistent myths about what is and is not safe to put online and giving you down-to-earth advice about managing privacy in a very open world — cyberspace.

Other Stuff to Check Out

www.dfc.org/
www.cdt.org
www.cpsr.org
www.junkbusters.com
www.zerojunkmail.com
www.crypto.com

Appendix

About the CD

Here's some of what you can find on the *Job Searching Online For Dummies* CD-ROM:

- ✔ MindSpring Internet Access, a popular Internet service
- ✔ BBEdit Lite, a freeware text editor for Mac OS computers that's useful for HTML editing
- ✔ A clickable list of the *Job Searching Online For Dummies* Internet Directory links

System Requirements

Make sure that your computer meets the minimum system requirements listed below. If your computer doesn't match up to most of these requirements, you may have problems using the contents of the CD.

- ✔ A PC with a 486 or faster processor, or a Mac OS computer with a 68030 or faster processor.
- ✔ Microsoft Windows 3.1 or later, or Mac OS system software 7.5 or later.
- ✔ At least 8MB of total RAM installed on your computer. For best performance, I recommend that Windows 95-equipped PCs and Mac OS computers with PowerPC processors have at least 16MB of RAM installed.
- ✔ At least 205MB (Windows) or 65MB (Mac) of hard drive space available to install all the software from this CD. (You'll need less space if you don't install every program.)
- ✔ A CD-ROM drive — double speed (2x) or faster.
- ✔ A sound card for PCs. (Mac OS computers have built-in sound support.)
- ✔ A monitor capable of displaying at least 256 colors or grayscale.
- ✔ A modem with a speed of at least 14,400 bps.

If you need more information on the basics, check out *PCs For Dummies,* 5th Edition, by Dan Gookin; *Macs For Dummies,* 5th Edition, by David Pogue; *Windows 98 For Dummies,* by Andy Rathbone; *Windows 95 For Dummies,* 2nd Edition by Andy Rathbone; or *Windows 3.11 For Dummies,* 4rd Edition, by Andy Rathbone (all published by IDG Books Worldwide, Inc.).

How to Use the CD Using Microsoft Windows

To install the items from the CD to your hard drive, follow these steps:

1. **Insert the CD into your computer's CD-ROM drive.**

2. **Windows 3.1 or 3.11 users: From Program Manager, choose File⇨Run.**

   Windows 95 and 98 users: Click on the Start button and click on Run.

3. **In the dialog box that appears, type** D:\SETUP.EXE.

   Most of you probably have your CD-ROM drive listed as drive D under My Computer in Windows 95 or 98 or the File Manager in Windows 3.1. Type in the proper drive letter if your CD-ROM drive uses a different letter.

4. **Click on OK.**

   A license agreement window appears.

5. **I'm sure you'll want to use the CD, so read through the license agreement, nod your head, and then click on the Accept button. After you click on Accept, you'll never be bothered by the License Agreement window again.**

   From here, the CD interface appears. The CD interface is a little program that shows you what's on the CD and coordinates installing the programs and running the demos. The interface basically lets you click on a button or two to make things happen.

6. **The first screen you see is the Welcome screen. Click anywhere on this screen to enter the interface.**

   Now you're getting to the action. This next screen lists categories for the software on the CD.

7. **To view the items within a category, just click on the category's name.**

   A list of programs in the category appears.

8. **For more information about a program, click on the program's name.**

Be sure to read the information that appears. Sometimes a program requires you to do a few tricks on your computer first, and this screen tells you where to go for that information, if necessary.

9. **To install the program, click on the appropriate Install button. If you don't want to install the program, click on the Go Back button to return to the preceding screen.**

   You can always return to the preceding screen by clicking on the Go Back button. This allows you to browse the different categories and products and decide what you want to install.

   After you click on an install button, the CD interface drops to the background while the CD begins installation of the program you chose.

10. **To install other items, repeat Steps 7, 8, and 9.**

11. **When you're done installing programs, click on the Quit button to close the interface.**

   You can eject the CD now. Carefully place it back in the plastic jacket of the book for safekeeping.

To run some of the programs, you may need to keep the CD inside your CD-ROM drive. This is a Good Thing. Otherwise, the installed program would have required you to install a very large chunk of the program to your hard drive space, which would have kept you from installing other software.

How to Use the CD Using the Mac OS

To install the items from the CD to your hard drive, follow these steps:

1. **Insert the CD into your computer's CD-ROM drive.**

   In a moment, an icon representing the CD that you just inserted appears on your Mac desktop. Chances are, the icon looks like a CD-ROM.

2. **Double-click on the CD icon to show the CD's contents.**

3. **Double-click on the Read Me First icon.**

   This text file contains information about the CD's programs and any last-minute instructions that you need to know about installing the programs on the CD that I don't cover in this appendix.

4. **To install most programs, just drag the program's folder from the CD window and drop it on your hard drive icon.**

5. **Some programs come with installer programs. With those, you simply open the program's folder on the CD and double-click on the icon with the word *Install* or *Installer.***

After you have installed the programs that you want, you can eject the CD. Carefully place it back in the plastic jacket of the book for safekeeping.

Using the Directory Links

For your convenience, I have put all the URLs that are listed in the *Job Searching Online For Dummies* Internet Directory on the CD. You can open the links in your Web browser in just a mouse click!

Links to every site reviewed in this book are available on the CD-ROM. To use these links pages, follow these steps:

1. **With the CD-ROM in your drive, launch your Web browser.**

2. **If you have Microsoft Internet Explorer, choose File⇨Open File.**

   An Open dialog box appears.

3. **Select the Links.htm file.**

   If you're using Windows, type **D:\LINKS.HTM**. (If your CD-ROM drive is not D:\, be sure to use the correct letter for your drive.)

   If you're using Mac OS, use the Open dialog box to display the contents of the CD-ROM. Select the Links.htm file and press Return or Enter.

4. **Click on a link for any site that you want to visit.**

   Doing so opens a second browser window that takes you to the Web site you've selected. The links page remains open in the original browser window so that you can toggle back to it to select another link. Each time you select a new link, the Web site selected pops up in that second browser window — so don't worry that you're going to end up with several browser windows open at one time.

What You'll Find

Here's a summary of the software on this CD. If you use Windows, the CD interface helps you install software easily. (If you have no idea what I'm talking about when I say "CD interface," flip back a page or two to find the section "How to Use the CD Using Microsoft Windows.")

If you use a Mac OS computer, you can enjoy the ease of the Mac interface to quickly install the programs.

Acrobat Reader 3.01

For Windows 3.1, Windows 95, and Mac OS. Adobe Acrobat Reader is a free program that opens portable document format (PDF) files. PDFs are handy ways to publish electronic documents that contain the same formatting and graphics of a printed document. To find out more, you can check out the Adobe Web site at www.adobe.com.

BBEdit Lite 4.0.1 and BBEdit 4.5 Demo

For Mac OS. BBEdit Lite, from Bare Bones Software, Inc., is a Macintosh freeware text editor with powerful features that make creating HTML scripts for your Web pages easy.

The commercial version of this program, BBEdit 4.5, has stronger HTML editing features. I've included a demo version of BBEdit 4.5 on the CD. This demo is fully featured but cannot save files. You can find out more, or register your version of BBEdit 4.5, at the Bare Bones Web site at www.barebones.com.

Eudora Light 3.1.3

For Windows 3.1, Windows 95, and Mac OS. Eudora Light, by Qualcomm, is a freeware version of the commercially available Eudora Pro Internet e-mail program. Find out more information about Eudora Pro and Eudora Light at www.eudora.com. Because using e-mail is a critical component of your job search, you may get a lot of benefits from this particular program.

Free Agent 1.11

For Windows 3.1 and Windows 95. Free Agent, from Forté Inc., is a popular Usenet newsgroup program that lets you read and participate in Usenet discussions. Current versions of the Netscape Communicator and Internet Explorer Web browsers have built-in newsreaders, so Free Agent is a "bonus" for you to try. Check out the Web site at www.forteinc.com.

HTML Web Weaver Lite 3.0.1

For Mac OS. This is the shareware version of Miracle Software's commercially available World Wide Web Weaver. HTML Web Weaver is simple to use, and it doesn't hog a bunch of space on your hard drive. HTML Web Weaver doesn't have the full functionality of the commercial version, but it's a great tool nonetheless. To discover more, or to purchase the commercial version, check out the Web site at www.miracleinc.com.

HTML Pro 1.08

For Mac OS. HTML Pro is yet another Macintosh Web page editor that lets you work on the graphical view of a page and the source HTML code at the same time. More information is available at the HTML Pro Web site: www.acc.umu.se/~r2d2/files/HTML_Pro_info.html.

HotDog

For Windows 3.1 and Windows 95. HotDog, from Sausage Software, is a "straight" HTML editor, which means that you work directly with HTML tags to create a Web page. This is a great program if you want to get very creative with your Web page and know HTML well. For more information or to register your version of HotDog, check out the Web site at www.sausage.com.

InterNews 2.0.2

For Mac OS. InterNews from Moonrise Software is a shareware Usenet newsgroup program that lets you read and participate in Usenet discussions. Current versions of the Netscape Communicator and Internet Explorer Web browsers have built-in newsreaders, but InterNews is small and fast, with lots of nice features, if you prefer to read newsgroups without going through the World Wide Web. To learn more or to register your copy, check out the Web site at www.dartmouth.edu/~moonrise/.

Internet Assistant for Microsoft Word

For Windows 95. Internet Assistants are free tools that work with Microsoft products. This Assistant allows you to instantly format a Microsoft Word document into an HTML document. If you have a resume all set to go, then the MS Word Internet Assistant can translate it instantly for you and make it Web-ready.

Microsoft Internet Explorer 4.0

For Windows 3.1, Windows 95, and Mac OS. This is a top-notch Web browser from Microsoft. You can use the version on the CD for all your job search surfing! For more information and the latest version, please check www.microsoft.com/ie/.

MindSpring Internet Access

For Windows 3.1, Windows 95, and Mac OS. MindSpring Internet Access is a free commercial product that gets you signed up to the MindSpring Internet service provider. If you don't already have Internet access, MindSpring is an excellent ISP that offers Internet access for a low monthly fee. If you're already on the Internet but would like to learn more about MindSpring and the different service options it offers, you can go to its Web site at www.mindspring.com.

When you install MindSpring, the installation program asks you for a key code. Enter **DUMY8579** into the dialog box. Make sure to use all capital letters, just as it's shown here.

If you already have an Internet service provider, installing MindSpring may replace your current settings. You may no longer be able to access the Internet through your original provider.

Netscape Communicator 4.0

For Windows 3.1, Windows 95, and Mac OS. Netscape Communicator is a sophisticated, popular browser made by Netscape. For more information about this well-known browser, please visit www.netscape.com.

PageMill 2.0

For Windows 3.1, Windows 95, and Mac OS. PageMill is a sophisticated but easy-to-use WYSIWYG editor. As you type, you see what your finished Web page will look like. For more information, you can visit the Adobe site (the makers of PageMill) at www.adobe.com.

If You've Got Problems (Of the CD Kind)

I tried my best to compile programs that work on most computers with the minimum system requirements. Alas, your computer may differ, and some programs may not work properly for some reason.

The two likeliest problems are that you don't have enough memory (RAM) for the programs you want to use, or you have other programs running that are affecting installation or running of a program. If you get error messages such as `Not enough memory` or `Setup cannot continue`, try one or more of these methods and then try using the software again:

- **Turn off any anti-virus software that you have on your computer.** Installers sometimes mimic virus activity and may make your computer incorrectly believe that it is being infected by a virus.

- **Close all running programs.** The more programs you're running, the less memory is available to other programs. Installers also typically update files and programs. So if you keep other programs running, installation may not work properly.

- **In Windows, close the CD interface and run demos or installations directly from Windows Explorer.** The interface itself can tie up system memory or even conflict with certain kinds of interactive demos. Use Windows Explorer to browse the files on the CD and launch installers or demos.

- **Have your local computer store add more RAM to your computer.** This is, admittedly, a drastic and somewhat expensive step. However, if you have a Windows 95 PC or a Mac OS computer with a PowerPC chip, adding more memory can really help the speed of your computer and enable more programs to run at the same time.

If you still have trouble installing the items from the CD, please call the IDG Books Worldwide Customer Service phone number: 800-762-2974 (outside the U.S.: 317-596-5430).

Index

(continued)

(continued)

IDG Books Worldwide, Inc., End-User License Agreement

• •

READ THIS. You should carefully read these terms and conditions before opening the software packet(s) included with this book ("Book"). This is a license agreement ("Agreement") between you and IDG Books Worldwide, Inc. ("IDGB"). By opening the accompanying software packet(s), you acknowledge that you have read and accept the following terms and conditions. If you do not agree and do not want to be bound by such terms and conditions, promptly return the Book and the unopened software packet(s) to the place you obtained them for a full refund.

1. **License Grant.** IDGB grants to you (either an individual or entity) a nonexclusive license to use one copy of the enclosed software program(s) (collectively, the "Software") solely for your own personal or business purposes on a single computer (whether a standard computer or a workstation component of a multiuser network). The Software is in use on a computer when it is loaded into temporary memory (RAM) or installed into permanent memory (hard disk, CD-ROM, or other storage device). IDGB reserves all rights not expressly granted herein.

2. **Ownership.** IDGB is the owner of all right, title, and interest, including copyright, in and to the compilation of the Software recorded on the disk(s) or CD-ROM ("Software Media"). Copyright to the individual programs recorded on the Software Media is owned by the author or other authorized copyright owner of each program. Ownership of the Software and all proprietary rights relating thereto remain with IDGB and its licensers.

3. **Restrictions on Use and Transfer.**

   (a) You may only (i) make one copy of the Software for backup or archival purposes, or (ii) transfer the Software to a single hard disk, provided that you keep the original for backup or archival purposes. You may not (i) rent or lease the Software, (ii) copy or reproduce the Software through a LAN or other network system or through any computer subscriber system or bulletin-board system, or (iii) modify, adapt, or create derivative works based on the Software.

   (b) You may not reverse engineer, decompile, or disassemble the Software. You may transfer the Software and user documentation on a permanent basis, provided that the transferee agrees to accept the terms and conditions of this Agreement and you retain no copies. If the Software is an update or has been updated, any transfer must include the most recent update and all prior versions.

4. **Restrictions on Use of Individual Programs.** You must follow the individual requirements and restrictions detailed for each individual program in the "About the CD" appendix of this Book. These limitations are also contained in the individual license agreements recorded on the Software Media. These limitations may include a requirement that after using the program for a specified period of time, the user must pay a registration fee or discontinue use. By opening the Software packet(s), you will be agreeing to abide by the licenses and restrictions for these individual programs that are detailed in the "About the CD" appendix and on the Software Media. None of the material on this Software Media or listed in this Book may ever be redistributed, in original or modified form, for commercial purposes.

5. Limited Warranty.

(a) IDGB warrants that the Software and Software Media are free from defects in materials and workmanship under normal use for a period of sixty (60) days from the date of purchase of this Book. If IDGB receives notification within the warranty period of defects in materials or workmanship, IDGB will replace the defective Software Media.

(b) IDGB AND THE AUTHOR OF THE BOOK DISCLAIM ALL OTHER WARRANTIES, EXPRESS OR IMPLIED, INCLUDING WITHOUT LIMITATION IMPLIED WARRANTIES OF MERCHANTABILITY AND FITNESS FOR A PARTICULAR PURPOSE, WITH RESPECT TO THE SOFTWARE, THE PROGRAMS, THE SOURCE CODE CONTAINED THEREIN, AND/OR THE TECHNIQUES DE-SCRIBED IN THIS BOOK. IDGB DOES NOT WARRANT THAT THE FUNCTIONS CONTAINED IN THE SOFTWARE WILL MEET YOUR REQUIREMENTS OR THAT THE OPERATION OF THE SOFTWARE WILL BE ERROR FREE.

(c) This limited warranty gives you specific legal rights, and you may have other rights that vary from jurisdiction to jurisdiction.

6. Remedies.

(a) IDGB's entire liability and your exclusive remedy for defects in materials and workmanship shall be limited to replacement of the Software Media, which may be returned to IDGB with a copy of your receipt at the following address: Software Media Fulfillment Department, Attn.: _Job Searching Online For Dummies,_ IDG Books Worldwide, Inc., 7260 Shadeland Station, Ste. 100, Indianapolis, IN 46256, or call 800-762-2974. Please allow three to four weeks for delivery. This Limited Warranty is void if failure of the Software Media has resulted from accident, abuse, or misapplication. Any replacement Software Media will be warranted for the remainder of the original warranty period or thirty (30) days, whichever is longer.

(b) In no event shall IDGB or the author be liable for any damages whatsoever (including without limitation damages for loss of business profits, business interruption, loss of business informa-tion, or any other pecuniary loss) arising from the use of or inability to use the Book or the Software, even if IDGB has been advised of the possibility of such damages.

(c) Because some jurisdictions do not allow the exclusion or limitation of liability for consequential or incidental damages, the above limitation or exclusion may not apply to you.

7. U.S. Government Restricted Rights.
Use, duplication, or disclosure of the Software by the U.S. Government is subject to restrictions stated in paragraph (c)(1)(ii) of the Rights in Technical Data and Computer Software clause of DFARS 252.227-7013, and in subparagraphs (a) through (d) of the Commercial Computer–Restricted Rights clause at FAR 52.227-19, and in similar clauses in the NASA FAR supplement, when applicable.

8. General.
This Agreement constitutes the entire understanding of the parties and revokes and supersedes all prior agreements, oral or written, between them and may not be modified or amended except in a writing signed by both parties hereto that specifically refers to this Agreement. This Agreement shall take precedence over any other documents that may be in conflict herewith. If any one or more provisions contained in this Agreement are held by any court or tribunal to be invalid, illegal, or otherwise unenforceable, each and every other provision shall remain in full force and effect.

Installation Instructions

To install the items from the CD to your hard drive using Microsoft Windows, follow these steps:

1. **Insert the CD into your computer's CD-ROM drive.**

2. **Windows 3.1 or 3.11 users: From Program Manager, choose File⇨Run. Windows 95 users: Click on the Start button and click on Run.**

3. **In the dialog box that appears, type** D:\SETUP.EXE **(type in the proper drive letter if your CD-ROM drive uses a different letter).**

4. **Click on OK.**

5. **Read through the license agreement that appears, nod your head, and then click on the Accept button.**

6. **Click anywhere on the Welcome screen to enter the CD interface.**

7. **To view the items within a software category, click on the category's name.**

8. **For more information about a program in that category, click on the program's name.**

9. **To install the program, click on the appropriate Install button. If you don't want to install the program, click the Go Back button to return to the preceding screen.**

10. **To install other items, repeat Steps 7, 8, and 9.**

11. **When you're done installing programs, click on the Quit button and eject the CD. Carefully place it back in its plastic jacket for safekeeping.**

To install the items from the CD to your hard drive using the Mac OS, follow these steps:

1. **Insert the CD into your computer's CD-ROM drive.**

2. **Double-click on the CD icon to show the CD's contents.**

3. **Double-click on the Read Me First icon and read the text file.**

4. **To install most programs, just drag the program's folder from the CD window and drop it on your hard drive icon.**

    Other programs come with installer programs. With those, you simply open the program's folder on the CD and double-click on the icon with the word *Install* or *Installer*.

5. **After you have installed the programs that you want, eject the CD. Carefully place it back in the plastic jacket of the book for safekeeping.**

IDG BOOKS WORLDWIDE BOOK REGISTRATION

Register This Book and Win!

We want to hear from you!

Visit **http://my2cents.dummies.com** to register this book and tell us how you liked it!

- ✔ Get entered in our monthly prize giveaway.

- ✔ Give us feedback about this book — tell us what you like best, what you like least, or maybe what you'd like to ask the author and us to change!

- ✔ Let us know any other ...*For Dummies*® topics that interest you.

Your feedback helps us determine what books to publish, tells us what coverage to add as we revise our books, and lets us know whether we're meeting your needs as a ...*For Dummies* reader. You're our most valuable resource, and what you have to say is important to us!

Not on the Web yet? It's easy to get started with *Dummies 101*®: *The Internet For Windows*® *95* or *The Internet For Dummies*®, 5th Edition, at local retailers everywhere.

Or let us know what you think by sending us a letter at the following address:

...*For Dummies* Book Registration
Dummies Press
7260 Shadeland Station, Suite 100
Indianapolis, IN 46256-3945
Fax 317-596-5498

BUSINESS AND
GENERAL
REFERENCE
BOOK SERIES
FROM IDG

COMPUTER
BOOK SERIES
FROM IDG